Labor Divided

SUNY Series in
American Labor History

Robert Asher
and
Charles Stephenson
EDITORS

Labor Divided:
Race and Ethnicity in United States Labor Struggles
1835–1960

ROBERT ASHER AND CHARLES STEPHENSON
EDITORS

State University of New York Press

Permissions

John J. Bukowczyk's essay appeared in *Labor History* (25:1, 53–82) and is reprinted here with the kind permission of the editor of *Labor History.*

Gary Gerstle's essay is a revised version of a chapter in his book, *Working-Class Americanism: The Politics of Labor in a Textile City, 1914–1960* (Cambridge University Press, 1989), and appears here with the kind permission of Cambridge University Press.

Rudolph Vecoli's essay appeared in George E. Pozzetta, ed., *Pane E Lavoro* (The Multicultural History Society of Toronto, 1980) and is reprinted here with the kind permission of the author.

Published by
State University of New York Press, Albany

©1990 State University of New York

For information, address State University of New York
Press, State University Plaza, Albany, NY 12246

Library of Congress Cataloging-in Publication Data

Labor divided : race and ethnicity in United States labor struggles,
    1835–1960 / Robert Asher and Charles Stephenson, editors.
        p. cm. – (SUNY series in American labor history)
    Includes index.
    ISBN 0-88706-970-3. ISBN 0-88706-972-X (pbk.)
    1. Labor and laboring classes – United States – History. 2. Trade
unions – United States – History   3. Minorities – United States –
History. 4. Ethnicity – United States – History. I. Asher, Robert.
II. Stephenson, Charles. III. Series.
HD8081.A5L33 1990
305.5'62'0973 – dc19   88-26334
                                                                    CIP

10   9   8   7   6   5   4   3   2   1

To the memory of Julian Asher, master teacher

and

To George Bischoff and to the memory of
Hilda Bischoff, German immigrants and
Americans, who lived these stories; and to
Frank and Betty, the children who benefited
from their work and from their love.

Contents

Acknowledgments

Ronald Takaki, Rudolph Vecoli, Jr., and John H. M. Laslett helped the editors locate many of the contributors to this collection. Ronald Takaki, Irwin Yellowitz, A. William Hoglund, Paul Buhle, Steven Merlino, and Steven Streeter made suggestions that improved the introduction. Rebecca Mlynarczyk and Carol J. Williams rigorously critiqued the style of the introduction and helped to improve its clarity. Malcolm Willison, our copy editor, gave the manuscript his usual thorough scrutiny. Peggy Gifford has encouraged and supported the concept of this anthology. The late Julian Asher inspired much of the effort that went into developing an anthology that provides the kind of specific, concrete detail about historical experiences that enables readers to grasp the flavor of life and struggle in the past. His life was dedicated to effective teaching and to progressive politics. Hopefully this volume will make a contribution to both goals.

PART I

INTRODUCTION

CHAPTER 1

American Capitalism, Labor Organization, and the Racial/ Ethnic Factor: An Exploration

ROBERT ASHER AND CHARLES STEPHENSON

I

In the summer of 1986 Americans shared in a celebration of self-congratulation commemorating the centennial of the Statue of Liberty. Everywhere the mass media reminded us of the substance—and inevitability—of the "American Dream." Numerous stories were written by or about immigrants, all with a common theme: America is the land of opportunity, the best country in the world, a place where immigrants improved their lot over what they would have achieved by staying in their country of birth or by emigrating somewhere else. Judging by these stories, there was no dark side.

But there was. "No one in the black community is really excited about the Statue of Liberty," said Atlanta Mayor and former United Nations Ambassador Andrew Young. "We came here on slave ships, not via Ellis Island."[1] Besides the forced immigration of the Black African labor force, there were many immigrants who entered the United States as contract laborers of one type or another, their freedom severely circumscribed until their contracts expired. (Even after Congressional legislation banned the practice, many workers, especially Mexicans, were brought into the United States as contract laborers.) And yet America *was* a land of opportunity for many immigrants. English Puritans came, seeking religious autonomy. The Irish arrived, fleeing starvation induced by colonialism, the commercialization of agriculture and the potato famine. German democrats whose side "lost" in the manuevering during the Revolution of 1848, and who faced a bleak future in the period of repression of dissidents that followed the collapse of the constitutional movement, hoped to find political freedom and economic opportunity in the United States. Skilled industrial workers – from England, Scotland, northern Italy, Germany and the Austro-Hungarian Empire, Scandinavia and the Low Countries – were attracted by the higher wages and abundant jobs in their specialties that were to be found in the world's most extensive and dynamic national economy. Asian workers from India, China, Japan, Korea, and the Philippines were attracted by the relatively high wages paid in the United States to workers at the bottom of the primary labor markets and in secondary labor markets – wages that were, even at their lowest, much higher than wages in any Asian country. Similarly Southern Italians, Sicilians, Mexicans, and immigrants from the Caribbean entered the United States, seeking an alternative to grinding poverty in their homelands, while Jewish and Armenian immigrants hoped to find refuge from genocidal assaults endorsed and executed by the Russian and Turkish governments.

During the last one hundred and forty years the United States' labor force has been formed and replenished by an unusually diverse mix of racial and ethnic groups. Many of the essays in this volume examine the consequences of this heterogeneity; they analyze both the divisive effect of inter-ethnic and inter-racial conflict among working people and the positive effects of strong ethnic identification on worker mobilization for protection and advancement. The essays selected for this volume are all case studies of these tendencies. We have tried to correct the usual bias towards workers of European backgrounds in historical anthologies focusing on workers and ethnicity. To present a more balanced picture we have included six essays about workers, both men and women, who are non-white and non-European in background. These workers have been subjected to much more discrimination than their European counterparts; and it was – and is – the failure to incorporate these workers (and native stock women) into the labor movement, on a plane of equality of access to jobs and union power, that has greatly weakened American labor.

This volume begins with a section on non-white workers from Asia, treating the experience of Hawaiian, Chinese, Japanese, Korean, Portuguese, and Filipino workers in Hawaii, Los Angeles, and Chicago.

The next section deals with the experiences of African-American and Hispanic workers in Alabama, El Paso, and New York City. The emphasis then shifts to European immigrants, including French Canadians who migrated to the United States from Eastern Canada.

The totality of the phenomenon of ethnic and racial diversity in the American labor force, and its effect on economic action by workers in this nation, cannot be neatly encapsulated the way a baseball game can be summed up by giving the final score. Ethnic and racial diversity have had both negative and positive effects. Ethnic and racial diversity undermined workers' efforts in the United States to secure humane treatment, higher wages, and other improvements in working conditions. But it must be remembered that no single villain was responsible for this failure. Nor was the unequal distribution of wealth and power in this nation caused by any particular racial or ethnic group, neither immigrants nor second- nor third-generation Americans. The market forces unleashed by the evolution of world capitalism and the existence of economic elites who held great economic and political power, disproportionate to their mere numbers, exerted much more influence on the fate of American workers than did the skill and racial/ethnic divisions that separated them.

It is commonplace to view the labor force of the United States as being *unusually* fragmented by ethnic and racial divisions. This heterogeneity was clearly encountered more often in American workplaces than anywhere else in the industrial world. But labor relations in many other industrial nations—especially Germany, the Balkans, and France (after World War I)—were complicated by major ethnic divisions, especially between skilled, native-born workers and immigrant machine operators and day laborers. In Germany and France, Polish immigrant workers formed separate ethnic unions. In England divisions between Irish Catholic and English Protestant textile workers were strained by intense religious conflict in the 1860s and the 1870s. In short, the phenomenon of explosive mixtures of racial and nationality groups at many work sites that was found in the United States was replicated, albeit not as frequently, in most other industrial nations.[2] In the years after World War II, migration of workers from the Caribbean, Africa, and Asia further increased the diversity of the labor force in the United States, created major racial divisions in the English and continental European labor forces, and also ethnically and racially diversified the labor forces of many Third World nations. Thus, an anthology focusing on the American experience with racial and ethnic heterogeneity sheds light on historical and current social/economic processes throughout the world.

II

Wherever it existed, ethnic and racial diversity placed many obstacles in the way of cooperative action to solve common problems, and hindered the formation of labor unions and the maintenance of class unity within unions. Veteran labor organizers, including those who were not racists and nativists, all agreed that ethnic and racial heterogeneity frequently presented major difficulties. Thus in 1890 Terrance Powderly, Grand Master of the Knights of Labor, wrote to a friend — out of impatience and frustration — that he had found it difficult to communicate effectively with immigrant coal miners in Pennsylvania to tell them that they were being asked to scab during a strike by union miners:[3]

> When I published a notice for men to stay away...and stated that Poles and Italians were being sent there...I had three or four Poles and Hungarians jump on my back for saying that men of these nationalities went out there...I am hanged if I know what to make of them, for if you call them Poles they will tell you they are Hungarians, call them Hungarians and they will say they are Lithuanians, but *whatever they are, they are being imposed on and made use of to injure themselves and all others who toil.* [emphasis added]

Writing in the *American Federationist* in 1910, American Federation of Labor President Samuel Gompers complained that[4]

> American labor has had to bear the burden of competition with an immigration that in the last decade has brought to the population a net increase of at least five million laborers, of whom an enormous percentage was totally illiterate, the great majority ignorant of the English language, and nearly all so poor on arrival that a month's idleness would have brought them face to face with starvation. To this class has been mostly due the undermining of American labor in certain industries...and much of the hostility to the American Federation of Labor....

Late in 1933, Rose Pesotta, a radical organizer for the International Ladies' Garment Workers' Union, told union president David Dubinsky[5] of her efforts to encourage the

> more class conscious workers...to entrench themselves in the organization. When I say CLASS CONSCIOUS, I say it advisedly, because we have Race Conscious workers and they have got a dose now that will last them a lifetime.

Specifically, Pesotta observed that organizing Mexican clothing workers in Los Angeles was difficult because Mexican workers transferred their antagonism towards Jewish bosses to Jewish garment workers: "All bosses [in the opinion of Mexicans]...are Jews and all Jews are bosses – hence they are doubly hated."[6] Such racial and ethnic divisions had an important effect on the consciousness of American workers, helping to prevent them from becoming a self-conscious class in the sense that Marx used the term to denote a group that was both aware of its common bond of opposition to the capitalists who owned the means of production and was capable of acting as a unit to advance its class interests.

The skilled workers in most craft unions and in positions of power in the American Federation of Labor frequently were reluctant to organize the "new immigrants" from Eastern and Southern Europe who came to America in mounting numbers after 1880. Rather, ethnic militants – especially foreign-born socialists and anarchists – took the lead in mobilizing "new immigrants" into independent proto-unions which threatened to become "dual unions" that would compete with unions chartered by the AFL. Sometimes the existence of such bodies forced AFL unions to mute their nativism and to incorporate immigrant workers into the established labor movement. But many AFL unions, especially those of skilled minorities within trades like textiles, where low-paid labor predominated, would have nothing to do with immigrant workers. The "dual unions" organized by militant immigrant leaders and native-born radicals (who often were affiliated with the Socialist Party of America and/or the Industrial Workers of the World) fought many difficult battles to advance the interests of immigrant production workers. Many of these conflicts were three-way confrontations between immigrant workers, capital, and AFL craft unions.[7]

The essays in this volume discuss the experiences of workers as producers, members of the agricultural and industrial proletariat created by the growth of capitalism. Class formation is not a static process: under capitalism – the most dynamic economic system that has yet evolved – the working classes (and other classes) are highly variegated and are continually being formed and reconstituted. Internal and international migration were (and are) essential to the mobility of labor that capitalism needed for flexible (and profitable) production. Capitalism created and then exploited a fluid, mobile labor supply that could be summoned and dismissed at will. (Under the economic systems that preceded capitalism, labor – whether slave or serf – was generally bound by law to live and work in specific locales and to work for a given owner or on specific lands.)

The American labor force grew through natural reproduction and through immigration. The United States opened its doors to foreign migrants because the nation's rapidly expanding economy needed labor – the labor of the highly skilled and of those who were willing, because they had no choice, to perform repetitive work that required brawn and stamina. Young people, especially males, were recruited and funnelled into the middle- and low-skill jobs that became proportionately more numerous as the division of labor and the degree of mechanization intensified under capitalism. Young people also migrated internally, from farm to factory, as mechanized agriculture displaced many rural workers.

Capitalism in the United States worked best when there were too many workers for the jobs available. The reason is simple: with a labor surplus, workers would compete with each other for jobs and generally be willing to accept wages lower than they wanted in order to obtain a job. Public policy encouraging massive immigration was not accidental, and when fear of political radicalism led to demands to close off immigration from Eastern Europe, Congress and public authorities responded in a pragmatic way, crafting an immigration law in 1924 that did not cut off the supply of skilled industrial workers and professionals from Western Europe. And workers from the Philippines and Puerto Rico could enter because they lived in American territories. In subsequent years, when American businesses needed a fresh supply of low-wage labor, state and federal authorities allowed millions of poor Mexicans to move across the Southwestern border and disperse throughout the nation.

In colonial times, the labor force was composed of three principal groups: English (predominantly Protestant), German, and Black African peoples. The latter were transported, against their will, to fill the demand for agricultural and craft labor in the Southern colonies, which were suffering from a severe labor shortage induced largely by the brutal treatment of English-born indentured servants. In the nineteenth century, massive immigration greatly increased the racial and ethnic diversity of the labor force, bringing in large numbers of Catholic and non-English-speaking peoples from Europe and East Asia.

American capitalists understood the potential divisiveness of racial and ethnic heterogeneity; employers consciously pursued a variety of strategies to divide their workers along racial and ethnic lines. Some employers segregated workers into ethnic and racial groups within work gangs or within work rooms. Ronald Takaki's essay in this volume (Chapter 2) demonstrates that on Hawaiian sugar plantations in the late-nineteenth and early-twentieth centuries employers "systematically developed an ethnically diverse plantation working class in order to create divisions among labor and reinforce management control." The plantation owners turned to a different ethnic group whenever they found that any one ethnic group was beginning to predominate, a situation that often led to successful worker resistance to an intense work pace and also facilitated overt union organizing. This led ultimately to a mixed labor force comprised of Japanese, Filipino, Korean, and Portuguese workers. At one point the planters also made efforts to introduce American Blacks. To divide and conquer, the Hawaiian planters also created an elaborate system of job hierarchies and paid their multi-ethnic labor force different rates for work in the same job classifications.

In a series of classic articles Herbert Gutman demonstrated that midwestern coal mine owners in the 1870s deliberately recruited Black or Italian strikebreakers who would be unsympathetic to the pleas for class unity made by the striking Yankee, English, and Irish miners.[8] In 1915 the Rochester *Post Express* would comment, in the midst of a strike of predominantly Jewish garment workers, that the planned introduction of Italian strikebreakers was designed "to create a race feeling between the Italian and Jew and to terrorize the non Italian element."[9] During World War I, the managers of the Chicago slaughterhouses and meatpacking factories deliberately mixed anti-union Black workers with unionized Polish workers in an attempt to create racial tensions that the employers knew would undermine the effectiveness of the Amalgamated Meat Cutters and Butcher Workmen's Union. The owners of the worsted mills of Lawrence, Massachusetts, and the steel companies of the industrial heartland deliberately excluded the more recent immigrants and Blacks from higher-paying jobs. Lawrence employers used yet another strategy in 1918 when worker discontent threatened to erupt into strikes that united workers of different wage and skill levels and ethnic strata: employers offered wage increases only to more highly-skilled native-born or "old immigrant" workers.[10]

Rational economic behavior for American capitalists meant an assiduous search for ways to pay workers less. Employers used intimidation, outright theft of worker earnings, avoidance of costly safety procedures, and many other techniques to reduce production costs. However, the quickest way to augment profit margins was to lower workers' wages; and the most effective way to accomplish this was to glut labor markets. Among the methods used to accomplish this was the hiring of labor recruiters who went to Europe and Asia to lure foreign labor to the United States. Extensive advertising in European newspapers and thousands of flyers also were used to try to convince workers to emigrate to the United States. To preserve the benefits they derived from a large influx of foreign-born labor most American corporations fought the attempts by many organized workers in the United States – native-born and immigrant alike – to protect their jobs by calling for literacy tests and nationality quotas to limit immigration.

Immigrant workers offered employers special advantages. Many immigrants came from low-wage regions; they were initially satisfied that American labor markets paid significantly more at all skill levels than employers had in the immigrants' countries of origin.[11] It is clear that during the last one hundred years of significant labor migration to industrial nations there has been an inverse relationship between a nation's level of economic development and the rate of worker emigration. Wage levels in more developed nations also were higher than in nations that were largely agricultural. American-born workers complained that many immigrant workers were willing to work for low wages and endure a low standard of living: a Wisconsin blacksmith noted ironically in 1887 that "immigrants work for almost nothing, and seem to be able to live on wind – something which I cannot do."[12] Moreover, since many immigrant workers intended (especially in the years before World War I) to save as much of their wages as possible during a relatively short sojourn in the United States and then return to their nation of origin, they were willing in the short run to tolerate substandard living conditions.

In some years between 1900 and 1914, re-emigration rates are estimated to have ranged between 40 and 60 per cent, especially for single male workers. These figures do not tell us much about the average length of stay in the United States for these workers, many of whom undoubtedly were part of an international group of migrants who circulated between countries in Europe, Latin America, Asia, and North America. Such international mobility had significant political and economic consequences for immigrant workers: they were aliens who could be deported by means of proceedings that did not give the potential deportee the civil rights that were accorded, at least in theory, to citizens of the United States. Especially during the periods of intense worker militancy in the wake of both World Wars, many immigrant workers were threatened with deportation for alleged seditious activity, were arrested, often without legal warrants, and were deported on the flimsiest of evidence. Between November of 1919 and January of 1920 thousands of immigrant workers – including many who actually were citizens – were arrested, beaten brutally, and held without bail, often simply because they had participated actively in labor strikes.[13] As Mario Garcia demonstrates in his account of

Southwestern refinery workers (Chapter 5), the threat of deportation was used a generation later to intimidate unionizing immigrant and native Mexican and Mexican-American labor. In the copper refineries of El Paso, Texas in the late 1930s and during World War II, migrants who daily crossed the border to work in the copper factories faced the threat of deportation or blocked access to jobs. This threat led union organizers to tell alien copper workers to avoid talking about union affairs while they were at work and were being observed by company managers.

Employment of non-citizens also reduced costs for businesses, because when these workers were killed in industrial accidents it often was very difficult for their dependents abroad to initiate suits against negligent employers. Alien workers who had entered the United States illegally obviously were unable to sue employers for industrial injuries since legal action would alert immigration authorities to the aliens' presence. When the states began passing workmen's compensation laws after 1910, many state legislatures included provisions that awarded less compensation to alien or naturalized workers' dependents living abroad than to dependents residing in the United States. This "cost-saving" feature of immigrant labor was particularly important to capitalists—a great many firms assigned immigrant workers to the most hazardous jobs.[14]

In a provocative analysis of the role of immigrant labor in contemporary European society, Manuel Castells has argued that "the utility of immigrant labour to capital derives primarily from the fact that it can act towards it as though the labour movement does not exist."[15] Castells may have overstated his case, but his analysis does point to a significant advantage for American employers who hired immigrant workers. Most immigrant workers, whether they came from urban or rural environments, could not be organized as easily as most native-born workers; language barriers impeded communication, ethnic and racial antagonisms arose in mixed work groups, and the workers often were unfamiliar with trade unions. There are two important exceptions to this generalization: First, American employers in the mining and textile industries hired many English workers even though the English were known to be militant trade unionists. Employers had no choice—they faced an absolute shortage of workers with the skills these English possessed. Second, immigrant workers' strong sense of group solidarity, which was often accentuated by the phenomenon of chain migration that led to the clustering of immigrants from the same European village or group of villages, gave them great cohesion when they became militant in reaction to work-place experiences in the United States. When employers, like the Chicago stockyards employers, hired very large numbers of workers from one ethnic group, e.g., Polish workers hired after 1900, they created a mass of workers of similar national heritage and linguistic background who could be galvanized into vigorous action.

It was clear to many workers, including immigrant and second-generation workers who strongly identified with the ethnic and racial group of their parents and kin, that continued immigration glutted American labor markets, driving down wages and frequently making union organizing more difficult. Workers already present in the United States often sought to bar immigrants from being hired, especially by government, and tried to prevent further immigration. Craft workers—whether Scottish coal miners, American steelworkers, Italian shoe repairers, or German brewers—all favored, at some point in the years between 1870 and 1910, some type of immigration restriction, whether through coercive or cooperative mechanisms. John Laslett (Chapter 9) discovered that Scottish immigrant miners already working in the northern Illinois coal fields proposed exchanging union cards with their peers in Scotland and then using membership in a common union to set up a system of immigration controls to prevent miners from either nation from emigrating to the other during periods of economic recession when unemployment glutted labor markets. In short, the operation of labor markets not only led to friction between members of different racial and ethnic groups but also produced antagonisms between members of the same ethnic or racial group that ran along the lines of "old-timer" vs. "newcomer," or employed workers versus potential migrants who would increase the supply of labor in a given labor market.

Proponents of "split labor market" theory (especially Edna Bonacich) argue that economic factors—the existence of high-wage and low-wage labor markets—are the primary cause of ethnic and racial separation of workers, exacerbating whatever friction already existed between workers of different ethnic and racial groups. They see racial and ethnic conflict as "rooted in differences in the price of labor," especially between high-priced and cheap labor. But Bonacich pushes her point too far when she argues that "language and cultural differences...are not formidable obstacles to communication and cooperation in the long run."[16] The intensity of inter-ethnic conflict, and the ease with which employers in the United States (and in other nations) have created and manipulated inter-ethnic and inter-racial tensions between workers, suggests that intrinsic racial and ethnic differences are much more potent than split labor market theorists allow.

Moreover, as structuralist historians like Mike Davis have pointed out, beginning with the massive immigration of Catholic workers (predominantly Irish, but with significant numbers of Germans) to the United States, between 1840 and 1860 there emerged *"two corporatist sub-cultures*, organized along a religious divide" and operating through many community-based voluntary organizations – churches, fraternal associations, and revolving credit associations.[17] On the one hand, there was a militant, often statist, evangelical Protestant subculture, which included most native-American workers and easily absorbed English immigrants; on the other side emerged a defensive, anti-state, Catholic subculture that included many more immigrants. Additional immigration, including migrants from the Orient and Latin America, and a new wave of European immigration after the Civil War, would further complicate the American scene. Jewish and Asian workers, both first and second generation, formed their own subcultures, especially since Catholic and Protestant workers were so hostile. After 1890 workers in the new stream of Catholic immigration from Mexico and Southern and Eastern Europe were aliented both economically and socially, at the workplace and on the community level. The Irish-German Catholic Church hierarchy refused to give them respect and position. Most established trade unions, dominated by American, Irish, and German officials, were similarly hostile.

However, we must not lose sight of the way that diverse racial and ethnic groups were able to coalesce to pursue similar goals and to organize unified action to achieve their aims. Ethnic homogeneity and the residential clustering of workers of the same ethnic group often facilitated their organization into labor unions. Jewish immigrant workers unionized in the United States in proportions significantly higher than other Southern and Eastern European immigrant nationalities because the Jews were highly literate and came from European communities that had responded to ghettoization by forming tightly knit religious and mutual aid organizations, including ethnic (Jewish) unions.[18] Victor Greene has demonstrated that ethnic community organizations of Slavic coal miners facilitated the immigrant miners' unionization and their disciplined, militant action during strikes.[19] Dorothee Schneider's contribution to this volume (Chapter 10) on the experience of immigrant German brewery workers in New York City in the 1880s reveals the Old World traditions of German brewers, including tightly knit worker associations (initially state-sponsored); these and the fact that the brewers lived in close ethnic communities made union building relatively easy once the brewers began to articulate common interests distinct from those of their German employers.

Ethnic identification also created significant disunity among workers in different segments of the brewing industry. English and Irish immigrants, who dominated the labor force of ale and porter (dark ale) breweries, did not want to join the same locals as German workers who made lager beer. Thus a structural division that coincided with ethnic groupings developed among unions of brewery workers; separate locals were established for lager beer workers on the one hand and for ale and porter workers on the other. This division undermined the ability of German lager beer brewers to secure the absolutely essential aid of other brewery workers and workers of other ethnic groups. After a period of cooperation with their workers' union, employers in the New York City lager beer trade initiated an open shop drive in 1888, attempting to smash the brewers' union. Only a city-wide working-class boycott of lager beer would have given the workers in that trade a chance to save their union. But the German brewery workers could not find allies within their trade and were denied aid by workers of other ethnic groups in other occupations. Ethnic differences were too great to be surmounted at this time.

Rudolph Vecoli's essay (Chapter 14) on the 1919 Lawrence strike also illustrates the dialectic of strong intra-ethnic identification and divisive inter-ethnic rivalry. The strike at the mills in Lawrence was not the first major labor action there. The Industrial Workers of the World aided Lawrence workers during a massive strike in 1912, which was followed by an equally intense walkout in Paterson, New Jersey. In each case the Wobblies supplied an answer to the pessimists who despaired of inter-ethnic cooperation. The IWW followed the simple (but uncommon) expedient in its Eastern organizing of designating organizers to speak and translate for each language group among the immigrant workers. In Lawrence in 1912, the IWW created a strike committee structured on the basis of nationality representation, with each ethnic group included, irrespective of its size. Vecoli tells us that in the 1919 Lawrence strike the striking workers, sixty percent of whom were immigrant women, joyously participated in singing the Internationale and other songs, each nationality singing in its own language, but together. The result was not cacophony but harmony.

Similarly, the United Mine Workers of America, the largest industrial union before the rise of the steelworker and autoworker unions in the 1930s, was particularly adept at preserving inter-ethnic unity. Especially in the critical period of organizational growth between 1900 and 1902, UMW leaders, many of whom were Socialists and/or former Populists and Chartists, openly criticized ethnic slurs and biases. During the 1902 anthracite strike, UMW President John Mitchell worked hard to prevent any discrimination in the dispersement of strike benefits. The resulting unity demonstrated that explosive ethnic differences could be defused by direct decisive leadership action.[20]

But even when immigrant workers were organized by leaders who explicitly tried to counteract ethnic prejudice, there were problems. In Lawrence, the Irish and French-Canadian workers, strongly influenced by their dislike of other European immigrants and by the attacks on immigrant radicalism made by the local Catholic church, refused to join either the 1912 or the 1919 walkout. Wage increases were won in both strikes, but in the aftermath of each strike a stable union organization could not be maintained: Management fired most activists and also continued to pit the favored Irish and French Canadians against the Italians, Poles, Portuguese, and Greeks.[21]

Achieving racial and ethnic unity in both large factories and small workshops was essential to the building and maintenance of union power. In his study of multi-ethnic organizing in the Chicago packinghouses, James Barrett (Chapter 13) found that Irish women workers nourished a tradition of union militancy that was infused by Irish nationalism. As more and more Slavic workers entered the labor force, ethnic fraternal organizations were important vehicles for organizing the new workers. On the other hand, Barrett argues that the reality of ethnic and racial separation, and especially the divisions between Black and white workers, whether immigrant or native-born, led to a stratified approach to union organization in the World War I period. Because socialist and militant non-socialist union leaders feared that Black workers would be submerged and exploited if they joined a stockyards/packinghouse union organized along industrial lines, the leaders decided on neighborhood locals, which implied a policy of de facto racial segregation, since in Chicago, as in so many industrial cities, intense racism forced Black workers into single-race neighborhoods.

Raymond Lou (Chapter 3) examines the nativism of Los Angeles trade unionists, whose fear of competition with Chinese workers reached such levels in the 1860s that it was generalized into a vendetta against Chinese farmers and vegetable peddlers, who were in a trade that native-born workers did not even try to enter! When no native-born workers stepped forward when the Chinese went on strike to protest high license fees enacted in an attempt to drive them out of business, the exclusionists tried to recruit native workers to take the place of the Chinese; the effort failed miserably. The irrationality of the Los Angeles workers revealed the special intensity of intraclass rivalries based on racial differences, especially between white and non-white workers. Anti-Oriental sentiment among California's workers was so intense that it became a major ingredient in the political appeal of the state's Socialist working-class leaders and its mainstream politicians.[22]

Barbara Posadas' study (Chapter 4) of the experience of Chicago's Filipino immigrants in the service trades reveals the way members of one non-white ethnic group absorbed the prejudices of the dominant native culture against native-born Black workers. Major hotels in Chicago deliberately stratified their labor forces along ethnic lines. Black workers were given the lowest-paying jobs; Irish and German workers were placed in the top jobs. Filipinos, many of whom had high school educations or were students working their way through college, often were asked by the better-paid American and Irish workers to help with arithmetic calculations. The Filipinos complied, but deeply resented the fact that, despite their superior education, they were placed in lower-paying jobs. Posadas also discusses the tactics of the Pullman Sleeping Car Company, which deliberately hired Filipino workers to try to create competition and racial friction between Black workers and the foreign-born newcomers. Initially the union of the Black Pullman Car workers, the Brotherhood of Sleeping Car Porters, disdained organizing the Filipinos. But in 1937, in a major shift of policy, the Brotherhood's Black leaders decided to forge a racial "popular front" and begin organizing and defending the rights of the Filipino workers. Posadas shows that racial friction between Blacks and Filipinos did not disappear, but nonetheless cooperation and mutual respect emerged as a generally united labor force achieved significant gains in wages and protection against punitive and unfair disciplinary action.

In his account of union activity among Black and white iron ore miners in Alabama, Horace Huntley (Chapter 7) shows that the Mine, Mill and Smelter Workers Union, which was strongly influenced by the racial egalitarianism of its Marxist and liberal national and local leaders, succeeded in building an effective interracial union. By the 1930s the union contained a Black majority and a white minority. But when the center and the right wing of the American Labor movement launched an anti-left purge in the wake of World War II, the leaders of the United Steelworkers of America, who sought to displace the Mine, Mill and Smelter Workers Union, tried to utilize the racism of those white workers in the Alabama locals of the union who had never been happy as a minority within a predominantly Black union. Representatives of the Steelworkers went beyond internal challenges to Black leaders, to scabbing and cooperation with company unions. Red-baiting was mixed with race-baiting. While most Black workers resisted the red-baiting of the CIO, and while the local NAACP supported the Mine, Mill Union, the Steelworkers unseated the union in a hard-fought representation election. Huntley documents, in chilling detail, the kind of harassment that was directed against non-racist white workers who bravely refused to accept divisive, vicious racial stereotypes of inferiority and superiority that were used by management and by organizers of the United Steelworkers of America in their effort to destroy the radical Mine, Mill and Smelter Workers Union.

Throughout the nineteenth and twentieth centuries, race-baiting had been used by employers in all sections of the nation to try to divide Black and white workers who were engaged in united action. In the South, incipient textile strikes were often nipped in the bud by the threat to import Black strikebreakers.[23] On occasion, white and Black workers resisted this tactic. This was especially true in New Orleans during the 1892 General Strike and in the first decade of the twentieth century when Black and white screwmen and longshoremen defended their agreement to share work equally between the two races, an equality that was reflected in racially balanced union negotiating committees. By standing firm against the attempts of employers and politicians to disrupt this interracial alliance, New Orleans port workers enjoyed production standards that protected them against the speed-up that was implemented in all other Southern ports.[24]

Some historians have hypothesized that many immigrant workers – with the exception of those who were committed radicals before they left their homelands – were not militant trade unionists until they had lived in the United States for several years and had decided that they would make the United States their permanent home. Having made that decision, they were willing to engage in militant confrontations with employers to seek union recognition and better wages and working conditions. David Brody concludes that the major organizational drive among immigrant steelworkers in 1918 and 1919 succeeded because World War I had just this impact on the Slavic immigrants who filled so many of the middle- and low-skilled positions in the nation's steel mills.[25] Gary Gerstle's research (Chapter 11) suggests that in Woonsocket, Rhode Island, French-Canadian workers' ties to their homeland in Quebec were strengthened by strong organizational links to the conservative Quebec Catholic Church that supervised the priests who ran Woonsocket's ethnic church. Until the 1930s, when Canadian workers in Woonsocket were caught up in the national wave of union organizing, they remained relatively indifferent to trade unions. By contrast, John Cumbler (Chapter 8) found that in Fall River, Massachusetts, in the 1860s and 1870s, newly arrived French-Canadian immigrants were unwilling to join trade unions; but contact with a very militant trade-union movement strongly influenced by English-born leaders convinced the French Canadians, by the 1880s, that the local textile unions could help them improve their lot. Consequently the French Canadian workers joined in the major Fall River strikes of the 1880s.

Cumbler reminds us that, contrary to most views, up to forty percent of the immigrants to America in the nineteenth and early twentieth centuries were skilled craftsmen, many of them experienced industrial workers. Like most immigrants, the English about whom Cumbler writes brought with them "a substantial array of cultural and institutional supports." Fall River was a community in which English and native-born workers established a rich institutional life, especially in the Odd Fellows and other fraternal lodges they created. Keeping in touch with the British labor movement by subscribing to the militant pro-union English newspaper, the *Cotton Factory Times*, the English in Fall River were instrumental in leading a vigorous trade union movement that in the 1860s and 1870s staged some of the most successful strikes ever conducted by American textile workers. Many of these workers also clearly expressed their opposition to the capitalist wage-labor system. The problem that they and so many other native-born and immigrant workers had was in coalescing around a common strategy and a common vision of an alternative political economy. In Fall River many textile workers tried to form producers' cooperatives, as did native-born shoeworkers in many New England communities. For a time, the Fall River cooperatives were very successful, but ultimately they failed, as did most undercapitalized worker ventures that sought to create an autonomy that was not possible as long as a worldwide competitive market system existed.

As the historical studies in this volume suggest, scholars must be careful of hasty generalizations about the propensities of immigrants as a whole or about members of specific ethnic groups. Worker consciousness is a product of experience and culture, which includes both the memory of past experiences and interpretations of present circumstances. There has been a great deal of variation in the experiences of workers in different locations, each with their own distinctive social structure, institutions, leadership elements, business enterprises, and economic conditions. Only by examining each social-geographical entity in which immigrant workers lived and worked, together with their cultural legacies, is it possible to understand their varying attitudes towards trade unionism and political ideologies.

"Red Scare," the anti-union, anti-Catholic Ku Klux Klan, often with financial aid from open-shop employers, thrived in many midwestern industrial regions, pitting Protestant workers against Catholic workers. A horrified Dayton, Ohio Socialist was chastened by the sight of a massive Klan rally in Dayton:[29]

> As I watched those muffled and masked thousands pouring along the street, flaunting their symbols of "Americanism" with the contrary insignia of the "Invisible Empire," the thought came to me: What a fearful weapon in the unscrupulous hands are these great blind forces of religious antagonism and racial prejudice! How oddly we Socialists underestimated the enduring quality of primitive influences....

According to most businessmen, unions were not "American." John Bukowczyk (Chapter 15) offers us insight into the interplay during this era between working-class protest, ethnicity, and local politics in Bayonne, New Jersey, a major East Coast oil refining center. Polish immigrants were hired initially as strikebreakers, but soon came to dominate refinery employment. Ethnic community institutions were critical in the daily life of workers, and often acted to support actions based on class, aiding mass strikes. But ethnicity also overlapped with and was confused with class by both workers and the middle class. Employers came to see ethnicity as "dangerous and volatile...a thing to be eradicated." In this they received significant support from other quarters, especially coupled ethnic businessmen and professionals.

In Bayonne, the conservatism of liberal democracy—its particular genius—worked in three principal ways. First, there were the measures of welfare capitalism—that clever blend of benefits and rhetoric designed to convince workers of a "partnership" between capital and labor. Second, especially after the strikes of 1915, the public schools embarked upon a vigorous program of "Americaniza-tion" intended to squeeze out the last vestiges of obstreperous ethnic-ity. Third, and at the same time, a massive political movement was launched to convince immigrants to become citizens and to then vote for anti-radical candidates. These three campaigns worked together to achieve the desired ends. Ultimately the support of middle-class Poles in Bayonne was the key, both in terms of political involvement and in terms of supporting "Americanization" programs, thus proving that class loyalties were stronger than ethnic bonds. "Pro-labor" became, by definition, "pro-business." Middle-class hegemony had been achieved.

Of course, there was repression aplenty in Europe, especially after World War I. Labor's road everywhere was difficult at best. Continued economic dislocations and political repression in Ireland and Great

III

All economic and political movements that focus on a militant ideology calling for vigorous confrontation with established power structures generally are led by a small number of intellectuals and accomplished organizers who do more of the planning and spend more time discussing tactics and strategy than does the rank and file. It is hardly surprising therefore, that in Woonsocket, as Gerstle demonstrates in his study of ethnic radicalism (Chapter 11) there were two relatively small groups of activists—a cadre of Belgian-born skilled workers who were dedicated Social Democrats, and a group of second-generation French-Canadian militants who believed in "bread and butter" trade unionism but were hostile to socialism. But even the latter group appeared "radical" to mill owners because the trade unionists challenged the norms of mill owners who did not want workers to have any independent representative organization that would infringe, even to the smallest extent, on the autonomy of management.

Veteran European union organizers often migrated to the United States, where they applied the tactics and ideologies they had absorbed abroad. English and French militants, the socialists, anarchists, and syndicalists who emigrated from Italy (often fleeing to avoid incarceration), and Russian and Polish radicals (particularly Jews) who came to America, especially after the 1905 revolution was crushed—all made the United States their home and provided dynamic leadership at all levels of the labor movement. These Europeans also had a strong desire to build on the American tradition of independent labor political action, promoting Marxist or non-Socialist parties that were explicitly working-class institutions.

Examining Scottish immigrant miners who first arrived in the United States during the Civil War, Laslett (Chapter 9) finds that the labor-relations strategies they favored evolved as they had in Scotland. At first exercising a considerable degree of job control, the miners favored labor-management cooperation; then, as technological changes gave management the upper hand in labor relations, the miners, whether in Scotland or the United States, turned first to militant strike activity and then, a generation later, to radical politics, supporting the Independent Labour Party (and then the Labour Party) in Scotland and the Socialist Labor Party (and then the Socialist Party of America) in the United States.

In industrialized nations, organized religion—especially the Catholic Church—influenced the political and economic consciousness of many workers. In Europe many Catholic laymen and church officials were politically active, striving for the adoption of welfare-state policies and building Catholic labor unions that favored evolutionary, not revolutionary, change. But in the United States the Church rarely exercised real power directly in the national political arena.

By the 1880s the Church was willing to endorse "respectable" labor unions. But as the mass-production labor force was being formed, with largely "new immigrant" workers from nationalities that the Irish- and German-dominated American Catholic Church had excluded from power, the Church sometimes became decidedly right wing—attacking as dangerous hotbeds of radicalism the militant labor unions that mobilized the "new immigrant" mass-production workers. The Church also desired to offset charges that it and its immigrant flock were "un-American." In Europe, the Church often pushed the center parties to the left, forcing conservatives to accept some restrictions on the prerogatives of capital. In the United States, its political pressure was almost always to the right. However, the Catholic church in the United States, dominated as it was by a conservative Irish hierarchy, which in the nineteenth century had incorporated only German Catholics into positions of power, could not control many Italian, Polish, and Slavic priests. Some of the latter were proponents of trade unionism, even when it took on a radical tone.

Time and again we find elite groups in the United States voicing concern about immigrants' lack of "Americanism" and devising methods to "Americanize" them. In every case, that Americanism was cast in the image of the American bourgeoisie, who viewed themselves as the product of a unique national culture that offered the individual the opportunity to excell and to accumulate great wealth and power. This was an unbridled capitalism in which American businessmen envisioned no legitimate role for collective organizations of workers. As Andrew Carnegie put it upon learning that the union of the steelworkers at his Homestead plant had been crushed in 1892: "Life Worth Living Again." Addressing "Americanization from the bottom up," Barrett (Chapter 13) shows the true character of the struggle over "Americanism." The immigrants who worked in the stockyards and packinghouses *were* good Americans, but their views conflicted with those of the country's owners. The conflict was over who would define what "American" was; the conflict was over which classes would control the country, over whose country it was to be.

The charge that the unions formed by workers in the United States were alien, un-American institutions, was an old one. In a famous verdict delivered after the 1836 conspiracy conviction of a group of striking shoemakers in New York City, the presiding judge expostulated that:[26]

In this favored land of law and liberty, workers have no need of artificial combination. Every worker knows, or ought to know, that he has no need of artificial combinations. They are of foreign origin, and, I am led to believe, upheld mainly by foreigners.

In the years after the Civil War most of the American daily press, and innumerable Protestant ministers, politicans, and businessmen all railed against the alleged influence of alien troublemakers in stirring up organized working-class action, on the picket line or at the polls. During periods of intense labor militance, repression of unions often was justified by the allegation that the nation was in danger of being "overthrown" by foreign radicals. Thus the press held that the railroad strikes of 1877 were the work of agents of the Paris Commune, that anarchists were responsible for the strikes of 1886 and that the strike wave of 1919—the most intense in American history—was the work of the Bolshevik agents.

Many conservative, anti-Socialist union leaders, of Yankee, Irish and German stock, were apprehensive that the "new immigrants" from Southern and Eastern Europe, whom Socialist politician Victor Berger in 1911 had called "modern white coolies," could not be good trade union material until they were deradicalized, a difficult task that most union leaders were loathe to undertake.[27] Listen to the rhetoric of an "optimist" on this question, James A. Henson, who told the 1913 convention of the Illinois State Federation of Labor that organized labor was[28]

the melting pot of America. We melt the raw, crude immigrant into a good citizen. We put it in our bylaws, we inculcate it in his mind, and as a result of that kind of method since I became a member of organized labor we have evoluted into men of intelligence, and the revolution is now going on, not with bullets made of lead, but with bullets made of mentality.

In the 1920s anti-union, open-shop-drives were draped in the rhetoric of patriotism. The "American Plan" favored by big business meant no trade unions. And in the aftermath of World War I and the

Britain during the 1920s, and the crackdown on unions in the wake of the British General Strike of 1926 (which was smashed by the military) encouraged many Irish and British workers, especially militants, to emigrate to the United States. Steve Babson (Chapter 12) points to the importance of the dynamic contribution these militants, most of them skilled metalworkers, made to the organization in the 1930s of American automobile workers into a militant industrial union, the United Automobile Workers of America (UAW).

In the 1930s ethnicity was not as potent as it had been in the past. But it still mattered, as did race. Addressing delegates to the 1937 convention of the United Electrical Workers, Mike Quill, leader of the multi-racial, multi-ethnic Transport Workers Union, warned that opponents of trade unionism[30]

> are going to cast the American worker against the foreign-born, the white against the negro [sic], the Catholics against the Protestants, the men of one belief against the men of another. They will raise the question of the isms to the high heavens, but you should go out of here determined that the one important ism is the question of honest trade unionism.

Many CIO unions found that language barriers made it necessary—an asset—to establish some ethnic locals. (They had been commonplace in the years between 1880 and 1920.) But there was also a new element present in the CIO's appeal to many ethnics, a "Pan-Catholicism" that urged all Catholic workers to submerge their national rivalries and join in a crusade for social justice that has been sanctioned by their common God. By the 1930s a sizable number of Catholic bishops, some with their sees in major industrial cities, e g , Detroit, had become vigorous proponents of trade unionism.[31] This does not mean that ethnic and racial differences disappeared; but their divisive effects were somewhat reduced, especially while the political left, which stressed racial egalitarianism more than any other element in the labor movement, was still a potent force within the labor movement. The post-World War II purge of the left from the labor movement, facilitated by the Taft-Hartley Act of 1947, gave American businessmen the kind of centrist labor movement they could tolerate as long as American economic preeminance allowed business a high level of earnings.

Any careful reader of newspaper accounts of internal union politics in the 1980s will understand, however, that ethnic and racial schisms still play an important role in dividing organized workers. Altagracia Ortiz presents a case study of ethnic disunity in the post-

World War II era (Chapter 6). The International Ladies' Garment Workers' Union (ILGWU) was one of the most progressive labor organizations in the country, and it operated in a highly competitive industry that had always been hard to unionize. The ILGWU had been a union of predominantly Jewish and European-born Catholic workers. As thousands of Puerto Ricans arrived in New York City after 1917 and entered the garment trade after 1930, and especially after World War II, the combination of economic stress and well-established racial prejudice against Third World Hispanics led the leadership of the ILGWU to treat its Puerto Rican members as second-class citizens. Italian members were allowed to maintain their foreign-language locals, in which all business was conducted in Italian; Puerto Ricans were not. Nor did the union adequately service the complaints its Hispanic members made about pay discrimination and other management abuses. The rules governing election to the union's executive board were rigged to prevent Puerto Ricans from obtaining positions of power within the union. Very few Hispanics were appointed as managers of union locals that had significant Hispanic membership. Moreover, the ILGWU excluded Puerto Ricans from training programs, preventing them from being taught the skills that would allow them to be promoted to higher-paying skilled jobs. In the mid-1950s Puerto Rican members in the ILGWU openly rebelled against this condition, staging public demonstrations and publishing pamphlets detailing their complaints. The only significant concession made by the ILGWU Executive Board was to hire a benefits clerk who spoke Spanish and to publish a Spanish-language edition of the union's newspaper. Today's garment industry is employing thousands of Asian women, who are equally subordinated by the patriarchical leaders of the needle trades unions.

IV

Both historically and in today's increasingly competitive world economy, capital continues to utilize existing divisions within the working classes and tries to create new ones, especially by lobbying for more flexible immigration policies that allow the recruitment of needed skilled workers and that augment the size and ethnic diversity of the reserve army of labor. This tactic helps prevent strong challenges to the authority of elites to make decisions about wages, hours, working conditions, fringe benefits, the level and location of employment, and the kinds of goods and services produced. Seeking lower production costs and to retard workers' organized collective power, business will, whenever possible, augment the labor pool with internal migrants and external immigrants, especially those from impoverished regions—whether they are allowed permanent entry into the United States or are given a "third class" status as temporary workers, which has been the fate of millions of Hispanic members of the American working classes.

In today's world of rapid communication and transportation capabilities, capital often shifts production sites to Third World locales where it can tap surplus labor, especially women without significant industrial experience who have been socialized in highly patriarchal societies that stress obedience to male authority. Migration of capital allows many companies to produce in a low-wage environment that is often union-free or is organized by state-directed unions. Whether business brings immigrant workers to a particular production site or moves capital to areas of tractable, low-wage labor, the same basic process is followed to allow production for profit at the lowest possible cost.

Immigrants who have entered and continue to enter the American labor force are participants in this process, a process that they have often tried to resist or to turn to their own advantage. Immigrants to the United States have been among the most fortunate in the history of the world—despite the disdain often displayed toward them by the host society, a disdain that is manifested by host societies all over Europe as well—if only because they have taken up residence in the nation that during the last eighty years has had the highest level of real wages in the world. These immigrants often have viewed the United States as a land of opportunity where they could live at a higher level of material culture and with more education available to their children then in their homelands.

But immigrants and their offspring, especially if they were non-white, also suffered grievously as they were psychologically traumatized and physically mangled because of prejudice and the drive of business owners to produce for profit. American employers have always used workers from racial and ethnic groups in the lowest income strata for the most dangerous and unpleasant jobs. For example, Black steelworkers have always been disproportionately concentrated in blast furnace jobs, which are hazardous because furnace emissions cause more occupational diseases than any other job in the steel industry. Black workers have taken these jobs because they suffered from higher unemployment rates than workers of any other racial or ethnic group and were therefore desperate for work.

During the 1930s many immigrant workers and their descendants became part of a unique left-liberal political coalition, allied with the

Democratic Party, which forced American capitalists to accept labor unions—albeit non-radical unions—and made reluctant business-men and politicians accept the principle and basic institutions of a welfare state that would provide a higher level of security for at least some of the nation's proletariat. In so doing, the immigrants often drew on the inspiration of their own communal institutions and were propelled by their anger against American and ethnic entre-preneurs' using the high levels of Depression-induced unemployment to intensify the exploitation of workers. Second-generation members of the "new immigration," Blacks, and a small number of recent arrivals from the ranks of the left wing of the British trade union movement, played a crucial role, along with native Socialists, Com-munists, and militant trade unionists, in building industrial unions in the mass production industries.

For the last fifteen years, the American labor force has been in the midst of a dramatic transformation, as rapid technological change reconstitutes the character of work and labor markets, creating an especially large number of less skilled jobs in manufacturing, retail, and service trades. New production and record-keeping technologies have given employers more control over the labor process than they have ever had. Ever larger numbers of workers are now inter-changeable, and therefore more easily exploited, as the job skills they need to master and the discretion they need to exercise at work have been reduced, in many instances drastically. Because new computer-based technologies enable employers to monitor closely the quan-titative and qualitative performance of workers at all times, employers have been able to intensify work speed and raise production stan-dards. Workers whose jobs have been eliminated by new production technologies have generally endured significant periods of unemploy-ment and have only been able to find work that pays on average 15 to 20 percent less than their former jobs. These developments have made many workers much less willing to strike or to protest against wage and work standard "give backs." Wage levels have been stagnant for almost an entire generation, and the pace of work, as well as work-related stress, has increased markedly.[32]

At the same time, immigration has turned sharply upward, once more bringing large numbers of workers from low-wage, Third World, especially Asian and Hispanic, countries into the American economy. For the first time in the history of industrial America, non-white groups constitute the majority, in most places in the nation, of the immigrant labor force. The structural assimilation of non-whites into all American institutions, including the labor movement, has always proceeded much more slowly then has the incorporation of peoples of European nationalities. Given the historical record of extreme prejudice manifested against non-white workers, it is highly doubtful that either today's rank and file or the national leaders of the AFL-CIO, enmeshed as they are in a Democratic Party that still reflects racism in all sections of the nation, will rise to the challenge of organizing these new workers.

In today's Asian and Hispanic communities in the United States, radical activists are largely absent. Most Asian and Hispanic radicals have "stayed home," either because they have risen to power in successful revolutions in their countries of origin or because they are actively involved in ongoing revolutionary movements. Thus, the immigrant ethnic radicals who played such a pivotal role in organizing the European immigrants in the United States between 1840 and 1940 have few current counterparts within the Asian and Hispanic working-class communities in the United States.

As the economy switches from a manufacturing/extractive to a service economy, the proliferation of innumerable small-scale service businesses makes organizing low-paid service workers much more difficult than it is to mobilize workers who labor in large factories. As the feminization of the labor force intensifies, large numbers of immigrant and second-generation working women come from cultures that emphasize the subordination of women to patriarchal authority and are hostile to women's labor activism. Some scholars believe that such cultural structures make women workers more likely to defer to the authority of male supervisors in the work place.[33] Such workers are less likely to engage in shop floor protests against exploitation and are reluctant to join unions.

In the short run, native-born workers, including the offspring of the once-despised "new immigrants" from Southern and Eastern Europe, may benefit from the segmentation of the American labor market. In the long run, a labor movement that represents a shrinking proportion of the labor force and the voting public will be less able to protect even the interests of the better-off strata of the working population. Without adequate economic and political mobilization unorganized workers employed in secondary labor markets — which are becoming so important as job-formation proceeds vigorously in the service trades — will suffer. Income polarization within American society can be expected to intensify; and American labor will become more and more divided.

PART II

NON-WHITE WORKERS
IN THE UNITED STATES

Asian

CHAPTER 2

Ethnicity and Class in Hawaii: The Plantation Labor Experience, 1835–1920

RONALD TAKAKI

Hawaii, Hawaii	Hawaii, Hawaii,
To yoo	Like a dream:
Yume mite	So I came –
Kita ga	but my tears
Nagasu	are flowing now
Namida mo	In the canefields.
Kibi no naka	

–Work song of Japanese
plantation laborers

Not all immigrants to the United States came from Europe, and the history of labor in this country was not wholly continental. Leaving their homes in Asia, many of them had sailed east to work on the sugar plantations of Hawaii. Due to the enormous demand for labor to cultivate sugar cane, over two hundred thousand people were recruited and transported to the islands between 1850 and 1920. They came from all over the world – Puerto Rico, Portugal, Germany, Norway, and even Russia. But most of them, over eighty percent of the entire plantation work force, were from Asia, specifically China, Japan, Korea, and the Philippines. These immigrants, together with native laborers, made possible the tremendous expansion of the sugar industry on Hawaii, from the first crop of twenty-five acres producing 30 tons of sugar in 1838 to 214,000 acres of cultivated cane yielding 556,871 tons in 1920.

These men and women working on Hawaii's plantations transformed the islands, and in a 1920 strike pamphlet they proudly claimed an important place in history. "When we first came to Hawaii," they noted, "these islands were covered with ohia forests, guava fields and areas of wild grass. Day and night did we work, cutting trees and burning grass, clearing lands and cultivating fields until we made the plantations what they are today."[1]

But now decades later, as we study their history, we need to know more about the making of Hawaii's multi-ethnic working class. Aware of the racial and ethnic diversity of American society generally, we need to ask how planters on the islands viewed and treated the workers representing a variety of nationalities. And we need to understand how the laborers themselves thought, felt, and responded in terms of ethnic and class consciousness.

The ethnic diversification of labor in Hawaii began almost as early as the sugar industry itself. In 1835, William Hooper of Boston founded the first plantation on the islands, and he recorded in his diary his thoughts on one of the purposes of his plantation in Koloa, Kauai:[2]

> Just one year to day since I commenced work on this plantation, during which I have had more annoyances from the chiefs and difficulty with the natives (from the fact of this land being the first that has ever been cultivated, on the plan of *free* labour, at these islands) than I ever tho't it possible for one white man to bear, nevertheless I have succeeded in bringing about a place, which if followed up by other foreign residents, will eventually emancipate the natives from the miserable system of "chief labour" which has ever existed at these Islands, and which if not broken up, will be an effectual preventitive to the progress of civilization, industry and national prosperity.... The tract of land... [was developed] for the purpose of breaking up the system aforesaid or in other words to serve as an entering wedge... [to] upset the whole system.

Clearly, a sense of mission lay behind Hooper's energetic enterprise: his plantation was the "entering wedge" of capitalism, designed to split apart, irrevocably, the ancient system of Hawaiian society.

Initially Hooper employed Hawaiians, but frustrated because he could not convert them into docile and efficient modern agricultural workers, he turned to Chinese as the solution to his labor problem. In a letter to Ladd and Company, the corporate owners of the plantation, he wrote in 1836: "We may deem it, at a future day, necessary to locate some halfdozen Chinese on the land, if the establishment grows it will require them." Shortly afterward, he began to use Chinese laborers; in 1838, he wrote: "A colony of Chinese would, probably, put the plantation in order, to be perpetuated, sooner and with less trouble than any other class of husbandmen."[3]

After 1850, as the sugar industry expanded and as the Hawaiian population declined due mainly to diseases, planters increasingly turned to imported laborers – the Chinese first, then other groups. Many planters viewed laborers simply as commodities they needed for production, and recruited workers wherever they could find them. In their business memos and requisitions, they submitted orders, side by side, for materials and for men.

On August 22, 1889, for example, Theo. Davies and Company sent C. McLennan, manager of the Laupahoehoe Plantation, a memorandum that acknowledged receipt of an order for:

> tobacco
> Portuguese labourers. we have ordered 20 men for you.
> lumber
> 7 ft iron bar
> wool mattress
> olive oil

On July 2, 1890, the Davies Company wrote McLennan regarding an order for bonemeal, canvas, "Japanese laborers," macaroni, and a "Chinaman." Other business correspondence specified orders for lime, thread, knives, shoe laces, and Chinese laborers. A letter from the Davies Company to McLennan on January 3, 1898, confirmed a list of orders, which included: "DRIED BLOOD [fertilizer]." "LABORERS. We will book your order for 75 Japanese to come as soon as possible." "MULES & HORSES." Similar memoranda filled the business correspondence of other agencies. On October 12, 1894, William G. Irwin wrote to George C. Hewitt of the Hutchinson Plantation to acknowledge receipt of orders for pipe coverings, insulators, bolts, bone meal (300 tons), and Chinese labor (40 men). A letter from the vice president of H. Hackfield and Company (now American Factors) to George Wilcox of the Grove Farm Plantation on May 5, 1908, had itemized sections, listed alphabetically, for "Fertilizer" and "Filipinos."[4]

This evidence supports the thesis that the making of Hawaii's multi-ethnic work force sprang from an economic need for labor. But while planters placed orders for labor as if it were a commodity or tool, they were also aware of the workers' nationality or ethnicity. In fact, they systematically developed an ethnically diverse plantation working class in order to create divisions among the laborers and reinforce management control. Robert Hall, manager of the Niulii Plantation, noted the "frequent occurrence" of strikes on plantations where workers were mostly of one nationality, and recommended a "judicious mixture" of nationalities to "modify the effect of a strike." Manager George F. Renton of the Hawi Plantation warned his fellow planters that strikes would occur as long as workers could combine, and urged them to employ as many nationalities as possible on each plantation and thus "offset" the power of any one nationality. George H. Fairfield, manager of the Makee Sugar Company, stated the planters' divide-and-rule strategy even more bluntly: "Keep a variety of laborers, that is different nationalities, and thus prevent any concerted action in case of strikes, for their a few [sic], if any cases of Japs, Chinese, and Portuguese entering into a strike as a unit."[5]

During the 1880s, as planters increasingly relied on Chinese laborers, they realized they had created a predominantly Chinese working class. To correct this imbalance, they introduced Portuguese laborers. "We need them," the *Planters' Monthly* declared, "especially as an offset to the Chinese; not that the Chinese are undesirable – far from it – but we lay great stress on the necessity of having our labor mixed. By employing different nationalities, there is less danger of collusion among laborers, and the employers...secure better discipline." The most important "different nationality" that the planters used to check the threat of Chinese labor solidarity was the Japanese. In 1886, A. S. Cleghorn, the Inspector-General of Immigration, reported that the Chinese workers, organized into "secret societies," had been able to increase their wages. But the recent introduction of the Japanese, he added, had served as "the principle check upon the Chinese, in keeping down the price of labor."[6]

Within a few years, however, the majority of the plantation laborers were Japanese. Fearful that the Japanese were "getting too much of an upper hand in the labor market," planters resumed the importation of Chinese to reduce their dependency on Japanese labor. They thought "discipline would be easier and labor more tractable if Chinese were present or obtainable in sufficient numbers to play off against the Japanese in case of disputes." In their business correspondence, planters frankly stated the purpose for importing Chinese labor: G. C. Hewitt, manager of the Hutchinson Plantation, wrote to W. G. Irwin and Company on March 16, 1896: "Our order for *40 Japs* – given you in our letter of the 6th inst., is now *void*. 25 Chinese, which are expected to arrive in April will fill all our back orders for labor to date." A few months later, H. Hackfield and Company informed George Wilcox of the Grove Farm Plantation: "Regarding the proportion of Chinese and Japanese laborers we beg to advise, that the Hawaiian Sugar Planters' Association and the Bureau of Immigration have agreed up 2/3rd of the former and 1/3 of the latter. For your private information we mention, that the reason for this increasing the percentage of the Chinese laborers is due to the desire of breaking up the preponderance of the Japanese element."[7]

In 1900, however, planters could no longer import Chinese laborers, for Hawaii had been annexed to the United States and federal laws prohibiting Chinese immigration had been extended to the new territory. Worried the "Japs" were "getting too numerous," planters scrambled for new sources of labor. "There is a movement on foot," wrote the director of H. Hackfield and Company to George Wilcox on December 22, 1900, "to introduce Puerto Rican laborers, as also some Italians, Portuguese, and Negroes from the South....We would ask you to let us know at your earliest convenience how many laborers of each nationality you need." Planter John Hind had already visited the Southern states and had returned "fully convinced of the feasibility of bringing Negroes to the islands as field hands." In 1901, some two hundred blacks from Tennessee were brought to Hawaii.[8]

Planters thought the ideal situation would be to have a work force divided "about equally between two Oriental nationalities," and viewed Korea as a potential new source of labor. In the late 1890s, sugar growers scanned the horizon of the labor market in Asia and seriously discussed proposals for the importation of Korean laborers. On November 19, 1896, for example, Theo. Davies and Company wrote to C. McLennan: "It has been proposed that the planters should have another source from which to obtain Asiatic laborers, lest the supply of Chinese or Japanese should be interfered with so that it might become impossible for us to get any one or either nationality. The source from which it is suggested that we get a new supply is Corea." Shortly after the annexation of Hawaii, planters and their business agents in Honolulu developed a plan to import a "trial shipment of Coreans" in order to "offset" the "large numbers of Japanese" in Hawaii. They sought to "mix the labor races" on their plantations. Thinking they would have "but little chance to get the Chinese to do this with," they decided to "get Koreans here" and "pit" them against the "excess of Japanese." The introduction of Koreans, planters stated in their correspondence, was "necessary" in order to make certain the Japanese laborers would not become "so independent in their relations with their managers and bosses" as to form "a combination to put up wages."[9]

Determined to create an ethnically diversified plantation work force, planters' began to import Korean laborers in 1902. A month after the arrival of 102 Koreans in January of the following year, Walter Giffard, Secretary and Treasurer of William G. Irwin and Company, predicted: "The Korean immigration scheme which has been inaugurated will in due course give us an element which will go far towards not only assisting labor requirements but will be of great service in counter-acting the evil effects in the labor market caused by too great a preponderance of Japanese." The director of Theo. Davies and Company wrote C. McLennan: "Corean laborers must be introduced here in small numbers so that we may not be depending so exclusively on Japanese." More important, he added, the Koreans were "not likely to combine with the Japanese at any attempt at strikes." The manager of the Hutchinson Plantation, angry at Japanese workers for demanding higher wages and leaving the plantation for the mainland, asked the Irwin Company to send him Korean laborers quickly: "In our opinion, it would be advisable, as soon as circumstances permit, to get a large number of Koreans in the country at say $12.50 a month, and drive the Japs out."[10]

But the planters' hopes to use Koreans to drive out the Japanese were dashed in 1905 when the Korean government terminated Korean emigration. A year later, after a Japanese strike at Waipahu on Oahu, the *Pacific Commercial Advertiser* condemned the Japanese as an "obstreperous and unruly lot." "To discharge every Jap and put on newly-imported laborers of another race would be a most impressive object lesson to the little brown men on the plantations," the editor declared. "It would subdue their dangerous faith in their own indispensability." A few months later, planters sent Albert F. Judd to the Philippines to initiate the importation of Filipino laborers, and, on December 20, 1906, he personally led the first fifteen Filipinos down the gangplank of the S. S. Doric in Honolulu. As he displayed them on the dock, Judd announced that if the Filipino were treated right, he would be a first-class laborer, "possibly not as good as the Chinaman or the Jap, but steady, faithful and willing to do his best for any boss for whom he had a liking." The manager of the Olaa Plantation, where the first Filipino laborers were sent, reported that he was pleased with the newcomers. Pitting the Filipinos against the Japanese, he recommended that more Filipinos be added to the plantation's labor force in order to bolster the "Filipino colony" numerically and help them continue to "stand up well" against Japanese efforts to exercise "a bad influence" on them.[11]

Planters followed the course charted for them by Judd. The Gentlemen's Agreement of 1907 restricted the migration of Japanese laborers to the United States, and the Japanese strike of 1909 demonstrated to the planters their dangerous dependency on a predominantly Japanese work force. Consequently growers saw the Philippines, which had been annexed to the United States at the end of the Spanish-American War in 1898, as "the only available source of a permanent labor supply and the only hope of the future." Recruiting Filipinos by the thousands, planters used them in the same way they had earlier used the Chinese and Koreans: to control and discipline Japanese plantation laborers. The manager of the Hawaiian Agricultural Company, for example, complained to C. Brewer and Company about the high wages which the "Japs" on his plantation were demanding. On August 7, 1913, he wrote to the agency in Honolulu: "If possible for you to arrange it I should very much like to get say 25 new Filipinos to put into our day gang....In this way perhaps we can stir up the Japs a bit." Twenty days later, he wrote again to C. Brewer and Company, stating that he was "very pleased" to receive the shipment of 30 Filipinos, and hoped "this increase" would bring the Japanese workers to "their senses."[12]

Thus planters developed a transnational labor supply for political as well as economic purposes, and diversified their labor force ethnically. The ethnic composition of the plantation working class changed significantly between 1872 and 1920 – from predominantly Hawaiian (82.8%) with a small percentage of Chinese, to mostly Japanese (73.4%) in 1902, to primarily Japanese (43.9%) and Filipino (29.4%) in 1920, with much smaller representations of principally Korean, Portuguese, and Chinese (as Table 2.1 shows). This ethnic diversification of the work force led directly to the making of Hawaii as a cosmopolitan society (see Table 2.2).

To strengthen their authority over their ethnically diverse workers, planters developed an occupational structure stratifying plantation employment according to race. One of the policies of the Hawaiian Sugar Planters Association was to restrict skilled positions to "American citizens, or those eligible for citizenship." This restriction had a racial function, for it excluded from skilled occupations Asians or immigrants regarded as not "white" according to federal law, and hence ineligible to become naturalized citizens. This structure of racial/occupational stratification was clearly visible in Hawaii in 1915. Japanese workers were mostly field hands and mill laborers. There were only 1 Japanese, 1 Hawaiian, and 3 part-Hawaiian mill engineers on all the islands; the remaining 41 mill engineers (89 percent) were of European descent. Racial differences were particularly evident in supevisory positions: of the 377 overseers, only 2 were Chinese and 17 Japanese; 313 of all overseers (83 percnt) were white. Field and mill laborers, predominantly Asians, took orders from *lunas* (overseers), usually white men. Planters also instituted a differential wage system, paying different wage rates to different nationalities for the same work. Japanese cane cutters, for example, were paid $0.99 a day, while Filipino cane cutters received only $0.69.[13]

In their strategy to control their workers, planters cultivated national consciousness and a strong sense of ethnicity in order to pit different groups of workers against each other. During the 1850s, planters used Chinese laborers as an "example" for the native workers. They hoped the Hawaiians would become "naturally jealous" and "ambitious" to outdo the model Chinese laborers. Planters noted how pleased they were to find that the "coolies" worked harder than the natives and condescendingly called the Hawaiians *wahine! wahine!* or "women! women!"[14]

This practice of promoting competition between different groups continued as planters expanded the ethnic diversity of their work force, and it became the policy of the Hawaiian Sugar Planters Association (HSPA). The Association sent a circular to plantation managers, showing that nearly 20 percent of the work time of the average laborer was "unavailable" to the plantations. Calling this loss

TABLE 2.1
Plantation Employees by Ethnicity

	1872	1882	1892	1902	1908	1912	1920
Chinese	446	5,037	2,617	3,937	2,916	2,744	2,378
	11.5%	49.1%	12.7%	9.3%	6.2%	5.7%	5.3%
Filipino	–	–	–	–	141	4,630	13,061
					0.3%	9.7%	29.4%
Hawaiian &	3,186	2,575	1,717	1,493	1,309	1,297	1,322
Part Hawaiian	82.8%	25.1%	8.3%	3.5%	2.7%	2.7%	2.9%
Japanese	–	15	13,019	31,029	32,771	28,123	19,474
		0.1%	63.3%	73.4%	69.8%	59.4%	43.9%
Korean	–	–	–	–	2,125	1,666	1,982
					4.5%	3.5%	4.4%
Portuguese	–	637	2,526	2,669	3,807	4,378	3,086
		6.2%	12.3%	6.3%	8.1%	9.2%	6.9%
Puerto Rican	–	–	–	2,036	1,989	1,695	1,422
				4.8%	4.2%	3.5%	3.2%
Spanish	–	–	–	–	750	1,587	313
					1.5%	3.3%	0.7%
Other	–	834	409	1,032	970	940	876
Caucasian		8.1%	1.9%	2.4%	2.0%	1.9%	1.9%
All Others	214[a]	145	248	46	140	283	373
	5.5%	1.4%	1.2%	0.1%	0.3%	0.5%	0.8%
Totals	3,846	9,243	20,536	42,242	46,908	47,343	44,287

Sources: R. Adams, *The Peoples of Hawaii* (Honolulu, 1933), p. 26; *Hawaiian Annual for 1921* (Honolulu, 1920), p. 17; *Pacific Commercial Advertiser*, June 27, 1874. .Spanish and Portuguese are listed separately from other Caucasians.
[a]Including "foreign." *PCA*, June 24, 1874.

of time "enormous," the Association then recommended the use of a "race pride" program which had been tried on one of the plantations:

> At the place where the section luna meets his men in the morning, is a board on which the timekeeper places each morning the daily attendance of the previous day. This is listed by nationalities, the idea being to bring up the attendance of Filipinos and Spaniards to that of the Japanese. This appeal to race pride has, we understand, produced good results in the few months the plan has been in operation.

Foremen also made direct appeals to the laborers' sense of national identity. They told Filipinos, for example: "Work hard and be thrifty and don't get into trouble. Don't show laziness – that would look bad on us Filipinos." One Filipino workgang leader, giving instructions in their Ilocano language, said: "We are all Filipinos, brothers. We all know how to hoe. So, let's do a good job and show the people of other nations what we can do. Let us not shame our skin!"[15]

Pitted against each other by the divide-and-control strategy of the planters, workers of different nationalities found themselves empha

TABLE 2.2
Population of Hawaii by Ethnicity

	1853	1872	1884	1890	1900	1910	1920
Other	1,600	2,520	6,612	6,620	8,547	14,867	19,708
Caucasian	2.2%	4.5%	8.3%	6.9%	5.4%	7.7%	7.7%
Chinese	364	2,038	18,254	16,752	25,767	21,674	23,507
	0.5%	3.6%	22.6%	18.6%	16.7%	11.3%	9.2%
Filipino	–	–	–	–	–	2,361	21,031
						1.2%	8.2%
Hawaiian & Part Hawaiian	71,019	51,531	44,232	40,622	39,656	38,547	41,750
	97.1%	90.6%	54.9%	45.1%	24.4%	20.1%	16.3%
Japanese	–	–	116	12,610	61,111	79,675	109,274
			0.1%	14.0%	39.7%	41.5%	42.7%
Korean	–	–	–	–	–	4,533	4,950
						2.4%	1.9%
Portuguese[a]	87	424	9,967	12,719	18,272	22,301	27,002
	0.1%	0.7%	12.3%	14.1%	11.9%	11.6%	10.6%
Puerto Rican	–	–	–	–	–	4,890	5,602
						2.5%	2.2%
All Others	62	384	1,397	1,067	648	1,071	658
	0.1%	0.7%	1.7%	1.2%	0.5%	0.6%	0.2%
Totals	73,132	56,897	80,578	90,390	154,001	199,919	244,482

Source: Andrew Lind, *Hawaii's People* (Honolulu, 1974), p. 28.

[a]Portuguese are listed separately from other Caucasians.

sizing their ethnic identities and interests. Inter-ethnic tensions led to fist fights in the fields, and sometimes exploded into violent mass clashes. On the Spreckelsville Plantation on Maui in 1898, for example, three hundred Japanese, wielding sticks and clubs, drove a hundred Chinese laborers from the camps. A year later, during a riot involving Chinese and Japanese workers on the Kahuku Plantation on Oahu, sixty Chinese were wounded and four killed.[16]

The strong sense of ethnicity among the workers was reinforced by segregated plantation housing and camps. A Korean laborer recalled how all of the workers, living in "one big camp," were "segregated racially—the Japanese occupying one building, the Chinese another, etc." Workers also were placed in separated ethnic camps. According to one camp resident on Maui, the plantation resembled a "pyramid." The manager's big house was located on the highest slope, with the houses of the foreman tiered below it. Farther down the slope was the Japanese camp, and at the bottom were the Filipinos.[17]

In their separate camps, workers of each nationality transplanted the cultures of their homelands to Hawaii. They organized their own educational and religious institutions. Japanese laborers, for example, founded Buddhist temples and established Japanese language schools for their children. The plantation became a multi-ethnic and multicultural society in miniature.

Divided by the political strategy of the planters and by their cultural identities, workers defined their class interests in terms of ethnicity. Initially they organized themselves into "blood unions"-- labor associations based on ethnic membership. Thus the Japanese belonged to a Japanese union and Filipinos to the Filipino union.

The most important manifestation of "blood unionism" was the Japanese strike of 1909. This four-month-long struggle was totally Japanese—strikers, leadership, and community support. The strikers demanded higher wages and equal pay for equal work. They angrily noted that Portuguese laborers were paid $22.50 per month but Japanese only $18.00 for the same kind of work. They argued that:

"The wage is a reward for services done," "and a just wage is that which compensates [the] labor[er] to the full value of the service rendered by him....If a laborer comes from Japan and he performs the same quantity of work of the same quality within the same period of time as those who hail from the opposite side of the world, what good reason is there to discriminate one as against the other? It is not the color of his skin...that grow[s] cane in the field. It is the labor that grows cane."[18]

Japanese strikers were also protesting against the harsh conditions on the plantations – conditions described in their work songs:

Hawaii, Hawaii	Hawaii, Hawaii –
Kita mirya	But when I came
jigoku	what I saw
Boshi ga	was hell:
enma de	The boss was Satan,
Luna ga oni.	The lunas his helpers.[19]

The strike involved seven thousand Japanese plantation laborers on Oahu, and thousands of Japanese workers on the other islands supported their striking compatriots, sending them money and food. Japanese business organizations such as the Honolulu Retail Merchants Association contributed financially to the strike fund, and the Physicians Association, an organization of Japanese doctors, gave free medical service to strikers and their families. An intense Japanese nationalism inflamed the strike. Strikers stridently shouted "banzais" at rallies, and were urged to commit themselves to the spirit of old Japan –"yamato damashi." They must "stick together" as Japanese in order to win the strike.[20]

The Japanese workers did struggle in solidarity but did not win. The planters had the government arrest the Japanese strike leaders for "conspiracy"; then they broke the strike by hiring Koreans, Hawaiians, Chinese, and Portuguese as scabs, and imported massive numbers of Filipino laborers. Three months after they had ended the strike, the planters eliminated the differential wage system, raising the wages of Japanese workers.

An ethnically based strike seemed to make good sense and strategy to Japanese plantation laborers in 1909, for they constituted 70 percent of the entire work force, Filipinos less than 1 percent. But the very solidarity of the Japanese made it possible for planters to use laborers of other ethnic groups to break their "Japanese" strike.

Eleven years later, Japanese workers found that they had been reduced proportionately to only 44 percent of the labor force, while Filipino workers had been increased enormously to 30 percent. Organized into separate unions, workers of both nationalities came to realize that the labor movement in Hawaii and its strike and other labor actions would have to be based on inter-ethnic working-class unity.

In December 1919 the Japanese Federation of Labor and the Filipino Federation of Labor separately submitted demands for higher wages to the Hawaiian Sugar Planters Association, which promptly rejected them. The Japanese Federation of Labor immediately asked the planters to reconsider their decision, and agreed to declare a strike after all "peaceful methods" had been tried. The Japanese Federation leaders knew there was "no other way but to strike." "Let's rise and open the eyes of the capitalists," they said. "Let's cooperate with the Filipinos"—"back them up with our fund" and "our whole force." The Japanese leaders thought both labor federations should not act precipitously, however. Rather, both unions should prepare for a long strike and plan a successful strategy.[21]

But the Filipino Federation of Labor felt the time for action had arrived. Consequently, on January 19, 1920, Pablo Manlapit, head of the Filipino union, unilaterally issued an order for the Filipinos to strike, and urged the Japanese to join them. In his appeal to the Japanese Federation of Labor, Manlapit eloquently called for inter-ethnic working-class solidarity: "This is the opportunity that the Japanese should grasp, to show that they are in harmony with and willing to cooperate with other nationalities in this territory, concerning the principles of organized labor.... We should work on this strike shoulder to shoulder."[22]

Meanwhile on the plantations, three thousand Filipino workers at Aiea, Waipahu, Ewa, and Kahuku went out on strike. They set up picket lines and urged Japanese laborers to join them. "What's the matter? Why you *hanahana*[work]?" the Filipino strikers asked their Japanese co-workers. Several Japanese newspapers issued a call for Japanese support for the striking Filipinos. The Japanese-language *Hawaii Shimpo* scolded Japanese workers for their hesitation: "Our sincere and desperate voices are also their voices. Their righteous indignation is our righteous indignation.... Fellow Japanese laborers! Don't be a race of unreliable, dishonest people! Their problem is your problem!" The *Hawaii Hochi* advised Japanese laborers to strike immediately, for the "best policy" to make the strike effective was to have "laborers from different countries" take "action together." Between Filipinos and Japanese, the *Hawaii Choho* declared, there were "no barriers of nationality, race, or color." On January 26, the Japanese Federation of Labor ordered the strike to begin on February 1. United in struggle, eighty-three hundred Filipino and Japanese strikers—77 percent of the entire plantation work force on Oahu—brought plantation operations to a sudden halt.[23]

Aware of the seriousness of the challenge they faced and determined to break the strike, the planters quickly turned to their time-tested strategy of divide and control. The president of C. Brewer and Company, one of the corporate owners of sugar plantations, informed a plantation manager: "We are inclined to think that the best prospect, in connection with this strike, is the fact that two organizations, not entirely in harmony with each other, are connected with it, and if either of them falls out of line, the end will be in sight." The planters isolated the Filipino leadership from the Japanese Federation and created distrust between the two unions. Through an attorney, they offered Manlapit a bribe, and suddenly, to the surprise of both the Filipino and Japanese strikers, Manlapit called off the strike, condemning it as a Japanese action to cripple the industries of Hawaii.

But many Filipinos stayed out on strike with the Japanese. Planters escalated their attack on the Japanese, slandering Japanese strikers as puppets of the Japanese government, seeking to "Japanise" the islands. They used ethnicity as an issue to attack the Japanese strikers. In a letter to a plantation manager on February 20, 1920, R. D. Mead, Director of the HSPA's Bureau of Labor, described the plan for ideological warfare against the Japanese strike leaders. "In order to let the plantation laborers know they are being duped and to make them realize what they are losing by allowing themselves to be misled by the agitating newspapers and strike leaders, we have commenced a program of propaganda....There is absolutely no race so susceptible to ridicule as the Japanese...."[24]

To break the strike directly, planters enlisted Koreans, Hawaiians and Portuguese as strikebreakers. Serving forty-eight-hour eviction notices to the strikers, planters forced them to leave their homes and find shelter in empty lots in Honolulu; crowded into encampments during the height of the influenza epidemic, thousands of workers and their family members fell ill and one hundred and fifty of them died. Under such harsh and chaotic conditions, the strikers could not hold out indefinitely, and were compelled to call off the strike in July.

Though they had been soundly beaten, they had learned a valuable lesson from the 1920 strike. Filipinos and Japanese, joined by Spanish, Portuguese, and Chinese laborers, had participated in the first important inter-ethnic working-class struggle in Hawaii. They had been integrated in the labor process, as one of their work songs expressed so clearly:

> "Awake! stir your bones! Rouse up!"
>   Shrieks the Five o'Clock Whistle.
>   "Don't dream you can nestle
> For one more sweet nap.
> Or your eardrums I'll rap
> With my steam-hammer tap
>   Till they burst.
> Br-r-row-aw-i-e-ur-ur-rup!
> Wake up! wake up! wake up! w-a-k-e-u-u-u-up!

> Filipino and Japanee;
> Porto Rican and Portugee;
> Korean, Kanaka and Chinese;
> Everybody whoever you be
> On the whole plantation —
> Wake up! wake up! wake up! w-ak-e-u-u-u-up!
> Br-r-ow-aw-i-e-ur-ur-rup!

Men and women of different ethnicities, remembering how the five a.m. whistle had awakened all of them and how they had labored together in the fields and mills, now had fought together to realize the same goal.[25]

During the strike, feeling a new sense of cooperation and unity which transcended ethnic boundaries, the leaders of the Japanese Federation of Labor questioned the existence of two separate labor unions, one for the Japanese and another for the Filipinos, and suggested the consolidation of the two federations into one union. They insisted that Japanese workers must affiliate with "Filipino, American, and Hawaiian" workers, for as long as all of them were laborers they "should mutually cooperate in safeguarding their standards of living." On April 23, the Japanese Federation of Labor decided to become an inter-racial union and change its name to the Hawaii Laborers' Association — a name which gave the union a regional rather than an ethnic identity and which emphasized its class basis.[26]

One of the leaders of the Hawaii Laborers' Association expressed the new class consciousness emerging among plantation laborers of all nationalities: The fact that the "capitalists were *haoles* [Caucasians]" and the "laborers Japanese and Filipinos" was a "mere coincidence," explained Takashi Tsutsumi. Japanese and Filipinos had acted as "laborers" in "a solid body"; as workers, they were aware of "capitalistic tyranny over industry, the general awakening of labor throughout the world." Noting that the Russian working class had "conquered a nation," the American Federation of Labor had become a powerful force on the mainland, and workers in Europe had struck for their rights, Tsutsumi declared: "Even the laborers of the utterly isolated islands of Hawaii were moved by this world spirit."[27]

What the workers had learned from the 1920 strike, Tsutsumi continued, was the need to build "a big, powerful and non-racial labor organization" which could "effectively cope with the capitalists." Such a union would bring together "laborers of all nationalities." The 1920 strike had provided the vision, the basis for the new union: In this struggle, Japanese and Filipino workers had cooperated against the planters. "This is the feature that distinguishes the recent movement from all others," Tsutsumi observed. "There is no labor movement that surpasses the recent movement of Japanese and Filipinos." Tsutsumi predicted that the "big" inter-racial union would emerge within ten years, based on an "Hawaiian-born" leadership. "When that day comes," he declared, "the strike of 1920 would surely be looked upon as most significant."[28]

This possibility of class unity in a multi-ethnic working class was explored by the son of a plantation laborer—Milton Murrayama—in his novel *All I Asking For Is My Body*. During a strike of Filipino workers on a Maui plantation in the 1930s, the manager recruited Japanese boys as scabs. The youngsters viewed the situation as a chance to make extra money. But one day a discussion on the strike erupted in an eighth-grade class. "What's freedom?" asked Tubby Takeshita, and the teacher and students agreed that freedom meant being your "own boss," not "part of a pecking order." And they saw that workers were at the bottom of the pecking order and were getting a "raw deal." "You gotta stick together even more if you the underdog," Tubby said. And the teacher asked: "How much together? Filipino labor, period? Japanese labor, period? Or all labor?"[29]

What happened in Hawaii needs to be compared to the experiences of workers on the mainland. Imported from different countries to fill the "orders" of the planters for men as well as macaroni and pitted against each other to keep wages low and labor disciplined, workers in Hawaii gradually realized the need for a new politics: While retaining the richness of their cultural diversity, they also had to develop a deeper understanding of their working class identity and interests. On the mainland, too, laborers representing racial and ethnic diversity—Asians, Blacks, Chicanos, and whites—found themselves forming an American working class, Walt Whitman's "vast, surging, hopeful army of workers."[30] They, too, often experienced intergroup competition and conflict in the labor market, occupational stratification, a dual wage system, and racial hierarchy. They, too, had to confront questions of ethnicity and class, and to ask: "How much together?" Thus, the experiences of working men and women in Hawaii, while apparently unique and exceptional, may illustrate more sharply certain larger contours and patterns in the history of laborers in America.

CHAPTER 3

Chinese-American Agricultural Workers and the Anti-Chinese Movement in Los Angeles, 1870–1890

RAYMOND LOU

During the latter half of the nineteenth century, Chinese immigrants in California were subjected to an intense campaign to exclude them from participating in the labor market. This essay examines how a group of Chinese American workers in Southern California countered these attempts to deny them their livelihood. It investigates the history of agricultural workers in Los Angeles County from 1870 to 1900.[1]

From the beginning of Chinese-American settlement in the Los Angeles region in the late 1860s to the turn of the century, agricultural occupations like farming, gardening, vending produce, and ranching were the largest area of employment for the Chinese-American community. In 1880, occupations in agriculture accounted for 31 percent of the population. By the turn of the century, this figure increased to 44 percent. In comparison, the next largest area of employment, the laundry industry, was a distant second at 19 percent.[2]

There are several reasons for this concentration. An important factor was job discrimination generated by the anti-Chinese movement. Chinese workers were excluded from all but the most menial occupations. In 1880, only four areas of livelihood accounted for 87 percent of all jobs: agriculture, laundry, domestic housework, and day labor. For most Chinese workers, economic mobility had to be achieved in one of these four areas. Few workers could accumulate enough capital to become a merchant or manufacturer. Incomes varied from twenty-five to fifty dollars a month. Day laborers were paid about one dollar per day. Domestics, received between forty and fifty dollars per month.[3] Laundry workers earned around thirty dollars per month.

Although agricultural work paid little more than day labor, many workers sought to enter this field because of its potential for higher income. Entry into domestic service and the laundry industry was limited. There was low demand for domestics.[4] Even with the comparatively low wage for Chinese servants, Euro-American households with live-in domestics were a distinct minority. Moreover, the skills necessary for a houseworker and/or to cook in a Euro-American house were acquired only through apprenticeship, training that relatively few Chinese could afford. The laundry industry, in spite of offering higher wages than agriculture, was less desirable. As early as the 1880s, the hand laundry business began to decline. Faced with competition from an increasing number of mechanized steam laundries, Chinese hand laundries were forced to lower prices and expand services. Hence, workers were faced with long hours under very poor working conditions.[5]

Agricultural laborers also faced long hours of strenuous work. However, work in the fields was not closely supervised; workers were usually delegated responsibility for their own work tasks. Since most farms were located in the countryside, farmhands were not subjected to daily racial harassment from Euro-Americans. Workers were also provided with room and board, whereas other workers were required to provide for themselves.

Work conditions aside, the agricultural sector was attractive because it offered more opportunity for upward mobility than laundry or domestic work. About all one could aspire to as a service worker was to be hired as a cook in one of the major hotels or restaurants of the city. These positions were the most highly paid in the area yet even the Chinese-American workers who held these positions had little job security. During times of anti-Chinese agitation, these positions were primary targets for elimination.[6]

Laundry workers were limited to two positions: washer and ironer. A good ironer was able to earn more than a washerman.[7] The real opportunity for economic mobility for laundrymen rested in their establishment of their own businesses. But although the capital required for opening a laundry was minor compared to a retail shop, it was usually beyond the savings ability of a worker.[8] Few workers formed cooperatives or partnerships to finance their own laundries.[9] Two other factors that may have limited the number of independent

With the Euro-American community united in opposition to the Chinese, city officials thought they would be able to disperse the Chinese population with minimal effort. One of the first acts initiated by the City Council, in January 1879, was an ordinance to increase the license fees for Chinese vendors to an burdensome level.[25] Licenses for Chinese farm vendors were increased from $3 to $20 a month.[26] The rationale was straightforward: make it economically unfeasible for Chinese to remain in the county. However, the anti-Chinese leaders did not anticipate that their initial foray would precipitate a conflict with farmers and vendors that would last into the 1890s.

The Chinese did not passively accept such discrimination—they went on strike.[27] By denying the entire town their services, the farmers and vendors demonstrated their resolve for fair treatment as well as the fact that they were an integral part of the local community. At first, the strike appeared to have succeeded. The Council's special committee on licenses recommended lowering the fee for vegetable peddlers to its original rate of $3 a month until May 1 when it would rise to $5 a month.[28]

Since farmers and vendors had previously paid the monthly license fee of $3 without major protest, there is reason to believe the matter would have rested there had the Council acted upon the committee's recommendation. Instead, the Council reaffirmed its intention to increase fees. Perhaps smarting from the display of unity by the Chinese and the public sentiment that the strike generated against the tax hike, the anti-Chinese office-holders attempted to regain the upper hand by refusing to negotiate. At the next meeting, the Council voted again to increase fees for Chinese vendors. In a demonstration of its contempt for the Chinese and their supporters, the Council raised the tax by an additional $5. The license for Chinese vendors was now $25 a month.[29] In response, the Chinese agricultural workers reconvened their strike and remained on strike until the Council relented. Only after the rates were lowered did the Chinese resume their service.[30]

Chinese-American farmers and vendors had little choice in deciding to resist the Council's nativistic assault. Had they paid the monthly tax, they would have been left with a net of $5 to $10 after taxes. It was in this period that the anti-Chinese leaders realized their charges of unfair economic competition were essentially groundless, for no one stepped in to provide the city with produce. Subsequently, the exclusionists intensified efforts to recruit whites into the agricultural sector.[31]

After produce deliveries were resumed—to the relief of the townsfolk—peace did not return for either the Chinese farmers or their customers. Anti-Chinese officials continued to try to reestablish

laundries were the increasing number of Euro-American-owned steam laundries, and the established Chinese entrepreneurs, who formed an exclusive local Chinese laundry association in answer to the decline of the industry. The Chinese entrepreneurs association attempted to regulate the number of laundries in the city.[10] This further reduced the likelihood of a worker becoming an owner.

Agricultural day laborers could remain as hired hands and resign themselves to tenuous jobs and a limited life, or they could try for some degree of security by renting farm land or by sharecropping.[11] The data indicate the latter was a popular choice.[12] Financially, becoming a farmer was less difficult than other entrepreneural possibilities. By sharecropping, a laborer could turn to farming with a minimal cash outlay. Hard labor was a more important factor in success than cash. The most common route for agricultural laborers to become farmers was to form partnerships. This arrangement allowed higher earnings, but of course required more capital than sharecropping. With several partners, raising the necessary money for rent, equipment, and seed was not an impossible task. In the initial stages of the vegetable farming business, growers usually marketed their own crops. As the city grew and the demand for produce expanded, farmers sold their crops to independent retail vendors, thus permitting more time in the fields.

Besides financial gain, the cooperative ventures in farming had other benefits for workers. An attractive feature of partnerships was that the workload was democratically shared. An observer of Chinese agriculturalists reported that he was not able to detect a "boss" or driver on the many farms that he visited.[13] According to his account, the work was divided equally, with no evidence of favoritism. Other chores such as cooking and cleaning also seemed to be equally shared among the partners. Decision making was performed collectively. Partners decided together on which crops to grow and how the farming was to be done.

Vendors were the marketing corps of the farming industry. They were responsible for over half of the industry's gross income in 1895. Vendors were the industry's mainstay prior to the development of interstate markets. The bulk of farming revenues in the early period was earned by selling vegetables to individual households. Although prices of vegetables were low, this market was so attractive that many farmers elected to bypass the wholesale outlet provided by local canneries.[14]

The examination of this category raises questions about whether farmers and vendors—theoretically in the independent petite bourgeoisie—should be considered as part of the working classes.

Chinese-American farmers and vendors occupy a gray area in this tax-onomy. They were not wage earners, yet they were not capitalists. Like the typical worker, they earned their keep with their labor. Unlike industrial workers, farmers and vendors sold a product that represented their labor. Their position was comparable to that of artisans who were self-employed or operated small shops.

These distinctions were inconsequential in so far as nineteenth-century Euro-American blue-collar workers were concerned; for them the relevant category was race. It did not matter if Chinese immigrants were of the same class or not. What mattered was the Euro-Americans' own class position, a position which they thought could be bettered by excluding Chinese workers.

As early as 1872, during the beginning stages of Chinese-American settlement in Los Angeles, a popular complaint was that Chinese vegetable farmers and peddlers had "almost a monopoly" on the business of vegetable production.[15] Chinese growers were, in fact, the major employers of agricultural workers in the Los Angeles area; by the mid-nineties, Chinese farms were conservatively estimated to number between 90 and 180. Farms varied in size from 20 to 189 acres, with the average farm encompassing about 80 acres.[16] Chinese American farmers accounted for the bulk of the crops in onions, potatoes, cauliflower, cabbage, beets, corn and small fruits.[17] Estimated gross annual income of these crops was over $500,000; A sizable portion of this income was derived from sales to the wholesale market. In 1895, the Santa Fe and Southern Pacific railroads each shipped to the East 25 million pounds of vegetables grown by Chinese farmers.[18]

These figures might at first sight seem to give justification to the often-heard charges by the anti-Chinese movement that the Chinese were taking over the state's agriculture and driving the Euro-American working man to despair. A common interpretation by American historians is that the Chinese-Americans created unemployment by underbidding the wages of Euro-American workers. This is also said to have driven down wage rates. But this was not the case in Los Angeles, at any rate.[19] As suggested above, Chinese workers were not employed in areas where they competed with Euro-American labor-ers. Like other people of color throughout American history, Chinese-American laborers were compelled to find work in areas neglected by their Euro-American counterparts. During this period a frequent lament was that the Chinese would never be driven out because white workers would not do the kinds of work done by Chinese laborers. Chinese-American workers gravitated to the "occupational vacuums" in the local labor market. Here the Chinese could make a living wage.

The primary reason why Euro-American workers usually avoided competing with the Chinese in this work was the low pay and long hours. Although retail sales generated over half of the annual income of this sector, approximately $260,000 in 1895, the actual earnings were small. Six days a week farmers and vendors worked from sun-up to sun-down; on the seventh day, the farmer took a half day off.[20] Each day vendors and farmers would load their wagons with nine or ten sacks of fresh vegetables and fruits. If the contents were sold, each sack brought approximately 50 cents. Hence, on a good day each wagon could gross around $5 per day in retail sales. After operating expenses were deducted, farmers and vendors had earned about $2 or $3. Since it has been estimated that the typical vegetable farm required a minimum of one worker for every 10 acres, one vendor wagon marketed the produce from 10 to 12 acres per year. Each ven-dor in effect marketed the output of one farmer per week, hence, each farmer and his vendor netted between $1 and $1.50 per day.[21]

The success of Chinese farmers and vendors was determined by how well they met the public demand for their services. In this respect, the workers were totally dependent upon the market place for their livelihood. Chinese farmers had to remain competitive or become unemployed. The literature of the period indicates that Chinese farmers were highly regarded for the quality of their produce, dependability, and reasonable prices.[22]

The first attempt to curtail the growth of farmers and vendors occurred in the summer of 1876 when the Los Angeles City Council required vegetable peddlers to acquire a business license before sell-ing in the city limits.[23] The ordinance was the result of an anti-Chinese petition presented before the Council at their previous session. It asked that the Council take action against "certain nuisances on the part of our Chinese population." The "nuisances" in question were Chinese vegetable vendors. A special committee of the Council agreed with the petitioners: To insure that the intent of the ordinance would not be misunderstood by white farmers, licenses were required only of Chinese product vendors.[24]

The anti-Chinese movement consolidated its forces during the 1878 election campaign as their political vehicle, the Workingman's Party, enjoyed landslide victories throughout the state. Swept into Los Angeles city offices on an anti-Chinese platform, local party members initiated discriminatory measures against Chinese farmer-workers. Their ultimate goal was total exclusion. Interpreting their political victory as a mandate for their actions, anti-Chinese officials began to implement plans to produce a Southern California society devoid of Chinese settlers.

their authority by harassing Chinese farmers and vendors. One method was the frequent examination of licenses by authorities. As a result of this close scrutiny, several Chinese vendors were arrested for possessing invalid permits.[32] However, these arrests allowed the farmers and vendors to test the legitimacy of the license tax by appealing to the higher courts. This was a costly maneuver for the city, for the litigation remained in the courts for months. One of the ironies of the courtroom debate was created by the farmers, who retained as their counsel Stephen M. White, a young attorney active in the anti-Chinese movement who later was elected to the U.S. Senate.[33] Evidently White did not allow the contradiction to interfere with his courtroom performance. The Chinese won their case. Modifications were made in the license ordinance.

But the court proceedings did not put an end to discriminatory taxes. On April 14, 1879, the City Council again voted to raise vendor licenses. At this session, licenses for Chinese vendors were raised from $3 to $5 a month. Again, the farmers went on strike. This time the Chinese stated they would pay no more than $3 a month.[34]

By Fall 1879, the anti-Chinese movement was no closer to the goal of ousting the Chinese agriculturalists than at the start of their campaign. In fact, the opposite occurred. The number of Chinese farmers and vendors increased. The anti-Chinese agitators were not yet discouraged; they persisted in their campaign. The Chinese showed no sign of tiring either. But the strikes had placed them in a precarious position. If they continued to strike, they risked alienating their public supporters. These had been an important element in their successful resistance. Had the townsfolk sided with the leadership of the anti-Chinese movement, the farmers could have been expelled easily by boycotting their services. Thus the farmers knew they had to devise other means of protest. The first required the enlistment of those who most benefitted from their services: the homemakers of the community. Here the Chinese succeeded. In an action that must have raised many an eyebrow, a group of Euro-American women descended upon a Council meeting to petition the councillors to stop their harassment of farmers and vendors.[35]

The next step taken by the agricultualists was to test the constitutionality of the license ordinance itself. On July 26, 1880, a group of 15 Chinese vegetable vendors had themselves arrested for violating the license ordinance of the city.[36] Their defense, handled by attorney C. M. Wilson, was ingenious. At issue was a state law, passed by the Legislature on April 12, 1880, which prohibited the issue of licenses "by the State, or any county, or town, or municipal corporation, to any alien not eligible to become an elector of this State." Chinese, of course, were excluded from becoming citizens of the United States; hence, they were "not eligible to become an elector...."[37] The local vendors reasoned that if they could not legally be licensed they could not legally be required to pay license fees.

At the preliminary hearing, the first defendant, Ah Tan, demanded a jury trial.[38] After several delays, Ah Tan was found guilty of operating without a license and fined $40.[39] In this case, the presiding judge skirted the issue of constitutionality and ruled only on the violation of the city ordinance. It was not until a month later, when Superior Court Judge Sepulveda adjudicated a similar test case, that the state law was found unconstitutional: Sepulveda ruled that by denying licenses to Chinese-Americans, the State was in conflict with the Fourteenth Amendment. The local press hailed Sepulveda's decision because it meant that Chinese had no recourse and were obligated to pay license fees.[40] The impact of this ruling was felt throughout the state. After Sepulveda's ruling, the anti-Chinese forces breathed a sigh of relief, for a strict interpretation of the law would have exempted Chinese from paying for business licenses.[41]

It is revealing that the Sepulveda ruling was celebrated as a victory for the anti-Chinese movement. In the two-year struggle between members of the Workingmen's Party and Chinese-American agricultural cooperative workers, the stated goals of the former changed from eradication of the latter to enforcing their payment of license fees. Moreover, the tax rates changed from an extraordinarily high level to one in proportion to the fees levied on Euro-American businesses. In 1883, the license fee for vendors was lower than in 1876, the year that fees were initiated. Small vendors who functioned with a push cart or similar vehicle were charged $5 per quarter year. Larger operators who used horse-drawn wagons were charged $40 per quarter.[42]

The local exclusion movement was resuscitated by the outbreak of anti-Chinese violence throughout the West during the winter of 1885-86. Violent expulsions of Chinese settlers began with an isolated incident, the Rock Springs Massacre in which 28 Chinese were killed, but quickly spread across the Western States.[43] The Rock Springs Massacre became a cause célèbre. The rioters were portrayed as simple working men who defended themselves from economic impoverishment. The local press defended the attackers. The judicial system contributed to the legitimation of Chinese expulsion, by refusing to indict any of the instigators.[44] Forceful expulsions followed in numerous towns and cities throughout the West. Encouraged by this turn of events, Southern Californians began to develop new strategies for expelling the Chinese from the region.

Early in 1886, the Los Angeles Trades Council sponsored a series of mass meetings to organize a drive to oust the Chinese. By February their plans had taken shape. The Trades Council adopted a resolution calling for a citywide boycott of all Chinese. The boycott was scheduled to commence on May 1 and to continue until the "Chinese question" had been wiped out. The plan had essentially two components. First was ending patronage of "the Chinese vegetable gardens, the Chinese laundries, and all laundries, restaurants, hotels and other establishments where Chinese are employed." Plans for the second phase addressed the central problem that had earlier hampered the effectiveness of the anti-Chinese movement. The Trades Council and its associates would "encourage and support persons other than Chinese engaged in the cultivation of vegetables and small fruits...."[45] In other words, although Chinese workers were already segregated into noncompetitive economic activities, nevertheless they were targeted for removal.

In the campaign against the Chinese farmers, the boycott effort was a significant departure from the previous tactic of high taxation. The levying of taxes can be seen as an indirect method of driving the Chinese from the region. Even the exclusion movement depended on the municipal legislature and executive to enact laws that would directly facilitate Chinese removal. Their enforcement by the police and judicial system was necessary for them to take effect. While the City Council operated with the approval of the townsfolk in passing the license ordinances, this did not require active participation from the townsfolk. The exclusion movement was essentially an operation sanctioned and implemented by the state.

In contrast, the boycott necessitated direct citizen participation. The Euro-American residents of the city were being asked to sign pledges to boycott all Chinese businesses and services. The boycott meant that Euro-Americans would have to make sacrifices. In the previous mobilizations against Chinese farmers and vendors, the townsfolk did not have to take a stand. They could have remained passive supporters or neutral without detracting from the movement's claim of overwhelming support. Now they were being asked to become active in the movement, to do without services and goods to which they had become accustomed. This was a real test of commitment.

The stakes were very high. The anti-Chinese movement elected to bypass its traditional source of strength, intervention by the state and its judicial apparatus, to appeal directly to the public. The exclusionists were calling upon what they considered their ultimate weapon, a society united against the presence of Chinese workers, for one final assault. It was, in the tradition of the West, a showdown. Two opponents would confront each other to settle their dispute. After the boycott, there would be no need for debate, for there would be a winner and a loser. The anti-Chinese leaders were determined to win.

Boycotts were not new to Angelenos. As early as 1877, the concept of "non-intercourse" was proposed as a means of starving out the Chinese.[46] The concept was not complex. It was based on simple logic: No work: No money: No Chinese. But despite its simplicity, it was not successful. A variation on this theme was introduced five years later when it was suggested that all Euro-Americans cease giving their patronage to Chinese retail merchants. That effort ended with the same outcome as the previous one.[47] To prevent a recurrence of these results, the boycott organizers devised an elaborate campaign to enlist the cooperation of the townspeople. Their efforts were well received by the press and local supporters. The boycott was launched on May 1.

Yet the boycott of 1886 failed. Within 10 days the debacle of the boycott's proponents was obvious to all observers.[48] Its organizers were embarrassed.[49] The Trades Council was not able to generate the necessary level of mass support for its undertaking. While the local politicos and the press endorsed the boycott and issued several pleas for white workers to take over Chinese positions, the bottom line was the continued patronage of Chinese services by the townsfolk.[50] The Chinese were able to maintain their rapport with Euro-American middle class consumers.[51]

Two important allies whose continued support was instrumental in the success of the Chinese farmers and vendors were the Women's Club of Los Angeles and an ecumenical women's federation, both middle class organizations. Alarmed over possible ramifications of the boycott, club members called for a mass meeting to discuss the Trades Council resolution.[52] Over two hundred women of various classes attended the meeting. The women discussed what their role should be in the boycott. Many felt that Euro-American men expected women to perform all the laborious task usually done by Chinese. Moreover, the women thought that men expected these services from them for free. This led to discussion about the political economy of Chinese labor.

What came out of their discussion was a strong sense of identification of women with the Chinese. Women saw themselves in the same class as the Chinese. They discovered that they performed similar labor tasks for similar wages or none at all. They labored under similar conditions, and their underpaid labor subsidized the same group of people: white men. Some women pointed out that working women were the primary beneficiaries of the labor of Chinese. The Chinese were responsible for developing the service industry in California. The wages obtained by Chinese workers set the industry standards for wage earners, including women. Working women received higher wages as a result of these standards. The Chinese "put a money value on woman's work....[53]

The point was made that homemakers benefitted directly from Chinese labor. Chinese laborers relieved women of the onerous chores of washing and ironing. Even moderate-income families could afford the luxury of having their wash done by neighborhood Chinese laundries. If the laundries were forced out of business, far fewer families could manage the rates charged by steam laundries. Because of the very large number (said to be "hundreds") of boarding houses in Los Angeles run by women, the matter of cooking and cleaning done by Chinese workers was of great importance. It was said that the ordinary work in boarding houses was "utterly beyond any woman's strength." Housekeepers were said to be "quite willing to try white men but none apply."[54] Vegetable vendors saved the homemaker time from shopping, since vendors made their daily rounds in all neighborhoods. The supply of fresh vegetable contributed to the general health of the populaton.

The women concluded that it was not in their best interests to support the boycott. They found Euro-American men unrealistic in their expectations and out of touch with the political economy of the region. The presence of Chinese settlers was not an economic drain to the society. On the contrary, they found the Chinese benefitting the society at large and women in particular.

The move to oust the farmers and vendors rapidly dissipated after the 1886 boycott collapsed. Between 1886 and the turn of the century, the anti-Chinese movement was only able to mobilize once more for a brief period in 1893. The galvanizing issue here was the passage of the Geary Act. Its enactment by Congress required all Chinese residents to register with federal authorities and to possess U.S. identity papers. Chinese-Americans throughout the country, in a mass act of civil disobedience, refused to comply. Local exclusionists saw this as an ideal moment to rid themselves of the Chinese. They sought to have Chinese workers arrested and deported for not having the necessary documents to prove the legality of their residency in the U.S. The excitement quickly died, however, when the federal government granted protesters a six-month grace period to register. Most Chinese residents, after the U.S. Supreme Court upheld the Geary Act, had no alternative but to register to avoid deportation.[55]

Chinese farmers and vendors were able to withstand the organized attacks on their position in the local economy by countering with collective efforts of their own. In this respect, their manifestations of group consciousness are unmistakable. They saw themselves as a distinct group of workers with common interests. They saw themselves as a group targeted for elimination. They realized that their life chances were dependent upon their ability as a collective body to resist the exclusion movement. Had they not been successful in combining their individual resources as well as enlisting the support of the Euro-American community, it is doubtful they would have been able to continue to function in the city.

Anti-Chinese forces, on the other hand, saw themselves as a group of workers whose potential for upward mobility was impeded by the presence of Chinese laborers. Whether this was true was not important. It was important for them as Euro-American workers to enhance their class position by establishing more leverage in the labor market. They sought to accomplish this by excluding Chinese workers. That they accomplished this is a matter of record. [56] That they enhanced their class position is a matter of debate.[57] Why they continued to object to the presence of Chinese is the main question. The exclusion of Chinese workers from the competitive West Coast labor market did not result in improvements to the quality of other workers' lives. Their class position continued to be eroded by industrialization and the growing population. Cyclic downturns in the economy continued to occur in the last two decades of the century. To compensate for their lack of control over their own destinies, they attempted to assert mastery over what they regarded as an element responsible for their own powerlessness. The mobilizations to expel Chinese farmers and vendors from Los Angeles were characteristic of this tendency.

The amount of energy the Euro-American working-class movement expended in harassing farmers and vendors during this period is of particular interest in light of the fact that the Chinese were not competitors and were providing services that Euro-American workers were not. Moreover, in comparison with other Chinese-American workers, farmers and vendors were a poor selection as targets. For example, laundrymen would have been better subjects to focus attention upon. The characteristics of laundrymen and their operations were subject to constant vilification in the local press. Complaints ranged from poor quality washing to endangering the health of the entire society.[58] An example of the latter is the charge of infecting customers with syphilis through the laundrymen's practice of spraying clothes prior to ironing by spurting water from their mouths.[59] The location of laundries in white neighborhoods and along popular thoroughfares was highly objectionable to exclusionists. The waste water runoff, which often produced muddy yards and noxious odors, the constant din of washing and ironing, and the sight of clothing hanging out to dry were reasons their neighbors argued for their removal. Another factor that rendered laundrymen a more logical target was the presence of alternative laundry businesses. Euro-Americans owned and operated steam laundries that proudly advertised "No Chinese Labor."[60]

The targeting of farmers and vendors, however, was a different matter. There were few issues that detractors could use to gain sympathy for the cause of ousting Chinese cooperative agricultural workers. Whereas anti-Chinese advocates could find causes to question the sanitary standards of laundries, one of the few health issues raised about farmers and vendors during this period occurred during a smallpox scare when the Chinese were suspected of being carriers.[61] The ubiquitous arguments about economimc competition were not valid. Chinese-American farmers and vendors displaced no other workers; hence, they could not be accused of depressing wages. Their daily presence in the city was not a factor in arguments for their exclusion; it is evident from literature of the period that their daily deliveries of fresh produce were welcome.[62] Unlike laundrymen, Chinese-American farmers and vendors, for the most part, did not reside in the city and had no permanent structures or equipment that could be singled out as eyesores or safety hazards. Vendors came in the morning and left in the afternoon.

Perhaps it was for these very reasons, their lack of negative characteristics and the degree to which the Euro-American community accepted them, that the anti-Chinese movement seemed so determined to eliminate Chinese-American farmers and vendors. The success of the Chinese farm cooperative workers in gaining acceptance must have been threatening to the ideologues of the exclusion movement, for such phenomenon had the potential of undermining its intellectual basis. It was fundamental to the anti-Chinese movement that the two groups, Chinese and Euro-Americans, could not co-exist without endangering the future of humankind. In Los Angeles a group of Chinese-American farmer workers was disproving that assertion. Moreover, the fact that these men could mount sufficient political pressure to compel the governing body of the municipality to remove anti-Chinese regulations was a sobering experience. In fact, because of their high degree of interaction with the larger society and their demonstrated willingness to organize and participate in the making of local political decisions, Chinese-American farmer-workers were found particularly objectionable. Laundrymen and day laborers did not demonstrate the same propensity for organization or interaction; hence, they were not subjected to the same degree of harassment although they were equally visible, if not more so, to the exclusionists.

This is not to say that Chinese-American laundrymen and laborers were not targeted for removal by the exclusionists. Chinese-American settlers, regardless of occupation, were seen as a collective group of illegitimate participants in the American society. Because of their race, Chinese-Americans were highly visible. Laundrymen, farmers, cooks, domestics, laborers, and other workers were subjected to the daily stress of racist interaction. While the level of harassment against cooperative farmers was more severe than others, this occurred because of the organized resistance of this group to exclusionist tactics. The characteristics of the agricultural workplace and the distribution network of vendors lent an organizational advantage to farm workers. Hence, anti-Chinese agitators directed their attention to their removal.

The truce that emerged in the 1890s between the two parties was in part due to the exclusionists' recognition that Chinese farmer-workers were an integral part of the society and to the fact that the exclusion laws of the earlier decade were beginning to reduce the number of Chinese immigrants. The local Chinese-American population in fact, had begun to shrink. It was as if the anti-Chinese advocates realized they no longer needed to push for the expulsion of Chinese settlers, for the exclusion laws guaranteed that within a generation the Chinese-American population would dwindle to an insignificant level. The changes wrought by the laws were becoming visible. The Chinese-American farmers and vendors who were now commonplace on the city streets were growing older, and no younger Chinese-Americans were replacing them. All the exclusionists had to do was sit back and wait.

CHAPTER 4

Ethnic Life and Labor in Chicago's Pre-World-War-II Filipino Community

BARBARA M. POSADAS

In lore and in legend the Statue of Liberty, her torch lifted high overhead, has long been an American symbol of mythic proportions to newcomers surging through the Ellis Island portals. Liberty's promise came less clearly defined on the West Coast where, over the decades, millions of Asians have streamed through various ports of entry. No single image, captured as they got ready to land, would dominate the first memories of those arriving from the Pacific. Similar hopes—and fears—they felt undoubedly, waiting to be realized or put to rest over the months and years ahead. But for the men disembarking from the United States' Pacific island colony, the Philippines, during the first third of the twentieth century, only a few hours on American soil were needed to implant the impact of color in the new land—a hostilely insulting word, a hastily printed sign—"Whites Only."[1]

Over time, the realities of color in America remained far from subtle. Color denied the lodging that money might have bought. Color restricted employment to the most menial of jobs. Color defined the boundaries of friendship and of love. Color masked the differences of class. Yet color provided a common bond, as well, reinforcing the ethnic ties of heritage and language, obscuring provincial differences, lessening the impact of loneliness in an all too hostile world, and sustaining camaraderie in the workplace.

During the years between the turn of the century and passage of the Tydings-McDuffie Act in 1934, America's imperial rule in the

63

Philippines brought a privileged status to her colonials. As nationals of the United States, Filipinos escaped the restrictive force of immigration law until a mid-1930s decision to grant Philippine independence within a decade simultaneously imposed a fifty-per-year quota on further immigration of Filipinos.[2] The new limitation effectively defined the first cohort of Filipino immigration to the United States as the "old-timers," a generation set apart in time and in experience from the massive Filipino migration of the post-1965 era.[3]

During the early decades of the century, thousands of young, single male Filipinos came to sojourn in the United States, never intending to stay permanently. The goals of education and employment – keys to a better life – set most in motion. Keys cut in the United States would unlock Philippine doors to opportunity, enabling a triumphant return to parents and sweethearts abandoned only temporarily. These goals cut across the divisions of class in Philippine society. Sons of poor farmers and wealthy landowners alike responded to the lure of American promise in these years. Many sought the dollars to be earned as field hands in Hawaii, as farm laborers on the West Coast, and as service workers in private homes, clubs, restaurants, and hotels. Others coveted the competitive edge in salary and status which an American college degree offered in comparison with a diploma earned in the Philippines. By the mid-1930s, almost 120,000 Filipinos had migrated to Hawaii in the hope of securing cash for land purchases, bridal doweries, or family support back in the Islands. A smaller number, almost 45,000, had come to the mainland, 81 percent locating in the Pacific Coast states where agricultural and service workers and aspiring students became the West Coast's newest Asian minority.[4]

In analyzing the early Filipino experience in the United States, scholars have devoted most of their attention to the West Coast and Hawaiian migrants, many of whom arrived poorly educated and remained in transient jobs throughout their lives.[5] My work in general and this article in particular, however, diverge from the main thrust of most previous inquiries by concentrating on Filipinos living in the city of Chicago during the period between the early 1900s, when young Filipino college students first began arriving in the United States, and the mid-1940s, when World War II wrought changes in attitudes and experiences.[6] Focusing on an alternative pattern of Filipino immigration and accommodation, in the Second City of the United States, is important for several reasons. First, it permits assessment of a segment of the old-timers' generation that was more highly educated, more occupationally successful, and less subject to legal restriction than its counterpart on the Pacific Coast. Second, it allows investigation of how Filipinos functioned both as minority group members and as ethnics in contrast to Chicago's substantial Black and white immigrant populations. Third, it records the transition in status and self-consciousness among the Filipinos themselves as these migrants changed from sojourners to permanent residents, a process by no means unique among immigrants to America, but one conditioned by the special characteristics of the Filipino old-timers and by the time and setting of their arrival in the Middle West.

Reminiscences of the Filipino old-timers and their wives, collected through oral interviews conducted in the Chicago area and in the Philippines since 1979, constitute the heart of this study.

Approximately a dozen Filipinos first came to the Chicago area between 1903 and 1907 as participants in the *pensionado* program, which provided government-funded scholarships for study at colleges and universities in the United States. Nationally, the select group numbered approximately two hundred young men and slightly less than a dozen young women who were drawn from each of the Islands' more than fifty provinces. The *pensionados* were widely scattered throughout the United States. Those in the Midwest included at least a dozen at Chicago-area schools, and others nearby in Illinois at the University of Illinois and at the normal schools at DeKalb, Bloomington, and Macomb. Indiana University, Notre Dame, Purdue, and Iowa State also drew handfuls of Filipino students.[7]

In addition to assured tuition, the *pensionados* were supplied with expense money sufficient to ensure their full-time enrollment without part-time work and their graduation within five years. The young Filipinos, mostly in law and medicine, were closely supervised by agents of the Bureau of Insular Affairs who placed them as boarders with carefully screened American families near campus; these agents monitored the Filipino students' academic progress and general adjustment to life in the United States, and urged travel in the United States during summer vacations. During the century's first decade, Americans, who had not yet tired of their imperial responsibilities, warmly welcomed these diligent symbols of the nation's success in its mission overseas.[8] Their academic achievements stood in sharp contrast to the portrayal of Filipinos as primitive barbarians at the 1901 Pan-American Exposition in Buffalo and at the 1904 Louisiana Purchase Exposition in St. Louis. The *pensionados* themselves protested against the Philippine Reservation at the St. Louis Fair, contending that its series of ethnological villages over-emphasized "the 'wild tribes,'" thus inaccurately propelling Igorots and Negritos into prominence as typical Filipinos. This inaccurate impression also served to bolster the notion of racial superiority by which many Americans justified colonial experimentation on their "little brown brothers." For many Americans, however, the contrast between G-string-clad tribesmen and Filipinos on campus probably called to mind a "before-and-after."[9]

In the 1910s and 1920s Philippines, the *pensionados*, all of whom had returned by 1912, became role models for succeeding generations, particularly as secondary education in the Philippines expanded during these years. By 1924, 7.9 percent of secondary-school-age Filipinos, those between the ages of fourteen and seventeen, were enrolled in high school, in contrast with 27.2 percent across the United States. Although few children of farm tenants or unskilled laborers might enter, and fewer still graduate, secondary schooling was not limited to the offspring of the wealthy. Education was increasingly seen as crucial to those aspiring to future mobility, to the children of small farmers, managers and clerks, artisans and skilled laborers. High school graduation pointed the way toward Philippine higher education, toward religious colleges founded in the Spanish colonial era or toward the newly established, publicly-funded University of the Philippines.[10]

In addition, the *pensionados'* success motivated some other Filipinos to reach farther, toward colleges and universities in the United States. American teachers encouraged these dreams by stressing that those lacking the secure financing of family money or increasingly rare scholarships might work part-time in America to help earn their way. Parents, siblings, and other family members pooled resources by mortgaging or selling land or using the savings of a lifetime to fund the journey. As time passed, others could call upon brothers already in the United States for assistance with passage money.[11] Many travelled in "steerage where the beds were placed top and bottom in rows like they are in the army."[12] On board the S. S. President Cleveland in the summer of 1926, Benny Feria found approximately fifty workers bound for Hawaii and two hundred and seventy students continuing on to San Francisco.

Some young Filipinos arrived on the West Coast with enough money to travel to chosen schools elsewhere in the nation, meet first tuition payments, buy books, and find a place to live. Others disembarked with little more than the money for a night's lodging in their pockets and more quickly confronted the restrictions of color in cheap rooming houses and menial jobs. One young Filipino, reduced to the role of his family's servant girl back home, cried after washing dishes to earn a meal during his first week in Seattle.[13] Another worked his way East on a crew repairing railroad tracks.[14]

By the middle 1920s Chicago was even more of a magnet for Filipino students than it had been at the turn of the century. The concentration of universities in the region, many of which had been attended by the *pensionados* and earlier students, doubtless supplied the initial attraction. But the metropolitan area itself proved to be even more enticing, not least because of its promise of part-time employment for self-supporting students, employment available year-round for those living in the city and in the summer for those on campuses some distance away. In practice, those enrolled as tiny minorities in Ann Arbor, Madison, Urbana, and West Lafayette were more likely to complete their college preparation and return to the Islands than were those in the Chicago area who increasingly favored such less prominent institutions as Crane Junior College, Lewis Institute, and DePaul University, either for their commercial programs or the availability of evening courses for students who worked full-time during the day. Living in Chicago and working there enabled young Filipinos to call themselves students whether university registrars recognized them as such or not.[15]

It is impossible to determine precisely the number of Filipinos living in Chicago or the proportion of students among them. Estimates vary from a high of six hundred students, 75 percent of the total Filipino population in Chicago in 1924, to a low of 155 students in the state eight years later in the depths of the Depression, when in hard economic times few could maintain even part-time enrollment. Federal censuses record the shifting total Filipino population in Chicago, 154 in 1920; 1,796 in 1930; and 1,740 in 1940. Informal estimates by those in the community in the early 1930s placed the number as high as five thousand. Whatever their actual numbers, or their student status, Filipinos forged and then modified bonds based on ethnicity during these years, as they moved their mental world from the transience of studying overseas to the unforeseen permanence of family and work in an alien land.[16]

As foreign students, young Filipinos continued to draw upon a sense of common national heritage in their extracurricular life. In 1906, two dozen Filipinos launched what became an annual celebration of the Philippine national holiday in memory of José Rizal on the campus of the University of Chicago. Twenty years later, at Crane Junior College, sixty "mostly self-supported students" created the Crane Filipino Club, whose musical ensemble played throughout the Chicago area. A Filipino Medical Students' Association, organized in 1923, united aspiring physicians from several medical schools to offer assistance to Filipino compatriots in school or out. This range of activities, which eventually included rival organizations representing different Philippine provinces, grew, along with the student population, in ways not possible on Midwestern campuses outside Chicago enrolling only a few Filipinos. By the 1920s over a dozen clubs had formed the Filipino Association of Chicago, Inc. as an umbrella organization which, until 1933, ran a Club House, first in the Near West Side, and then, as the Filipinos shifted neighborhood, in the city's Near North Side.[17]

If their numbers provided support for a vibrant associational life, however, other factors conspired to complicate life for the Filipino foreign student in the Second City. The student's struggle for academic success frequently collided with the young man's pursuit of excitement. Temptations to shirk school work lurked everywhere: in the fancy clothes, gambling dens, and pool halls that took his money; in the dime-a-dance girls who might take his virtue as well. By 1932, sociologist Paul G. Cressey's study of "commercialized recreation" in Chicago linked "The Filipino and the Taxi-Dance Hall" in a separate chapter focused on the "problem."[18] A Filipino who won at the "Chinese gambling place" at Clark and Van Buren on the edge of Chicago's Loop customarily bought a bottle of whiskey to share with his luckless friends and might expect a warm welcome at the Filipino-owned combination barber shop and pool hall across the street.[19] As his family prepared for his eightieth birthday party in 1982, Jose Marasigian reflected: "We didn't care for tomorrow. We were still young."[20]

Those who succeeded and could return to the Philippines confident of a warm welcome, with diploma in hand, had learned to be single-minded in the pursuit of their goal. Conserving time and money became as important as studying itself. Filipino educator Pedro T. Orata recalled the difficulties of life as a student in the early 1920s, working as a waiter in the Women's Residence Hall at the University of Illinois in Urbana during the academic year and coming to Chicago for summer jobs. After eight hours at a Montgomery Ward store, Orata earned "dinner and a little cash for washing dishes for three hours each evening" at the Harmony Cafeteria downtown. To save on carfare, Orata, the son of a small farmer who died just after his son began his American education, walked everywhere. The trek back to his room on the West side, after eleven hours of labor, took over an hour and a half. "I still wonder how I did it. When I graduated at Illinois four years later in 1924 — without losing a term — my diploma read 'with final honors.'" Orata's success as an undergraduate eased his years in graduate school during the following three years. The Philippine government awarded him a partial scholarship of fifty dollars per month. At the University of Illinois, while working on his master's degree, he held "a graduate scholarship which included free tuition...and three hundred dollars a year." During work on his doctorate at Ohio State University, a student assistantship provided support. "Happy to return to the Philippines in 1927," Orata used the difference between the paid-for first-class and his actual third-class passage home to buy books for his work as a teacher there.[21]

Prior to the crash of 1929, Filipinos found work easily in Chicago—in the homes of wealthy Chicagoans, in their clubs, and in the restaurants and hotels that catered to those with money. In prosperous times, few remained dishwashers for long. Their jobs as butlers, chauffeurs, waiters, and cooks—and the absence of the West Coast alternative in farm labor—typed Filipinos into service occupations, limiting their mobility, yet providing a form of continuing education that shaped their group reputation and molded their perception of themselves, the city, and their place within it. Filipinos were increasingly viewed as quick learners and good workers—neat, mannerly, and precise in their attention to detail.[22] Filipinos who "made the grade" eased the way for those who followed. When he first reported for work in the linen department of the LaSalle Hotel, Benny Feria was surprised to find that "there were two old-timer Filipinos in the same department where I was assigned ...I knew then that the job was more secure." Feria remained at the LaSalle for "almost seven years," meeting "all kinds of people...from all walks of life."[23]

Filipinos who worked in a personal capacity for wealthy Chicagoans glimpsed the best of life in the Second City. As the personal butler and as the cook in the Lake Forest home of the coffee magnate and owner of the Blackhawk hockey team, Frederick L. McLaughlin, provincemates Alipio G. Posadas and Pedro L. Cabillener each earned fifty dollars per month, room and board, and a weekly day off and round-trip train ticket to Chicago. Already known as a "sharp dresser" among his peers, Posadas had responsibility for his employer's wardrobe and expanded his own knowledge of fine tailoring and expensive fabrics through McLaughlin's clothing. On the estate's tennis court, Posadas improved his game as the practice partner of McLaughlin's wife, the former dancer Irene Castle.[24] Work for the wealthy established a deferential relationship by no means unfamiliar in Philippine society, where patron-client alliances confirmed the status of the elite and gave their favorites modest advantages in return for subservience.[25] In Chicago, such affiliation could give access to racially restricted places and provide help in dealing with the bureaucracy and the law. If dark-skinned Filipinos were fair game, their employers generally were not. Years after the incident, one elderly Filipino remembered with considerable satisfaction that the mere mention of his employer's name quickly blunted the antagonism of the policeman who had stopped his car on Lake Shore Drive and had found a white woman in his company.[26] Filipinos never aspired to the wealth of their employer-patrons, but ties to the important generated a sense of status and pride. Even as an adult, the daughter of one Filipino recalled her family's visits to the Lake Shore Drive home of the widow of her father's employer – she and her sister and brother, scrubbed and in their finest, and, of course, on their best behavior in the antique-filled sitting room. Each Christmas package arrived from a store they had never entered – Saks Fifth Avenue.[27] In this limited way, Filipinos distanced their world from Chicago's immigrant slums and black ghetto, even if their own patterns of residence typically placed them in marginal areas and their contact with the elite was more often transitory than lasting.

During these years, the racial climate in Chicago made particularly appealing the establishment of an advantageous line of demarcation between Filipinos on one hand and those of lesser education or darker skin color on the other. By the years immediately following the First World War, race had become fixed as a primary organizing element in the city's economic and spatial arrangements. Racial antagonism had replaced the class conflict of late-nineteenth-century labor violence as Chicago's most visible problem. Since 1900, the number of Black Chicagoans had skyrocketed from just over 30,000 to almost 234,000 in a city of 3.3 million. Blacks in Chicago became concentrated – in a South side ghetto that constituted a "city within a city." They became conspicuous as well, particularly as unskilled laborers in Chicago's industries, from which they had generally been excluded prior to World War I. By 1920, 48.8 percent of the Black male labor force worked in manufacturing or trade, holding jobs which might take them through white areas on the journey to work or place them in contact with whites on the job. Chicago's race riot of 1919 unleashed tension over these fundamental changes.[28]

Consciousness of the black-and-white dichotomy of American racial prejudice formed in the minds of many Filipinos long before migration. Rather than the history of their own nation, colonial Filipinos studied a past which proclaimed the achievements of American political leaders and businessmen. Slavery was also a part of United States history, and its presentation by American teachers and texts would have a lasting impact on Filipino interaction with Blacks in the United States, particularly as consciousness of their own status as a minority crystalized through bitter experience. In attempt-

ing to define the attitudes of many of his compatriots, Filipino
Methodist minister Fernando A. Laxamana noted:

> Somehow,...by osmosis, you begin to say Negroes must be terrible to
> be enslaved and to be treated like that, so I'm not going to associate
> with such people who are relegated to being almost animals. And if
> I'm going to be acceptable to the American white[s], I better share
> their prejudice. Otherwise, if I associate with the blacks against whom
> they are prejudiced, I'll be included in that. I have enough prejudice
> [against me] as an Oriental. Why should I add some more by
> associating with the blacks?[29]

In fact, given the de facto residential and social segregation of
Chicago, Filipinos had few opportunities for contact with Black
Chicagoans. Though restricted in their access to housing by its cost
and their color, Filipinos found sufficient space outside the Black Belt,
space which drew them into contact with white ethnics. During their
earliest years as self-supporting students in the city, they, like many
European immigrants before them, made the polyglot Near West Side
their first neighborhood, drawing on the ties of family, town, and province in choosing apartment-mates.[30]

Just as homesick Filipinos in college towns sometimes found
"American 'mothers'" to guide them and ease their loneliness, so too
West Side Filipinos, buffeted by rising joblessness in the Depression,
found their own Jewish mother who dispensed tender care and
chicken soup to those in need. To middle-aged, chunky Ida Nasberg,
who ran a dry cleaning business in the neighborhood with her husband, Isadore, the young Filipinos were "all my children....My
home is their home,.. They are just babies separated from their
mothers[s]."[31]

More generally, however, racial interaction on the Near West Side
was problematic. In November 1931, less than a half mile south of
Mother Nasberg's flat, Felomino Montigo and Adriano Elanparo "were
viciously attacked by a mob of hoodlums" as they were walking from
their streetcar stop to their boarding house. Elanparo was "knocked
unconscious by a bat." Montigo, pursued by the assailants from whom
he had momentarily escaped, was "shot dead."[32] At the time, neither
the *Chicago Tribune* nor the *Filipino Nation* speculated on the identity
of those responsible, but shortly thereafter, in reporting the mid-1930s
shift of Filipinos from the West Side to the Near North Side in his
study of *Orientals in American Life*, Albert W. Palmer linked the move
to "gangs of Italian hoodlums [who] systematically broke the windows
of their [Filipino] clubhouse."[33]

Filipino community life centered in the Near North Side from the early 1930s through World War II. Approximately a mile and a half north of the Loop and even closer to Chicago's elite Gold Coast along Astor Street and Lake Shore Drive, the area offered proximity to the service-sector jobs available to Filipinos. Free of notable ethnic identity, this relatively transient locale of walk-up apartments, converted flats and apartment-hotels, near the city's largest YMCA, tolerated a Filipino presence more easily than had the Near West Side where turf was often in contest.[34]

The move to the Near North Side, which occurred gradually during these years as early Chicago Filipinos shifted place and newcomers enlarged their total number, underscored themes of change within the Filipino community itself. As the Depression worsened and menial jobs became more scarce, even the fictional notion of student status based on self-support evaporated. Immediate needs consumed any thought of future goals. In their twenties, the Filipinos had been casual sojourners in quest of adenture and buoyed by a tenacious, youthful belief in the future. But, as hard times stretched months into years, the Filipinos and their dreams aged. If the permanence of their situation was as yet unspeakable, they were stranded nonetheless.

Ironically, coping under these conditions heightened the stratification of Filipinos within their own community. Those in want continued congregating on the Near North Side where the Filipino Community Center on LaSalle Street, an outgrowth of the YMCA's longstanding socio-religious effort among foreign students, now functioned as Filipino Chicago's own settlement house by ministering to those in physical want. Loyalties to province and barriers of dialect diminished as homeless Filipinos ate from the same soup pot and slept side by side on cots under thin blankets in the Center's dormitory. Others crammed into overcrowded apartments nearby where those with a dollar or two sustained the rest. But continuing employment at a living wage increasingly set the luckiest Filipinos above their less fortunate compatriots and financed their movement to slightly better neighborhoods. During these years, a job with the post office or the Pullman Company defined a Filipino "elite."[35]

As early as the mid-1920s, post office and Pullman work claimed status as the best employment to which Filipinos could generally aspire in Chicago. Comparatively, the federal civil service offered better wages than Pullman. As a postal clerk, a Filipino who finished a probationary period as a substitute could earn "pretty handsome money," $1700 in his first year as a regular employee, and could also confidently await $100 yearly raises until he reached a maximum of

$2400. In contrast, a Pullman worker was assured only $780 to start. While tips were expected to supplement this figure, their total amount varied greatly, depending on the clientele of a particular "run."[36]

Employment by Pullman held another disadvantage as well. The railroading pattern of runs and lay-overs foreclosed enrollment in school. In contrast, a postal worker's schedule permitted attendance. Baldomero Olivera, who arrived in Chicago in 1928 and passed the post office's civil service exam on his eighteenth birthday, recalled his good fortune – and hard work: "Those of us who went to the post office had evening jobs and... we could go to morning class. ... It was tough; it wasn't easy at all. ... From the time you punch the clock to the time you left, why you're really working – no wasted minutes over there." From four or five in the afternoon until one in the morning, Olivera sorted mail for six and a half years while earning the Northwestern journalism degree which would launch his half-century career as a respected newspaperman and writer in the Philippines. Filipinos such as Olivera's older brother, Francisco, had "no chance." Despite their "chance," however, a relatively small proportion of the estimated two hundred Filipinos at the Chicago post office completed college study–"not more than twenty finished and came home with a degree.[37] Thus, Filipinos working for the Post Office and for Pullman won elite status among their compatriots not for their achievement of original educational goals established in the Philippines, but rather for their success in accommodating to the realities of life and labor in the United States.

During the Depression, these men were more likely than the under- or unemployed to break from the Near North Side area of settlement by finding apartments farther north and in the Near Northwest Side, or more rarely by buying small homes in marginal suburban areas. The steadily employed, along with the tiny group of Filipino professionals and small businessmen, were also more likely to continue in the community's various clubs. Thus, their distancing from their less fortunate brothers was hierarchical as well as spatial. Enjoying a vantage point as director of the Filipino Community Center in the mid-1930s, the Rev. Laxamana perceived that while the Center still drew affluent and poor together, especially on holidays, the "successful" in their fine clothes stood apart. With the basics of daily living assured, they had the time to be officers in community organizations and the money to devote to community activities. Attendance at banquets and dances, always formal affairs, demanded tickets and tuxedos, and, for those escorting ladies, taxis and corsages as well.[38] Over time, these men found reason to plant roots in Chicago. For some, job and community sufficed, but for others, the establishing of a family, most frequently through marriage to an American woman, also furthered stability.[39]

Whatever their status within the Filipino community, whatever the extent of their individual successes or failures within the world of their countrymen, within the broader context, Filipinos in Chicago were defined by their race as a minority. Theirs was a minority of numbers as well as of color. Neither white nor Black, Filipinos forged a collective group identity by contrast with the city's dominant races. In the workplace, where contacts with whites and Blacks occurred most systematically, Filipinos generally sought accommodation; they sought the security of place that dark skins and small numbers might make tenuous. To find and keep a job, especially a "good" job, required individual effort, but also sometimes collective action. At times the daily struggle engendered camaraderie among Filipinos in organizations based on common labor – unity shaped from within. At other times their exertions generated hostility, protests against their collective presence – conflict defined from without.

In the years prior to World War II, conflict in the occupational sphere occurred in a variety of settings. Not always overt, such conflict is documented with difficulty today, particularly in those instances that pitted an individual Filipino or a tiny group against non-Filipino co-workers. Labor in the unorganized kitchens and dining rooms of restaurants, hotels, and clubs produced bitter memories more often than written complaints.

Two illustrative incidents come from Benny Feria's memoir, *Filipino Son*. New to Chicago in the late 1920s, Feria found his first job in the city as a dishwasher in a restaurant far north of the central business district. As the only Filipino in the establishment, Feria "performed willingly and well...and this attitude and efficiency won for me golden opinions from my employer and chef."[40] But while a young waitress from Wisconsin, Betty, befriended him, other co-workers resented his presence. "One waitress, a pretty girl with sharp tongue and wit, tried to make me uncomfortable. A bus boy vied with her in criticizing the 'funny lingo' I used...."[41] After Feria's "promotion" to bus boy, tension increased, in no small part because of Betty's obvious fondness for him. "I never knew quite how it happened, but suddenly I felt a jerk at my ankle, and, thrown off balance, down I went sprawling between the tables, while the heavy tray I was carrying clattered to the floor, scattering remnants of food over chairs, tables and diners.[42] Accommodation impossible, Feria lost his job.

In his next position as a linenman at the LaSalle Hotel, Feria found a more secure niche in a department that included two other Filipinos and two European immigrants. "It was nice for a change to work in a place where people of other races were respected and where race prejudice was not practiced.[43] Yet while he would not call it "prejudice," Feria chafed at the segmentation produced by color:

> In this hotel, the only job that a Negro could hold...was either that of garbage collector or a porter....The Mexicans were employed as dishwashers and vegetable men and some as bus boys and waiters on room service department. The Filipinos were either bus boys or linen-man and that was as far as they could get. The whites held the best jobs in this hotel. In our department...the two white boys were the assistants of the boss...[but] they could hardly write a sentence. In making their reports during inventory...the Filipinos working with them made their report cards for them. The Filipinos did all the book-keeping for them with less pay.[44]

Despite the fact that the white immigrants in his department "were very nice to us Filipinos," Feria's relegation to a subordinate role obviously rankled.[45] But in contrast with his earlier disaster in the restaurant, Feria found working conditions at the LaSalle Hotel to be a vast improvement. Earning $95.00 per month and two meals each day, Feria enjoyed a day off on Thursdays and a half day on Sundays. His boss worked with him "when he knew that there was lots of work to be done. He was simple and understanding in every way"[46] If work at the LaSalle Hotel failed to offer Benny Feria the recognition which he coveted, and confirmed the meaning of color in America, it nonetheless provided immediate financial security and a relatively pleasant daily environment – all this once a man made the required internal compromise and accepted his place.

In their quest for security of place and income, Filipinos employed by the Pullman Company reached similar adjustments. (The Pullman Company built, owned, and operated the sleeping cars attached to passenger trains.) Yet because their numbers were larger, the road to accommodation was less solitary, if no less difficult. Filipinos were first hired by Pullman for work in private railroad cars during the Autumn of 1925, just two months after a group of disgruntled Black porters convinced New York radical activist A. Philip Randolph to lead their struggle for unionization.[47] Pullman's employment of Filipinos was both an experiment and a threat. By the mid-1920s, Blacks had been Pullman porters for over fifty years. In that time, the Pullman porters' collective reputation for service as "George" had become fixed. Having a Black servant who kept his place while attending to every passenger's needs and whims became part of the elegance and thrill of first-class rail travel.[48] Black monopoly of the occupation had never before been challenged. Could Filipinos successfully break through the Black service model fixed in the white passenger's mind? And could the presence of Filipinos frighten away the specter of the black Brotherhood?

For the dozen years from the Filipinos' initial hiring to the first contract between Pullman and the Brotherhood in 1937, the company kept Filipinos separate from Blacks by creating another job classification—attendant—as an alternative to porter. During these early years, Filipino "attendants," operating out of Pullman's Commissary Department, replaced buffet porters in running club, observation, and combination (lounge-bedroom) cars. As the Commissary's dining car operations expanded in the Depression years of the early 1930s, more Filipino attendants, cooks, and bus boys—all eager for jobs—were added to the service.[49] Despite this separation of black from brown, however, in the minds of the unionists Filipinos were "scabs" who now occupied the most lucrative Pullman jobs open to men of color. By February 1926, Randolph demanded "elimination of Filipinos hired in violation of seniority rules."[50]

In time, as the Brotherhood struggled for recognition, the union's official attitude toward Filipinos moderated:

> We want our Filipino brothers to understand that it is necessary for them to join the Brotherhood....While they have been put on the cars in violation of seniority rights, so long as they are there, they must be organized....The only security of the Filipinos as well as the Negro Pullman porter is organization in one common union, fighting for one common objective: namely, more wages, a 240-hour month and humane working conditions.[51]

In the two-year period between certification of the Brotherhood as the representative of Pullman porters in July 1935 and the signing of the first contract in August 1937, the union worked to recruit Filipino workers, a task made somewhat easier by the 1937 agreement that recognized the Brotherhood as the bargaining agent for attendants as well as porters, established a separate seniority list for attendants, and preserved the attendants' advantageous pay rate as well. But the task of organizing Filipinos moved slowly. Status-conscious Filipinos saw little common identity with America's Black minority and generally remained reluctant to join a Black union, despite the appeals of their countryman, Brotherhood activist Cypriano Samonte, whose marriage to a Black woman gave him entré to Black Chicago—where other Filipinos were loathe to be.[52]

Most Filipinos gave a tenuous allegiance to the union paying dues and sometimes attending meetings but rarely appearing at social events—only after the Brotherhood began to extend to Filipinos its defense of "paid up" members. In a critical case decided by the National Railroad Adjustment Board (NRAB) in August 1938, Brotherhood Vice-President Milton P. Webster successfully fought Pullman's reassignment of a Filipino club car attendant—and recent union member—to kitchen work "because he could not speak and understand the English language fluently enough."[53] Pascual, a four-year veteran with Pullman, had obviously been punished as a warning to other Filipinos contemplating Brotherhood membership.

Thereafter, the Brotherhood waged other battles in behalf of its Filipino members before both the company's disciplinary board and the NARB. One type of case is particularly indicative of the underlying separation between Blacks and Filipinos despite their common employment and union membership. In these disciplinary cases, the Brotherhood unsuccessfully defended various Filipino attendants who had received thirty-day suspensions for refusing to work on temporarily assigned cars with more beds to make than their usual cars. Filipinos generally claimed that the work on the substitute cars was "too heavy"; attendants vigorously resisted doing a porter's job.[54]

At a company hearing, in defending Attendant F. J. Domantay, Webster pressed the underlying historical basis of a distinction between attendants and porters:

> This Attendant is small in stature, was hired by the Company when they were hiring Filipino Attendants with full knowledge of the fact that they were small in stature, and it was not anticipated that these men should handle heavy Pullman cars with berths and rooms. The average Club Car assignment at the time these men were hired when they were classified as Attendants carried either no sleeping car space, or just one or two rooms. These men were hired with the view of handling that service, and before the contract of 1937 between the Company and its employes [sic] of this class they were properly and deliberately selected to handle these Club Car assignments where there was either no sleeping car space or very little sleeping car space.[55]

As in other similar cases, the December 1944 decision that concluded this hearing went against Attendant Domantay. The NARB ultimately held that while the contract classified "Pullman service employe [sic] [separately as porters, attendants, maids, and bus boys], there is nothing therein which purports to separate the work of the classes of employes therein mentioned."[56] Work on club cars, even those with some sleeping space, was less onerous and more likely to produce substantial tips than work on cars with sleeping space alone, but in addition the negative symbolic value of "making beds" should not be underestimated. Filipino interviewees frequently defined the passage of time in Pullman service with this task: "In the later years, we were trained to make beds," Domingo C. Manzon remarked. Others bristled at being mislabeled "porter."[57]

How then did Filipinos interact with Blacks in the workplace? A fairly clear picture emerges. Overt conflict between the two groups cannot be discerned. If Filipinos ranked their place in the company — and in America — above that occupied by Blacks, they nonetheless depended on the black Brotherhood for improved conditions and defense. In addition, over time, Filipinos came largely to share with their Black co-workers a similarly negative view of Pullman management. Both groups felt the impact of long hours, low wages, and harsh discipline enforced by a network of inspectors, spotters, and spies. Both Blacks and Filipinos sought ways around rules and regulations. Some in each group challenged company control by stealing from Pullman. The Filipinos called it "palocso," making it into an ethnic practice, but Blacks used the same techniques.[58] Who taught whom remains a mystery.

The potential for conflict at Pullman was further limited by the isolation of many workers at work, or their separation by color. A club car attendant, for example, worked alone in a single car and was required to alternate hours of sleep with the attendant in the next car so that both cars were watched throughout the night. Dining and café cars pulled together a larger staff: an attendant running-in-charge, bus boys, and cooks. The actual extent of the interracial mixing of crews is unknown, but it probably rose over time, after the union contract broke the Commissary Department in Chicago as a Filipino preserve and especially after World War II (and Philippine independence) when new hires of a younger cohort were uniformly Black.[59] A 1944 disciplinary case involving the practice of "palocso" reveals an all-Filipino crew of five.[60] Speaking of a later era, Domingo C. Manzon recalled his experience as an attendant in-charge of a racially mixed café car crew: "We [Filipinos] worked very well with them [Blacks]....I have a chef call[ed] Frank Collier and two Black boys as waiters, ... Brownie and ... Eddie, ... my right-hand man....Frank did not stay too long on the job, as he was bumped off the job, by seniority basis, by one of our boys, Del Rosario, who had accumulated seniority over the years he worked."[61] On layovers at the opposite end of a round-trip run, interracial crews ate together and stayed in the same hotel if personal preference dictated.[62]

Thus, the Pullman/Brotherhood setting permitted development – or maintenance – of personal patterns of friendship, tolerance, or hostility. Manzon defined the limits of his interaction: "I have very special friends among the porters...that I'd have loved to invite them in my home, but I didn't, as they live on the South side, whereas I live in the North side."[63] Florentino Bella remarked: "After a while there were a lot of colored workers. They're all right....I have some good friends. I have no trouble with them. Some of them were pretty good."[64] At the other extreme, another Filipino attendant, who had long been a Pullman mangement favorite and had been asked to attempt formation of a Filipino union in 1935, pronounced: "I can't get along with them because...in general the Negroes are lazy....They just don't believe in sanitation, neatness....They're just jealous because the average American people, they don't like them. I can't blame them. I don't like them either."[65]

Camaraderie, when supplied within the framework of occupation, was organized almost exclusively on an ethnic basis. During the late 1940s and early 1950s, a Filipino Pullman Club collected dues, sold tickets, held dances and picnics, and thereby served the needs of fraternity more than it did labor solidarity.[66] The Filipino Postal Club of Chicago provided similar social activities for its approximately one hundred members and, during the Depression, contributed to both the Governor's Emergency Relief Fund and the direct assistance of "needy Filipinos." In addition, Postal Club members protested the American Legion demand that non-citizens be dismissed from the federal civil service in favor of out-of-work Americans.[67] Defined by the world into which they migrated as neither white nor Black and ineligible for naturalization until the late 1940s, Filipinos – even the most successful among them – defined themselves as a group and continued to feel most comfortable with each other.

World War II marked a watershed for the Filipino old-timers. Most of the men working for the Post Office and for Pullman, if not already past the age for military service, were nonetheless deferred on the basis of the essential nature of their employment. By the middle of the war, the Filipino Community Center ceased operations, its relief function no longer necessary. Unemployment faded as the nation's labor pool shrank and Filipinos found jobs as civilians in Chicago or relocated to areas of greater promise. Others became soldiers. As an army chaplain, Rev. Laxamana, who had directed the Community Center's operations for a decade, followed the troops from island to island across the Pacific, ministering to their spiritual needs and burying the fallen.[68] In uniform or not, Filipinos enjoyed a previously unknown toleration and respect based on the common struggle of the United States and the Philippines against the Japanese foe.[69]

In the decades following the war, color would nonetheless continue to define the Filipinos in Chicago. If bigotry was less strident, it still persisted in restricted opportunities for improved housing and employment. In these areas, in the fundamental fabric of the Filipinos' lives, accommodation remained an ongoing process, its direction still dictated in large measure by the quest for security. Immediate survival was now rarely in question, but the long-term needs of family and old age claimed attention.

As they aged, many Filipinos turned inward from the wider ethnic community, dancing less frequently at Rizal Day celebrations to commemorate the national hero of their homeland, seeing family and old friends more exclusively. Yet pride in ethnicity and confidence in its supportive capacity occasionally surfaced – in the grey-haired veterans in uniform, a shrinking number marching proudly in Memorial Day parades as American Legion Filipino Post No. 590;[70] and in the comfortably retired old-timers who pooled thousands for the downpayment on a new Filipino American community center,[71] as in years past, when they had pooled pennies to purchase the neck bones for the soup pot from which all were welcome to eat.

Hispanics

CHAPTER 5

Border Proletarians: Mexican-Americans and the International Union of Mine, Mill, and Smelter Workers, 1939–1946

MARIO T. GARCÍA

Along with the constantly diminishing number of the magnates of capital, who usurp and monopolise all advantages of this process of transformation, grows the mass of misery, oppression, slavery, degradation, exploitation; but with this too grows the revolt of the working-class always increasing in numbers, and disciplined, united, organized by the very mechanism of the process of capitalist production itself.

Karl Marx, *Capital*, Vol. I.

What the type of analysis used here suggests is that the exploitation of clearly marked groups in a variety of different ways is integral to capitalism and that ethnic groups unite and act together because they have been subjected to distinct and differentiated types of exploitation.

John Rex, "Race,"
A Dictionary of Marxist Thought

While the history and contributions of Black workers to the rise of the CIO during the 1930s and 1940s is being recognized, that of other racial minorities, such as Mexican-Americans,* is less well known.[1] Yet

---

*Ethnic labels used in the article are defined as follows: "Mexican" refers to persons of Mexican descent, whether U.S. citizens or not; "Mexicano" refers specifically to Mexican nationals; "Mexican-American" refers to U.S. citizens of Mexican descent; and, finally, "Anglo" refers to white U.S. citizens.

in certain industries affected by CIO organizing, such as steel, auto, meatpacking, longshore operations, furniture manufacturing, fruit canning, and non-ferrous mining and smelting, Mexican-Americans represented sizeable sections of the American working class.

This study is an attempt to integrate the history of Mexican-American workers into the larger labor and union history of the United States. It examines the indispensable role of Mexican-American workers in El Paso, Texas – the border proletarians – in the formation of the CIO along the United States–Mexican border and, in particular, the successful and symbiotic relationship involving class and ethnic solidarity between Mexican-Americans and the International Union of Mine, Mill, and Smelter workers. It is a study of how class, race, and ethnicity have functioned in a particular labor market: the Southwest and border country. Class, race, and ethnicity were manipulated by Southwestern capitalists to profit from cheap Mexican labor and the proximity of a poor country like Mexico. Yet class, race, and ethnic bonds also provided the organic foundation for Mexican-American labor struggles.

I

Located on the United States–Mexican border along the shores of the Rio Grande, El Paso exemplified the organizing problems that the Mine Mill Union confronted in the Southwest. Since the late nineteenth century, the railroads had made this former desert hamlet into a major southwestern commercial, mining, and ranching center which had reached almost one hundred thousand people by 1920. Employers and entrepreneurs flocked to the border to take advantage of the city's location and, as important, its cheap labor market.

Poverty and political revolution led to a great migration from Mexico to the border between 1900 and the 1920s. As immigrant workers, Mexicans were grateful for employment in border industries, as the Southwest economy, feeding raw materials to U.S. industries, became integrated with the rest of the United States. In El Paso, the railroads, retail and wholesale houses, construction firms, urban services, and the expansive smelting plant of the Guggenheim-owned American Smelting and Refining Company (AS & R) employed thousands of Mexican immigrant workers as a non-skilled and low-skilled labor force that came to compose one-half of the city's population.

Employers profited from the work of Mexicans by paying them the lowest wages in the city. Facing both class and racial exploitation and discrimination – or what some scholars term a segmented or split labor market and what Mario Barrera calls "colonized labor"– Mexican immigrant workers were funnelled into a dual occupational structure and a dual wage system. In comparison to Anglo workers, Mexicans were primarily restricted to non-skilled dead-end manual jobs – the so-called "Mexican jobs"– and received for their labor what also came to be known as "Mexican wages": lower wages than Anglo workers and lower than comparable work in areas outside the border district. Early border unionization, principally by the mostly conservative, elitist, and white American Federation of Labor (AFL), added to this dichotomy by excluding Mexican immigrant workers from more skilled and better-paying positions.[2]

The Great Depression, commencing in 1929, contributed to the burdens of Mexican labor and labor in general in the Southwest. Unemployment affected thousands of workers, especially the more vulnerable, such as those of Mexican descent. Those not holding U.S. citizenship faced deportation and repatriation pressures as many Southwestern communities sought to deal with unemployment and increased job competition by victimizing Mexicans.[3]

But dependent on cheap Mexican labor and with a majority of its population Mexican, El Paso minimized this forced expulsion and continued to survive on the basis of cheap and unorganized Mexican labor. Two key border industries that displayed this reliance were the AS & R plant and the newer Phelps Dodge Corporation refinery that began operations in El Paso in 1930. The largest industries in the city, with the biggest payrolls, both tapped the mining areas of Arizona, New Mexico, and northern Mexico for supplies of lead, gold, silver, zinc, and copper to be smelted and refined in the border city before being shipped to the industrial sections of the United States, as well as to Europe.[4]

Surviving the Depression and expanding with the outbreak of World War II, the AS & R smelter and the Phelps-Dodge refinery employed hundreds of Mexican-Americans and Mexicano workers from both sides of the border. Each plant in the late 1930s employed between five hundred and six hundred workers. As with other Mexicans in the mining and smelting industries of the Southwest, those in El Paso continued to face both class and racial exploitation and oppression. "On the job, Chicanos were restricted to common labor positions," one historian writes, "featuring sub-standard job classifications and pay scales and lacking standard seniority provisions."[5] Of approximately five hundred employees at AS & R, about four hundred were Mexican Americans or Mexican nationals and almost all were common laborers.[6] Nicaraguan-born Humberto Silex, an early Mine Mill organizer in El Paso, recalls that most employers in the 1930s paid as little as nine to ten cents an hour. When Silex first worked at the

AS & R plant in 1937, Mexican common labor received $2.06 for a 10- to 12-hour day, and worked six days a week with no vacation time. By comparison, when Silex had earlier worked in a Chicago smelter he had received $6 to $7 a day.[7] "The working conditions were the worst," Silex further notes. Workers faced hard, dirty, dangerous labor conditions. Managers employed few safety precautions, and workers often faced injuries due to burns or falls.[8]

AS & R bosses forced their workers to purchase provisions at the company store. "If you didn't owe the store some money you were bound to be laid off pretty soon," Silex remembers. "Every payday something was docked from your check."[9] Many workers at the smelter had to live in dilapidated housing adjacent to the plant. AS & R leased the land to its employees, who constructed their own shacks. Smeltertown, as the area came to be called, lacked general sanitation. Until the late 1930s and 1940s, when the federal government financed new housing projects in the de facto segregated Mexican neighborhoods of South El Paso, most smelter workers could not afford to pay the rents. Those who lived across the border in Juárez possessed no better, and probably worse, housing.[10]

Mexican workers encountered further discrimination in job mobility. Silex, for example, although already an experienced fireman when first hired, began as a helper with an Anglo fireman and an Anglo assistant. Both Anglos had less experience than Silex, but received higher wages. Management paid the assistant a dollar more than Silex and after a few months promoted him to fireman while Silex remained a helper. When finally upgraded in a job reclassification, Silex still did not receive the accompanying wage increase. Management paid Mexicans with semi-skilled jobs only one cent more per hour than common laborers. With such low wages, workers found it difficult to provide for their family needs and children often went without necessities such as shoes.[11]

To circumvent New Deal labor legislation, such as the Wagner Act, and to prevent Congress of Industrial Organizations (CIO) organizing, the smelter in 1939 encouraged a "company union" affiliated with the AFL. Ostensibly representing both the smaller number of Anglo craft workers and the larger mass of Mexican laborers, the Metal Trades Council was under the control of Anglo leaders, including some plant supervisors. The first contract signed by the "union" provided only a 1½-cent-per-hour raise for common laborers.[12] Paternalistic in its attitude toward the Mexican workers, the union constituted an additional form of labor control in the plant. "More harmonious relations have been brought about between workers and employers because of the willingness of the management to reach an agreement," an Anglo leader of the union claimed.[13]

Conditions at the Phelps Dodge refinery were no better. J. B. Chávez, who became one of the key Mexican-American leaders of the Mine Mill Union in El Paso and the Southwest, remembered the state of affairs when he first began work at Phelps Dodge in 1937. Job discrimination and job segregation were the norm at the plant. Chávez hired on as a furnace laborer while an equally inexperienced Anglo received an initial job as a furnace pipeman, a more skilled position. A dual job system based on race created a dual wage system. Mexicans received less pay then Anglo workers. Chávez obtained about 17¼ cents an hour while the Anglo hired at the same time received substantially more. "He was getting a dime more than I was because he was a *gabacho* [Anglo] and I was a Chicano." In Chávez's particular section of the plant, other Mexicans worked predominantly as common laborers. All worked a 40-hour week.

Conditions, as at the AS & R plant, were hard and dangerous. Injuries were common, but the workers got no health benefits. A Mexican worker laid off due to an injury often was not rehired. Protective equipment such as safety shoes could only be purchased on credit from a downtown store that provided a "kickback" to a Captain Simpson, the head of security at Phelps Dodge.

Simpson, an ex-Texas Ranger, also forced Mexican workers to buy raffle tickets at a dollar a ticket for used radios he bought. If a worker refused to participate in Simpson's raffles, he would be fired. No Mexican ever won the raffle.

Unlike the AS & R smelter, Phelps Dodge did not even allow a company union. The one Anglo AFL union, the Bricklayers, had been crushed after the bricklayers had gone on strike. The company simply promoted and trained other workers to replace them.[14]

II

The CIO began organizing in El Paso in 1939. In this effort, the CIO, through unions such as Mine Mill, utilized to its advantage the race, ethnic, and class characteristics of the El Paso labor market. It first supported a strike by Mexican bakery workers against nine South El Paso bakers. Organized in the Benito Juárez Bakers Union No. 913, seventy workers struck on July 6 when bakery owners refused to concede higher wages and an 8-hour working day. The bakeries continued to operate with non-union labor and management personnel.

Assisted by M. J. Dineen, the CIO representative in El Paso, the union charged that the bakeries were using the strike as an excuse to raise their prices. Dineen called on city officials to mediate the dispute by establishing a conciliation board. He further requested the U.S. Department of Labor and the regional office of the National Labor Relations Board (NLRB) to assist in settling the strike. However, Saul O. Paredes, the secretary of the El Paso Bakers Association, refused Dineen's offer and instead charged that Communist agitators from Juárez, across the border, had infiltrated the bakery workers and were the cause of the labor disturbance. Within two days, a total of 160 bakers and their helpers left their jobs and walked the picket lines. The owners responded by placing guards on their trucks after three of their vehicles had been damaged. Dineen at the same time accused the recalcitrant owners of hiring 15- and 16-year-old boys as strikebreakers and then refusing to pay them for their labor.[15].

Despite the friction, representatives of the workers and the owners, aided by the Mexican Consul, tentatively agreed to end the strike. The compromise involved a 90-day truce, during which the strikers would return to work while a permanent settlement would be negotiated. When both the workers and owners refused to sanction the agreement, a federal labor conciliator stepped in and by July 15 had worked out new, and this time satisfactory, terms between four of the bakeries and their employees. The workers would return to their jobs in return for new wage and hour agreements during a 90-day grace period while other grievances were settled. The owners agreed to a small wage increase and an 8-hour day. Master bakers would now receive $3.60 a day compared to a previous $3.25 to $3.50 for a 10- to 14-hour day. Oven and bench workers would receive $2.80, up from $2.25 to $2.50 a day for 10- to 14-hours work. With the other remaining bakeries refusing to settle, the workers still on strike opened their own bakery, the El Paso Co-operative Bakery.

The CIO failed to achieve a victory for all the strikers or to consolidate union recognition. Yet its first foray into El Paso had been moderately successful.[16] Boosted by this effort, the CIO challenged the AFL by organizing Mexican-Americans construction workers employed in building federal housing projects. Certain Mexican-American workers assisted in this as well as other CIO activities by forming the Union of Protective Latin Americans.[17]

Initial contacts between the CIO and the Mexican smelter and refinery workers took place in late 1939 when a representative of the Packinghouse Workers arrived in El Paso to organize the local meat-packing plant. Silex described conditions at the smelter and the CIO organizer promised to see about having a representative of Mine Mill come to El Paso and organize both the smelter and the refinery. A couple of months later, James Robinson, a long-time activist in Mine Mill and the father of Reid Robinson, the current President of the union, arrived in the border city. The elder Robinson met with Silex and agreed that Mine Mill would undertake the effort to organize in El Paso.

However, a problem that both Robinson and Silex faced was Robinson's inability to speak Spanish and Silex's lack of union experience. Both agreed to take advantage of El Paso's border location and the particular nature of labor within a bi-national context: In a show of international labor solidarity, they asked the progressive Confederaión de Trabajadores Mexicanos (CTM) in Juárez to loan one of their organizers to Mine Mill in El Paso. A CTM organizer would be helpful not only in providing Spanish-speaking labor experience, but also because of the many smelter and refinery workers living across the border in Juárez. The CTM assigned José Oaxaca to the task. A second CTM organizer later joined Oaxaca in El Paso. Oaxaca, Robinson, and Silex organized initial small-scale meetings in the *barrio*. Others gradually agreed to join the union, either in Local 501 of the refinery or Local 509 of the AS & R Smelter. These recruits in turn encouraged their relatives and friends to join the union.[18]

At Phelps Dodge, J. B. Chávez recalls that he was recruited by Alfonso Medina, who had earlier enrolled in Mine Mill. Chávez joined because of adverse working conditions at the plant and because his own father had been a member of the miners union in Mexico. Chávez notes that the main organizers at Phelps Dodge were Mexican-Americans like himself rather than Mexican nationals.[19] This was a key distinction since, unlike earlier periods when Mexican immigrant workers who led and participated in strikes could be threatened with deportation, Mexican-Americans, as U.S. citizens, had greater legal and constitutional protections. Moreover, Mexican-American workers like Chávez planned permanent residence in the United States, as opposed to many immigrant workers who expected to return to Mexico.

As the growing majority of people of Mexican descent in the United States, Mexican-Americans, either as unionists or as civil rights activists, by the 1930s and 1940s assumed key leadership roles in their communities and begun to wage protracted struggles for equality and justice. This collection of leaders I term the "Mexican-American Generation."[20] "One of the first things we were told when we started to organize," Chávez stresses, "[was] that if we weren't U.S. citizens we should not be very outspoken or active, but the rest who were citizens should be very involved."[21]

At the AS & R smelter, Silex as secretary of Local 509 recruited Mexican-American leaders such as Ceferino Anchondo, who as a fireman had belonged to the AFL company union. His recruitment by Mine-Mill convinced still other Mexican-American and *Mexicano* workers to join the union.[22] Silex explained to workers the benefits to be gained from joining a CIO union rather than the AFL. A CIO union treated all workers as equals regardless of job and organized both craft and unskilled workers together in one union. An AFL union, such as the one at AS & R, unfairly divided workers by job and discriminated against unskilled labor. Silex recalls that most Mexican workers preferred the CIO form of union. He and other Mine-Mill organizers further informed workers that Mine-Mill would be better able to achieve higher wages and more satisfactory working conditions. "We told them how a contract that gave the workers a cent-and-a half wasn't anything."

Silex remembers the main objectives of Mine Mill in El Paso:

> We wanted equal treatment. We demanded that companies such as
> American Smelting and Phelps Dodge that had plants, mines, and
> refineries all over the United States and in other parts of the world
> because they were large monopolies...that they pay us the same
> wages paid in Nebraska, in California. While in the smelter in San
> Francisco the workers received $5 dollars a day, here workers
> received only $2 dollars a day. The same company paid the wages, the
> same work was involved, although perhaps under more difficult con-
> ditions. Hence, we asked for equality of wages and of work with other
> plants in other locations. We also asked for vacation time and shift
> differentials.[23]

Still, it was not easy to recruit members to the Mine Mill Union. One of the biggest challenges involved the presence in the plants of sizable numbers of Mexican nationals living in Juárez. About half of the workers commuted from that neighboring border city. Many stayed away from the union for fear of being harassed by U.S. immigration officials. To overcome these hurdles, Mine Mill, besides relying on CTM organizers in El Paso, utilized Spanish-speaking Mexican-American members who together with CTM officials in Juárez visited the homes of AS & R and Phelps Dodge workers south of the border and encouraged them to join the union. This particular method of border organizing succeeded. Mine Mill also pursued its border strategy by securing the assistance of the Mexican Consul in El Paso who recommended that Mexican nationals become union members.[24] Besides signing up workers inside the plants, organizers such as J. B. Chávez held union meetings in the numeros *cantinas* (bars) of South and East El Paso, common recreational centers for Mexicans in the city.[25]

Although Mine Mill succeeded in recruiting a good number of workers at both plants by 1940, it faced increasing hostility by company officials as well as by local law enforcement authorities. AS & R management, for example, did everything it could to break Mine Mill unionizing efforts – including laying off workers who signed with the union. Bosses singled out leaders such as Silex, whom they discharged in July 1940. Awaiting an NLRB decision on his firing, Silex found it difficult to obtain another job or to keep one due to what he considered "blacklisting" by the El Paso Chamber of Commerce. "Everywhere I went to work, they would give me a job and in a few days...they would say, 'well, we don't need you. You're a troublemaker.'"[26] J. B. Chávez recalls that at one meeting of Local 501, Phelps Dodge managers succeeded in intimidating many workers by waiting outside the assembly hall to record which employees attended.[27] Moreover, management secured the assistance of local immigration officials who harassed Mexican nationals working either at AS & R or Phelps Dodge by threatening to deport them if they joined Mine-Mill.[28]

El Paso law enforcement officials led by County Sheriff Chris P. Fox added to the unionizing difficulties of Mine Mill. Discovering where the locals met, Sheriff Fox ordered his men to frighten the workers away. "We couldn't have an open meeting anywhere," Silex explains:

> We even had to paint the windows of the places where we held meetings. As soon as the sheriff or the police found out where we were they would send men and cars to walk and drive around the place. The workers were scared. Probably one-half of them were born here in the U.S., but didn't know their rights. So we had a hell of a time for several years.[29]

Mine Mill also faced increased competition from the AFL which, with the apparent sanction of both the AS & R and P-D, commenced drives to sign up Mexican-American workers. As one reporter noted: "El Paso has become the battleground of a jurisdictional struggle between the CIO and AFL for labor supremacy in the Southwest."[30]

Besides these anti-union tactics, "red-baiting" by linking Communism with the CIO and with Mexican "aliens" proved another obstacle for Mine Mill. El Paso's "Red Scare" was led by Sheriff Fox. Considering the CIO a front for the Communist Party, Fox expressed alarm at CIO efforts in the bakery strike. However, his main efforts at linking the CIO with the Communist Party began in early March 1940, when without formal charges he arrested and held without bond six men whom he claimed were spreading Communism in El

Paso. Fox alleged that a letter sent by the Communist organizer in the Southwest to the head of the CP in Juárez urged a "hands across the border" policy between Juárez and El Paso Communists. The letter, according to Fox, stated that CIO unions in El Paso should eventually become part of the Communist movement. Fox claimed that U.S. and Mexican Communists had been lecturing to workers on what the sheriff called "cultural orientation."

He considered such activity and propaganda to be seditious and noted that since the bakery strike he had been investigating Communist activity in El Paso and had informed the House Un-American Activities Committee (HUAC) of the possible Communist threat along the border. Fox obtained information on the CIO from his employment of a Mexican-American labor spy, J. G. Escajeda. To corroborate Sheriff Fox's allegations, a special investigator for HUAC arrived in El Paso to study the growth of Communism in the border city.[31]

After making his arrests, Sheriff Fox, along with Acting County Attorney W. H. Fryer, requested a court of inquiry before a local Justice of the Peace. The court subpoenaed thirteen persons, including the six arrested by Fox. Two of the arrested, Frank Sener and Domingo López, both were CIO organizers. A third, Alfredo Casares, was accused of distributing Communist and CIO pamphlets in El Paso urging workers to join both organizations. Miguel Oaxaca, head of the CTM in Juárez, was described as a "writer" of Communist literature. Finally, Guadalupe Pedroza, an El Paso barber living in Juárez, and Joseph Mack Waller, an alleged CP official in El Paso, completed the list of detainees. Denying any link between the local court of inquiry and HUAC, attorney Fryer engaged not only in red-baiting but in what one historian terms the "Brown Scare" by attempting to link Communism in El Paso with the presence of Mexican "aliens":

> The Immigration and other government officers have been alert to the international aspect of the Communists [sic] activities here, and their cooperation with Sheriff Fox has been invaluable. The audacity of aliens in coming into El Paso to actively, though secretly, attempt to plow the ground for the planting of the Soviet seed has been surprising. The more surprising fact, however, is that they have been aided and abetted by American citizens.[32]

In his testimony, Fox accused various people of subversive Communist activity. He charged that Communist leaders in El Paso several months earlier had borne arms in attending a meeting in a south side Catholic church hall with the intention of shooting anyone who objected to their distributing Communist literature. Fox reiterated that he had been investigating Communist activity in El Paso since the bakers' strike. Fox further accused Katherine Winfrey, the wife of an inspector for the U.S. Bureau of International Revenue in El Paso, of being the "top" Communist in the city. The Sheriff added that Waller, one of the men arrested, had admitted to being both a Communist and a CIO official and that he had deliberately falsified the time of his joining the union in return for a promise that the CIO would fight his earlier dismissal from the Peyton Packing Company in El Paso. Fox's allegations were strengthened when Waller admitted to the falsification when called to testify before the proceedings. In addition, Fox charged that a large amount of Communist literature had been confiscated by his office.

"I had information," he also told County Attorney Fryer, "that the CTM...and the Juárez Communists were trying to inject themselves into the local labor movement." Fox also claimed knowledge about the formation of an El Paso unit of the Los Angeles–based Spanish-Speaking Congress "designed to instill in Mexican aliens living in the United States the principles of the Mexican Communist form of government." He attacked the CIO for authorizing local organizer Maurice Dineen to participate in what the Sheriff labeled the "May Day Communist celebration" held in Juárez the previous year and stated that the CIO had instructed Dineen to do so as a Communist and not as a CIO member. The Sheriff concluded his statement by affirming the link between Communists in El Paso and the presence of Mexican "aliens": "I began this investigation because I resented, openly and strongly, having Mexican aliens inject their form of government into our country."[33]

County Attorney Fryer called other subpoenaed witnesses and attempted to draw out implications of ties between the Communist Party and CIO organizing in El Paso. Fryer later said: "To my mind, the hearing in El Paso establishes the fact that when you scratch the hide of a CIO member you find a Communist." The Court of Inquiry ended its one-day deliberations with the presiding judge concluding that Communism needed to be "wiped out" and that criminal proceedings might be brought against one of the six men arrested. The Sheriff released three of the men arrested, but detained the others.[34] In his column for the El Paso *Herald-Post*, Dr. B. U. L. Conner reiterated the anti-labor sentiments voiced by both Fox and Fryer. "Labor unions are okay," he conceded, "but some of the labor leaders are either dumb, or nuts, the way they will get mixed up with Communism."[35]

The CIO responded to the arrests and to the red-baiting by attacking Fox's violations of basic constitutional rights. James Robinson castigated Fox's efforts to discredit CIO organizing by suggesting

Communist subversion. Robinson pointed out that evidence illegally seized and presented at the inquiry proved the opposite: The only un-American actions involved were those of the Sheriff. López and Casares, both U.S. citizens, had been apprehended without warrants or formal charges. The Sheriff had placed them in jail, recorded and fingerprinted them as prisoners, held them incommunicado for two days and three nights, and subjected them to the "third degree methods in an attempt to extort information of a connection between the local CIO and the Communist Party." Labor leaders labeled Fox's efforts as nothing more than a "witch hunt" and a "red scare" deliberately aimed at preventing labor organizing along the border. "The CIO is engaged in the organizing of the unorganized, underpaid, ill-clothed, ill-fed and ill-housed workers," they concluded, "and we know of no place in the United States where a correction of these abuses is more necessary than in El Paso."[36] In support, Homer Brooks, secretary of the Communist Party in Texas, noted that of the six arrested only one belonged to the Communist Party, a membership not forbidden by law. The issue was not the Communist Party and its legal right to exist and assist in the labor movement, Brooks proposed, but the overt violation of civil rights by Fox and his attempt to intimidate workers to keep them from exercising their right to unionize.[37]

Besides utilizing labor spies, Phelps Dodge harassed members of the union by firing those who attempted to sign up other workers. Not afraid to testify, one Mine-Mill member, Aurelio Zacarías, acknowledged that a Phelps Dodge foreman had warned him that if he continued with the union "I was going to have a lot of trouble with the company." Eduardo Valdívez testified that the same foreman had cautioned him against outside agitators who wanted to raise salaries in El Paso. This, the foreman alleged, would hurt workers rather than helping them. "Mr. Purdy told me that the cost of living would go up if Phelps-Dodge raised wages," Valdívez stated, "because all other companies would also have to pay more and that they would then charge more for commodities." The foreman told Valdívez that such agitators needed to be put in concentraton camps. Valdívez concluded his testimony by telling of seeing signs written by one employee that read: "CIO Is No Good." In addition, Mine Mill complained of efforts by Phelps Dodge to establish an AFL company union and to pressure workers to support it. Another Mine-Mill member, Domingo López, testified that officers and supervisors of Phelps Dodge directed the company union. The union won its first major victory in El Paso when in February 1941 the NLRB ordered Phelps Dodge to "cease and desist from discouraging workers at the El Paso plant" from organizing, to drop recognition of the company union, and to reinstate three discharged employees who had been active in Mine-Mill organizing.[38]

Successful in its challenge of Phelps Dodge before the NLRB, Mine Mill in 1941 filed similar complaints against the AS & R smelter. "We...have several witnesses," James Robinson wrote to a fellow Mine-Mill official, "who can prove that the A.F.L local at the Smelter is a company union." Unfortunately for the smelter workers, the NLRB in this case ruled in favor of the company and recognized the AFL affiliate as the bargaining agent for the workers.[39]

III

World War II, the war for the "Four Freedoms," provided progressive unions such as Mine Mill with additional ideological support, and inspiration for achieving union representation and equal justice for racial minorities. "Here in the southwest," wrote Antonio Salcido, the president of 501, "the victory of the Phelps Dodge workers under the CIO banner will be a blow in the face of all the fascist-minded employers who utilize racial and national discrimination as a means of paying starvation wages."[40]

Although enthusiastic, Mine-Mill organizers at Phelps Dodge found the road to an NLRB election to be rocky. Unable to collect adequate union dues from its El Paso locals, apparently the result of members' unfamiliarity with such contributions, the International dropped Silex as an organizer at Phelps Dodge in the midst of the drive to secure additional Mexican-American members. Before leaving, Silex along with others at the Phelps Dodge plant had succeeded in enrolling large numbers of workers. In late May 1942, Local 501 petitioned the NLRB for an election. "Workers here are tired of the medieval labor policy of Phelps Dodge," organizer Harry Hafner noted, "and are building the Union so as to get rid of the 50-cent hourly wage minimum, discrimination policy against Spanish-Americans, lack of seniority and promotion rights and refusal of the company to set up a joint labor-management production committee."[41]

During the last week of June, Mine Mill secured an election at Phelps Dodge and won decisively. Out of 385 ballots cast, Mine Mill received 267 votes, while 107 workers voted for the AFL union. Ten votes were challenged and one was void. Besides Phelps Dodge, Mine Mill through Local 509 won union recognition at the smaller El Paso Brick Company with its predominantly Mexican-American labor force.[42]

Mine Mill turned to achieving a similar victory at the AS & R smelter. Silex, who had been rehired at the plant, led the campaign, along with Ceferino Anchondo and outside organizers Leo Ortiz and Jess Nichols, the International representative. To prevent Mine Mill from achieving recognition, AS & R bolstered the AFL company union by providing a 50-cent pay increase in July 1942.[43] Secret on-the-job organizing work, however, succeeded in signing up over one hundred members.[44] Outside of the smelter, the union staged mass meetings at Smeltertown, where workers and their families could attend. Organizer Nichols, apparently able to speak Spanish, visited workers in their homes both in El Paso and Juárez and convinced many to sign up with Mine Mill.[45] In late 1942, Local 509 petitioned the NLRB for an election. The union scored a second major victory when the majority of workers voted it their representative.[46]

Part of Mine Mill's successful organizational strategy in El Paso and in other Southwestern locations consisted of the close links developed by its Mexican-American leadership with the labor movement in Mexico and along the border. Silex, for example, fostered relations with the Mexican Miners' Union in Chihauhua and, of course, with the CTM in Juarez. Such ties helped not only in union organizing, but in creating a communications network that helped influence Mexicano workers not to scab at either the smelter or the refinery. Mexican-American leaders, such as Leo Ortiz, further understood that labor rallies around Mexican holidays such as the *Dieciseis de Septiembre* (16th of September), Mexican Independence Day, represented good organizing tactics among Mexican-American workers in the Southwest. Ethnicity and culture, along with working-class solidarity, had to be tapped.

In addition, in 1942, Mine Mill helped organize a highly successful international Labor Day celebration supported by the CIO and AFL in El Paso along with Mexican workers in the CTM. Local 509 raised funds for the event by hosting a dance, and Silex traveled to Chihuahua to encourage CTM participation. The celebration expressed international labor unity and provided support for the war effort. The chairman of the International Labor Day Celebration Committee told organized labor members in El Paso,

As you know, our country as well as Mexico has declared war against a common enemy. Many of us are unable to shoulder a gun or fight in the front-line trenches, but we can in various ways make our selves felt in the home front. The Committee feels that this celebration will give us the opportunity, in an indirect way, to "slap a Jap" and make some contributions to the war effort by marching with our Brothers from Mexico and showing to the world the solidarity of Labor from these two greatest American countries.[47]

On July 4th of that same year, Mine Mill and the Railroad Brotherhood had hosted another international labor day celebration which featured Lombardo Toledano, the great Mexican labor leader.[48]

Following election victories at Phelps Dodge and AS & R, Mine Mill at both plants commenced negotiations on the signing of contracts. But Phelps Dodge refused to recognize the Grievance Committee formed by the union or to establish a Labor and Management Production Committee as called for by the War Production Board. Instead, Phelps Dodge continued to favor the AFL company union. Moreover, Phelps Dodge refused arbitration on grievances as recommended by the War Labor Board. Specific worker grievances at Phelps Dodge included management's penalizing workers for absences beyond their control by laying them off without pay for several days. Any worker absent for three days had to undergo a complete physical by the company doctor before resuming work. Phelps Dodge ignored seniority and forced older and more experienced workers to quit.

Wages and working conditions, of course, continued to be major grievances. In a report to the Fair Employment Practices Commission that held hearings in El Paso in 1942 on discrimination against Spanish-speaking workers, Leo Ortiz and Harry Hafner addressed the dual wage and job system sponsored by employers such as Phelps Dodge throughout the Southwest and especially in the border country. They observed that about four hundred workers labored in the El Paso plant, of which about two hundred were of Mexican descent, 75 were Blacks, and the rest Anglos. The company practiced job and wage discrimination by paying lower wages in El Paso than in other copper refining areas, by denying certain jobs to Mexicans and Blacks, and by paying higher wages to Anglo workers hired at the same time as Mexicans and Blacks.[49]

Similar if not worse conditions existed in other Southwestern locations, such as the Silver City area of southern New Mexico dominated by the Kenecott Copper Company. "This company has always maintained a special rate for Mexicans," Ortiz and Hafner told the commission, and

has refused them promotions, and has refused to hire them for certain jobs in open mine pits, such as shovel operators, drivers, craftsmen, mechanics, locomotive engineers, and firemen. The only classification open to Spanish-speaking workers are truckmen, powder men, mechanical helpers and general laborers. There is a difference in what an Anglo laborer is paid and what a Mexican laborer is paid for the same job. The minimum pay for Anglo workers is, I believe, about $6.50. In both plants, that is, the mine and smelter, the total number of employees is 2,000. In many instances Mexican workers have trained Anglo workers to do certain jobs in mine and smelter, while the Anglo student was getting a higher rate of pay than the man who was training him. The Anglo was promoted to the vacant job. The vacant job is denied to the qualified Mexican worker. In the Smelter, Mexican workers are limited to certain positions beyond which they can not be promoted. They can not work as craftsmen, mechanics, furnace men, tappers, or mill operators, etc., and jobs of like category. New Anglo workers are imported from the outside to fill vacant jobs and are trained by qualified Mexican workers who are available to fill these jobs. An Anglo worker who is hired will not work on a job called "labor." That job will be handled in all cases by Mexican workers.[50]

Ortiz and Hafner noted that segregated company housing separated Anglos and Mexican workers and provided inferior conditions for the latter. Mexican workers relaxed in separate and unequal recreation facilities. Mexicans received treatment in separate wards in company hospitals. Finally, some companies forced their Mexican worker to relieve themselves in separate toilet facilities.[51]

In October 1943, Local 501 received from the War Labor Board a favorable decision granting a wage increase of 11½ cents an hour retroactive to October 1942. Each worker received back pay of almost two hundred dollars. As a show of their loyalty to the war effort, union members with some of their wage increase purchased $12,000 worth of war bonds, and voted unanimously to donate one day's pay to the Community War Chest. "Now we no longer have any fear of the company," organizer Nichols wrote to the Denver office, "or any reactionary groups who might attempt to disrupt our organization."[52] Throughout the Southwest, Mine Mill won various grievance cases during the war years for its mostly Mexican-American members. Sensitive, however, to the charge that Mine Mill was only a "Mexican Union," the Union News of Morenci, Arizona, emphasized that Mine Mill had also won cases for its minority of Anglo members.[53]

After a year and a half of negotiations, Phelps Dodge in January 1944 agreed to a contract. The following year, despite many of the same obstacles, Local 509 at the AS & R smelter likewise secured a contract. And later in June 1945, Mine Mill through Local 509 won an election and contract at the smaller Southwestern Portland Cement Company.[54]

Under provisions of the Phelps Dodge contract, similar to the one at AS & R, the company recognized Local 501 as the sole bargaining agent for the plant's production and maintenance workers, and agreed not to discriminate against union members. The contract provided for a union check-off to insure that the union received dues from members. Working hours were set at 40 hours per week and any employee working more than eight hours per day would be paid 1½ times the hourly wage. The company consented to an immediate wage increase of 11¼ cents an hour. Workers would receive one week's vacation at full pay. Seniority would be recognized with regard to advancement, retention, and reemployment. Phelps Dodge further agreed "that there shall be no discrimination against any employee because of race, creed, color or national origin." Signed among others by J. B. Chávez, the contract was published in both English and Spanish.[55]

IV

Although Mine Mill in El Paso succeeded in renewing contracts with both Phelps Dodge and AS & R during the remainder of the war, Mexican-American employees of the plants persisted in condemning the continued dual job and wage system that affected them. These structural inequities plus the International's drive to achieve higher wages for all its members following the war led to the first significant strike carried out by Mexican-American members of Mine Mill in El Paso, which proved to be a major test for Mexican-American union leaders.[56]

In February 1946, the International announced that, unless eighteen AS & R plants agreed to increased wages for workers plus acceptance of industrywide bargaining, the union would call a nationwide strike. Mine Mill called for the equalization of wages for common labor throughout the AS & R plants and the end of regional wage differences. The union demanded in El Paso a 30 cents an hour increase for laborers that would raise their pay to $9.90 a day and insisted on a reduction of work hours that had once again gone up to 48 hours. It made similar demands on the Phelps Dodge Corporation. At Phelps Dodge, Mine Mill demanded a $2-a-day pay increase from the $4.90 minimum then being paid. However, both AS & R and Phelps Dodge rejected the wage increase and industrywide bargaining. Wages at the AS & R smelter, plant manager R. P. Bradford insisted, represented the "highest wages or equal to the highest wages in any industrial plant in the area." He noted that AS & R had offered an increase of 8¾ cents an hour for laborers and 5 cents for more skilled labor. Bradford discounted the idea of ending regional wage differentials and defended them on the basis of cost-of-living differences. As for work hours, he observed that the current 48-hour week would soon revert to a 40-hour one as more labor became available in the postwar adjustment period. Bradford reiterated that management was prepared to discuss issues, but only at the local level.[57]

On February 25, 1946, Mine Mill struck the eighteen AS & R plants throughout the United States. It would be a long strike. In El Paso, out of 650 employees – 550 workers – almost all Mexican-Americans or Mexican nationals – left their jobs. Laboratory and technical workers along with plant supervisors and foremen remained on duty. Local 509, avoiding mass picketing, only stationed "observers" outside of the plant. José Morales, Vice President of the local, termed the strike a "peaceful one." Most workers stayed at home or in the union hall at Smeltertown, as production at the smelter came to a halt. The *Herald-Post* criticized the strike and attempted to split Local 509 from the International by suggesting that it was not worth it for members to lose more than three thousand dollars a day for a nationwide contract that would only benefit union leaders. "That is sacrificing a lot of bread, beans and beef in an attempt to gain a point – a nationwide contract," the paper editorialized, "in which most of the workers have little personal interest."[58] A week later, members of Local 501 at the Phelps Dodge refinery also walked out.[59]

Locals 501 and 509, led by Mexican-American officers, prepared for a lengthy strike by maintaining union solidarity and morale. Strikers continued day and night picketing at both plants as a show of force and to prevent employment of strikebreakers. Lines of twenty to thirty strikers on average picketed at Phelps Dodge. A joint strike committee linked both locals together, with Silex, representing Local 509, as chairman of the committee, along with Ignacio Tovar and J. B. Chávez of 501 as vice-chairmen.[60]

Picketing successfully discouraged strikebreakers and prevented management from using surplus labor along the border to break the strike. Both locals secured the cooperation of the CTM in Juárez, which promised not to allow workers to cross the border to scab at either plant. As a show of international solidarity, over five hundred Mine-Mill members from El Paso led by Humberto Silex marched with 10,000 Mexican workers in the May Day celebration in Juárez. Mine Mill strikers along with CTM members carried signs supporting the strike against AS & R and Phelps Dodge along with placards urging United Nations unity and action against Franco in Spain. Other Mine-

Mill locals along the border, such as Local 470 in Douglas, Arizona, likewise received support from unionists and residents on the Mexican side of the border.[61]

The locals organized community rallies at which they solicited support and countered the hostile press by taking their case directly to the public. At one large rally, attended by between fifteen hundred and two thousand people, President Robinson defended the strikers by pointing out that the workers had patriotically stayed on the job throughout the war and now deserved better treatment. Addressing the Mexican-American members of Mine Mill, Robinson first praised the efforts of the Southern Conference for Human Welfare which had representatives at the rally. "You of Spanish-speaking origin know you always get the dirtiest, lowest paid jobs in El Paso," he proclaimed. "But slowly democracy is coming to the South, with the aid of such organizations as the CIO and the Southern Conference for Human Welfare."[62]

Locals 501 and 509 printed and distributed thousands of leaflets in both English and Spanish throughout the city and mailed circular letters requesting support from business and professional people.[63] They also responded to negative editorials in the local press. The El Paso *Herald-Post* red-baited Mine Mill by asserting that its leadership was on the "pink side." It commented that Reid Robinson in his speech at Liberty Hall had criticized Winston Churchill but not Joseph Stalin.[64] Replying, J. B. Chávez charged the *Herald-Post* with red-baiting: "Your statement that the leadership of the union is on the pink side has a familiar ring." Some Senators and congressmen had similarly criticized Churchill without doing so to Stalin. "Does that make our congressmen 'pink' too? Communists, maybe?" Chávez concluded by stressing the patriotic character of Mine-Mill members:

> We do not question your right to any opinion you may wish to hold regarding the union, its membership or leadership, but we object to any attempt, even by indirection or innuendo to picture this union before the public as unpatriotic or subversive. The record of the IUMM & SW and its membership in the war just ended is sufficient refutation of any such ideas.[65]

By June 1946, the strike against AS & R was settled. Within three days, Phelps Dodge also agreed to a contract. José S. Cordero, Acting President of Local 501, co-signed the agreement in El Paso and presented the terms to an approving membership. Almost identical to the AS & R contract, the one with Phelps Dodge gave workers an 18½-cents-an-hour increase with a majority of employees receiving an additional 7½ cents an hour. Along with Cordero, members of the negotiating team that met with local management included F. G. Villa, J. Aveno, Silex, A. Martínez, and E. Valverde. They and other members of the local greeted the end of the strike with elation. Avena, a shipping department worker, commented to a reporter:

> I'll be glad to go back to work. I'm tired of staying home during the day and reading the funny papers to my two kids. My wife has been asking me when I'll start working. Now my kids will be able to go to the picture show again, and get their allowances back.[66]

Francisco G. Villa, general chairman of the local strike committee, declared, "I'm happy the way things have turned out. That's the American way of fighting, when workers and company men can get together and talk things out." And Fred Rodríguez exclaimed: "Now I'll be able to buy my wife some dresses and shoes."[67]

The new wage rates, while not completely eliminating the dual wage system affecting Mexican-American workers, did aid in closing the gap between El Paso wages and those paid in other parts of the country. Locally, it made members of Mine Mill among the highest-paid industrial workers. "The vicious and discriminating wage differentials of the Southwest were struck a telling blow by additional increases won for workers at the El Paso plant," *The Union* noted of the AS & R contract. "Here the extra raises ranged as high as 7½ cents over the general increase, and will total as much as 26 cents an hour in some cases." And in commenting on the Phelps Dodge contract, *The Union* also celebrated the blow against the "Mexican wage":

> The raise, along with a similar raise for common labor at the AS & R properties in the Southwest earlier this month, has wrestled from the corporations' hands one of the most vicious weapons in their anti-labor arsenals – the discriminating wage differentials designed to keep common labor rates at oppressively low standards to bolster the old employer myth of racial and national "inequality."[68]

Adding to the sense of victory, Local 509, led by Humberto Silex along with a committee composed entirely of Mexican-Americans, two months later successfully negotiated a new contract with the Southwestern Portland Cement Company similar to those with AS & R and Phelps Dodge. Average wage increases amounted to $12.78 a week, raising the common laborers' weekly pay to $46.54. "These new high levels of take-home pay have broken all records for this notorious low-wage area of El Paso," *The Union* observed, "where discrimination against Spanish-American workers had previously been the chief weapon of the bosses."[69]

V

The 1946 strike solidified Mine Mill's position in El Paso. The strike and indeed the entire struggle to bring CIO unionization to the border revealed the collective strength of Mexican-American workers in their effort to eradicate humiliating class, race, and ethnic discrimination through such forms of labor control as the "Mexican job" and the "Mexican wage." Part of a larger and younger generation of Americans of Mexican descent – the Mexican-American Generation – that came of age during the Depression and World War II, Mine Mill leaders such as Silex, Anchondo, Chavez, and Tovar, as well as many of the rank and file, recognized as part of their "American heritage" the right to job opportunities and pay equal to other U.S. workers.[70]

Their "Americanization," however, did not betray their class and ethnic solidarity with Mexican nationals who worked alongside them and joined the struggle to unionize the plants. Although part of a progressive union, considered by some to be "leftist," Mexican-American members did not possess a revolutionary class consciousness. But they identified with collective struggles as workers. Class solidarity was supported by increased ethnic awareness as Mexican-Americans and Mexican nationals revolted against their dual exploitation. Workers of Mexican descent, whether U.S. citizens or Mexican nationals, related to one another along both job and ethnic lines. A Mexican worker at either AS & R or Phelps Dodge labored together with other Mexican workers, went home with other Mexican workers, drank in *cantinas* with other Mexican workers, and lived in the *barrio* with other Mexican workers. Border conditions created an expanding Mexican working class on both sides of the border, but also made it difficult to divide that class by playing on diverse ethnic prejudices, as occurred in more heterogeneous ethnic working-class communities in the East and Midwest. The working class in El Paso, with the exception of a distinct minority of skilled Anglo workers, was composed predominantly of Mexicans. The smelter and refinery might have been able to exploit differences between Mexican-American and Mexican nationals. However, ethnic and even family ties, as well as an international consciousness encouraged by the Mine Mill Union, prevented such possible dichotomies.

Further key variables in Mine Mill's success among Mexican-Americans included the union's ability to adapt to the particular class and ethnic character of the border country and to a more favorable climate for unionization in mass industries due to labor support by the New Deal. Moreover, multi-national corporations such as AS & R and Phelps Dodge proved in the end more flexible in a period of wartime economic expansion to adjust to unionization; this would be less true for locally owned industries. While CIO unionization in both the smelter and refinery initiated the move to eradicate "Mexican jobs" and "Mexican wages" in these two border industries, it did not affect many other Mexican workers in El Paso. Class and race segmentation founded on cheap labor continued to characterize the border city's labor market. In fact, job and wage improvements for some workers due to unionization in time created a chasm between better-off Mexican-American union members and Mexican immigrant workers, especially the undocumented, who flocked to the border.

Still, the courageous and successful struggle to establish the International Union of Mine, Mill and Smelter Workers in El Paso and elsewhere in the Southwest represented a historic leap forward. Unionization brought relative material gains and economic security as well as another step in the evolution of a Mexican-American working class in the United States.[71] Mexican-American workers in Mine Mill were not yet a class totally conscious of itself as a class, but they understood that only as a collective movement and through struggles against employers rather than through individual measures could they gain some of the fruits of their production. Power relationships between workers and bosses may not have been fundamentally altered through these struggles, but workers did gain greater leverage and protection against the most overt forms of labor exploitation. The history of the U.S. working class, especially in the 1930s and 1940s, is rich with the pluralistic struggles by many ethnic workers to obtain a better life. In the Southwest and other regions Mexican-Americans, through supportive unions such as Mine Mill, formed and continue to form an important part of that movement.[72] No labor strategy in the United States, and particularly in the Southwest, can succeed without attention to this legacy and to the continued growth of the Mexican working class north of the border.

CHAPTER 6

Puerto Rican Workers in the Garment Industry of New York City, 1920–1960

ALTAGRACIA ORTIZ

Throughout its history, the ready-made garment business, one of the oldest and most important sectors of the industrial economy of New York City, almost always has depended on immigrant workers. For nearly two hundred years, abundant and "cheap" foreign-born labor allowed clothing manufacturers to expand their businesses and make New York City the garment center of the world. During the early and mid-nineteenth century, waves of migrations brought Irish and German seamstresses and tailors who worked in the city's first clothes shops.[1] In the 1880s and the 1890s the industry began to employ skilled Jewish tailors who emigrated from eastern Europe – mainly Russia. In the late nineteenth century, large numbers of Italian garment workers entered the industry.

The first Puerto Rican needleworkers began arriving in the United States after the U.S. occupation of Puerto Rico in 1898. These women were usually skilled handsewers, embroiderers or professional seamstresses. The bulk of these workers were "homeworkers," sometimes also called pieceworkers because they either completely made or finished a piece of work at home. By the 1920s Puerto Rican women were an identifiable segment of the labor force in the needle trades, but it was not until the late 1940s and early 1950s that the great majority of Puerto Rican garment workers entered the outside labor force.[2] By this time almost all workers in the industry had been organized by the International Ladies' Garment Workers' Union (ILGWU).[3]

At the beginning of the century the skilled Puerto Rican seamstresses who sailed into New York brought with them centuries-old needlecraft techniques they had learned from their mothers and grandmothers. In later years the primary public schools in Puerto Rico were instrumental in teaching most girls on the island a variety of sewing skills.[4] During the 1920s and 1930s many of these women gained their experience in the flourishing "homework" industry on Puerto Rico, in the shops owned by Puerto Rican entrepreneurs (like Maria Luisa Arcelay of Mayaguez), or in the clothing factories that were being established in Puerto Rico by United States investors.[5] Many of the adults who emigrated to New York in the 1940s and 1950s had had some previous experience in the "cottage" or manufacturing industries of Puerto Rico.[6]

Early in the twentieth century, Puerto Rican *operadoras* (factory workers) in New York City picked up bundles of partly constructed garments – dresses, blouses, skirts, undergarments, handkerchiefs – at an agent's warehouse or a local factory. Then, with the aid of young daughters, sisters, or other adult females, they finished the garments at home. The experience of some of these women have been documented by Virginia Sanchez Korrol in her study of New York's Puerto Rican community during the first half of the twentieth century.[7]

Some Puerto Rican women dedicated themselves exclusively to needlework at home because of the belief that a women's most important role was to take care of her family personally. Besides permitting mothers to care for their young children, homework allowed the *operadoras* independence in their work schedules and enabled them to supplement the low salaries of their husbands. In 1937 Julia Gonzales, who was expecting a baby, began to hem handkerchiefs for a Mexican woman who owned a factory on Eighth Avenue in Manhattan. Gonzalez' husband worked only three out of every four weeks for the WPA, and earned only $15 a week. She "would work a little in the morning and some more at night. The rest of the time was devoted to housework, cooking, and cleaning. . . . " Clara Rodriguez, a homeworker with four children, took up needlework to help support her growing family. At first she hemmed handkerchiefs at thirteen cents a dozen. She admitted this was a low wage, but then the subway fare "to pick up more piecework was only five cents." Later, she sewed blouse collars on her sewing machine, and gave her children the chore of counting and turning them inside out. For this, she was paid twenty-five cents a dozen, extra money that "helped us to buy little extras – or helped stretch my husband's earnings."[8]

In spite of the apparent advantages that homework held for immigrant Puerto Rican women, it was extremely exploitive, involving long hours of work for very low pay – wages usually ranging from $5 to $12 a week.[9] However, few of the women interviewed by Sanchez Korrol thought of themselves as exploited workers. Some were aware that factory owners or contractors were making huge profits as a result of their work, but none of these homeworkers protested their exploitation. It should be noted that homeworkers in New York City were paid higher wages than those in Puerto Rico. In the late 1930s homeworkers on the Island made an average of a nickel an hour; and for an entire garment, such as a blouse, a homeworkers received 25 or 35 cents. If a piece of garment was damaged, the worker had to pay for the material. Sometimes workers were paid in groceries, or there were delays in wage payments and in getting work bundles. Agents were known to keep the wage increases of workers.[10]

During the 1930s law enforcement actions by the New York State Department of Labor, as well as increased union activity, began to curtail the homework industry in New York. The total numbers of workers involved – including Puerto Ricans – declined sharply. But in 1936 and 1937, the numbers of Puerto Rican homeworkers again began to increase. This is verified by the research of Lawrence Chenault, who studied the Puerto Rican immigration of the 1930s. Chenault reports that Puerto Rican participation in the homework industry involved 402 workers in 1933, 318 in 1934, 228 in 1935, and 327 in 1936.[11] Chenault also observed that the proportion of Puerto Rican homeworkers to all other groups was greater in 1936 and 1937 than in 1933. But in some homework industries – men's clothing in particular – there were no Puerto Rican workers.[12]

In the 1940s and thereafter, the practice of doing needlework at home was continued by Puerto Rican workers.[13] To supplement their income, some factory workers brought home pieces of garments to decorate or to finish. Georgina Feliciano, an industrious needleworker, helped her husband raise five children by hemming and decorating scarfs and sewing pockets on skirts.[14] Dan Wakefield, a journalist who documented Puerto Rican life in East Harlem during the 1950s, noted that:

> People come closer to memories of home with the farmed-out
> needlework of garment shops . . . [for] needlework has long been a
> widely practiced skill on the island, and the small, often fly-by-night
> dress shops in Spanish Harlem constitute a main chance for employ-
> ment within the neighborhood. It is nearly all women's work, and
> very few girls grow up in these streets without getting a touch of it.[15]

One of these young women, a seamstress by the name of Rosie Flores, was trained by her mother to do piecework at the age of eleven. Rosie's mother brought home blouses, belts, and other simple garments for her to finish. Her aunt also helped teach her, and she "got real good" at it. At the age of sixteen she entered the garment factory where her mother worked.[16]

This was probably the most significant outcome of the homework experience in the Puerto Rican community in New York City – the preparation of Puerto Rican women for factory work in the garment industry. After 1920 most skilled needleworkers who were employed outside the home began to enter this industry. This trend was made clear by a 1925 Census which showed that 600 – that is, 17.2% – of the 3,496 women, listed as living in the Puerto Rican community of East Harlem at that time and working in the production sector of the city's economy, were skilled seamstresses and dressmakers who had factory jobs.[17] The reports of the Department of Labor of Puerto Rico, which in 1930 established an employment office in Harlem to help Puerto Ricans solve the unemployment crisis created by the Depression, indicated that some 699 needleworkers and handsewers, 694 garment workers, and 229 miscellaneous factory and machine workers – all of them women – were integrated into the garment industry between 1930 and 1936. The total number of women placed in this industry amounted to slightly over 40% of all the women serviced by the agency in Harlem.[18]

Little is known of these first pioneer factory workers, but recent studies have begun to explore some of the problems that confronted these workers. Some Puerto Rican women already had jobs when they arrived, because garment employers brought them here directly from Puerto Rico to work in their factories, or soon got one, because relatives secured a spot for them in the places where they worked. But many had to search through newspaper advertisements, walk the streets of the garment center or the Lower East Side, or seek one of the few employment agencies that existed in order to find a job. The fact that many did not speak or understand English well or did not know how to travel through the city compounded the problem of finding and keeping a job. To cope with these problems, Puerto Rican immigrant women developed informal "network" systems, consisting of friends and relatives, that provided the mutual assistance that garment workers needed to survive in the city during these years. These close friends and relatives enabled immigrant Puerto Rican women to find work, to ride the unfamiliar system of transportation, to communicate with English-speaking employers and co-workers, and if the woman had children, to care for her young while she worked.[19]

These community-oriented network systems, however, did not help Puerto Rican garment workers combat the iniquitous practices of employers in the industry. Traditionally, the garment industry was characterized by low-wage labor, poor working conditions, and inhumane treatment of workers. In 1900 the International Ladies' Garment Workers' Union (ILGWU) was organized in New York City and became an affiliate of the American Federation of Labor (AFL). Before the local was organized, according to Pauline Newman, an old-time organizer of the Dressmakers' Local 22, dressmakers worked fourteen hours a day and sometimes seven days a week during the busy or "high" season. There was no overtime pay, but to keep the workers happy employers gave out five-cent pies as compensation for the long hours. Many shops were fire-traps: heated by pot-bellied stoves in the middle of the floor, surrounded by rags, pieces of fabric or paper, lighted by gas jets in poorly ventilated rooms, lacking fire escapes, accessible only by broken stairs. Because of the long hours workers were forced to sleep on top of work bundles.[20] In some factories the workers even had to pay for the chairs they sat on, and were charged for the lockers and electricity they used. Frequently, the time clocks and paychecks were altered to shortchange the workers.[21]

Led by Jewish and Italian syndicalist and socialist trade unionists, the ILGWU mobilized its members to strike for shorter hours, better work facilities, and higher wages.[22] In 1909 and 1910 the ILGWU's militant female shop stewards and organizers staged two mass strikes, the first on behalf of some twenty thousand waistmakers, and the second in support of sixty thousand cloakmakers. The final settlement of these strikes in 1910 resulted in the recognition of the ILGWU by garment employers as the collective bargaining agent for their garment workers. In exchange, the ILGWU ratified—with some workers bitterly protesting—Louis D. Brandeis' famous "Protocol of Peace," which bound the union to a no-strike contract as long as the Protocol, establishing a grievance and arbitration mechanism, was accepted by both labor and management.[23]

Dissidents within the ILGWU, especially syndicalists, opposed written contracts on the grounds that they unduly limited workers' freedom to engage in wildcat strikes, used to protest and end employer contract violations and to bring a fast halt to hazardous working conditions, sexual harassment, and physical intimidation. Contracts like the Protocol also banned the sympathy strikes that promoted class consciousness by allowing workers in one branch of the garment trade to come to the aid of workers in other branches or even other industries.

The radicals in the ILGWU also emphasized ethnic and racial egalitarianism. But as pragmatists, they understood that ethnic/linguistic divisions among recently arrived immigrant workers were so strong that initially it would be necessary to organize the newcomers into separate nationality locals.[24]

As a union of very low-paid workers, whose supply was constantly augmented by immigration, the ILGWU was not in a position to bring its workers dramatic wage increases. ILGWU leaders understood the limitations imposed on their union's power by the economics of the garment industry. With a shop size that was significantly smaller than in the men's clothing trade, the women's clothing industry was especially vulnerable to intense competition between employers – including non-union employers in small towns in the hinterland – competition that drove down wage rates. However, like many unions in low-wage industries, the ILGWU protected the interests of union members by taking up the grievance cases of workers who were improperly paid and disciplined, by pressing employers to improve safety and sanitary conditions, and by protesting on behalf of union members who were sexually harassed. The ILGWU also established a benefit fund that paid members modest but welcome unemployment, sickness, and death benefits.[25]

In the 1920s, as American agriculture entered a crisis that would last until World War II, the labor of thousands of women who had worked on U.S. farms was suddenly made available to employers of needleworkers. As "outwork" in non-union shops increased, severely weakening the ILGWU, the union was also rent by a bitter struggle between Socialist and Communist factions which brought the union to the verge of financial bankruptcy and dissolution. By 1927, the ILGWU was a paper tiger, heavily dependent on the monetary relief tendered by the Executive Council of the American Federation of Labor.[26]

There had always been a marked gender-based division of labor within the garment trade and within the ILGWU. Most of the skilled workers were male; the overwhelming majority of the rest of the organized industry labor force was female. Skilled male workers became the leaders of the most powerful locals – including those initially organized by women – and of the international, whose top officials were drawn largely from Local Number 10, the almost completely male cutters' local. The ILGWU's shop stewards were largely women; but the officers of its locals were almost all men, and men predominated among the delegates at union conventions. While most of the union's top officials were Jewish or Italian socialists, who believed in social insurance and collective working class political action in support of the Socialist Party of America, the union's leaders had an Achilles heel – sexism – that severely limited their vision of worker solidarity, leading them to take a condescending view of the bulk of the union's rank and file, which was female. This was clear to Rose Pesotta, a feminist and a syndicalist, who was one of the union's most talented organizers. In 1926 she was appointed to the token union Vice-Presidency reserved for a women. She succeeded Fannie Cohen, who had been forced out of the post because she advocated a democratic shop delegate system of governance for the union's locals, a system that would have transferred power from local officials (largely male) and the General Executive Board (largely male) to the rank and file (largely female). Pesotta recalled being told by union President Benjamin Schlesinger (in the 1920s) that she would have been better off getting married and staying home to raise babies.[27]

The union's male officers held tightly onto power within the union, imposing a standard of political, ethnic, and sexual homogeneity for the union officials that created a power structure dominated by anti-communist Jewish and Italian males. Puerto Rican and Black workers, irrespective of gender, and women, irrespective of nationality, were almost completely excluded from the best-paying jobs (e.g., cutters and pressers) and from the leadership positions within the union. Undoubtedly, after the 1920s the ILGWU's leaders ran scared, fearful of more internecine warfare within the union if new, potentially radical elements were recruited. The ILGWU's ageing leaders became more bureacratically oriented, losing touch with their youthful shop floor work experiences. As holders of leadership posts that brought them social and political recognition and enjoyable daily work routines far removed from the noise, heat, and dust of the workshop, these men were reluctant to share their power with any new intraunion factions that might demand their place in the sun. After 1929, the ILGWU's leaders became militantly Zionist and more politically conservative, relegating domestic problems to second place behind international developments that affected the survival of Israel. In 1935 the ILGWU had seceded from the AFL to join the militant Congress of Industrial Organizations (CIO). But in 1940, the ILGWU rejoined the AFL because of jurisdictional battles with the Amalgamated Clothing Workers of America and because many Communists were active in the CIO. Back in the AFL fold, the ILGWU's leaders were influenced by the racism of the AFL's dominant leaders, who tended to equate racial egalitarianism with radicalism, especially because Communists in the labor movement stressed racial equality so explicitly.[28]

The ILGWU did not begin actively to organize Puerto Rican garment workers until the early 1930s. As early as 1921 union members had complained that many Puerto Rican women were working in non-union shops; and some Puerto Rican workers had begun to join the union of their own accord. In the early years of the Depression, there was a significant return migration of Puerto Ricans as over eight thousand returned to the Island between 1930 and 1934. The Puerto Rican garment workers who remained in New York City continued to earn low wages and face discrimination.[29]

After the passage of the National Industrial Recovery Act in 1933, which ostensibly guaranteed workers the right to join unions, the ILGWU began a dynamic membership drive that added thousands of new workers, including more than two thousand Puerto Ricans. Most of the Puerto Ricans joined Dressmakers' Local 22; but here they made up only about five percent of the total membership. The bulk of the members of this local continued to be Jewish women. Puerto Ricans were also found in Childrens' Dressmakers' Local 91, Beltmakers' Local 40, Embroiderers' Local 66, Knitgoods Workers' Local 155, Neckwear Workers' Local 142, and Truck Drivers' Local 102. Puerto Ricans were organized into these locals – known to be the lowest paid units of ILGWU – because of the fear that non-unionized Puerto Ricans would work for wages lower than those the union had contracted for its own members. In jobs where Puerto Ricans did not pose a threat yet, such as pinking (edge-finishing) and shipping, there was no organization of workers.[30]

However, as Robert Laurentz has demonstrated, the ILGWU was unable to resolve any of the major problems of its Puerto Rican members. The ILGWU was silent on the issue of wage discrimination; consequently Puerto Rican women continued to receive lower wages than non-Hispanic white women. Puerto Rican workers were often humiliated by the imposition of fines and threats of dismissal if they did not obey the dictates of employers. The union assumed a passive role here, ignoring for the most part the complaints of some Puerto Rican women that they were being sexually harassed by their employers or foremen. The male leadership of the ILGWU possessed the same mentality of many of the men in those days that equated sexual harassment with "flattery." Nonetheless, at least one Puerto Rican women succeeded in getting the union to take up the issue on one occasion, and as a result the employer was forced to pay financial damages to the victim.[31]

Likewise, the ILGWU failed to prevent the acceleration of de-skilling, job-contracting, and relocation, changes which had begun long before Puerto Ricans entered the garment industry, but which during the 1930s and throughout subsequent decades, more and more adversely affected garment workers. De-skilling, for example, readily enabled Puerto Rican seamstresses to do "section-work"– the making of part of a garment – rather than the whole garment. In certain industries, such as the highly skilled, well-paid tailoring trades, section-work had begun during the first decades of the twentieth century, and was mainly in the hands of Jewish and Italian women; hence, it was called "women's work." The more intricate sewing operations were still done by professional Jewish or Italian male tailors. By the 1930s many Puerto Rican women started to replace other female workers in de-skilled jobs, and to earn the low wages that were characteristic of this semi-skilled labor. Laurentz argues that in addition to this: "Deskilling of the industry made it extremely difficult for any of these women to move up from lower-wage to higher-wage crafts.[32] Even if there had been no de-skilling in the garment business, the highly skilled, better-paid crafts, which included not only the specialized tailoring trades, but cutting in all trades as well, were male-dominated. This, coupled with existing discrimination, would have prevented Puerto Ricans from using these skilled crafts as a means of upward mobility during these years. Low-wage Puerto Rican workers, therefore, continued to work in most de-skilled shops, making women's and children's garments.

The economic crisis of the Depression forced many job manufacturers to distribute cut-up work to independent contractors, who would agree to make these garments for a specific price, using cheap non-union labor. The degree to which job contracting directly affected Puerto Rican garment workers has not been researched at all. We can presume, however, that Puerto Rican workers were probably found in the shops of these contractors and that their wages and working conditions were far below union standards. Laurentz found that the relocation of dress businesses outside of the city "tended to undermine the security of . . . Puerto Rican women who [had earlier] found thousands of positions in the New York City dress trade. . . . " Many of these women made inexpensive cotton dresses, an industry branch that paid an average of 72.5 cents an hour in New York City. Many dress manufacturers, however, found that labor costs outside of the city were lower – on the average 38.7 cents an hour – and they relocated to places with such less-expensive labor. Close to three hundred fifty dress businesses relocated to towns in Connecticut, New Jersey, and Pennsylvania in the 1930s. Many businesses, also, relocated to Puerto Rico. One Puerto Rican women told Laurentz in a 1978 interview that the children's dressmaking shop in which she worked took its business to Puerto Rico and left her without a job in New York City.[33]

The ILGWU did not succeed in eliminating any of the problems that confronted the Puerto Rican rank and file during the 1930s. The responsibility for this must be borne in part by the ILGWU leadership, which, under David Dubinsky—now more than ever—embraced Justice Brandeis' philosophy of "industrial peace." Elected President in 1932, Dubinsky quickly moved to implement that policy and prevent dissension within the union. To accomplish this, he eliminated the last vestiges of radicalism by purging the union of remaining Communists and radicals.[34] He also attempted to prevent the rise of future opposition by banning political discussion in the union and by forbidding the creation of special locals or groups among the rank and file. This last action affected the Spanish-speaking members who had recently joined the union. From 1933 to 1934 a group of them attempted to create a Spanish-speaking local in the dressmakers' industry because of "a deep feeling of discontent with the present administration of [Charles] Zimmerman," the head of Dressmakers' Local 22.[35] These workers complained that the situation in the shops revealed the union was not accomplishing much for them. They accused the Zimmerman "clique" of rigging the elections in Harlem, and of forcing them to vote for the so-called "progressive group." Hence, they demanded that the union recognize their right to organize and select their own leaders from their own ranks. They exhorted their co-workers to unite with a cry that must have been anathema to Dubinsky's ears:

> Spanish dressmakers let us fight with all our strength for the election of the left group candidates. They represent our platform for the enforcement of the decision on the minimum prices in all the shops, for the immediate attention of our complaints, for reduced dues to the unemployed dressmakers, against taxes, for the demands of the finishers, pinkers, and examiners and for unity of all workers of the trade.[36]

These workers, labeled "politically ambitious newcomers" by one scholar years later, failed to get recognition as a separate group within the organizational structure of the union.[37] Instead, Dubinsky instructed Saby Nehama, a Sephardic Jewish agent in Dressmakers' Local 22, to organize Spanish-speaking workers into a special department. At the 1934 annual convention Nehama and Zimmerman engineered the seating of two Puerto Rican women as bona fide delegates. Thus, the ILGWU leadership checkmated the Puerto Rican and other Spanish-speaking radicals of Local 22, and prevented them from becoming a viable source of leadership for other workers within the union. The rest of the Puerto Rican rank and file quietly acquiesced to Dubinsky's demands.[38] They had neither the members nor the power to challenge the ILGWU leaders who decided their fate during these critical years.

With the brief expansion of the garment industry during the late 1940s and early 1950s, many more Puerto Ricans were incorporated into the needlework trades, and subsequently into the ILGWU. The statistical analysis by Abraham J. Jaffee in 1953, based on the 1950 Census, indicates that 40 percent of the Puerto Rican female population was in the New York City labor force (as compared to 35% of the city's females); and that the greatest number of these women were employed as "operatives" in the manufacturing industries.[39] Carl Raushenbush noted in his occupational study of first- and second-generation Puerto Ricans that first-generation men were employed as "operatives" during this period.[40] Neither of these demographic accounts, however, helps us to determine the numbers or percentage of sewing-machine operators who worked in the garment industry. The 1979 Centro de Estudios Puertorriquenos study maintains that by the end of the 1950s the proportion of Puerto Rican female workers who were "operatives" (presumably garment factory operators) was 61.9 percent; and that "there were three women operatives for every four Puerto Rican men in the factories. . . . "[41] But in 1961 Clarence Senior placed the proportion of Puerto Rican working females who were operatives at 65.3 percent and of the working Puerto Rican males the semi-skilled operatives at 41.0 percent.[42] Again, there is no categorizing or definition of the term "operatives" in these statistical analyses from which we can extrapolate the numbers of garment operators. The ILGWU records and other studies of Puerto Rican immigration or Puerto Rican labor in the United States are just as vague on the question of the exact numbers of Puerto Ricans who participated in the garment industry during the decades after World War II.

The garment business, in spite of its short-lived period of expansion after World War II, was generally declining.[43] The Korean War brought an increased demand for clothing items, but the mid- and late-1950s saw a marked reduction in retail consumption of garment wear.[44] This decline was aggravated by increased competition from foreign imports — especially in neckwear, skirts, blouses, scarfs, and sweaters. The introduction of longer-lasting materials, such as acetates, nylons, and polyesters, also lowered consumer demand for clothes.[45]

These changes had a tremendous impact on the garment industry, and on its Puerto Rican labor force. Between 1950 and 1959 Puerto Ricans were coming to the United States at an average rate of 4,300 per year.[46] This was the largest migration wave ever to come to New York City from Puerto Rico. This means that the bulk of the Puerto Rican population that came to this country during the twentieth century came at a time when the garment industry – the city's biggest industrial employer of unskilled and semi-skilled immigrant labor – was waning. In addition, the garment manufacturers and jobbers had continued to use the de-skilling and subcontracting practices which they had introduced in earlier decades, and which were still legitimate ways of cutting down on labor costs.[47] During the 1950s and 1960s these adverse economic conditions also stimulated the trend toward relocation to areas where labor and other costs were cheaper.[48] To avoid New York's "high cost" of production, garment businesses, noticeably those in the lower-price brackets of the men's and women's apparel industries, began to move in greater numbers to New Jersey, Massachusetts, Pennsylvania, Ohio, Texas, California, and even to other countries.[49]

The Puerto Rican garment workers of the 1950s and 1960s continued to join and work with the ILGWU with the same high expectations as the garment workers of previous generations. Some, like Rosie Flores of East Harlem, joined the union because they felt the ILGWU would make a difference in their lives. During her 1959 interview with Dan Wakefield, Rosie happily enumerated her benefits as a union member:

> We get sick pay and holidays. . . . We even get paid when we have a baby – $150 for the time off and doctors' bills! And such a difference in the work, too. Not just getting paid more, but more relaxed. In the shops that don't have a union it's always a fight to get your work. . . . In our shops we divide it up, so whatever work there is for the day, we all have some. And then we get a minimum of $42.50 a week no matter what, but most of the time it's lots more, usually $70 or $80.[50]

Carlotta Rodriguez, a Puerto Rican labor organizer in East Harlem, also believed in the ILGWU. During the 1950s she helped Joseph Piscitello, who was the union's organizer for Harlem, to recruit workers in the remaining sweatshops. Many other workers supported the ILGWU and the organizational work that it was doing in Harlem and in other parts of the city.[51]

However, by the end of the 1950s, some Puerto Rican workers began to express disappointment with the ILGWU's conservative leadership and policies. In 1957 a group of protestors rejected the ILGWU as their bargaining agent, and along with Black workers, demonstrated in front of union headquarters. These workers were convinced that the union had not negotiated a fair contract for them; they petitioned the National Labor Relations Board to decertify the ILGWU as their representative. The following year there was another demonstration against the union, involving some two hundred members of Local 132 of the Bronx, employees of Plastic Wear, Inc., who criticized the ILGWU's leadership for conducting the Local's meetings in English, when 80 percent of its membership spoke only Spanish. In 1958 there was a second revolt–this one in the Q-T Knitwear Company factory in Brooklyn. In this case Puerto Rican workers accused the ILGWU of establishing an alliance with employers that was detrimental to their interests–in other words, of negotiating a "sweetheart contract." Carrying signs that read: "WE'RE TIRED OF INDUSTRIAL PEACE. WE WANT INDUSTRIAL JUSTICE," they marched around the factory.[52]

The leaders of the ILGWU dismissed the demonstrations as the work of agitators, and denied any charges of discrimination. The union, they proclaimed, had always admitted Puerto Ricans into its ranks, and in some shops, especially in the skirt trade, had made a concerted effort to integrate them into the local. They maintained that Local 23, the skirt-makers' division of the ILGWU, began to organize Puerto Rican workers during the late 1940s, as soon as they started working in this industry branch. The increase in the number of Hispanic workers, however, led Local 23 to appoint three new Spanish-speaking business agents–all Sephardic Jews–to facilitate communication with Puerto Rican and other Latin American workers. In 1949 the ILGWU created the position of Education Director, who was to be fluent in Spanish, and whose main function was to set up a special educational program for Hispanic members of the union. As part of this program, the union initiated English classes for its members. This, the union leadership believed, would help Puerto Ricans get jobs in the better price-line shops, where little Spanish was spoken, and of course, would facilitate the integration of Puerto Rican workers into full participation in union membership and activities.

Among the activities Local 23 offered its members were: lectures, visits to historic places, an annual spring dance, and an annual weekend outing for shop chairpersons–some of whom were Puerto Ricans. Through these social activities the union hoped to create a feeling of solidarity and cohesiveness. The union also initiated a program of political education in this local to develop union consciousness. Workers were informed of special legislation affecting workers. They were urged to participate in elections and signature drives to support such bills. A significant part of this political program envisioned the development of a core of Hispanic leaders who would become active in union affairs. To keep its entire local membership informed of union activities and benefits, the ILGWU distributed its Spanish-language edition of *Justice*, the union's bimonthly publication.

On a more personal level, Local 23 ran a counseling program to help Puerto Ricans with individual problems, and for a while had a Spanish-speaking clerk to inform members of their health care benefits.

In 1959 Roy B. Helfgott presented a report to the New York State Commission Against Discrimination, announcing that the ILGWU had successfully integrated almost all Puerto Rican skirt-workers into Local 23, and that of the 8,036 members, one-half were Latin American, most of whom were Puerto Ricans.[53] There were still problems with union membership retention, payment of dues, and full participation in union activities; but the report emphasized that the vast majority of Puerto Ricans were active members of the local, and some were in leadership positions on the local's executive board and its various committees.

Recent research has shown, however, that the ILGWU nevertheless subordinated Puerto Ricans in the occupational ladder of the industry and in the leadership structure of the union. This discrimination was especially obvious in the lack of adequate representation of Puerto Ricans in the top leadership positions of the union. It should be noted that Black workers complained vociferously about exactly the same pattern of subordination.[54] Jews, and to a lesser extent Italian-Americans, had held these positions in the past, but as their numbers among workers in the industry began to decline, they established an exclusionary electoral process that prevented other groups from occupying important decision-making posts.[55] The eligibility rules for candidates for President, Secretary-Treasurer, or membership on the General Executive Board were the strictest among all the labor unions in the nation.[56] This severely limited the number of challengers, especially among the newcomers to the union. Since political groups or caucuses were not allowed to convene until three months before the annual convention, it was difficult for contending candidates to meet with the rank and file to present their platforms. Those in office, however, could meet with the members as often as they wished. Exclusivist appointment methods also prevented Puerto Ricans from becoming local managers or agents in the lower ranks of the ILGWU. Vacancies, transfers or new appointments were deliberately given to Jewish members of the union, and sometimes to Italians in order to balance out the power structure of the old members.[57] Even in areas such as East Harlem, where Puerto Rican garment workers were clearly in the majority, the union did not alter its policy, and maintained a non-Puerto Rican representative. Thus the Puerto Rican rank and file, consisting mainly of female workers, were excluded from full participation in union activities.[58] The ILGWU continued to blatantly disregard the language needs of its Spanish-speaking members. In 1954 it allowed another Spanish club within the Dressmakers' Local 22 to be created in order to meet the needs of its members. But the union's top leaders refused to allow a Spanish-language local, claiming this would fragment the garment labor movement. Yet the ILGWU allowed the two Italian locals – Local 89, the Italian Dressmakers' Union and Local 48, the Italian Cloakmakers' Union – to operate until the mid-1970s, in spite of the New York State Anti-Discriminatory Act of 1945 and the Equal Employment Section of the Civil Rights Act of 1964, both of which had declared all nationality locals illegal.[59] The Italian locals controlled some of the better-paid jobs in the industry and constituted a source of power for the Italian workers, whose numbers had also begun to decline at this time. The ILGWU, likewise, did not appoint a Spanish-speaking agent to the Harlem area, where a good number of workers did not speak English. Joseph Piscitello, who had been Harlem organizer since 1933 when the Italians made up the greatest number of workers, knew no Spanish. He admitted:

> This is a problem, you see, because they can't understand English, a lot of them, and we can't make them understand about the things they should have and why they should have a vision. . . . But, you see, the Puerto Ricans, they don't have the education that we have. . . . They're just not educated, you see, except for some elite like Miss Rodriguez here. But mostly they're backward.[60]

Perhaps if Piscitello had been able to communicate directly in Spanish with the Puerto Rican workers, rather than through Carlotta Rodriguez, the workers may not have seemed so "backward." Puerto Rican workers resented this kind of attitude on the part of union representatives, and their 1957 and 1958 protests against the union clearly showed this. But the union continued to appoint and keep people like Piscitello, denied the Puerto Rican members the right to organize their own locals, and refused to translate contracts and minutes for the Spanish-speaking membership.

Puerto Rican male workers, most of whom entered the industry in the decade of the 1950s as shipping clerks, packers, delivery men, order pickers, and push-boys, experienced further discrimination when the ILGWU refused recognition of Local 60A, the shippers and packers local, as an independent unit. Local 60A had been organized in the early 1950s as an appendage to Local 60, the pressers' local. But the manager of Local 60 represented 60A at all union functions. Since most of the members of Local 60A were Puerto Ricans and Blacks, the

ILGWU contended that the creation of a separate local for these workers would result in "discrimination."[61] Yet the existence of Italian Locals 89 and 48, and of Local 10, consisting of highly paid and highly skilled cutters, who maintained an almost all-white local through the use of "selective" training practices, was not, according to the ILGWU, discriminatory. Throughout the 1950s, therefore, Puerto Rican male workers, earning on an average about fifty dollars a week, continued to be represented by a local whose members made about five dollars an hour.[62] As late as 1969 a Puerto Rican shipping clerk who worked for Stacy Ames, a women's apparel company in Long Island City, complained of the lack of Local 60A activity in his shop. The union representatives never showed him his contract; he was simply told that he would be earning $76 a week; instead, he was paid only $67. Local 60A held only three meetings a year, and when it did meet, workers were discouraged from raising pertinent questions about their wages.[63] Although Puerto Rican shippers and packers complained about these problems, and struggled to make the ILGWU leadership more sensitive to their needs, they did not succeed.

Originally, a worker was trained in a skilled trade by a friend or was recommended for training by local union officials. Will Herberg's 1953 study on ethnic group tensions in the dress industry noted that the union had tried to get Jewish and Italian skilled workers to "bring up" Puerto Ricans into the better trades. These attempts failed; and Herberg believed that "ethnic clannishness"– that is, the reluctance of the "old-timers" to accept Puerto Ricans as their equal, was mainly responsible. But Herberg maintained, nonetheless, that there was no "oppression" in the garment industry, and that the advancement of Puerto Ricans was not "altogether barred." It was his opinion that Puerto Ricans were not interested in advancing themselves in the skilled trades anyway. This is a classic example of the phenomenon of "blaming the victim" that sociologist William Ryan has identified.[64]

In 1959, Roy B. Helfgott concluded that in the dressmakers' crafts Puerto Ricans were found in the less-skilled, lower-priced jobs, "and in this industry their advancement to higher skills was not proceeding very rapidly." He noted that in the better shops "with few exceptions, unlike the Jewish and Italian men of earlier days, they do not become highly skilled tailor system workers on dresses or 'cloaks.' As a result, a shortage of skilled sewing machine operators is developing."[65]

Even when the shortage of trained skilled workers became an acute problem during the 1960s, the union did not adopt a position favoring the advancement of Puerto Rican workers in the garment trade. At 1962 hearings before a subcommittee of the House Committee on Education and Labor that was studying discrimination in the

ILGWU, Dubinsky and other union officials insisted that the union was not an "employment agency," and that consequently, it was not its responsibility to train workers for the industry.[66] Later, when the federal government recommended subsidizing training programs in the garment industries in order to create employment opportunities for minorities, the ILGWU objected on the grounds that this could cause instability because the industry depended greatly on inexperienced labor.[67] Union leaders believed that workers who needed specific skills could be trained by individual employers, mostly supposedly in small businesses, where advancement in a skill was certainly possible, or they could learn the trade at the Fashion Institute of Technology High School, where the union held "grading" classes. As a result of the ILGWU's opposition, federally funded programs were not implemented throughout the industry. In the coat and suit business, however, the ILGWU finally relented, and in 1966 declared that minorities could be trained; but Dubinsky made it very clear to Secretary of Labor Willard Wirtz, who had personally appealed to the union to alter its "non-training" policy, that training in the coat and suit trade was to be an exception. During the decade of the 1960s the ILGWU did not make any great efforts to train Puerto Ricans for better-paid jobs in other needle-trade industries.

The union's discriminatory training policies had dire consequences for Puerto Rican garment workers and for the garment industry in New York City in general. Puerto Rican workers continued to perform semi-skilled work, which was paid at a much cheaper rate than skilled craft work; and most were unable to enter the better-paid trades for lack of skills. Herbert Hill, the National Association for the Advancement of Colored People labor relations attorney and a special consultant at the Congressional hearings, bitterly criticized the union's position, noting that evidence clearly indicated that the garment industry still had great need for more skilled labor, and that contrary to the ILGWU leadership's perception, the industry was becoming one of big businesses that required new needlework skills. He included the ILGWU among "those labor unions which in the past were important vehicles for improving the economic condition of workers [but] now use their power to prevent the entry of certain groups of workers into the labor market or to lock these groups permanently in unrewarding menial and unskilled job categories.[68] Laurentz argues that "the shortage of skilled operators was basically caused, not by the ILGWU, but by employers who found it more profitable to exploit the lack of opportunities for blacks and Puerto Ricans by deskilling garment operations, lowering wages, or leaving workers jobless as they relocated in lower-wage areas."[69] But he does blame the ILGWU for allowing the union locals to discriminate against Puerto Ricans. Some of these locals, such as the cutters' Local 89, consisted mainly of white male workers, who because of the skills they possessed, made very good wages and found a high degree of stability in the job market. These locals refused to train Puerto Ricans for available positions; the union did not challenge their discriminatory practices.[70]

The discrimination that Puerto Ricans experienced in the ILGWU and in the garment factories eventually affected the entire Puerto Rican community. In the past workers from different cultural backgrounds had been able to move up into higher-paying jobs throughout the garment industry. Jewish and Italian skilled workers, for example, had helped other workers to obtain better paying jobs. This process enabled low-income workers to increase their earnings, and ultimately served as a vehicle for the upward mobility of their group in the economic ladder of the city. When Puerto Ricans entered the industry, however, their path to a better life was blocked by the negative attitudes of skilled workers from other ethnic groups who felt threatened by the presence of the new work force, and by the changes that were occurring in the industry. As a result, the Puerto Rican community was not able to benefit as much from the skilled labor of its garment workers as earlier groups had done.[71]

Although most Puerto Ricans did not significantly improve their economic status through their labor in the garment trades during these years, the garment industry certainly profitted from this renewed source of immigrant labor. Some scholars even argue that had it not been for the availability of cheap Puerto Rican labor, the garment industry in New York City would not have survived during the decades of the 1950s and 1960s. This was particularly true in the more standardized sections of the industry, such as the dress, skirt, and underwear businesses. Herberg's brief study of the dress industry clearly indicated that by the early 1950s Puerto Ricans, along with Blacks, had begun to replace the older Jewish and Italian workers in the dressmaking trade.[72] By the end of the decade Puerto Ricans had become predominant not only in this industry, but in the skirt and undergarment sectors, too. Their importance in these trades was recorded by Helfgott in his 1959 reports on women's and children's apparel. These studies – one for the New York State Commission Against Discrimination and the other for the Metropolitan Region Association – singled out Puerto Ricans as the most important source of labor in the skirt and undergarment industries.[73] In the undergarment factories they already had replaced the older ethnic groups as early as the 1940s. Helfgott doubted that Puerto Rican immigrants would continue as the main source of labor for the garment industry in New York City. Even at this time, when the Puerto Rican migration to the United States was quite large, he noted that in some of the shops, the number of Puerto Ricans was not sufficient to meet the labor needs of employers. He attributed this shortage both to the lack of skilled workers in some trades that we noted earlier, but also to the fact that Puerto Ricans had begun to settle in other areas in the United States. He observed that a

> significant fact about Puerto Rican migration to the continental United
> States is that New York's share of it has skidded from 95 per cent to
> 65 per cent between 1946 and 1956. . . . The opening of new job
> opportunities in other areas explains the steadily declining proportion
> of migrants in New York.[74]

Indeed, demographic reports of the late 1950s showed an increasing trend toward the relocation of Puerto Ricans to places outside the metropolitan region, particularly to industrial sites where Puerto Rican males could find employment.[75]

Raymond Vernon, the director of the 1956–1959 study of the New York City metropolitan region, also remarked on the importance of Puerto Rican labor in the manufacturing industries in the area. Although he did not believe that immigrant labor at this time was as crucial in the development of the area as earlier waves of migration, he still considered Puerto Rican immigrant labor as having "some significance." The Puerto Rican laborer, with more information than earlier immigrants "has been able to present himself [or herself] for employment at times corresponding with the existence of employment opportunities." Puerto Ricans, however, did not come to New York City "to take on any job at any price." Thus, "the 10,000 or 15,000 Puerto Rican immigrants who have been added annually to the New York labor force in recent years have made barely a ripple on the New York wage structure."[76] It was Vernon's opinion, therefore, that Puerto Rican immigrants had not made much of a difference in the supply of low-wage labor in New York City. Moreover, Puerto Ricans had begun to develop skills and take on higher paying jobs or, as Helfgott had pointed out, to move to other cities – Philadelphia, Baltimore, Chicago – in search of better job opportunities.[77]

In spite of migration trends that had Puerto Ricans settling in places outside of New York City during the late 1950s and 1960s, many Puerto Ricans continued to work in the area, particularly in low-wage and less-skilled manufacturing industries. Clara E. Rodriguez, who studied the degree of integration of Puerto Rican workers into these industries, especially the garment industry, writes that:

> The significance of the manufacturing industries to the welfare of the
> city cannot be overemphasized. There is a renewed awareness of the
> importance of the garment industry as the largest employer in the
> city. . . . And as important as manufacturing is to the city, Puerto
> Ricans are to manufacturing. Despite the imposed marginality of the
> Puerto Rican community in decision-making, if there were an exodus
> of Puerto Ricans, the city would be in serious straits. Puerto Ricans
> provide the unacknowledged, but indispensable, role of perhaps all
> previous immigrant groups and blacks – that of workers supporting the
> base of the economic system.[78]

Rodriguez is convinced that the involement of Puerto Ricans in the
garment industry during the 1950s, 1960s, and early 1970s was crucial
to the survival of this sector of the city's economy. At a time when
competition from other areas would have driven many of the garment
businesses out of New York, Puerto Rican workers tipped the scale on
behalf of the city by providing the low-pay labor that investors
required in order to stay in New York. Rodriguez argues that: "Without
this source of cheap labor many more firms would have left the city;
those that stayed would have had to reduce their production. In this
sense, New York's claim to be the garment capital of the world rests
upon Puerto Rican shoulders."[79] Rodriguez did not ignore the role of
earlier immigrants, recognizing that the arrival of low-wage laborers
increased the "surplus value of capitalists," and made it possible for
these capitalists to expand their businesses. Puerto Ricans in time
"assumed the role of previous immigrant groups – that of depressing
wage levels and increasing the ranks of the industrial reserve army."[80]

Lest it should be construed that Rodriguez' statement implies that
the large number of Puerto Ricans in the New York City work force
was solely responsible for the low wages in the garment industry, it
should be noted that the ILGWU had adopted a policy of wage
restraint since the years after World War II, fearing that garment
businesses would relocate outside the city at a much faster rate than
they had been doing.[81] Moreover, garment manufacturers had been
the group that took the initiative in reorganizing garment production
to encourage a more advanced division of labor that produced an even
higher ratio of unskilled to skilled jobs.

For Puerto Rican families, the availability of jobs in the Ladies'
garment trade was a mixed blessing. They filled the "inferior" jobs of
the secondary labor market, a market historically characterized by
high turnover of workers and very exploitative economic and social
conditions. But needlework employment helped preserve stability in
the Puerto Rican household. As Federico Ribes Tovar has noted,

The [Puerto Rican] men, without any preparation whatever, often could not find work, and it was the Puerto Rican woman who saved the situation. In the garment workshops of New York there was always a demand for operators. She did not take long to learn the operation of the machines and her wages sufficed to feed the family, though poorly.[82]

However, Lourdes Miranda King, a leader in the Puerto Rican woman's movement in the United States, warns that we must not interpret this as evidence of a "success myth" for Puerto Rican women: "For many reasons, Puerto Rican women found employment more readily. Sexist attitudes permitted hiring a woman for a lower wage than a Puerto Rican man. Either they were seen as less of a threat in the white male hierarchy, or the available opportunities were so-called 'women's jobs'–this is, unskilled."[83] However, the idea of "female success" is incorrect, since statistics indicate that Puerto Rican women in general had much higher unemployment rates than men. As the 1979 Centro de Estudios Puertorriquenos interpretation concluded,

The idea that Puerto Rican women have been at an advantage, either in access to the labor market, in job status, or in earnings, in ways that would undermine family relations or the manhood of male household heads thus seems to rest on a slim foundation. What these crude figures [comparative statistics on the participation of Puerto Rican men and women in the labor market] do convey is a sense that women have been migrating and taking jobs, not as occasional or privileged earners, but as a mobilizable reserve driven by the need to work shoulder to shoulder with men in factories and at . . . very low wages.[84]

African-American

The Red Scare and Black Workers in Alabama: The International Union of Mine, Mill, and Smelter Workers, 1945-1953

HORACE HUNTLEY

During the late 1940s and early 1950s, several left-wing labor organizations came under vigorous attack from both within and outside the labor movement. At the Congress of Industrial Organizations national convention in Cleveland, Ohio, in 1949, CIO President Philip Murray declared, "There is enough room within the CIO movement to differ about many subjects, many ideas, questions of reform within the CIO, economics, social and trade-union policy—yes, plenty of room, plenty of room, but there is no room with[in] the CIO for communism." At this convention the CIO amended its constitution to allow for expulsion of "Communist-dominated" unions from the organization.[1]

One of the unions that was labelled "communist" and expelled from the CIO was the International Union of Mine, Mill and Smelter Workers. This essay will address that expulsion, and also consider Black workers' attitudes toward the Mine Mill union as the "communist" issue was used to destroy the union in Alabama.

The left-wing unions affiliated with the CIO had been under constant internal and external pressure from the inception of the CIO. The CIO had been successful in organizing industrial workers in the 1930s partly because of its left-wing organizers; just as important, however, was the militancy of workers facing the increase in exploitation that accompanied the Depression, the aid tendered by Section 7a of the National Industrial Recovery Act (1933) and the more potent National Labor Relations Act (1935), and the growing acceptance of labor unions by the middle classes in the United States. According to Philip Foner, the National Association of Manufacturers led the Red Scare of 1937–1938 by distributing two million copies of a pamphlet entitled *Join the CIO and Help Build a Soviet America*.[2] The attitude displayed by the NAM intensified after World War Two. Attacks on the left escalated to the point where James Forrestal, Under Secretary of the Navy and later Secretary of Defense, could warn of the "Communist infiltration" into every facet of domestic life, including the attempts to take over the motion picture and radio broadcasting industries, the press, the church – and, of course the labor movement.[3]

Between 1943 and 1947 the labor movement was bombarded with a variety of anti-labor proposals from the executive and legislative branches of government, including suggested legislation to revoke the bargaining rights of any union violating a no-strike provision, to make unions subject to suits from "damaged employers" resulting from broken contracts, to make it impossible for employees to sue employers for back pay, and to institute the anti-labor injunction that had been banned by the 1932 Norris–La Guardia Act.[4]

The country's political leaders were frustrated by a segment of the labor movement that dared to challenge these efforts. During the war years, much of organized labor adhered to the "unity" program in behalf of the war effort; John L. Lewis and the United Mine Workers (UMW) had been criticized severely by Philip Murray and other labor leaders for their wartime strikes.[5] In 1944 President Roosevelt was supported for re-election by most union leaders, even though he had endorsed the "Little Steel Formula Wage Freeze," had proposed labor conscription for men up to the age of 65, and had made attempts to break mine and railroad strikes. His labor supporters expected repayment after the war.

It was not to come. President Roosevelt died in April 1945, and with his death also died the hopes for better labor relations after the war. Workers began pressing for relief from the anti-labor wage restrictions with which they had been so thoroughly disenchanted during the war. When Congress and President Truman refused to act, a rapid upsurge in strikes took place. Between January 1 and May 30, 1945, even before the war had ended, thirteen times as many workers voted for strikes in National Labor Relations Board (NLRB) polls than in the same period the previous year (42,992 in 1944, 558, 570 in 1945).[6]

The business and political leadership's explanation for this increased labor strike activity was "Communist infiltration." By 1947 the attacks upon "Communists" in the labor movement had intensified. The House Un-American Activities Committee opened hearings on the issue, and many people were harassed because of their leftist political beliefs. The U.S. Chamber of Commerce stepped up its attacks and became an effective lobbyist for the passage of the repressive Taft-Hartley Bill (1947), which, among other restrictions, required union officials to sign affidavits stating that they were not members of the Communist Party.

Efforts also were under way to organize a self-purge in labor. The Mine Mill union offers a particularly vivid example of the actions generated against the left through the McCarthyism of more conservative labor leaders. Charges were brought against the union by William Steinbery, President of the American Radio Association and a member of the CIO Executive Board. A two-day hearing was held before a three-man committee commissioned by Philip Murray; the committee recommended "that the executive board exercise the powers granted to it by article VI, section 10, of the CIO constitution and, by virtue of those powers, revoke the certificate of affiliation heretofore granted to the Mine, Mill, and Smelter Workers and expel it from the CIO." Shortly thereafter the CIO expelled ten other unions for their alleged Communist connection. The official charge in all eleven cases was that those unions' policies and activities were "consistently directed toward the achievement of the program or the purposes of the Communist Party, rather than the objectives and policies set forth in the Constitution of the CIO."

Three of the most notable accounts of this left-wing struggle in the CIO are found in Max Kampelman's *The Communist Party vs. the CIO*, David Saposs' *Communism in American Unions*, and Vernon Jensen's *Nonferrous Metals Industry Unionism*. All three accounts portray the left-wing unions as villains in this struggle. From its earliest days in the Alabama ore mines the Mine Mill union had engendered the wrath both of red-baiters and of race-baiters who attacked the union's advocacy of racial equality as not representing workers' needs and simply reflecting its being a puppet of Moscow. These conclusions reflected the hysteria of the times. The weakness of these studies stems from their acceptance of the official reports of the CIO without question, and from ignoring the questions raised and positions taken by the unions' rank and file.

From the perspective of the local power structure in Alabama, communism, labor questions and questions of race were inextricably bound together. Law-enforcement officials habitually acted to repress promptly any hint of radical thought. When someone was suspected of being a communist or possessing "inflammatory literature," a "liquor warrant" ordinarily was issued by the city or county authorities to allow a search of that person's premises. Arthur Green, Solicitor of the Bessemer Cutoff Company, candidly admitted, "If we want to search and don't have anything sure on the person, then we send a liquor warrant and search the house anyway." The formality of obtaining a liquor warrant generally was reserved for searches of whites' homes; police rarely bothered to obtain a warrant when Black homes were to be searched.[8]

Private efforts were more direct. In the case of one "well-known Communist," steelworker organizer Blaine Owens was taken "over the mountain," beaten until he lost consciousness and left to die. Atlanta detective E. S. Carlton, who filed an affidavit with a U.S. Senate Committee investigating Violations of Free Speech, reported that an adviser to the president of the Tennessee Coal and Iron Company told him that TCI had Owen abducted and beaten.[9]

The Birmingham Red Scare was one of long standing. As early as May 1934, a *Birmingham News* front-page article entitled "Police, Sheriff's Office and Grand Jury Will Open War on Radicals," linked the Communist Party with strike violence in the iron ore district. On May 7 the police department had raided a Southside apartment and arrested five white men and one Black woman. These arrests were referred to by the Chief of Police as "a round-up of Communist leaders in this district." The article further stated that "Every member of the department was ordered to jail every communist suspect." The Sheriff of Jefferson County stated that "there can be no doubt that professional agitators are responsible for the major part of our industrial trouble in Jefferson County."[10] Evidence against those arrested was meager, for the press had been enlisted in the anti-communist/anti-union campaign and tended to sensationalize accounts of alleged local communist activity.

Labor analyst F. Ray Marshall also contends that a Communist base was established among Blacks in the iron-ore mining district of Birmingham.[11] The present author has found little to support his contention. Nevertheless, there is ample evidence of a Black presence in the Party outside the mining camps. In 1933, for example, Robert Washington, who had worked for various steel, coal, railroad, and trucking companies in the Birmingham area, became an organizer for International Labor Defense, a Communist-dominated legal defense group. In September 1934, Washington and Willie Foster, another union organizer, were arrested in Selma for attempting to organize a sharecropper's union. The men were released the following night, but at different times. Washington's fate rested with a mob of armed white men who were waiting for him outside the jail. They took him several miles into the woods, where he was questioned about his ILD membership, and beaten. The men finally released him with a threat to kill him if he ever returned to Dallas County. The other Black man, Willie Foster, was never seen or heard from again after leaving the jail; apparently he was murdered.[12]

The case of Helen Long, a Black woman who joined the Communist Party in the early 1930s because of its call for relief for the unemployed, also illustrates the threats faced by Party members. About five o'clock one morning, while she and her husband were asleep, five men who identified themselves as Birmingham police officers stormed into their home and confiscated newspapers and a list of the names of some of her associates. When he reported to work later that morning, Mr. Long was fired from his job at Stockham Pipe and Fitting and informed that he would never be able to get another job there because they could no longer trust him.[13]

Harriet Flood, a Black woman who lived in Bessemer, encountered similar difficulties. In 1935 she went to the WPA for a job and was assigned to a sewing-room project. About two hundred women worked there and approximately twenty were active union members. Ms. Flood joined the Women's Auxiliary of the Hodcarriers Union. In April 1935, the District Council of the Union called a strike to protest a proposed two-week layoff without pay and to demand removal of a Tennessee Coal and Iron official who had been loaned to the state to help administer the program. Ms. Flood gave a vivid description of her activities and those of other women on the picket line in a statement filed with the U.S. Senate Committee on Education and Labor. The two most vocal Black women reportedly were beaten by several white men. The women bled profusely from the head after being attacked by WPA supervisors and policemen, and the pickets were dispersed by trucks speeding into their midst. The strike eventually was settled, but some union leaders were not allowed to return to work.[14]

Finally, the two most noted cases of Black Communists in the Birmingham area are those of Angelo Herndon and Hosea Hudson. Herndon was a coal miner and Hudson, a steelworker; both were avowed Communists and were forced to leave the district because of their organizational efforts among industrial workers.

The persons described above were atypical, not because of their activities, but rather because their experiences became part of the public record. Stories of common harassment generally were not recorded but instead became part of the oral tradition of people in the area. Historians and journalists have argued correctly that few Southern Blacks actually joined the Communist Party, but the importance of the Party in Southern struggles of the 1930s cannot be measured simply by membership statistics.[15]

Accounts of Blacks and Communists are numerous, and most point to the fact that the Communist Party failed to analyze properly the plight of Black Americans. The two most noted accounts, both published in 1951, are Wilson Record's *The Negro and the Communist Party* and William A. Nolan's *Communism vs. the Negro*. Each concluded that the impact of the Party upon the majority of Blacks had been minimal because of this analytical failure. In *Blacks in America*, James McPherson and others argued that, "As the most obviously oppressed and exploited minority in the United States, Black Americans, according to Communist theory, should have been ripe for revolution."[16] This assessment is probably correct; but even in such fertile ground, the Party failed to take advantage of the opportunity.

The position of the Communist Party on the question and method of achieving Black equality had traditionally been ambivalent. Prior to 1928, the Party condemned the NAACP and Urban League's stance of moderation, and charged that their appeal was limited to the Black middle class and was made without regard for the Black working man and woman. Since the earlier Communist tactic of "boring from within" had proven to be impractical, the Party organized to oppose these groups openly. The Party looked more favorably upon Marcus Garvey's United Negro Improvement Association (UNIA) because it appealed to the Black working class. Communists had tried to infiltrate and gain control of Garvey's movement in an effort to divert it from its "Back to Africa" and "Negro Zionist" direction.[17] Party members in the movement were too few to gain any influence, however, and these attempts were unsuccessful.

After 1928, the Communist position changed, and they advocated "self-determination" of Blacks in the Black Belt of the Southern states. The party promoted union organization among sharecroppers and tenant farmers in the rural areas, and among industrial workers and the unemployed in the cities. The Southern base of operation for these organizing drives was Birmingham.[18] The Communist approach to solving the "Black problem" of America and the world changed several times after 1928, changes which caused conflicts of interest for many Blacks who had joined the Party, and which resulted in many becoming hostile to the Party. The fact still remains, however, that the Party's positions on race created an affinity between it and Blacks.

From its introduction to the Alabama iron ore mines in 1933, The Mine Mill union was termed the "Nigger Union" and accused of being

Communist-inspired. Such accusations were based on the union's Black majority membership and on its emphasis on equality within its ranks.[19] Observers frequently have failed to raise the appropriate questions with regard to Black participation in the Communist Party. On the labor front, the question should not be how many Blacks participated, but rather what the non-participants thought of those unions labeled Communist by leaders of other unions and the CIO.

The Mine Mill union initially was known as the Western Federation of Miners, which was the progenitor of the Industrial Workers of the World (IWW). These labor organizations believed in "One Big Union" of all workers, irrespective of occupational distinctions. They rejected the craft elitism espoused by the AFL. In 1916 the WFM changed its name to the International Union of Mine, Mill and Smelter Workers. Mine Mill was active during World War I but became moribund in the 1920s as the anti-union, open-shop "Americanism" drive of American businessmen put the labor movement, and especially industrial unions, on the ropes. After the passage of the New Deal legislation, Mine Mill successfully organized in the copper, lead, zinc, iron ore, and precious metal mines of the Western, Midwestern, Eastern and Southern states.

The backbone of the organizational efforts of Mine Mill in Alabama was in the iron ore mines, concentrated along a strip of land around Red Mountain in Jefferson County. The strip was some fifteen miles long and came within a few miles of Birmingham on the northeastern and Bessemer on the southwestern slope of the mountain. Despite this geographic proximity to the two cities, it was a physically isolated area because the mines and mining camps were situated away from principal highways. On the normal drive from Birmingham to Bessemer, for instance, one would not pass through these areas—it took a special effort to get there. Turning off the Bessemer highway enroute from Birmingham, crossing the railroad tracks, ascending and descending the hills, rounding curves and invariably passing through wooded areas was necessary before finding the mines and camps. Miners and their families occasionally went to Bessemer because it was close by and later because the Mine Mill Union District Office was located there.

The first Mine Mill local in Alabama was chartered in July 1933. It eventually became a force in the area, but this power was not realized until the workers had suffered through two strikes, prolonged layoffs, frequent company intimidation, constant harassment, and the loss of most white support.[20] After 1938, white membership in the Union increased significantly because an NLRB election victory gave Mine Mill company recognition and certification as the workers' sole collective bargaining agent.[21] This victory seemed a blessing, but ironically it signaled the beginning of the end for Mine Mill on Red Mountain. Some white miners became worried about the prominence of Black workers in the union. The various companies—Tennessee Coal and Iron, Sloss Sheffield, and Republic Steel—were aware of the white miners' uneasiness, and set out to nurture and exploit it. After 1938 T.C.I. reversed its hiring policy: previously it had mostly hired Blacks, but now it began hiring whites almost exclusively.[22]

White concern became more apparent when they tried and failed to wrest control from Blacks and reverse the union's racial policy of equal representation of Blacks and whites in union leadership positions.[23] Their discontent in Mine Mill persisted through the 1940s, but not until 1949 did those forces within the union become sufficiently powerful to successfully challenge the Black controlled Mine Mill union. As the improbability of a white takeover became apparent, whites began to consider seceding from Mine Mill and affiliating with another union.

These whites were motivated by a racism that manifested itself in a desire to dominate and control Black workers. Even in the South, however, this rationale could not be stated too openly, and some other equally resonant justification was needed. The issue of "Communism" met this need perfectly. On top of its already negative connotations, the Hitler–Stalin Pact of 1939–1941 had divided Communists from many of their previous allies in the labor movement. At Mine Mill national conventions since 1942, some International leaders had repeatedly been accused of being controlled by the Communist Party. Discontented Alabama whites joined the Connecticut locals in the effort "to rid the Union of all Communists." By 1946 this movement was in line with a national mood, as a number of other CIO affiliates were attempting to rid the movement of the "Red Menace."[24]

There had been aborted attempts at secession in the Mine Mill union prior to 1948. These were classified as minor internal rumblings because the locals were still predominantly Black, and most Black miners consistently favored Mine Mill over other unions attempting to acquire their union's membership. Black workers particularly appreciated the concrete benefits won by Mine Mill, and remembered that prior to the union's presence on the Mountain there had been no effective grievance procedures, no seniority, few health and safety regulations, no vacation with pay, and no portal-to-portal pay. In short, there had been no effective mechanism through which the workers could negotiate with management on an equitable basis. Mine Mill had ended their powerlessness.

Late in 1948 some whites in Alabama Mine Mill locals contacted the United Steelworkers of America (USWA) about possible affiliations. The CIO sent Homer Wilson, a former Mine Mill Executive Board member, to investigate the schism and to solidify support for the iron ore miners who wanted to secede from Mine Mill. Arriving at one of the secessionists' meetings on Red Mountain in Birmingham, Wilson found only whites in attendance and, when he suggested that a new USWA local would have to accept Blacks, the dissident miners became incensed. Wilson was soon relieved of his duty by the CIO and replaced with Van Jones, another former Mine Mill representative and executive Board member from District 5. Jones did not repeat Wilson's mistake, instead appealing to those workers by promising all-white locals of the Steelworker Union.[25] His arrival marked the effective beginning of the secessionists' struggle on Red Mountain.

Between January and Mid-March 1949, the secessionists mounted an intense campaign against Mine Mill. During this period neither the Steelworkers nor the CIO would acknowledge their role in the controversy. However, the USWA/CIO dispatched a representative to Birmingham who conducted an investigation and recommended that USWA charters be issued to the secessionists. Charters were issued against vehement protest by Mine Mill.[26]

The intensity of the struggle escalated, and it became apparent that the USWA/CIO would challenge Mine Mill by calling for a consent election. On April 4, 1949, an agreement for such an election was agreed upon between Mine Mill and the dissident whites, now called Industrial Union/CIO, and scheduled for April 21.[27] In addition to the winner of the election becoming sole representative for nearly four thousand iron ore miners employed by T.C.I., the prospect of workers of smaller companies following this lead undoubtedly loomed large in the minds of the leaders of both unions.

The election drive for the loyalty of Red Mountain iron ore miners was hotly contested as Mine Mill launched a counter-offensive against the USWA/CIO. A lengthy editorial in the *Iron Ore Miner*, a local Mine Mill paper, accused its opponents of inserting the race issue into the campaign, and summed up the union's position in pointing to the inevitability of what it called the "popsicle gang"[28] resorting to this tactic. It warned that race-baiting had been an effective company tactic in defeating independent unionism in the past; the union further emphasized that the close relationship between T.C.I. and the secessionist officials indicated that the dissidents were not a real union.

The newspaper attacked the argument that it was possible to organize a successful union on the basis of race. In order to have an effective organization the appeal must be to all workers regardless of race, the editor declared, and asserted, "Either White and Negro would win together or not at all." The editorial concluded by asking the question, who would be the real winner if the USWA/CIO won the election? The answer was T.C.I., because the champion of democratic unionism on Red Mountain would be rendered powerless.[29]

What was the most striking was the support that the Steelworkers and the CIO gave to such tactics. Dividing the workers by race was one of the oldest anti-union tactics in the corporate arsenal, and the *Iron Ore Miner* expressed its surprise at how the CIO and the USWA could support such efforts.[30]

Nine leaders of the affected Mine Mill locals had sent a joint statement of condemnation to CIO Director of Organization Allan Haywood in Washington, D.C., in March 1949, which strongly censured the CIO for encouraging and assisting the raiding of their union. The leaders answered their own question as to why had Black workers totally rejected overtures from the secessionists: "The leaders of this outfit were scabbing on Mine Mill strikes and/or leading the T.C.I. company union while [Blacks] were standing firm in Mine Mill during the years when it was tough to be a union member on Red Mountain." Notwithstanding the fact that Blacks made up nearly fifty percent of approximately four thousand miners employed by T.C.I., fewer than a dozen had joined the secessionists' cause, and indeed, only about fifteen percent of the white workers were actively supporting the dissidents' cause. Haywood was warned that these men had previously attempted and failed to destroy Mine Mill from within. For several years they had also resorted to labeling the union "Communist" and calling all whites who remained, "Nigger Lovers." The leaders concluded their letter by insisting angrily that if the CIO continued to support the secessionists in their "raiding, hoodlum-violence, promotion of race hatred, discrimination and company unionism," it was no better than the company, which had continually employed similar tactics against all independent unionism.[31]

During the last week of the campaign, the race issue became even more central. Mine Mill had been continually referred to as the "Nigger Union" and its white members, "Nigger Lovers," but it was not until the Ku Klux Klan rode in that the issue peaked. Some one hundred klansmen dressed in their familiar white robes and hoods drove past the Mine Mill District office in Bessemer and entered the controversy by waving torches and sounding their horns.[32] This was the first official Klan support for the USWA/CIO efforts. Undoubtedly, this involvement weighed heavily in the decision many white workers took on April 21.

The day before the election an altercation occurred at a radio station where both unions were broadcasting final messages. The Steelworkers/CIO described the incident as a simple fist-fight between two men. Mine Mill described it as a goon-squad attack upon their Secretary/Treasurer, Maurice Travis.[33] Regardless of the interpretation, it resulted in Travis' losing the sight in one eye. The balloting took place as scheduled; Rufus Paret, Director of the voluntary labor arbitration tribunal of the American Arbitration Association, stated that he had never witnessed such a bitter union election. According to his description, the intense campaigning continued throughout election day: "Airplanes with loudspeakers and airplanes towing banners were used by the conflicting unions, in addition to sound trucks on land, radio speeches and ordinary mass meetings."[34]

The election ended with Mine Mill losing by a vote of 2,696 to 2,233. The struggle, however, was not concluded. Black workers wished to retain Mine Mill at the workplace, even though the die had been cast against it. Frank Allen, a Black Mine Mill International Representative, reportedly was establishing committees to collect the dues that now could be paid only on a voluntary basis.[35] J. P. Mooney, a white International Representative, helped establish classes designed to teach Mine Mill officials how to file grievances, collect dues, and in effect maintain their locals while preparing for a future election to win back the bargaining-agent position.

Mooney also asserted that Philip Murray had lost the respect of "most of the real union men in the area."[36] This was especially significant because only a few years earlier the CIO had been highly regarded by the same Black workers. Philip Foner has noted that:

> the prestige of the CIO among black workers at the end of the [Second World] war stemmed in no small degree from the record of the so-called Communist dominated unions. But none of those unions was allowed to become involved in the CIO's Southern Organizing drive launched after the war.[37]

Not only had left-wing unions been excluded from participation in the Southern drive, they also were made the object of continued raiding by other CIO unions. As Black workers in the South, especially on Red Mountain, became aware of the raids, they began viewing the CIO with increased animosity. The consent election obviously failed to quell the many charges and counter-charges. According to the Steelworkers and the CIO, the key issue was that Mine Mill was a Communist front. Mine Mill defined the issue as simple "gangsterism" and raiding by fellow CIO unions.

These were among the issues debated in the following months before the CIO Executive Board in Washington. The meeting was held in closed session with only four Mine Mill representatives allowed to attend: President Clark, Vice-President Robinson, District 5 Executive Board Member Charles Wilson, and Marion Reynolds, a Black miner representing the rank and file. After the hearing, the Board passed a resolution censuring the Union because of its alleged Communist domination.[38] Ironically, the resolution accused Mine Mill of "using the Communist weapon of fear, intolerance, racial hatred, threats and other methods which have no place in the decent ranks of trade unionism." Black workers were appalled at such an accusation, since, demonstrably, it had been the white secessionists who had employed precisely those tactics so effectively. Mine Mill was expelled from the CIO in February 1950 for its reputed Communist connections.

Counter charges were forthcoming from Mine Mill, and efforts begun to have the U.S. House Committee on Education and Labor, headed by Congressman Adam Clayton Powell, hear testimony from the Mine Mill rank and file on charges of unfair labor practices and discrimination by the CIO and the Tennessee Coal and Iron Company.[39] Powell was known for his unceasing attacks on all forms of discrimination. He was a founding member and director of the New York Coordinating Committee, one of the more militant and successful protest movements of the 1930s and 1940s, which had been instrumental in pressuring Consolidated Edison, New York Telephone, members of the beverage industry, and various large drug stores to eliminate discriminatory hiring practices.[40] He had denounced the internment of Japanese-Americans during World War II and had introduced anti-lynching and anti-poll tax legislation.[41] But his committee did not investigate Mine Mill's charges. Given Powell's history of fighting discrimination, that is puzzling. Powell had once asserted that "there is no group in America, including the Christian Church, that practices racial brotherhood one-tenth as much as the Communist Party."[42]

The most likely explanation for Powell's failure to hold hearings lies in the Red Scare itself. With all of the anti-Communist hysteria and "witch hunts" taking place, the outcome of this and similar struggles were foregone conclusions, and the probability is that little could have been done to save Mine Mill. Still, a strong case might be made for holding hearings such as those proposed by Mine Mill in order to bring to light inherent contradictions in the American commitment to justice. In any case the hearings failed to materialize; but the CIO stood condemned in the eyes of Black workers on Red Mountain.

The expulsion of Mine Mill and other unions from the CIO was a severe blow to the cause of democratic unionism. In his study of unions in the nonferrous metals industry, Vernon Jensen concluded:

> The unfortunate thing is that the CIO carelessly, callously, or unwittingly neglected the basic desires of the rank and file among the miners and smelter workers. It was known, of course, that Mine Mill rank and file members were not communists and that they were good CIO unionists. Perhaps this knowledge led to the policy the CIO followed, and the belief that the rank and file would remain loyal to the CIO and leave Mine Mill and its leaders and affiliate with other CIO unions. On this score, the CIO made a serious error in judgement.[43]

The pivotal years for Mine Mill, nationally as well as in Alabama, were 1949 and 1950, evidenced by its loss of the T.C.I. miners, its censure and its expulsion by the CIO. However, its setbacks did not discourage the efforts to retain workers in its Alabama locals, nor did it deter the Union from its struggle to improve the condition of Blacks on and off the job.

Black miners continued to show their strong preference for Mine Mill over the USWA. An important issue in the continuing controversy was the attendance of white workers at Mine Mill meetings. The strategy of the Steelworkers was to draw the color line and completely isolate Blacks by intimidating whites into staying away from its rival's meetings. When several whites attended a meeting of the Muscoda local in Bessemer in the summer of 1949, for example, Steelworker supporters gathered for an attack on white Mine Mill union members after the meeting. Mine Mill called for protection from the city, county, and state law enforcement agencies: all agencies refused to answer the call. Rebuffed, the Black Mine Mill members called upon Blacks in the local community for assistance. They responded, and arrived armed for action, and the Steelworkers decided the time was not ripe for their proposed attack. This was the type of united effort that had prevented blood from flowing in the streets on many occasions.[44]

As a result of not joining the Steelworkers' Union, Black workers were subjected to increased harassment from the company, as well as from the Steelworkers. Amzi Parks, a veteran red ore miner, related a typical story of these difficulties to a Mine Mill representative in 1951:

I, Amzi Parks, have worked at the T.C.I. mines, Wenonah Division, for 25 years. I worked as a drag operator from 1930 to 1932. I lost that job between 1932 and 1934, but regained it in 1934 and held the same job until 1949. Then I was taken off the drag and placed on a shuttle car where I trained another man. After teaching this man to operate the car, he was given the job and I was sent to slope 8 to operate a drag for less money. On January 8, 1951, I was transferred to slope 7 and given the job of shuttle car operator again. On January 29, I was relieved of that duty again. Mr. Malcolm Smith, assistant Mine Foreman, came to me and suggested that if I wanted to drive the shuttle car again, that I should see the USWA representative, Mr. Kendricks. I refused and was put back on the drag with a decrease in pay. On March 26, 1951, I was again transferred and was given another shuttle car until April 14. I was instructed to teach another man how to operate the car. Upon completion of this training, I was again sent back to slope 7 on a drag and paid less money. Mr. Tom Clayton who is Mining Captain, came to me and said, Amzi, why don't you sign a Steel card so you won't be bothered anymore? I, Amzi Park, do feel that all of the office personnel and foremen are working with Steel [USWA] and whatever you go to the office to see about, even if its our age with the company, they send you to Sam Savage who is vice president of the Steel local who work among the Colored employees.[45]

This and similar accounts offer clear evidence of the continuing persecution of Mine Mill stalwarts. Black miners, however, were determined to hold on to something of their own, even against the rival union in its alliance with management. Mine Mill had meant a way of life that those workers refused to relinquish. But even with their dogged determination, the tide of Mine Mill's destiny was in motion and would not be altered.

Mine Mill launched a final attempt to regain its previous status as bargaining agent at T.C.I. in February 1952, by forcing a new election. This time Mine Mill lost by almost one thousand votes. After that defeat, Mine Mill officials accepted the apparent permanence of their loss and encouraged their members to join the Steelworkers' Union. Asbury Howard, Mine Mill Regional Director said, "It was time for us to become a part of that organization so that we could change its direction."[46] The persuasion was not an easy task, for Black workers' bitterness toward the Steelworkers continued, and some miners reaffirmed their vows never to join the Steelworkers' Union. Others did join, however reluctantly. One former miner conceded in retrospect that, "It was a mistake not to join with the Steelworkers after the defeat in 1949." He felt that failure had retarded the efforts of Blacks to receive better-paying jobs. Given the respect and admiration Black miners felt for Mine Mill and what it symbolized, however, it is doubtful that any other course of action was possible for them in 1949.

Mine Mill rapidly decreased in importance on Red Mountain, but the focus of former Mine Mill leaders shifted to the Bessemer NAACP, and that organization became more important and demanding. Eventually most Blacks who worked at those several companies which hired primarily Black workers became card-carrying members of the Bessemer branch of the NAACP. In several companies the NAACP actually commanded enough strength to receive a membership fee payroll deduction checkoff. A worker had to agree to this, but most did.[47]

Under the leadership of men in Mine Mill, a relatively effective voter registration campaign had been an ongoing concern in Bessemer. Now voter registration classes were held at schools and churches to prepare for the difficult questions asked of the newly registering; more often than not, Mine Millers were the class organizers, as well as providing transportation to the courthouse for the applicants to appear before the Board of Registrars to become eligible voters.[48] Although the Bessemer Voters League and the NAACP favored repeal of the poll tax, the two organizations encouraged Blacks to pay and to participate actively in political affairs. Campaigns to raise money for the poll tax were held so that people who could not afford to pay could still register to vote.[49]

A variety of Black organizations in Bessemer launched the "Committee for Building a Negro Community Center" in March 1953. Asbury Howard was elected chairman. While Howard credited all segments of the community with participation, he observed that the Mine Mill leadership had initiated the project. The International office of Mine Mill contributed $100.00 to the cause.[50]

The transfer of local Black activism from Mine Mill to the NAACP did not go unnoticed by the union's old enemies. At the 1953 Alabama State Convention of the NAACP, Van Jones, the white USWA organizer who initially assisted the secessionists from Mine Mill in 1948, asked the National NAACP to revoke the charter of the Bessemer branch.[51] His attack revived the "Red" issue, because the National NAACP had previously criticized the International Mine Mill union because of its alleged Communist connections.[52] Jones argued that, since the President and Vice-President of the Bessemer branch were also Mine Mill officials, the NAACP branch therefore had been successfully infiltrated and consequently was Communist-dominated. The NAACP State Convention rejected Jones' request and went on record as being in complete support of the branch and its leadership.[53] Nevertheless, the issue was serious enough that the NAACP national office launched an investigation. The investigators visited Bessemer, interviewed dozens of residents, and left satisfied that in this case the Communists were only "uppity Niggers" who dared to fight for Black rights in their community.[54] This time Steelworkers' efforts to red-bait Black activists had failed.

The Mine Mill union failed to regain its membership in the iron ore mines, but its influence remained evident in the Bessemer community for many years. As Marion Reynolds, former miner and Mine Mill official, stated, "Martin Luther King had to come, after what Mine Mill had done. They killed Mine Mill, but could not kill the spirit. Mine Mill will forever live!!!!"[55]

The salient question to be asked concerns not the source of Mine Mill's defeats, but of its success. What made it possible for the Mine Mill union to organize and to sustain itself on Red Mountain for nearly fifteen years? First, the union was aided by the National Industrial Recovery Act of 1933, the Wagner Act of 1935, and the Fair Labor Standards Act of 1938. Second, the International office of Mine Mill was alert to the necessity and the possibility of organizing in the iron ore mines, it realized the importance of Black workers in that effort, and it was militant enough to organize interracially. Third, the white workers that remained loyal to Mine Mill before and after 1938 were unusually courageous men, because they and their families were constantly under attack by opponents of the "Nigger Union." Finally, the most important factor in the success of Alabama Mine Mill locals was the perseverance of Black workers.

Even with courageous white supporters, empowering labor legislation, and its International office, Mine Mill would not have survived without the determined tenacity of the Black workers. After the initial setbacks suffered by the Union, it would have been easy for the workers to have succumbed to the many pressures upon them. But their tenacity, their fortitude, and their sacrifices made it possible to overcome those obstacles and to build a strong workers' organization. The strength to continue derived from the Black majority who set the tone and charted the direction of the locals. They worked heroically from Mine Mill's inception, when it was most unpopular to be a union man on Red Mountain. Those Black workers learned the business of operating their workers' organization and eventually that knowledge became instrumental in the wider arena of Black protest movements.

Black workers on Red Mountain knew what they wanted and focussed upon the best route to acquire it. In the labor movement, the left-wing unions closely mirrored their values, and an intense relationship developed between those workers and Mine Mill. Even red-baiting tactics were unable to extinguish Black workers' dedication to their union. One former Mine Mill worker later reflected philosophically about injustice, the red scare and "good white folk."

So many people say the Negro should pull himself up by his bootstrap. Well, they [whites] didn't pull up by theirs, and when they [whites] talk about the Negro people and how they ought to do this and qualify themselves and all, what they forget is that their skin is Black. They don't tell him how to change his Black skin. Well, we're proud of our skin being Black. We just don't want to be mistreated, and we don't need a Communist to tell us what is justice and what is injustice. We know! Nobody had to tell me when somebody is choking me. I know! If I'm going to wait for somebody to tell me that, then that's different. But I did tell them this: I've never known a Communist in the labor movement to bomb a worker's home. I've never known a Communist in the labor movement to mob a man inside a city hall, lynch him, and castrate him and everything else, even shoot him on sight. Now they do that in Russia, they say, but none of the Communists do that here. It's the good white man who does that, you see. So, why am I going to go out and fight somebody who doesn't do the thing that the good white folks have done?[56]

This statement captures the sentiments of Red Mountain's Black workers about their relationship with a "Communist-dominated" union. They often remarked that if communism was defined accurately by those white workers who suggested that it meant equality between the races, then they, Black workers were indeed communist.

Paul Robeson once said the, "We Negro people are very mature in our political understanding. We may not act at once upon all we sense and know—but we know." Black workers in Mine Mill knew—and they acted upon that knowledge.

PART III

EUROPEAN-ORIGIN WORKERS IN THE UNITED STATES

Northern and Western Europe

CHAPTER 8

Immigration, Ethnicity, and the American Working-Class Community: Fall River, 1850–1900

JOHN CUMBLER

Since the publication of Oscar Handlin's *Boston's Immigrants*, and especially with the influence of the "new labor history," historians of the American working class have been struggling to understand the influence of immigration on the experience of American workers. Not only did immigrants from Poland, Italy, Russia, Ireland, and Germany do much of the building and heavy work in America's industries, they also made up the membership of a significant portion of the unions, fraternal organizations, and working-class communities in the industrial cities and towns of America.

There has been a great deal of revision of Oscar Handlin's original thesis of peasants uprooted from their native soil by agricultural revolutions or starvation at home. But American labor historians are still at a loss to understand fully the significance and impact of the European experience on immigrants in America and on American institutions.[1] The picture of the European experience of the immigrant most often used by American historians draws upon the dichotomy between an impoverished peasant culture and an urban industrial life style.[2] According to this view, the immigrants suffered a traumatic shift in moving from one experience in Europe to the other in America. Some historians argue that immigrants were led to accept the conditions in America and to reject any radical alternative because, despite the hardships of the New World, conditions here were better than in Europe.[3] Other historians claim that the conflict between peasant life and industrial life gave rise to resistance to indus-

151

trialism and bred further conflict in the New World.[4] It has also been argued that the difficulty of the new world experience led to a sentimentalism about that of the "old country," and a nostalgic nationalism.[5]

Yet this framework still leaves the labor historian without a strong analytical handle for understanding the impact of the pre-immigration experience on immigrant labor. It also tends to obscure the role of immigrants who did not come to the New World as peasants but as artisans or industrial workers. As many as 40 percent of adult male immigrants between the years 1907 and 1910 came over as skilled craftsmen, stone cutters, blacksmiths, leather workers, shoemakers, spinners, weavers, tailors, or factory workers.[6] These immigrants brought with them a substantial array of cultural and institutional supports, as well as a consciousness of the role of artisans and workers in the production process. These experienced artisans and skilled workers took the lead in developing the institutions that dominated working-class communities. They were often the leaders of unions and strikes.[7] Because they played this vital role, we need to understand the values and institutional support systems of the skilled immigrant workers before migration as well as in America.[8]

What follows below is a limited attempt at a transatlantic study of a group of workers in Fall River, Massachusetts, rather than a comprehensive study of American and European working-class institutions. It is a suggestion of what can be done, which should provide some insights on what can be learned by such an international approach.

Fall River, Massachusetts, is a particularly apt place to study the continuities and transformations of the culture and institutions of the immigrant workers as they made the move from Europe to America. Fall River was the nation's largest center for cotton manufacturing during the late nineteenth century, drawing thousands of immigrants from Europe. Many of those immigrants brought with them experiences in cotton mills before they came, while others came directly from agricultural work. In either case they moved into factories and industrial communities that affected their lives just as they in turn affected the city they came to inhabit.

Fall River was an industrial city with one of the nation's largest foreign-born populations. Much of our understanding about immigrants has come from studies of immigrants who got off the boats in commercial port cities like New York, Philadelphia, and Boston. Although these studies are important, the majority of our immigrants did not settle in port cities but in industrial cities. Fall River was just such an industrial center. It was a working person's city, and it attracted working people.[9]

Fall River owed its development to a combination of local geographic advantages – humid climate and an even, fast-flowing river – and investment of outside capital. Using the city's waterpower, manufacturers quickly introduced textiles, the nation's first major capitalized industry. The city's favorable location between Boston and New York and its waterpower quickly moved Fall River into a position of national industrial preeminance.[10] The early mills of the first half of the nineteenth century depended upon local farmers, and their wives and children, for labor in the mills. But the success of Fall River's first mills encouraged the city to expand, especially in the fine cloth area, and this expansion eclipsed the local farmers as workers in the mills. In the 1850s and 1860s, the city grew rapidly as the mills began to import skilled English and Irish workers from Lancashire to work on the spinning mules, fix the looms, weave the finer cloth, and manage the more skilled positions in the mills. By 1875 almost nine thousand inhabitants of Fall River had been born in England and another nine thousand in Ireland. Many of them had spent several years in Lancashire textile mills before catching the boat from Liverpool to America, or were married to someone who had.[11] These immigrants made up the heart of Fall River's labor force and were in turn to dominate the city's labor movement and working-class organizations.

In January 1858, early arrivals from England formed the Mule Spinners Association and elected Patric Carrol as President and John McKeower as Secretary, both Lancashire Irish.[12] Another Fall River labor leader, Robert Howard, of English-Irish stock, came over to Fall River from Stockport in 1871. Before migrating, Howard was president of his local spinners and twiners union. Upon his arrival in Fall River, Howard continued his active union work. He vied for leadership with Robert Bowe, George Gunton, James Tansey, and John Golden in Fall River unions; all were Lancashire English or Irish.[13]

So strong was the influence of these immigrants from the British Isles that by the mid-1870s the name "Fall River" had become synonymous with America for Lancashire workers. Ben Brierley, a Lancashire writer on a voyage from Liverpool in the 1880s, noted this conversation with textile workers coming over in steerage:

> Where dun yo' come fro'?
> Oldham, an Mossley.
> Where are yo' going to?
> To Fall River.
> Hav' yo' shops to go to?
> Nawe, but we's friends there.[14]

As late as 1903 an English observer noted that Fall River "in the early morning is but a gateway to workaday Lancashire. Fall River is Lancashire in epitome."[15] The workers who left the mills of Lancashire to enter the mills of Fall River brought with them the traditions and institutions that had developed from a wide range of historical forces in Lancashire. The community they built and the institutions they supported in Fall River had a distinctive Lancashire heritage. Lancashire textile operatives developed a whole system of institutions, ranging from the most informal pub to the more formal workingmen's club, lodge, benefit society, cooperative, and union.[16]

The Lancashire Experience

Concerned over the developing dislocation of the new industrial age, the late-eighteenth-century English reformer, John Acland, put forth the idea of societies "for rendering the laboring classes independent by means of compulsory contributions to be applied on the principle of friendly societies."[17] English friendly societies were centered around ale houses, many of which were run by publicans who were ex-operatives who had been either blacklisted or forced out of work because of an accident or shift in employment. Utilization of these formal organizations and informal social institutions by workers soon concerned the authorities, especially since they functioned not to pacify workers but rather increased their ability to create collective pressure on employers and officials to address the interests of the workers. Even by 1800 some observers lamented that these institutions "had an obvious tendency to facilitate combinations for improper purposes in trade, religion, and politics." Sir Frederick Eden, an English reformer who published several reports on the poor at the turn of the century, went so far as to claim that friendly societies, originally proposed to ease social tensions by encouraging self-help, "ha[d] been perverted to purposes most inimical to social order, and that in manufacturing districts, dangerous meetings have been held under the disguise of benefit clubs for the relief of the sick workers."[18]

Because of the importance of the textile industry in the development of industrial capitalism, Lancashire, England, was one of the first areas of that nation to develop the kind of social institutions and patterns of settlement, work, capital, and population that came to typify industrial society. Furthermore, Lancashire experienced extensive immigration from underdeveloped regions of the Empire, particularly Ireland, which were themselves undergoing extensive economic and social dislocation. The traditional relationships between masters and artisans were breaking down as the increased power and control of the owners of capital led to a new age of factories and machines. Economic insecurity plagued the working class as periodic trade "busts" led to massive unemployment for those who had come to look on industrial labor as their sole resource. Large numbers of workers were inevitably involved in labor disputes, and conflicts over work and wages (previously scattered and individualized) moved to an increasingly mass scale. In addition, the increase in the scale of the productive enterprise, and its centralization in factory towns and cities, gave rise to large working class residential areas separate from both the middle and upper class of English society.

Within these areas workers developed their own social institutions. The separation of these institutions from the structure of bourgeois English society frightened the establishment; these working-class communities became the center for radical working-class activity. Lancashire had over eight hundred and twenty reported friendly societies in 1801, well over twice as many as London or Suffolk, and almost a third more than Middlesex. These clubs did not utilize their resources mainly for individual benefits. The Lancashire clubs spent less on sick benefits than clubs in other counties, and instead focussed more of their activity on supporting the growth of militant workers' organizations.[19] In the less industrialized areas such clubs functioned mainly as burial societies with no substantial political function, but in Lancashire they were important as an institutional framework independent of the middle class, within which workers could discuss job conditions and wages, laying the basis for feeling of class solidarity and the rudiments of class organization.[20]

The expansion and organization of the textile industry beyond the local level and small cottages into a large and regional structure forced members of the working class to wander from town to town searching for employment. It made them, as well, look to institutions that would help them link together with other workers facing similar conditions. Under such conditions the friendly societies and clubs provided not only a means for working-class agitation, but also an organizational infrastructure that allowed workingmen to develop lines of communication between different mills and communities.[21] Ultimately they were the formal structure upon which unions were built. Many of the local meetings of spinners which led to the formation of the spinners union in 1810 were held under the auspices of the friendly societies. The friendly societies, by maintaining members during periods of economic depression, reinforced class solidarity and, through aid during strikes, helped the union movement over the initial building period.[22]

A. Andrew of Oldham noted in 1825 that the "spinners club of the earlier period was held at a little public house . . . " that was a meeting place for both friendly and union organizations.[23] The first of the clubs in Lancashire were organized in Oldham and Manchester in 1795 and 1796, just when the factory system for spinners was beginning. Most of the members of these early clubs came from the mills located near the clubs. A leader of the strike of 1834 in Oldham suggested the relationship between the worker organization and the older clubs and friendly societies when he noted that the strike was organized by a central club which met in a local public house and was an outgrowth of the earlier friendly clubs.[24] As members of the friendly societies, the leaders of these early strikes, as E.P. Thompson notes, received valuable training and experience as leaders and organizers. The societies also provided much of the rules, discipline, and structural basis for the more overtly working-class organizations.[25]

When the Combinations Act was repealed, many of the friendly societies gave way to formal trade unions, although some still maintained close ties to their earlier form of organization. In some cases the relationship continued into the second half of the nineteenth century. Although unusual in the 1880s, when it was established by the amalgamation of three friendly societies, the Union of Stuff Pressurers typified the pattern that had existed earlier. The three precursor societies had existed at least since 1850 as informal gathering and socializing institutions.[26]

Following the repeal of the Combinations Act, workers acted to form new and more aggressive unions during the 1820s and 1840s. Manufacturers did not give in to worker militance, and used the courts to prosecute union men for "obstructing and molesting"; manufacturers also used the blacklist and yellow dog contracts to break the unions and drive out militant union members. The resulting struggle left many of the early unions in ruins and taught the Lancashire workmen not to abandon their traditional mechanisms for support and subterfuge. During the turbulent period between the late 1840s and the late 1860s many of Lancashire's workmen looked to the friendly societies and clubs to maintain the spirit of unionism and class solidarity.[27]

Inquiring into the conditions of cotton spinners in Preston in 1838, Henry Ashworth found that fewer than half of the spinners belonged to formal unions. In many cases the unions were thus reduced to relieving their sick members and contributing to the wants of other societies. Under these conditions, the friendly societies and clubs maintained unionism beyond the watchful eyes of the manufacturers.[28] Just as the Stuff Pressurers had been formed from three friendly societies in 1880, the Secretary of the Amicable and Brotherly Society of Calico Machine Printers (with headquarters in Manchester covering the surrounding districts) wrote to the Webbs that his organization had existed for over fifty years as both a union and a social club without registering or affiliating with any formal union.[29]

Besides the friendly societies there were other institutional mechanisms that English workers utilized for community solidarity and cohesion. J.J. Baerneither, in his nineteenth-century study of English working-class associations, was impressed by the strong separate lodges of the Independent Order of Odd Fellows and the Ancient Order of Foresters. Lancashire was an important center for these voluntary organizations as well as for the friendly societies. The largest Odd Fellows lodge was the working-class-dominated Manchester Unity Odd Fellows founded in 1822. The Grand United Order of Odd Fellows was also heavily working class and also centered in Manchester.[30]

Amid the general insecurity about jobs and the various ups and downs of employment that textile workers came to expect, the Odd Fellows functioned to tie textile workers into a network of information and communication. The Odd Fellow lodges, with their avowed objective of developing and strengthening brotherhood and union, were centers for conversation. They acted as forums for venting hostility and sharing information concerning wages and working conditions, as well as information about job prospects in the various mills in the district. As the cotton workers were forced to migrate to different regions because of layoffs or blacklisting, the lodges provided fellowship, information about housing, and a means for integrating into the new area. The increased scale and organization of the industrial economy of Lancashire encouraged the workers to look to and nurture institutions such as the Odd Fellows which provided a supralocal base for understanding and coping with the supralocal structure of the economy. These institutions also provided indigenous leaders with training and experience that they could utilize in more formal labor organizations.[31]

The role of the Odd Fellows, friendly societies, and Foresters was also assumed by another social institution of the English working class, the Workingmen's Club. Although the clubs, like the friendly societies, were begun by elite reformers as a means of influencing workers, most clubs were taken over by the workers themselves in the 1870s. Once in control, workers used the clubs as forums for working-class politics and as a means of attacking the English establishment, the Church of England, the Tory Party, and the capitalist class itself. Although much of the clubs' activities were social events, a clear working-class perspective on class antagonism and conflict emerged.[32]

Besides participating in social activities and organizations, the English working class looked to alternative economic institutions to try to deal with the difficult times from the early 1830s to the 1870s, when wages progressively fell and the buying power of the English cotton operatives deteriorated. In searching for means of avoiding the structure of capitalism and labor competition that was taking root around them, the workers maintained consumer cooperatives, building societies, and cooperative savings societies.[33]

The structures of alternative institutions had their roots in the informal socializing at the local public houses. They were built up through a network of working-class organizations into the formal trade union and the political party. As the Industrial Remuneration Conference of 1885 stated:

> The working men of Lancashire were tied into a whole system of unions, cooperatives, building . . . societies . . . trade unions with large reserve funds and their accident, sickness and out of work benefits, insurance and benefit societies. In most cases he or a member of his class works for or with these organizations after hours. They are staffed with working class members.[34]

Within a society in which notions of individual failure and success were deeply ingrained, the clubs, societies, pubs, and trade unions offered workers an analysis of their conditions which stressed the importance of collective action and the labor theory of value. These clubs, societies, and trade unions were institutional expressions of a value system at odds with the dominant bourgeois culture and ideology. They were viewed rightly with suspicion by reformers and conservatives alike.[35]

Through discussion and struggle, the workers shared their experiences and verbalized their feelings of being victims of and in conflict with the manufacturers and their system. The class perspective of these organizations was reinforced by the bitter experience of the workers in the mills themselves. In her novel, *Mary Barton*, Elizabeth Gaskell describes the tension and class feelings of Lancashire workers. Mary Barton's father is active in a number of clubs and a trade union. He

> was concerned about the differences between employers and the employed, an eternal subject of agitation in the manufacturing districts which . . . [broke] forth again with fresh violence at any

depression of trade, showing that in its apparent quiet, the ashes had still smoldered. . . . At all times it is a bewildering thing to the poor weaver to see his employer removing from house to house, each one grander than the last . . . while all the time the weaver who thinks he and his fellows are real makers of this wealth, is struggling on for bread for his children, though the vicissitudes of lower wages, short hours, fewer hands employed. . . . And when he knows trade is bad . . . large houses are still occupied, while the spinner and weavers' cottages stand empty, because the families that once occupied them are obliged to live in rooms or cellars.[36]

Like Mary's father, many of Lancashire's textile workers verbalized, in their clubs, societies, trade unions, and local pubs, grievances and the injustices of a society where the creators of wealth lived in constant fear and insecurity. Because of their insecurity and their lack of power and control over their future, these workers clung to the institutions which mitigated their conditions and reinforced their sense of the importance of their role in society as the producers of the wealth that was manifested in the grand houses of the mill owners.

Lancashire Irish

Depressed agricultural conditions in Ireland and the eclipse of the cottage textile industry in that country led to a constant migration of Irish into England, especially into Lancashire's textile district. Initially these immigrants came to work the agricultural harvest. But as conditions deteriorated in Ireland, more and more immigrants began to flow across the channel, and fewer and fewer returned home. The condition of economic insecurity that plagued English workers also beset the Irish. The Irish, like the English, looked to social institutions to support them in times of hardship and insecurity, and shared the English workers' hostility to the owners of the mills and the grand houses. There was tension between English and Irish workers in England, but this did not prevent the Irish workers, once they moved into the factory,from participating in the social institutions of the working-class community; the Irish also created their own institutions, which acted to reinforce their ethnic and class solidarity.

The Irish eventually filled a third of Manchester's working-class residential areas. They came into the mills in heaviest numbers during the Irish Famine years. These were the same years that the English workers were feeling the heavy pinch of the recessions of the 1840s. The Irish workers were more than a theoretical threat to English unionists. As one manufacturer stated in 1836: "The moment I have a turn out and am fast for hands I send to Ireland for ten, fifteen or twenty families."[37]

Although the threat of strikebreakers did keep up tension between Irish and English workers, the rising number of Irish workers in the mills eventually gave rise to Irish participation in unions and other social institutions of the working class and to support for strikes and union activities by Irish ethnic organizations. Moreover, the competition for jobs was mitigated by being stretched out over several generations. The first Irish immigrants who reached the mills of Lancashire did not directly compete with the skilled or semi-skilled English textile workers, but rather filled in at the bottom as unskilled labor, in positions that the unionized or skilled English were reluctant to take. It was only after a long apprenticeship at the unskilled jobs (an apprenticeship that often lasted a whole generation) that Irish workers moved into the move skilled positions. Thus, for the first Irish migrants there was a dual labor market; one for the Irish and one for the English.

The Irish also had the advantage of having several of their countrymen in the vanguard of the Chartist and union movements in Lancashire. And having migrated to the cotton mills of Lancashire when the cottage textile industry of Ireland first began to fall behind, many of these early migrants broke the ice for their countrymen, whether Catholic or Protestant. Bronterre O'Brien led the Chartists in Stockport. Robert Howard was elected president of his English local despite his Irish parentage. John Doherty came early from Ireland and established himself as one of the greatest leaders of the Lancashire cotton workers, paving the way for the acceptance of the later waves of Irish immigrants.[38]

Links in the Chain

Although historians of migration and immigration have emphasized the process of transportation links and the depositing of large number of immigrants on the doorsteps of the nation in its port cities, for many migrants the process of migration was not a process of dumping energetic but rootless peasants on the American shore. Workers who left Europe, whether artisans with limited but transferable skills, experienced industrial workers, or even some unskilled peasants, did not catch the first boat to any American port, but rather chose deliberately the city, community, and the work they were bound for in the New World.[39] Indeed, these immigrants knew a great deal about the world they were about to enter.

What was true of most immigrants was particularly true of industrial workers, such as whose who left Lancashire. Charlotte Erickson has noted that industrial workers made use of "an extension of the network of advice and assistance beyond the family. Most of these people found jobs with the help of workmates and friends from their own communities."[40] Most immigrants depended upon informal means of communication between friends and relatives. As John Greenwood told an American official, he hailed "from Lancashire, England" and his "destination is Fall River where [I] have acquaintances . . . John Thornston and his son."[41] Acquaintances, friends, and kin made up the chain of communication and the links of immigration upon which the immigrant made his way not to a strange new land, but rather to the colony, or community where he or she had ties that maintained the continuity between the source community and the destination community.

Not only did the English with their established institutional structure maintain developed lines of communication, but the Irish did as well. Fall River, like Lancashire, had an Irish population that by the 1860s was well integrated into the working-class structures of the city. Most Fall River Irish had lived part of their lives in England and arrived in Fall River along with the Lancashire English.[42] Both these groups brought their English experience in the mills, pubs, and social groups with them. They utilized their experience to build a militant trade union movement and a strong working-class community.[43]

The workers who left Lancashire and the workers who remained behind kept in close contact with each other and events on both sides of the Atlantic through letters and contacts with friends as well as through the labor papers that became important means of communication in the spreading textile industry. Lancashire, the center of English textile production, was also the source of the textile workers' major newspaper, the *Cotton Factory Times*. This weekly circulated widely among Lancashire workers and was used by workers on both sides of the Atlantic for information concerning the state of the trade, the cost of cotton, wage rates in the industry, strikes and union business, and social and political news of interest to the working class.

The first issue of the *Cotton Factory Times* in 1885 included an extensive article on "News From America," in which Fall River news predominated. The article included a comparison of wages and hours between Fall River and English mills. It discussed the institutional support systems that English workers had come to rely on, and their development in America. It noted the lack of a "wholesale association as in England," and discussed "the development of American cooperatives." The paper ended its maiden issue with advice to Lancashire workers: "No families should think of leaving England for America unless they have engaged places . . . and have sufficient means to tide them over."[44] Throughout the late nineteenth century the paper engaged a correspondent in Fall River to keep families, friends, and potential immigrants aware of what to expect in Fall River, especially in terms of wages and job conditions.[45]

Although the paper was primarily a Lancashire one, Fall River operatives began subscribing and regularly communicating through letters to the editor for folks back home. The paper extensively covered the bitter Fall River cotton mill strike of 1884 and the effect of the depression of the mid-1880s on the Fall River mills. In the sixth issue, an article by Robert Howard, identified as an American textile union official, discussed the impact of cheap labor on American conditions. In another article a commentator stressed that despite the general problems American workers were having, Fall River mills were considered the best for textile workers in terms of trade union rights and working conditions. This was especially so compared to Connecticut, where not only were there no unions, but workers were pushed and overworked.[46] The April 3, 1885, issue ran a special report on Robert Howard and his activity as a union leader in Fall River. In am article he sent in to the next issue, Howard explained the conditions of textile workers in America and their progress towards unionization. He explained that although American workers lagged behind their British counterparts in organizing themselves, they were making progress. He felt that soon American workers would be on a par with English workers in their labor solidarity.[47]

As a means of informing migrants about conditions and linking together Lancashire experience with Fall River conditions, the paper was a formal expression of the continuing flow of information. The writers to the paper from Fall River stressed this role. "My object was to say something of the cotton industry in this country for the benefit of the cotton operatives of Lancashire who are contemplating immigration to this country, ... Coming as I do from the heart of the cotton district of Lancashire and knowing something of the trade and difficulties of the operative classes there . . . , I feel warranted in saying to the discontented among operatives of Lancashire contemplating a voyage to this country . . . don't."[48] Letters such as this helped to rationalize the decision for or against migration. As conditions improved in Fall River, other letters reflected a more positive outlook for unionists and immigrants. One writer to the editor admitted that, although conditions in Fall River were not the best, they were not worse than those in England, and wages were good.[49] Besides information about wages and conditions, the paper continually reported on the activities in Fall River, from strikes to union meetings, and even the activities of the Fall River Cricket Club.[50] The paper provided information about jobs, conditions, and the institutions that the migrant could use to link up the experiences of the Old and New World.

In addition to their subscriptions to the *Cotton Factory Times*, English textile workers had formal institutions which they brought over from England. Not only did Fall River support several Odd Fellows lodges, which were familiar institutions to the English, but some of the lodges were chartered directly from Manchester. The Odd Fellows Lodge not only provided comradeship for the operatives in Fall River, but gave the new immigrants formal institutional support. Odd Fellows from Lancashire could depend upon friendship and contacts from the Fall River Lodges, as well as continuity with Old World traditions. In the Fall River Manchester Unity Lodge, all but one of the officers were textile workers or temporarily unemployed textile workers, mostly weavers.[51]

The Lancashire workers also brought with them the Ancient Order of Foresters, England's second largest fraternal society. In Fall River, the Foresters, like the Odd Fellows, were dominated by textile workers, many of whom were Irish, reflecting the interaction between the English and Irish within the institutional support system to which both groups looked as textile workers.[52]

The workers who came to Fall River from Lancashire were familiar with the importance of social institutions and trade unionism. Many of the workers had been blacklisted for union activism in England.[53] Local unions there provided Lancashire workers with migration grants, distributed according to seniority. Thus, the longer a worker had been a loyal union member, the more funds he could expect from his home union. (It is not clear if female unionists also got immigration grants.)[54]

Textile work, like mining, encouraged child labor at a very early age. It was accepted that a Lancashire child of a working-class family would be in the mills by the age of 10. Robert Howard, for example, was already an experienced spinner by the age of 15; by 26 he was a president of his local union. When blacklisted in England for his union activities, he then migrated to Fall River where he continued his union work. The migrants leaving Lancashire for Fall River, even those relatively young, most likely had at least several years of textile work and union experience behind them before arriving in the New World. These workers knew what to expect in the industrial community and in a mill, and they used that experience to build up their community and support systems.

The Fall River workers who came over from Lancashire found, as several letters to the *Cotton Factory Times* advised, that their position of dependence, and insecurity, and their low wages, had not been altered by the voyage across the Atlantic.[55] As they had in Lancashire, these workers looked not only to unions and fraternal organizations for amelioration of their situation, but also to institutions to counter the structure of a capitalist economy. Under the leadership of the spinners, the Fall River operatives built up an extensive cooperative system. In 1869 the Fall River Workingmen's Co-operative Association switched over to the system used in Rochdale, England, the hometown of James Tansey, a Lancashire Irishman and the secretary of the Fall River Carders. The Fall River Co-op grew so large that by 1879 it covered a whole block and was considered the most successful American example of the Rochdale system.[56] Although the cooperative system in Fall River finally fell victim to the same economic discipline that held the working class of the city in near poverty, it nonetheless gave the immigrants to the city an institutional framework that, although different from Lancashire, was nonetheless familiar.

Fall River, like Lancashire, had a wide network of pubs and taverns that acted as social centers for workers and as informal union halls. An observer in Fall River in the late 1870s noted that Lancashire-like taverns such as Harmony Hall, the Avon Arms, and St. George's Hall dotted the city's landscape and were filled with operatives who "go in and get their glass of beer as they do in the old country."[57] Many of these taverns, like their Lancashire counterparts, were operated by discharged mill operatives. Funds to set up the taverns, whether formal ones like St. George's or a saloon in a corner store or in a tenement basement, often came from union funds for blacklisted operatives.

A union official in Fall River stated in 1880 that "men who have been discharged from one mill and are unable to obtain work in any other, have to go into some other business. It was only the other day we gave a spinner one hundred dollars to go into another business, and he will probably open a liquor store."[58] In a study done to understand why Fall River was the center of militant unionism, a Massachusetts commission (although reflecting the middle-class bias of the investigators) indicated that the militance could be attributed to the socializing and drinking habits of the English and Irish immigrants in taverns. As one operative claimed, the drinking habits of Fall River's operatives stemmed from "the work we have to do, combined with the national tendencies of the English and Irish races."[59] The drinking itself was irrelevant to the militance of the workers, but the habits and traditions of using the pubs and taverns as social institutions of the working class and arenas for agitation were brought over from Lancashire and facilitated the process of union militance.

Just as social scientists have shown that laundry rooms in public housing projects in London serve as centers where tenants organize against the housing councils, and that churches in the black community in America are important social centers for black community organizing, so, too, pubs and taverns were centers for struggle for both Lancashire and Fall River textile operatives. Typical of this pattern was Coleman's tavern, located in a working-class residential area and continually disrupted by the police because of its reputation as a gathering point for unionists. In fact, during strikes, Coleman's was an important strategic center for coordination of the informal strike activity of harassing scabs and rallying support.[60]

The workers of Fall River also set up a workingmen's club which served as a center for political discussions. Charles Evans, a local "agitator" and blacklisted organizer of the weaver's union, often used the club as a forum for discussing the conditions of labor and the oppression of workers by the owners.[61] The club was much like the Lancashire workingmen's clubs, which also provided temperance centers (although serving beer) for the working class.[62]

Although both the English and the Irish joined in many of these formal social institutions, there were institutions — such as the Ancient Order of Hibernia — which supported the general working-class struggle while at the same time reinforcing separate ethnic identity. Like the Workingmen's Circles of Jewish workers that embraced unionism, socialism, and Yiddish traditions, the Ancient Order of Hibernia was an important social institution that supported Irish workers and acted as a disciplinary agent for those workers who abandoned class solidarity. The Irish workers in Fall River, as they had in Lancashire, linked together the interests of working-class struggle with their ethnic community. During the 1884 strike, the Hibernians not only held a benefit for the strikers, but also, claiming that strikebreaking was contrary to their principles of solidarity, fraternity, and a free Ireland, expelled members from the order who were "Knobsticking,"[63] Fall River also supported a cricket club and over twenty-five soccer clubs in the 1890s, which helped complete the Lancashire scene for those homesick for familiar sights.[64] Within the structure of these organizations, Lancashire workers found friends from home and a continuity of traditions and experiences.

Immigrant workers, through these organizations and informal institutions, transformed a New England town into the Oldham of America, a place where Lancashire writer Ben Brierly "soon forgeet wheere [he] war, an' fancied [h]'re i' England, an wur the only Yankee in th' company."[65] Fall River immigrants built unions as well as other working-class organizations that helped mitigate the harshness of Fall River's industrial system and their alienation from the new environment. The union movement that the Fall River operatives built was based upon a Lancashire experience and tradition and fitted to the new but recognizable environment of Fall River.

The *Cotton Factory Times* not only reinforced the continuity between Fall River and Lancashire unionism by regularly reporting on wages, strikes, and union meetings in Fall River, but also by stressing the gap between unionism in Fall River and Lancashire. It urged its readers in Fall River to bring the unionism of that city up to the level of Lancashire. The criticism was friendly, for the ties between Fall River and Lancashire were close and traditional. These went beyond institutions to individuals, and the paper regularly reported on the activities of Fall River labor leaders, most of whom were Lancashire-born.[66] These personal ties also helped to push the Fall River trade unionists to continue to struggle to maintain a visible level of union struggle, for their activities in Fall River were matched in the old country by both friends and family.

Workers as members of a common class share values, a way of life, and a structured relationship to the owners of the means of production. Consciousness of class emerges not just from that structured relationship, nor only from the shared experiences and way of life, but is also shaped by traditions and institutions. The traditions and institutions which the workers of Fall River brought over from Lancashire acted as arenas for the sharing of common experiences and the cementing of the city's workers into a class conscious of itself, and were agents for maintaining a proletarian culture. They welded the workers into a common community that viewed itself as the opponent of the manufacturers and as a separate entity within the city.[67]

By the end of the 1870s, those workers had stamped the city with their culture and institutions. In the late nineteenth century a middle-class writer said that

a great line divides the population into two classes . . . every man, woman and child in the city either is or is not an operative. If he or she is an operative he or she not only works, but also goes to church, buys, finds companions, dresses and lives as an operative. The designation is fastened upon each one and is laid off neither day or night. . . . The attitude of [Fall River's two classes, the operatives and the owners] is one of mutual suspicion, hatred and war. The unquestioned assumption is that their interests are necessarily opposed; their dealings with each other proceed upon that assumption.[68]

Thus the workers were conscious of their role as workers. In 1879, a conservative reformer was alarmed to find Fall River's workers had a "distrust, suspicion, and hostility regarding all who [did] not belong to their class."[69] It was the workers' institutions that fostered this hatred and suspicion, and provided a foundation for the workers' sense of commonality. As industrial workers with experience in industrial work and a developed resistance to the manufacturers, as well as a tradition of countervailing institutions, Fall River textile workers developed a system of institutions that fastened the designation of "operative" on workers. This system, although different from that developed in Lancashire, had its roots there. In Lancashire the Industrial Remuneration Conference reported that workers were "tied into a whole system of unions, cooperatives, building and benefit societies." In Fall River a worker "not only works, but also goes to church, buys, finds companions, dresses and lives as an operative," in other words, "tied into a whole system."

The workers of Lancashire, like the characters in *Mary Barton*, came to see themselves in opposition to the manufacturers. They felt that they produced wealth that the manufacturers denied them. "We are their slaves as long as we can work; we pile up their fortunes with the sweat of our brows; and yet we are to live as servants as if we were in two worlds."[70]

The institutions which they developed, whether formal ones such as unions and fraternal organizations, or informal ones such as gatherings at pubs and taverns, were not only manifestations of the workers' common identity in opposition to the manufacturers, but also structural supports for that opposition. When these Lancashire workers came to Fall River, they found that in their new environment the manufacturers still controlled the resources of the community, the mills, and in turn the jobs and the land, the housing and the formal institutions of exchange, the banks, and ultimately the state structure itself. In response the workers developed institutional forms outside the control of the manufacturers, institutions that were originally inspired by their Lancashire experience.

The institutions could not control the resources of a developed capitalist economy, but they could influence the use of those resources. Unions, as they had in Lancashire, struggled to alleviate the persistent economic insecurity that plagued the working class. They struggled to give workers access to a greater share of the wealth produced. Family, neighbors, and fraternal brothers maintained a network of information about job openings and housing opportunity. These networks, although not independent of the manufacturers' control over the jobs themselves, acted to give workers leverage. They were networks that transcended Fall River and reached back across the ocean to Lancashire itself. And they were networks that kept alive a sense of independence from the manufacturers' control.

The institutions, which grew up on the basis of the relationships of groups of people, had developed over time and were a product of a culture that expressed common interests, values, and norms. Lancashire workers brought that culture with them to Fall River. They recreated institutions there that were an expression of that culture. Thus, the new environment of Fall River was transformed by the continuing relationships between manufacturer and worker.

Although historians of American labor and social history have emphasized the immigrant experience, that experience has been seen as a peasant village experience, either uprooted or transplanted intact. Yet many of our early industrial workers had industrial or at least artisan experience in the Old World. These people created the communities and institutions in which peasants later came to settle and participate. Thus, in order to understand the development of American working-class communities and institutions, we must look at the industrial, as well as the peasant experience of the work force.

Moreover, we must remember that much of that experience took place in Europe. The transatlantic context is important not only because workers functioned in that context, but also because many viewed themselves in those terms. They did not abandon their traditions and institutions but utilized those that were appropriate and changed others to fit the new environment. The institutions which were brought over – and even those that were changed – in turn changed the setting into which they were transplanted, and helped form the working class communities that later immigrants would make their homes.[71]

The French Canadians

Some immigrants, of course, came from traditions that were neither industrial nor artisan. These immigrants often found themselves within an industrial community with developed institutions and sometimes with a hostile work force. In such conditions the response of these immigrants would differ from that of the English and Irish immigrants of Fall River. For example, in the late 1870s and 1880s the immigrants of Lancashire were replaced by immigrants from French Canada.

Like the English, the French Canadians were mostly textile workers, and they found themselves without access to control over the resources of the community. They experienced economic insecurity.

They too looked to traditions and institutions that would ameliorate their condition. But unlike the English, the French Canadians did not have developed working-class institutions. This created a vacuum in the French Canadian working-class community. That vacuum was partially filled by experienced ethnic leaders, but those leaders came heavily from the small French-Canadian middle class.

These leaders of the French-Canadian working-class community had no experience with friendly societies and fraternal organizations in their Québec homeland.[72] Instead, middle- and lower-middle-class French-Canadian ethnic leaders, particularly those who served a closed ethnic community, were encouraged by the closeness of their ethnic homeland to support the idea of maintaining their ethnic solidarity and the hope of returning to Canada. The historical experience of Catholic religious embattlement in Canada reinforced the authority of nationalist leaders. They in turn were encouraged by the hostility of the Irish Catholic hierarchy to French-Canadian Catholic nationalism.[73]

It was French-Canadian lawyers, doctors, and priests who dominated the French-Canadian ethnic organizations, such as the Société de St. Jean Baptiste, the Ligue des patriotes, and the Grande Napoléon. These middle-class ethnic leaders identified the interests of the French-Canadian population in ethnic terms and not in class terms, opposing unions, strikes, and class struggles. Unlike the Irish Ancient Order of Hibernia, therefore, the French-Canadian ethnic organizations did not link together ethnic interests with class interests. Although the ethnic community was a vehicle for controlling and protecting resources, particularly housing and jobs, from other ethnic groups, it did not provide a vehicle for addressing class-based experiences structured into the employer-employee relationship.

Because of the differences in their traditions before migration and in the institutions that they developed, the French-Canadian experience in Fall River differed from that of the Irish or English. But ultimately, the French-Canadian working class began to look to the institutions previously developed by the English and Irish. As their community established itself within the industrial environment, workers who became active in the struggle against the manufacturers developed experience and formally broke with the middle-class leaders. This tension led to divisions within the French-Canadian community. These divisions were class and generational. Older French Canadians looked to ethnic nationalism and the promise of the return to Québec as the solution to their economic and emotional insecurity, while younger workers began to join strikes and look to class solidarity as the salvation for their condition.[74]

Initially the divisions within the ethnic community were masked by the predominant role of the middle-class leaders, but they later became open. During the strike of 1884 the French-Canadian workers denounced the "false prophesy of the shopkeepers" who dominated their formal fraternal organizations and urged the workers to go back to work. Instead of following the anti-union lead of their ethnic leadership, the workers actively supported the strike.[75] Ultimately, French-Canadian workers began moving into the institutions of the Fall River working class, as well as developing within their own communities informal social institutions independent of their middle-class ethnic leaders. New working-class leaders emerged to challenge these ethnic leaders. The division between advocates of ethnic unity around the middle-class leaders and those who called for class unity around working-class leaders was never fully resolved, remaining an important dynamic within Fall River throughout the late nineteenth and early twentieth centuries. It was a dynamic that involved not only the French-Canadian community and historic traditions, but also those of the Lancashire workers, for their institutions remained important within the working class and influenced the French-Canadian workers as well.

The experience of the French-Canadian workers in Fall River did not duplicate that of the English and Irish, nor did the experience of later ethnic groups duplicate the French-Canadian experience. Yet the English and Irish experience radically affected the French Canadians. Each ethnic group brought with it traditions and experiences that affected the community in which they settled. Yet the community they settled in created new environments that changed the ethnic communities and were changed by them.

Because many of our early industrial communities were settled by immigrants with industrial experiences, it is important that we study the experience and institutions they brought with them, as well as the interaction between their communities and later immigrants who came to America to work in her mills and mines.

Scottish-Americans and the Beginnings of the Modern Class Struggle: Immigrant Coal Miners in Northern Illinois, 1865–1889

JOHN H. M. LASLETT

It is rarely possible to trace the exact geographical origins of a particular immigrant community, still less to ascertain all of the influences—cultural, occupational, religious, political—that governed its prior experiences, and that helped shape its course of action in the United States. When this can done, however, the information throws light on a number of questions to which historians can usually give only the vaguest of answers. Why did a particular group of workers emigrate? What were its hopes and expectations? How much better off was it in America compared to the home country? And how far was its attitude towards issues of class and class-conscious behavior determined by the conditions in the home country, and how far was this shaped by its subsequent experiences in the United States?

In this essay, I have attempted to probe these questions more deeply than usual by examining the background, class position, and attitudes towards collective action that were held by several hundred coal miners who migrated in the 1860s and 1870s from Larkhall, Wishaw, and other small mining towns near Glasgow, in the west of Scotland, to Braidwood, Streator, and other mining communities in the northern counties of Illinois. My argument, in brief is that these Scottish miners came to the United States partially to escape growing class antagonisms that were threatening to undermine their position as skilled workers, and to reassert the artisan independence that they had earlier enjoyed at home. At the social and political level they did secure a number of advantages in the United States that weakened their sense of identity as wage earners. But at the economic level, in their day-to-day work as miners, they encountered a level of class conflict that with the passage of time became just as severe as it had been in Scotland.

Scottish immigrants were not the only nationality to participate in the creation of mining towns on the northern Illinois prairie. In Streator they were outnumbered by English colliers, and Irish and Welsh miners also played an important role there. By the late 1880s, there was also a growing number of Bohemian, German, Italian, and other European immigrants in the mining camps, each of which developed their own forms of associational life in separate parts of town. But in Braidwood the Scots predominated; and since Braidwood and Streator were fairly typical of dozens of other small mining communities that British immigrants helped establish in Maryland, Pennsylvania, Ohio, and elsewhere during the post-Civil War period, understanding their social development gives us an indirect insight into similar mining towns elsewhere.[1]

In order to understand the class position of these Scottish miners, to see how this evolved after their coming to America, it is necessary first to describe the background and traditions that they brought with them to the United States from their native Lanarkshire. By 1850 there were approximately twenty-three thousand coal miners employed in the mining villages that dotted the Clyde valley near Glasgow. They worked either for large-scale ironmasters, who produced coal to fire their own blast furnaces; or for smaller-scale coalmasters, who sold their product either for domestic heating or for railroad consumption. It is a mistake to regard these miners, in premachine-mining days, as unskilled workers. To the contrary, they were as skilled as most urban craftsmen, even if their knowledge was intuitive, rather than gained through formal learning. Colliers had to know how to slice out the deepest undercut possible without bringing the coal face down on top of them; how to fit a pit prop snugly into the roof; and how deep to insert their blasting needle without killing their workmates and themselves.[2]

The labyrinthine tunnels and the instinctual nature of the miner's skills made supervision of his performance largely impossible. It was this that gave the Lanarkshire collier his vaunted independence. Primitive technology, the initial scarcity of labor, and the shallow depth of the mines in the early nineteenth century, when the skilled collier first came into his own, meant that he was able to maintain a degree of control over the labor process that was virtually unparalleled in other trades. Depending on the prevailing "price" or wage for mining a ton of coal, the miner would set his own "darg" (daily output); pause for a "social glass" when a particular tub was filled; and in the shallow pits of the early days come and go from the pit more or less as he pleased.[3]

Like other Victorian craftsmen, the Lanarkshire skilled miner was also more of a petty contractor than he was a wage laborer. Often he would employ his own "drawers" who pulled the coal hutches to and from the pit bottom, and sell his services on a piecework basis, with a fortnight's oral or written contract entered into with the manager of the mine. This left the collier free to move on, if he disliked a particular mine. "The principal trait in the character of the Scottish miner," wrote Thomas Stewart, the Larkall collier-poet, "is unyielding independence." Unlike the "cringeing slaves in other trades," Stewart asserted, the Lanarkshire colliers were "an independent, brave, and industrious portion of our Scottish peasantry."[4] This reference to peasants was no accident. Quite a few of the miners had family members who were former tenants or farmhands, or themselves worked in the fields at harvest time. "A number of them kept cows for the use of their families," wrote one contemporary, "and all of them had a pig."[5] Thus rural values and a feeling for the land were widespread.

The independence that the miner's skills gave him, together with his autonomy at the workplace, also encouraged a sense of proprietorship about the running of the mine. Like other mid-Victorian workers, the Scottish collier of this period upheld the idea of a rough equality between himself and the mine owners, a sense of mutual interest in which both collier and operator shared equally in the proceeds of the mine. "As the workmen view the matter," stated Alexander MacDonald, who was the most influential of the Scottish miners' leaders at this time, "money is the capital of the employer, labour is the capital of the workmen. . . . The great social problem of the day is to devise the means which shall secure an amicable adjustment – a fair division of profits among the respective capitalists."[6]

The central means by which the miners sought to maintain their share of these profits was by controlling cyclical fluctuations in miners' wages by influencing the supply of coal. This was to be done, first by restricting the output of coal by limiting the "darg"; and, second, by controlling or influencing the supply of labor, for example, by inhibiting the flow of unskilled Irish workers into the mines. Another tactic involved mutual acceptance by both masters and men of a wages policy known as the sliding scale. This meant negotiating wage agreements with employers whereby wages would rise as the price of coal (or, more especially, pig iron prices) rose on the Glasgow selling market, and declined when times got bad. Wage disputes should be settled, MacDonald maintained, by means of arbitration, or a gentlemanly agreement, not by means of strikes.[7]

This, then, was the traditional way of life that the Scottish colliers had created for themselves by about 1850. As capitalist relations in the mining industry became more complex, however, this life style came increasingly into conflict with the corporate interests of the large-scale iron and coal masters who now dominated the trade. Iron masters and large coal operators faced a wider, and hence more competitive market than their predecessors. Hence production delays, whether due to restricted dargs or the collier's preference for part-time work, brought a financial loss. Thus, by mid-century, ironmasters were in the forefront of a campaign to introduce managerial supervision into the coal mines, destroy the collier's influence over the production process, and turn him into a wage earner pure and simple. In the first of these tasks they were aided by advances in mining technology. Improved blasting powder increased output, and improved winding gear, coupled with greater depth of pit, meant that colliers could no longer come and go from the mine when they pleased.[8]

The Lanarkshire miners used a variety of means to defend themselves against these developments. They formed unions; established friendly societies to provide insurance against accidents, death, and unemployment; and took a keen interest in cooperative enterprise. At one level, this interest was manifested in cooperative groceries in the mining towns that were run on Rochdale principles, and in the establishment of building societies which enabled a few of the miners to buy their own homes.[9] At another level, it was reflected by an interest in land reform, as in the Irish-born William Cloughan's 1845 plea to the miners of Holytown to raise a fund for cooperative ownership of plots of land. This land would be used either for farming, or to raise enough livestock and produce to sustain the miners and their families during strikes. Nothing practical came of this proposal, however.[10]

Last, but by no means least, the miners turned towards emigration as a solution to their problems. In economic terms, the idea was to decrease the labor supply in Lanarkshire, so that the remaining miners would be in a stronger bargaining position at home. Beginning in the 1840s, some of them had already migrated to newly opened coal fields in British colonies such as Canada or Australia. But for many Scottish miners, like their English and Welsh counterparts, the United States became the primary destination. Political reformers among them had long admired Jacksonian advances in the suffrage; dissenters and free thinkers extolled the absence of an established church; and self-improvers looked to higher U.S. wages and free public education to deliver them from the bonds of poverty and ignorance.[11]

Some Scottish colliers may also have had special reasons for being attracted to the American Midwest during the Civil War years. In the early 1850s that region of the country, where many of the emerging coalfields lay, had been the cradle of the new Republican Party. Its more radical wing was dedicated to the principles of "free labor, free soil, free men."[12] All three of these principles were likely to evoke a sympathetic response in the hearts of men and women from semi-rural backgrounds who had sympathized with abolitionism, some of whose forebears had themselves been bonded in virtual perpetuity to their coal masters before the Scottish Emancipation Act of 1799. Illinois, in particular, was the state of Abraham Lincoln, the self-made son of toil who had praised labor as superior to capital. Moreover, Lincoln was the author not only of the 1863 Emancipation Proclamation for slaves but also of the Homestead Act of 1862, of which some emigrant miners were later to take advantage. In addition, there was the fact that the Civil War, when it broke out in 1861, drew many native-born American miners into the Union army, creating a scarcity of labor and driving wages up in the northern coal fields. By contrast, wages suffered a major decline in the Lanarkshire coalfield in the late 1850s.[13]

Not all of these Lanarkshire miners, of course, went to northern Illinois. Some went to Lonaconing or Frostburg, in the Maryland coal region;[14] others went to Schuylkill County, Pennsylvania;[15] still others to the Hocking Valley, in southeastern Ohio;[16] to Missouri, or to the Belleville field, near St. Louis in southwestern Illinois.[17] A number followed a peripatetic life out West, or even went to Canada, sampling many different coal camps before settling down. But Braidwood, Streator, and other smaller northern Illinois settlements like Gardner, Carbon Hill, and Coal City, which together made up the Wilmington coalfield, became for a time at the end of the 1860s—with an output of 228,000 tons in 1870—the largest single producer of coal in the American Midwest.

Described in 1865 as "nothing but a sea of tall grass" on the vast Midwestern prairie, by 1872 Braidwood had twelve separate coal pits, employing 2,041 miners.[18] In that year Andrew Cameron, the Scots-born editor of the Chicago *Workingmen's Advocate*, found Braidwood to be a good-sized town, with a population of over five thousand. "Churches, schoolhouses, hotels, and stores had arisen as if by magic," he reported, on a main street half a mile long. Yet the vast, shallow bed of three-foot seam coal that lay no more than fifty to eighty feet under and around the city had "been little more than cropped."[19] Streator, twenty miles to the southeast, although considerably smaller than Braidwood, had similar amenities.

For several years after they first settled in Braidwood, Streator, and other mining villages along the Illinois River, it seemed undeniable that the newly arrived miners had improved their position considerably over what it had been in Scotland, in both a social and a material sense. Take politics, for example. The mining villages from which the miners had come in the Clyde valley had, since their founding, been dominated by an established elite of gentry, clergy, and landed lairds who filled virtually all of the positions of authority as magistrates, poor-law overseers, and elected officials. Until the Third Parliamentary Reform Act of 1884, few of the miners could even vote. In Braidwood, by contrast, they made their political influence felt from the very first. W.H. Goodrich, Braidwood's first mayor, was an ex-mine superintendent of humble origins. Daniel McLaughlin, who was elected mayor several times in the 1870s, was a Scottish immigrant miner with an Irish background. The town sheriff – a crucial officer for the miners to have on their side during strikes – and several members of the city council were either practicing miners or ex-miners during the period under review; and in the years between 1887 and 1911 no less than twenty seats in the Illinois state legislature were held by working or former miners, most of them elected on the Republican ticket.[20]

The type and character of housing available to the miners was also clearly superior to what it had been in Scotland. In Lanarkshire, despite a number of showcase miners' cottages owned by Baird's and by the Coltness Iron Co., mostly tiny two-room company houses without proper ventilation or sanitation predominated.[21] In northern Illinois, by contrast, large numbers of miners were able to purchase their own homes. "The type of miner's house most frequently met with is a one-story frame, painted and plastered cottage, standing on a lot 50 x 150 feet deep," reported the Illinois Bureau of Labor Statistics in 1883. "Out towards the suburbs the lots are larger, some of the miners having two or three acres which they cultivate during the summer. . . . Their furniture usually consists of tables, chairs, bureau or stand, sometimes a rag carpet, and pictures and other common household goods."[22]

The reference here to the cultivation of "two or three acres" also showed the potential that cheap land and the wide open prairie provided for satisfying the Scottish collier's traditional attachment to rural values. Given the high rate of turnover among the mining population in places such as Braidwood, as well as the speculative land-buying habits of organizations such as the railroads, it is difficult to know just how many of the Scots colliers were able to take advantage of the

Homestead Act and actually buy farmland in the immediate area. An 1884 report on the town of Streator, however, did say that most of the miners there who had "got ahead in the world" had done so by becoming farmers.[23]

Initially at least, skilled Scots miners also had more opportunity to move up and out of the pits into positions of authority as mine managers or inspectors, state employees, or even mine owners in the United States than they had before emigrating. Of the pioneer mining generation in Braidwood, James Braidwood himself (after whom the town was named), Robert Fairbairn, and the brothers Frank and Richard Newsham and Richard and William Ramsey, for example, became owners of mining enterprises. Three other immigrants, Samuel Drew, William Mooney, and David Ross, studied law and were admitted to the Illinois bar. The great majority of the dozen or so state mine inspectors appointed in Illinois to supervise safety laws in this period were either English, Scottish, or Welsh. In Scotland at this time there were only two official mine inspectors, both appointed by Whitehall.[24]

The state-administered training programs for mine inspectors were also part of a public education system that, although rudimentary by modern American standards, was far more extensive in Illinois than it was in Scotland. There were parish schools in a number of the mining towns in Lanarkshire, but before the 1872 Education Act the number of places in them was far too small for the number of miners' children; they were heavily influenced by the Church of Scotland clergy; and they typically ended instruction at the age of 14.[25] Although at age 14 many sons of immigrant miners followed their fathers into the pits in Illinois, far more educational opportunities awaited the ambitious among them than for the "lad o' pairts" (men like Alexander MacDonald or the young Keir Hardie) who sought to climb out of the Scottish pits. In Illinois some attended public high school up to the age of graduation; others, industrial training schools, or mine schools; and a few even went to the University of Illinois.[26]

In the world of the mine itself, the first pits sunk in Braidwood and Streator were also relatively small family concerns that enabled the immigrant colliers to reassert their independence and pride of craft in ways that were no longer feasible in the Lanarkshire mines. The coal seams in northern Illinois were narrower than they were in the old country, but they were nearer the surface. This meant that only limited capital was needed to open a mine and that, for a time at least, little in the way of advanced technology was needed to operate each pit. The first coal company in the Braidwood area was the Eureka Coal Co. (1865), which employed 43 men. It was followed by the Chicago and Wilmington Co. (1866), the Diamond Coal Co. (1870), and by several others in subsequent years. In 1870 the three largest coal companies operating in the area employed, respectively, 109, 84, and 63 men. These were smaller numbers than those recorded in an 1863 survey of the Larkhall and Hamilton districts, in Lanarkshire, where there were nine collieries with an average workforce of 111 miners each.[27]

Other, still smaller mines (the exact number is unclear) were of the slope or drift variety, and were cut into the sides of creek bottoms along the Illinois, Vermilion, and Kankakee Rivers where outcrops of coal were exposed to view. In these pits, there was a relatively gradual incline for the men getting down to and back from the coal face. The result, for a time at least, was the establishment of informal work relations and workplace autonomy on an even more extensive scale than had previously existed in Scotland. In the fall of 1865, several letters written home by immigrants recently arrived in Illinois were reproduced in the *Glasgow Sentinel* describing the advantages of the new Illinois mines. "The work is much easier and lighter here than at home," wrote Thomas Rankin from Streator. "You would really be amused . . . to see me threading my way to the mine in the morning betwixt six and seven, and returning no later than three in the afternoon."[28] In his historical novel about Illinois coal mining, written many years later, Tom Tippett also caught the easy social relations that existed between mine owners and men in this early period. In it, skilled English miners worked alongside of mineowner "Old Bill," a former collier who had set himself up in business on his own.[29]

These social and workplace advantages did not mean that there was no social conflict in the northern Illinois coal towns in the immediate post–Civil-War period, either between the miners and mine owners, or among the colliers themselves. The presence of large numbers of bars – some said as many as eighty in Braidwood alone – led to drunken brawls, particularly on Sundays, which was the day after pay day. Ethnic and religious differences between Welsh Methodists and English Episcopalians, between Scottish Presbyterians and Irish Catholics, and between the Orange and the Green factions within these Celtic groups were also reflected in residential segregation between ethnic neighborhoods, in differences over such issues as temperance and parochial schools, and in political fights. After the closely contested Braidwood city elections of April 1875, for example, a mob stormed the polling booths and carried off the voting boxes. Twenty people were injured in a melee which, according to one local newspaper, "arrayed the various factions against each other:

Republicans vs. Democrats; Scotch vs. Irish, and more bitter still—
Orangemen vs. Catholics, between whom we all know there is little
love lost."[30].

Whatever social tensions there were within the mining community in normal times, however, during labor disputes that same community, including members of the trading and commercial classes,
gave virtually united support to the miners, when they found it
necessary to protest the policies of the operators. A good example of
this can be seen in the first serious strike that occurred in Braidwood,
in May 1868, when the operators cut piece rates from $1.50 to $1.25
a ton. The owners brought in seventy strike breakers from Chicago, as
well as some Pinkerton detectives to make sure they were permitted
to work. It is noteworthy, however, that before the miners gave in,
they formed a committee to secure material aid from the citizens of
Braidwood, as well as from neighboring towns. In addition, a local
resident miner who continued to work throughout the strike received,
in the words of one account, not "a single expression of sympathy"[31]
either from the strikers or from the townsfolk, a fact which revealed
the depth of community support for the strike. In other words,
whatever ethnic and cultural conflicts the miners may have
demonstrated in non-work contexts, these were overlaid by class unity
during critical struggles in the pits.

A still more striking fact about the 1868 dispute is that the leaders
of the Braidwood miners undertook the strike reluctantly, and only
after all other means for settling it had been exhausted. John James,
who had been one of Alexander MacDonald's lieutenants in Scotland,
called it "ruinous"[32] for both miners and operators, and expressed the
hope that future disputes could be settled more amicably. The Pinkerton detectives who had been brought in to maintain order proved
unnecessary, since the miners remained "intelligent, orderly, and
trustworthy" throughout.[33] The strikers secured further public support
when they decided to make use of the courts to sue the Chicago,
Wilmington and Vermilion Co. to try to secure back wages.

What the 1868 strike reveals, in fact, is that up to this time the
immigrant Scottish miners, along with their Anglo-Saxon and Celtic
allies, were trying to maintain the spirit of social harmony, of shared
responsibility, and of mutual respect between collier and coal owner
that they had looked for in Scotland in the 1850s. This vision was not
to be sustained for long, however. Some of the social advantages that
the immigrant miners secured, in areas such as home ownership or
educational opportunities, for example, were to remain permanently
with them. However, it was a very different story at the workplace.
By the end of the 1870s, and in some respects even earlier, the rapid

development of large-scale capitalist enterprise in the northern Illinois coal towns brought about the same kind of class separation, degradation of work, and bitter recriminations over the unfair distribution of profits made by the coal owners that had occurred in Scotland twenty years before.

The key to these developments, as in the Lanarkshire coal and iron industry in the earlier period, lay in a rapid expansion in the market for coal; in technological innovations which rendered obsolete the small slope or drift mines that had been present in the Wilmington field in its earliest years; and in the replacement of small, locally owned coal companies by large absentee-owned mining corporations. In the early days the Braidwood and Streator mines had enjoyed more or less unchallenged access to the Chicago coal market via the Chicago and Alton railroad line. By the Mid-1870s, however, numerous other railroads had been built, bringing higher grade coal to Chicago from newly opened southern Illinois coal mines, as well as permitting newer and larger coal companies to be established.[34]

By the end of 1873, for example, the Wilmington Coal Mining and Manufacturing Company had sunk a deep shaft mine in the newly laid out village of Diamond, southwest of Braidwood. In 1874 the Coalfield Coal Co., organized by a group of New York and Braidwood financiers, purchased one thousand acres of land along the railroad in Grundy County, leased 640 acres to the Wilmington Star Coal Co., and laid out the town of Coal City. In the early 1880s, the slumbering village of Braceville was rejuvenated when the Chicago, Milwaukee and St. Paul Railroad purchased 14,000 acres, and undertook large-scale mining operations nearby. In 1878 the coal companies of Will and Grundy Counties produced 478,000 tons of coal with a labor force of 5,422 men. For a brief period this made them the two largest coal-producing counties in Illinois.[35]

Technological innovations came about largely as the result of the ingenuity of Alexander Crombie, superintendent of the Wilmington Star Co., who in 1876 obtained a patent on "a machine for digging coal." The machine proved to be impractical, but it set a precedent for the development of more efficient coal-cutting equipment soon afterwards. Two years later Crombie invented a device to prevent the sudden and deadly descent of the miners' elevators when the cable broke. Later on, Richard Ransay of Braceville put together a new machine for "trimming" cars loaded with coal, reducing from seven to two the number of men needed for trimming.[36] These changes made it possible to increase both the efficiency and the scale of mining operations, as well as the number of miners employed at any one pit. In 1882, for example, the four largest coal companies in Grundy County employed, respectively, 330, 287, 234, and 150 miners. These were far larger figures than the numbers for the year 1870, and for the Scottish pits in which the men had worked earlier. All of these mines were shaft pits, using steam-driven machinery rather than horses to move the coal, and all of the shafts went down more than a hundred feet. All of them also had professionally trained supervisors: no more owner-managers of the "Old Bill" variety, working alongside their own men in the pit.[37]

In one way, the greater number of men employed underground increased, rather than diminished, their sense of solidarity; and it should not be inferred that the new steam winding gear and other inventions completely destroyed the skilled collier's autonomy in the workplace. According to one authority, that did not happen until some years later, when machine mining replaced most of the pick miner's hand skills, and when the hand-loading of coal had been replaced by the automatic moving belt.[38] Nevertheless, it can readily be seen that such changes gave the larger mining companies new weapons in their struggle to improve efficiency and cut labor costs by increasing the degree of control they exerted over their labor force, a struggle that had been rendered necessary by sharper competition in the coal market.

No company reflected this transition to modern corporate methods more clearly than the Chicago, Wilmington and Vermilion Co., which had been formed as a result of a merger of two earlier firms. Capitalized at two million dollars, by 1876 its five Braidwood shafts provided employment for more than half the 1,665 miners living in the town that year. Not only were the company's stockholders absentee owners in Boston and other Eastern cities, but both its President, James Monroe Walker, and its General Manager, A.L. Sweet, lived in Chicago, more than fifty miles from Braidwood.[39] The emergence of the C.W.& V. as the corporate giant of the northern Illinois coalfield symbolized the demise not only of the small, single-family firm that had characterized the pre–Civil-War – and in some ways pre-industrial – phase of American capitalism. It also symbolized the demise of the coal town as a harmonious, face-to-face community displaying a rough equality of wealth and mutual respect between miner and mine owner that had characterized the idea of the independent collier in Scotland, and that in America was associated with the ideals of republicanism.

Faced with growing competition, the C.W.& V. lost no time in promulgating new contract rules that severely affected its employees' established position in the mines. In the spring of 1873, it asserted unilaterally that the company had the right to shut down its pits at any time; that the men had to "perform a full day's work of ten hours"[40] unless they had special permission to do otherwise; and that the terms of employment would be determined solely by the company's officials. The resistance that the Braidwood miners made to these depradations was in most respects similar to what they had shown in Scotland: establishment of trade unions, efforts to persuade employers to withdraw these new rules through negotiation, and discussion of alternatives like cooperative production.[41]

One begins to find in the letters sent back home, from this period on, surprise and anger that the hopes and expectations that the miners had brought with them to America in the immediate post–Civil-War years had been profoundly disappointed. In June, 1873, for example, John Kemp, who was then Secretary of the Workmen's Benevolent Association (a miners' union largely confined to the East), expressed his concern at the dictatorial role that the C.W.& V. had now assumed, and compared it unfavorably with the earlier policies of the mining companies in the Pennsylvania coalfield. "The shadow of the struggle between labor and capital is . . . upon us," he wrote in a letter that was reprinted in the *Glasgow Sentinel*, "and it remains with combined wealth whether it is to be a peaceful struggle, or a bloody one. There will be no bloodshed with the men of labor. Ah, no; God forbid, for if there were, capital would accomplish its end with little or no struggle."[42]

Consistent with its earlier conciliatory policies, the Braidwood District union at first responded cautiously to the C.W. & V.'s demands. It suggested, as an alternative to the new pronunciamentos, that a joint committee of colliers and C.W. & V. representatives draw up the 1873–74 contract, that eight hours rather than ten constitute the working day, and that a Board of Arbitration made up of three miners, three operators, and an unbiased umpire adjudicate any grievances. The miners eschewed a strike, arguing, as they had in Scotland, that strikes were "injurious to the best interests of the employer and employee."[43] The company refused to compromise, however. On May 17, 1873, it announced a new contract mandating the ten-hour day, as well as the other new provisions. Divided, most C.W.& V. employees gave in, only to find that in early June the Eureka Coal Co., Braidwood's second largest firm, also insisted on the ten-hour day. In the summer of 1873, reflecting the decline in demand that the industrial depression of the mid-1870's was beginning to produce, these as well as other coal companies in Streator and elsewhere cut their men back to only five hours' work a day—a workday that could not possibly provide enough wages to sustain a miner and his family.[44]

Even in these circumstances, the miners confined themselves at first to expressions of moral outrage against the operators, with whom they still in some sense considered themselves to be in partnership. Yet, in a remarkable speech which he made to an outdoor mass meeting of Braidwood miners on August 9, 1873, Daniel McLaughlin expressed disillusionment for the first time with the principles of class harmony and mutual respect between employer and employee, which underlay the republican ideal. What is more, he did so in such a way as to contrast the position of the skilled miner in the United States and Scotland, to the advantage, not of the former, but of the latter. "Let me point out to you the standing of your craft in the old world, and ask you to compare them [sic] with yours," he said. "There, they have worked themselves up from a menial state of serfdom . . . by the power of their Association," that is, by the efforts of the Scottish Miners' Union. In Braidwood, by contrast, "under a system of government, the justest, the best, and [the one which] when properly administered admits of no inequalities, . . . your names are mentioned only with contempt by those who employ you and those outside of you. Such is the place which this society has assigned you in this land which we are accustomed to call 'The Glorious Republic of the West.'"[45]

As the depression deepened, the C.W. & V. adopted even more stringent policies. On May 31, 1874, it cut piece rates from $1.25 to $1.10 per ton. The Braidwood miners' union met and decided to accept a temporary reduction of fifteen cents on the rate for digging coal, but it refused to sign a contract making the reduction permanent for one year. The employers insisted, and this time, goaded beyond their patience, the miners voted to strike. Thus began the Braidwood stoppage of 1874, which has been described at length by Herbert Gutman. The C.W. & V. brought in strikebreakers, and armed Pinkerton guards to protect their property; Braidwood's mayor and city council, as well as its tradesmen, sided with the strikers. State militia were brought in after Streator miners were falsely accused of setting fire to several buildings, creating much bitterness. The compromise settlement reached on September 7, 1874, resulted in a minor wage cut that, given the depressed state of the mining industry generally, was generally regarded as a victory.[46]

Three years later, an even more extensive, nine-months miners' strike erupted, lasting from April 27, to November 23, 1877. This stoppage also overlapped with the bloody and violent national railroad strike that took place during the summer of that year. The 1877 Illinois miners' strike illustrated, even more than the 1874 dispute, the forebearance of the miners when faced with the increasingly repressive tactics of the coal operators, as well as their ongoing faith in the political power of the community to sustain them. At the same time it precipitated a division of opinion within the miners' leadership that revealed a further rapid decline in support for the mid-nineteenth ideal of mutual equality and respect between employer and employee. In its aftermath there also appeared the first faint glimmerings of a more radical solution to the miners' problem, one that responded to the third-party message of the Greenback Labor Party movement, while at the same time showing a more modern understanding of the meaning of the class struggle.

On May 1, 1877, the Chicago, Wilmington and Vermilion Co. announced a wage cut of twenty-five cents per ton, coupled with a demand that all miners in the company's employ promise not to join a union. Several thousand men in the operators' pits in Streator, as well as in Braidwood, walked out. First some white, then six hundred Black strikebreakers were brought in, protected by Pinkertons and special police, and armed for self-defence. Unwilling to counterpose class violence with class violence Mayor Daniel McLaughlin (as he had by now become), John Keir, Frank Lofty, and the other strike leaders disarmed the Negro strikebreakers and made them leave town. Accusing the Braidwood leaders of mis-treating the Blacks, Illinois Governor Cullom ordered General Ducat to Braidwood with a large force of state militia. Arriving on July 28, Ducat and his men confiscated the arms taken from the Black strikebreakers, and arrested McLaughlin on charges of exceeding his municipal authority. This effectively broke the strike. Although it limped on until November, it ended in catastrophic defeat. McLaughlin, Lofty, Keir, and a dozen other strike leaders were blacklisted, and the back of the Braidwood miners' union was broken for several years.[47]

There were further, even more serious, expressions of anger and disillusionment after the defeat of the 1877 strike, as the employers pressed home their advantage to break down still more any manifestations of collier independence. The Braidwood cooperative grocery failed during the course of the dispute. It was replaced by a company store. The right to graze cattle on the Chicago, Wilmington and Vermilion's land was withdrawn. Work discipline was increased not only by the use of the "yellow dog" contract and by blacklisting, but permits were also now required for miners to change employment from one of the company's pits to another. According to one account, for a time the C.W. & V. even fired all of its single white male employees, on the grounds that married men were less likely to cause trouble. Small wonder that one anonymous Braidwood miner, surveying the human suffering and the degradation of the miners and their families which followed the defeat, exclaimed bitterly: "We are often reminded by politicians of our glorious Constitution, and how every man is to be protected in his right to 'Life, Liberty, and the pursuit of happiness'. . . . [yet] Corporations can do and dictate to thousands what they shall eat, drink, and wear, and should anyone grumble at their lot, they must be discharged." "Oh, my country," the miner concluded, "what a mockery!"[48]

A similar note was struck in a series of letters written by John James in Braidwood to Scottish miners' leader Alexander MacDonald between 1874 and 1876, asking for advice on ways to halt the deteriorating position of the immigrant coal miners. In April 1874, James commented bitterly on the unemployment that miners all over the United States were suffering, and then averred that their situation was even worse than that of the Scottish colliers. "You have seen, and so have I," James wrote, "the miners on your side of the water sunk down low in the slough of despond, . . . but never in their lowest state have I seen them so much the victims of wanton oppression, as they are throughout the Western States of this country at present." As a means of limiting the supply of excess labor in the American mines, James advocated the exchange of trade union cards between the English and the American National Miners Associations, so that no new immigrant colliers would come across the Atlantic until the present crisis had passed. Nothing came of this suggestion, however.[49]

It might be objected that these observations were made during the course of the 1873–76 depression, and did not accurately reflect the miners' situation in normal times. But in January 1876, James wrote a further letter to MacDonald in which he specifically set aside the recession as a factor in comparing the status of miners in Scotland and America. Noting that the American Miners National Association, of which he was an officer, was struggling to survive in the face of severe employer repression, James regretfully announced his agreement with the opinion of MacDonald, expressed in an earlier letter, that, "Capitalists are the same the world over. The same desire to trample roughshod over the man who toils is evidenced here to a large extent. . . . I am thoroughly satisfied," James concluded, "that whether it be under a republic or an empire, labour, if it will have fair, honest dealings at the hands of its employer must put itself in a position to command it."[50]

James' views in this 1876 letter came nearer to accepting a class conflict analysis (as opposed to one based on mutual interest) of relations between miner and coal operator than any collier of his mid-Victorian background had hitherto done. Yet when it came to deciding what practical steps northern Illinois miners should take to resist the repressive stance that the Chicago, Wilmington and Vermilion Co. took toward them in the 1877 strike, it became clear that James could not bring himself to accept the adversarial policies that such an analysis prompted. In fact, a split occurred between him and Daniel McLaughlin over what tactics the union should pursue. James opposed calling the strike in the first place, considering it to be a rash undertaking. He was particularly critical of the actions of Braidwood Town Supervisor John Young (himself a miner) in imposing taxes on previously untaxed coal lands, believing that this was excessively punitive towards the mine operators. Still more important, James opposed the establishment of a secret Knights of Labor assembly in the city, as well as its corollary, the election of a citywide, Greenback-Labor third party ticket. He even joined in the red-baiting used by opponents of the party to discredit it. Ostracized by his former friends as a result, James left Braidwood permanently in 1880, becoming a mine manager for a time in Carthage, New Mexico. After taking other jobs, he retired and died in Santa Monica, California, in 1902.[51]

Daniel McLaughlin, on the other hand, was radicalized by the brutal defeat of the 1877 strike. He remained critical of strikes save as a weapon of last resort, and he continued to uphold setting wage rates by means of a sliding scale. McLaughlin also never became a socialist in quite the same way that some of the next generation of Illinois coal miners' leaders were to become. But he fully supported the program of the Independent Greenback-Labor party at the state and local level in the 1876–78 period. And in the winter of 1877 we find McLaughlin talking not only of the need for paper currency, of the need to deny free land to speculators, and of the need for free education for "rich and poor alike"– all standard parts of the Greenback-Labor program, but going further: "It does not require much logic or reason to prove that the wage workers and wealth producers are defrauded and robbed out of the just share of the wealth they create," the Scots immigrant leader said. "The basis of our social system requires to be remodelled and founded on industrial equality."[52]

In the short run the coal operators were to have the last word. McLaughlin himself had been mayor of Braidwood, at the head of a Greenback-Labor ticket, during the 1877 coal strike. During that strike, town supervisor John Young, as we have also seen, made use of his taxing power to defend the colliers' cause. And in the April 1878 Reed township election (Reed township contained the city of Braidwood), the miners again elected a full Greenback-Labor Party ticket, headed by none other than blacklisted supervisor Young. Again the miners seemed to triumph. But this time the Chicago, Wilmington, and Vermilion Company had had enough. It fired the ten miners who had led Young's campaign. In the May 1878 Braidwood city election, the coal company obtained a Republican/Democratic fusion ticket, illegally registered two hundred Black miners left behind as scab workers from the strike, and swept the miners out of office. It was a dazzling display of bourgeois class power.[53]

Still the miners would not give up. In June 1878, they held a grand picnic–complete with banners proclaiming "A Republic Forever," "Never a Monarchy," "We Use No Coercion to Get Votes"–and invited Chicago Bohemian socialist I.B. Belopdradsky to speak.[54] Two years later, at a July 4, 1880, picnic, they invited the still more radical Chicago anarchist Albert Parsons to address them.[55] All of this seemed to suggest that the northern Illinois miners were beginning to move towards an explicit abandonment of the Victorian ideal of class harmony, in favor of the acceptance of the Marxist idea of inevitable conflict between classes, and to a burgeoning committment to socialist politics. And so, up to a point, they were.

But two factors, in particular, militated against their going any further along this path during the time period covered by this essay. One was the collapse of the Greenback-Labor Party and the Workingmen's Party movement at the national level, which had taken place by the end of the decade.[56] The other was the growing ability of the miners to make use of the existing two-party system to force the Illinois state legislature to make legislative concessions to them on matters of mine safety, mine inspection, mine ventilation, and the like. As the 1880's progressed, the Illinois miners' unions made common cause with the fledgling Illinois State Federation of Labor to finance a joint legislative committee to lobby in Springfield at each legislative session.[57] In the long run, the members of both the main political parties responded to this pressure, in ways which appeared to preclude the need for the establishment of an independent labor party.

There were other obstacles to the development of a more modern understanding of the class struggle among the miners of northern Illinois in this period. One was the setback suffered by the Knights of Labor, and by radical forces generally, as a result of the Red Scare that followed the Haymarket riot in Chicago of May 1886, only fifty miles to the northeast.[58] Another was the further discrediting of radical causes that took place in response to the arrival of a number of Italian anarchists, as well as other new southern and eastern European immigrants in newer mining communities such as Spring Valley, some twenty miles to the west of Braidwood, in 1894.[59] A third was the inhibiting effect upon full-throated defiance of the employers that resulted from the 1886 signing of the Joint Interstate Agreement between miners' unions and the operators. Although it was more of a modern collective bargaining document than any of its predecessors, in acknowledging clear and mutually accepted differences of interest between mine owners and men, that agreement also contained elements of the older, class-collaborationist ideal.[60]

Besides all this, three more great strikes, the Spring Valley strike of 1889, and the two national coal strikes of 1894 and 1897, in both of which Illinois miners played a leading part, were to be necessary before a majority of miners in the state could be disabused of the older patterns of thought. And when a new generation of explicitly socialist miners did arise in Illinois, they remained a minority when compared to the unionized colliers as a whole. Nevertheless, in the end the patience of the radicals was rewarded. The socialists among the Illinois miners, led by such men as John H. Walker, Duncan MacDonald, and Adolph Germer, were never as successful in terms of third party politics as their counterparts were in Scotland. In 1908 the Miners Federation of Great Britain, and within it the Lanarkshire Miners county union, affiliated with the British Labor Party, thereby helping to transform it into the mass political party of the British working class. But, nevertheless, from approximately 1905 to 1926, and to some extent beyond, District 12 of the United Mine Workers of America, as the Illinois miners' union was then called, became the powerhouse of radicalism within the United Mine Workers of America.[61]

CHAPTER 10

The German Brewery Workers
of New York City
in the Late Nineteenth Century

DOROTHEE SCHNEIDER

Among the many industries flourishing in metropolitan New York during the second half of the nineteenth century, the brewing industry was one of the most insular. The workers in New York City's lager beer breweries were almost exclusively German-speaking, as were their bosses. Almost all of them learned their skills in the Old World and brought over social and organizational traditions that they were able to preserve in the homogeneous world of their craft in North America. However strong their penchant for tradition, though, workers (and bosses) in North American breweries also faced drastic changes during the second half of the nineteenth century. More than almost any other industry in metropolitan New York, brewing was undergoing fundamental technological change. The cohesion of immigrant traditions provided only a limited answer to the problems that hit the brewery workers: They faced unemployment, obsolescence of their skills, loss of responsibilities and of personal relations with their bosses, and increasing dependence on anonymous national corporations.

The existing historical literature has assumed that the brewery workers responded to the technological and organizational revolution in their trade by espousing socialism as union men.[1] I shall argue that the socialist rhetoric in New York and elsewhere coexisted (sometimes uneasily) with a deeply held traditional craft identity that persisted beneath attempts to become part of the socialist labor movement in the city. Encouraged by their employers to maintain their ideas of craft

189

superiority, and at first successful in perpetuating a *Gemeinschaft* of workers and employers, the brewery workers of New York City only reluctantly faced the long road of transformation leading from craft unions with restrictive admission policies to an industrial union structure to accommodate new classes of semi-skilled workers and immigrants from non-German backgrounds.

What were the traditions of German-American brewers in New York City? To begin with, brewing was an old craft in Central Europe. The Germanic tribes were already known as beer drinkers to the Romans. Brewing remained a home industry up to the late Middle ages; in contrast to other crafts, it did not develop into an independent urban trade with powerful guilds or independent self-regulation by the thirteenth and fourteenth centuries. Instead, brewers were closely dependent on local and regional authorities. Brewing remained a privilege awarded by princes, cities, or monasteries on a temporary basis as a form of political patronage. These authorities also set their own standards for licensing brewers, taxing them, and regulating the beer-making process itself. The Central European brewing craft was thus interwoven with the peculiarities of a feudal society: Brewers were linked to the privileged classes in a much more direct and dependent relationship than almost any other trade.[2]

The effects of this close connection between the ruling nobility and the development of the brewing trade were particularly evident in Bavaria where, from the sixteenth century on, the Elector (later King) of Bavaria himself centralized all brewing operations under his direct supervision – a policy that favored the development of Bavaria's brewing industry into Central Europe's largest and most modern by the mid-nineteenth century. The ingredients, brewing process, and licensing and taxation of breweries were regulated by various decrees. Protected from outside competition, Bavarian brewers had developed their popular effervescent lager beer by the early nineteenth century, and owned some of the wealthiest manufactories in that part of Europe.[3]

The second part of the nineteenth century witnessed the industrialization of the brewing industry in many parts of Germany. Firms in Berlin and Westphalia began to compete with breweries in Munich and Nuremberg for a national market. Freed from many of the government rules that had shaped the industry up to German unification in 1870–1871, Germany's large breweries entered the industrial age quickly. Small breweries soon began to have a difficult time competing with large and increasingly mechanized beer factories, and despite a steadily growing market, the overall number of breweries shrank by 10 percent in each decade after 1875. The demand for skilled workers also levelled off because of the increasing use of machinery. For journeymen brewers, the industrialization of their trade brought about diminished opportunities, and growing numbers attempted in the second half of the nineteenth century to continue their livelihood in North American breweries.[4]

The need to find a stable job in a brewery was not the only reason for Germany's skilled brewers' leaving their homeland. Their restricted and difficult lives and working conditions, despite the transformation of brewing into a modern industry, meant that the occupational mobility of most German brewery workers remained limited up to the mid-1890s by craft traditions and feudal regulations. Almost all workers in German breweries had to go through three to four years of apprenticeship to become brewers or maltsers, after which they had to earn a living as travelling journeymen for at least two more years before they could hire themselves out as skilled brewers. Throughout their training, journeymen brewers had to perform extremely taxing physical labor fourteen to sixteen hours a day, six days a week, plus six hours on Sunday. Monthly wages were meager, varying between 80 and 95 Marks a month ($20 – $24 according to contemporary exchange rates) during the 1880s.[5]

During their rare leisure hours brewers were usually under some kind of supervision by their employers. In small breweries brewers had to board with the owner himself; larger businesses forced their workers to live in a special hostel. Only married workers were exempt from this so called *Herbergszwang*, or compulsory dwelling in the hostel selected by one's employer. No wonder many workers elected to leave Germany: The promise of greater freedom across the Atlantic had real meaning for them.[6]

While for many workers emigration provided an answer to some of their problems, others attempted to form a brewery workers trade union in Germany. But the long, exhausting hours, the lack of a tradition of journeymen's organizing; and the isolation of the many workers in small breweries made it difficult to get them together. Early organizations of journeymen brewers, founded in the 1870s, were mutual help and social groups without political overtones. In 1885 a number of these local associations came together to found the national General German Brewers Union (*Allgemeiner Deutscher Brauer Verband*). Conflict between socialists and more conservative factions dogged it during the 1880s, and in 1889, it split apart. During the ensuing decade the growth of the brewery workers' movement in Germany was consistently hampered by this division, which reflected the divided consciousness of many brewery workers: steeped in the conservative traditions of their craft, many of them joined anti-socialist journeymen brewers associations that aimed at cooperating with the employers. Others aligned themselves with the socialist trade union movement in Germany as industrial workers. The socialists had organized a majority of workers in urban breweries and won a number of contracts there during the 1890s. But even the socialist brewery workers union remained one of the more conservative branches of the German trade union movement. In contrast to Germans in many other trades, the brewery workers could not serve as an inspiration for a progressive North American trade union movement.[7]

The German immigrant brewers who came to New York during the decades following the Civil War entered an industry that was already almost entirely German. In 1880 Manhattan had some fifty-seven breweries, Brooklyn, 38. About twenty ale and porter breweries were owned mostly by Irish and English immigrants, the rest by German-Americans. Most of the latter had arrived between 1845 and 1865; many had started out in the United States as skilled workers, eventually saving enough money to start a small business of their own, often with the help of relatives or a business partner; some brewers came from merchant families in the grain trades.

No matter what their specific occupational background, most of these German-Americans regarded themselves as craftsmen in a very specific traditional sense, especially in their relationship to their fellow brewers and their workers. Most German-American brewery owners tried to fit this mold, following the standards of a conservative community with high social homogeneity. With considerable success they had developed an image of paternalism and social responsibility by the 1880s which found few parallels in other metropolitan industries during the late nineteenth century. Brewery owners were well-known benefactors for conservative local charities such as churches and relief societies. They also regularly held festivities for their employees: New Years' dances and Christmas parties in the winter, picnics and boat rides in the summer. More than most American industrialists they took an interest in the welfare of their employees. Employee housing, support for brewery workers' widows and their families, and other voluntary support were more frequent than in most other industries. In the short run these measures were old-fashioned means to control the workers' mores; in the long run they maintained a craft-oriented community ethos and inhibited the formation of industrial labor organizations.[8]

Employment opportunities were favorable for German immigrant brewers at least until the 1890s. The relatively young lager beer industry in the United States did not train its own workers, but instead hired skilled immigrants, preferably Germans. Thus 73 percent of all brewery workers in New York City were German-born in 1880, while many of the rest were German-speaking workers from such areas as Austria, Switzerland, Alsace, or Bohemia. American-born children of German immigrants, on the other hand, rarely stayed in their fathers' occupation. Like their employers, the majority of German-American brewery workers came from South Germany, usually from semi-rural areas. Altogether, New York's brewery workers had remarkable continuity with their Old World culture; German was their language at home and at work, and non-German speakers had to learn German on the job.[9]

Continuity and homogeneity permitted a peculiar form of social organization among the brewery workers. Single brewers almost always lived in boarding houses set up by the employer – the New York equivalent of the brewers' hostel in Germany. Like their German counterparts, the brewery workers rarely choose their own lodging, but were required to stay in the boarding house with which their employer had a contract. As in Germany, employees were not at liberty to change accommodations so long as they stayed with the same employer. Thus the European *Herbergszwang* was maintained in America. Married brewery workers, especially those working in the large breweries of the upper East Side, often lived in tenements owned by their employer and managed by their boss's relative or brewing foreman. Outside the brewing industry such employer-sponsored and -supervised housing was extremely rare in nineteenth-century Manhattan. The arrangement heightened the New York City brewery workers' already considerable social isolation from other working-class groups.[10]

If the social world of American brewery workers resembled that of their German counterparts to a remarkable degree, the work itself, was also similar to what the Germans had hoped to leave behind. Despite mechanization, much physically arduous work remained in New York's breweries during the late nineteenth century, such as carrying materials, stirring the mash, and tending the machines. As in Germany, workdays were long and irregular during much of the year. They lasted from six in the morning to six at night, with frequent overtime after dinner. Sunday work was also the rule. The wages for these hours were not high; journeymen brewers were paid between $11 and $14 a week, while foremen received about $20. Brewery workers had to reckon with at least six weeks of layoffs during the winter, leaving yearly earnings between $500 and $650.[11]

What kept the immigrants coming was the hope not just of better wages or working conditions, but also of owning a brewery of one's own some day. But this had become largely a utopian dream by the 1870s. The New York brewing industry had by then become increasingly capital-intensive and mechanized, offering little room for the small entrepreneur. In contrast to their predecessors during the 1850s and 1860s, brewery workers wanting to start their own businesses in the 1880s needed to raise considerable sums to build a physical plant and to buy expensive steam-powered machinery such as artificial refrigeration equipment. Even established breweries had trouble staying profitable in competition with more efficient and larger businesses. The number of New York City breweries shrank by about 10 percent between 1880 and 1890. The restructuring of the brewing business not only eliminated the workers' chance to become independent operators; it also affected their status as wage earners, for mechanization resulted in a gradual elimination of diversity and skills, and, in time, elimination of jobs altogether. It also increased the general intensity of work. The rift between expectation and realities, traditional rules and new demands, became the prime source of discontent for New York's brewers, as it did for so many other workers.[12]

But the social isolation of the brewery workers, enforced by the long and exhausting work and its low wages, kept New York's brewers until relatively late from organizing a union. As late as 1881, New York's brewery workers had no labor organization of their own; they seemed untouched by the political activism that had swept through most other parts of the city's labor movement during the late 1870s.[13] Like their German colleagues, German-American brewery workers showed little interest in any type of organization devoted to labor interests before the 1880s.

The quiet and harmony surrounding the brewery workers' community of New York was suddenly shattered when four workers at Peter Doelger's brewery in mid-Manhattan died in an explosion at the brewery on January 6, 1881. The accident attracted a great deal of attention in the press, and the Mayor was pressured into setting up a commission to look into the causes of the accident and find out who was responsible for it. The commission's investigation shed light on the working conditions in New York's breweries for the first time, and revealed the miserable working and living conditions of the brewery workers, to whom nobody had previously paid much attention. But although the commission failed to find a culprit for the accident, and since it could not find out who was responsible for the almost total lack of safety precautions at the brewery, the incident had the effect of rousing the brewery workers to take action.[14]

When the German American socialist daily *New Yorker Volkszeitung* announced a gathering of brewery workers in February

of 1881, about three hundred of them showed up, and 120 immediately signed up as members of the newly founded Union of
Journeymen brewers (Union der Brauergehuelfen). Within two
months, hundreds of brewers had joined the new union, which
included workers from Manhattan, Brooklyn, Staten Island, and New
Jersey. Organized on a shop basis, the group had low dues and was
open to all brewers in the New York City area. But, in fact, membership in the group was limited to the German-speaking workers in lager
beer breweries. Union meetings and discussions were always conducted in German. The German character of the *Verein* reflected
closely the traditionality and the relative isolation of the New York
lager beer brewers from the rest of the city's labor movement, even
from non-Germanic workers in their own trade. American and Anglo-
Irish brewery workers from the ale and porter breweries, for example,
had no part in this first brewery workers movement in New York.[15]

Monthly dues entitled the members of the brewery workers
organization to union representation in case of conflict with their
employers. Unlike other organizations, the journeymen brewers union
had no benefit program and, at first, no political program. Instead, the
young organization concentrated all of its energies on attracting as
many new members as possible in order to fortify its claim as the sole
bargaining agent in New York City's breweries. Despite its low-key
politics, the union in its organizing drive met with considerable
resistance from the employers, which, however, did not at first
threaten the union's existence.[16] But in June of 1881, the union struck
for a twelve-hour day, launching a serious confrontation with the
employers. The brewery owners refused to accede to the workers'
demands for a shorter workday and an end to Sunday work. The difficulties of organizing a large-scale strike and beer boycott soon over-
whelmed the young labor union. With no system of strike support in
place and a sizable number of non-unionized workers in the
breweries, the brewery workers organization officially surrendered to
the employers in early July.[17] After this decisive defeat, the group
swiftly began to disintegrate, and by the fall of 1881 the union of
Journeymen Brewers had ceased to exist.[18]

It was not until the fall of 1884 that a small band of journeymen
brewers renewed their efforts to fight the long hours and low wages
of their trade by again founding a trade union. After the bitter experience of 1881, the group, which was affiliated with the Knights of
Labor, remained a secret organization, a fact that hampered its growth
considerably. The prospects of the brewery workers' organization
began to improve when the New York Central Labor Union
announced in late January 1885 that "it had worked out a specific
organizing plan for all brewery workers which looks very promising

and whose realization will be undertaken in the coming days." The systematic organizing attempt of the CLU was off to a successful start. A specially appointed committee held well-attended mass meetings for workers at specific lager beer breweries. At times as many as two-thirds of those present signed up with the union (which, though no longer a secret organization, kept a very low profile).[19] But in March 1885 the campaign ran into its first obstacle: Peter Doelger, owner of the brewery that was the site of the accident in 1881, dismissed all workers who had joined the new union. Although the CLU immediately called for a boycott of Doelger's beer, the organization had problems in winning the broad support necessary to fight Doelger effectively. Only four small breweries were completely organized. The majority of the city's skilled lager beer brewers were still not members of the union and were therefore hard to reach by the Central Labor Union. Even those few workers who were contacted feared dismissal if they sided openly with their colleagues. Confronted with seemingly united and hostile employers, the union seemed seriously endangered in the spring of 1885.[20]

In this difficult period the union benefitted from the crisis in which the metropolitan brewing industry found itself in 1885–1886. In the mid-1880s New York's brewery bosses faced severe competition in their home territory for the first time. A few large breweries in St.Louis and Milwaukee – the so-called shippers – had begun to expand their reach beyond the Midwest and sell in the New York area. In addition, a group of British investors bought a number of Midwestern breweries and began to market their product aggressively in competition with the big shippers. A price war ensued during which the wholesale price for beer fell by as much as 50 percent in some localities.[21]

The New York area brewers at first watched these events with considerable apprehension. But, in contrast to their Midwestern colleagues, they showed remarkable cohesion. In 1882 they had formed the United Lager Beer Brewers of New York and vicinity, an organization which successfully engineered a number of regional trade agreements. Prices were fixed for all member breweries and rebates for saloonkeepers were forbidden. Thus, at least among New York brewers, competition was kept to a minimum during much of the 1880s. Such concerted action was only possible because most of New York's breweries remained family businesses. Only two firms sold out to British investors and only one, George Ehret's brewery, began to market its beer outside the New York area. The city's brewers remained a cautious group, following a continuous but relatively unaggressive expansion strategy.

Instability, be it from unregulated competition or labor unrest, had to be avoided. In this situation a few key members of the United Lager Beer Brewers of New York and Vicinity (who also held office in the national parent group, the United States Brewers Association) began to seek an accommodation with the New York brewery workers union.[22]

In the summer of 1885 Henry Scharmann, a Brooklyn brewer, and Richard Katzenmayer, Secretary of the United Lager Beer Brewers, secretly paid a visit to union Secretary Louis Herbrandt. As Herbrandt later recalled they asked him if the union was "willing to make an agreement with the bosses." "Well, I was at that time astonished to hear something like that from a brewer boss," observed Herbrandt. He was also hesitant about accepting such an offer, for despite the help from the Central Labor Union, his own union's organization was still incomplete and its membership relatively small. The employers' confident response was that "they would attend to that," and Herbrandt finally indicated his organization's willingness to enter into an agreement with the brewery owners.[23]

During the following ten months, the members of the United Lager Beer Brewers embarked on a vigorous membership drive, encouraging their employees to join the brewery workers union. One worker later remembered that at his brewery "several times circulars were posted up, enjoining the men to join the union." Since the workers showed no intention of doing so, the owner decided "that on a certain day in February, they had to join the union, . . . and whoever did not join the union would be dismissed." With the aid of such drastic methods, twelve breweries in the New York area were organized by the end of 1885, and in late March 1886 the brewery workers in 56 New York area lager beer breweries had joined the brewery workers organization, which by then had over fifteen-hundred members – 90 percent of all the skilled lager beer brewers in Greater New York. The unionization campaign of the Central Labor Union had thus reached an enormously successful end. The fact that much of his success followed from an agreement of cooperation with the brewery owners remained unacknowledged. Instead, the Central Labor Union leaders attributed their success to their vigorous and convincing organizing work, and ignored or failed to perceive the role of the bosses in furthering their movement.[24]

During the organization of the brewery workers in 1885–1886, the brewer's union kept in the background. Union officials were never mentioned in the progress reports. Instead, the CLU's organizing committee coordinated and arranged everything. As a result, the entire campaign was somewhat de-politicized. Although the CLU had earlier gained a profile as a progressive, pro-socialist organization, it did not openly advocate a clear political program while coordinating and organizing the brewery workers. The brewery workers' union remained so much in the background that we know almost nothing about the political beliefs of its members during 1885 and early 1886. The only demand consistently brought up by the union was for the closed shop.[25]

The political profile of the union became more evident when, with most of New York's lager beer breweries organized, negotiations began in 1886 for a citywide contract between union representatives and the employers. The union's leaders gave the highest priority to the recognition of their organization as the sole legitimate representative of the workers, although to be sure they did not fail to demand shorter working hours and a general improvement of working conditions as well as higher wages. After a few weeks of secret negotiations, the union and the New York City area lager beer brewers signed an agreement covering the workers in 58 New York area breweries for one year.[26]

The contract clearly improved the lives of most New-York-area brewery workers. No worker would work more than 12 hours a day, Sunday work would be paid double, and wages would be fixed on a sliding scale ranging from $10 a week for apprentices to $18 for the most qualified workers. The agreement also contained a number of clauses eliminating oppressive rules that had circumscribed the lives of brewery workers: single workers would not have to live in employer-chosen boarding houses any more, and henceforth the union – and not saloonkeepers as was commonly the case before – would recommend workers to prospective employers. By helping to abolish the worst leftovers of quasi-feudal dependency for the brewery workers and improving their economic position, the union had won a major victory and had shown itself to be a pragmatic and forceful organization of skilled workers.

At the same time the contract contained a number of provisions giving the brewery workers union almost the role of a craftsmen's guild. It thus not only fixed the terms of apprenticeship for young brewers, but also determined that after three years of training apprentices would have to pass an examination given by the union in order to become full-fledged journeymen and union members. Journeymen brewers would broaden their skills by being promoted regularly to different (and better-paying) jobs within the brewery, a process overseen jointly by the union and the employers. Another important indication of the cooperative craft spirit of the agreement was the creation of an arbitration panel, consisting of three brewery workers (usually union officials) and four brewery owners, which would mediate all disputes.[27]

The agreement of 1886 marked the first time that an entire major New York industry was covered by a union contract. This momentous achievement should not obscure the fact that the contract reflected the split identity of the union and its members. On the one hand, the union had acted as a progressive force pushing up its members' working and living standards toward that of other organized skilled workers; on the other hand, the brewery workers had assumed the position of a craftsmen's guild guarding over the craft's continuity and the value of the brewer's skill. What really united the union members despite their profoundly divided, perhaps contradictory, politics, was their common culture: their union was an ethnic organization of Germans who continued to live in a close-knit, somewhat isolated community.

Nowhere did this amalgam of of traditional German craft-consciousness and progressive optimism become more obvious than during the flag dedication ceremony of New York's brewery workers union in the summer of 1887. The union's flag, which bore a very close resemblance to the banner of the Berlin Journeymen Brewers Union founded in 1885, was red, as the members proudly pointed out (and the employers noted with some misgivings). Stitched on the red silk was the squat figure of Gambrinus, legendary god of beer drinkers and beer makers from Roman times, with a large beer mug in his hands. He was surrounded by a garland of hops and traditional German brewer-guild inscriptions such as "Hops and Malt – May God Preserve Them" (*Hopfen und Malz – Gott erhalts!*) and the Union motto, "Victory through Struggle" (*Durch Kampf zum Sieg*). The President of the New York union interpreted the flag and its inscriptions as follows:

> With the extinction of the guilds, the brewers' flag also lost its significance and its bearers rested on their laurels for too long. But now the time of enlightenment has come, the brewers guild, which had been asleep for so long, has woken up and is demanding its rights. The flag is unfurled anew and flutters ahead of the fighting troops, just as in olden times, in its fight against the modern day robber barons.[28]

In an effort to overcome the isolation of its members, the brewery workers' union made an effort to become active in the New York City labor movement in the months after the first contract was signed. The union became more active in the Central Labor Union, through which it was involved in the mayoralty campaign for Henry George during the Fall of 1886. In the following years, the union consistently sided with the socialist unions in the Central Labor Union, in keeping with the strong socialist sympathies of its leaders. All in all, though, the brewery workers' union stayed in the background of the socialist labor movement of the city.[29]

The union's relations remained much more problematic with the Knights of Labor than with any other labor group. Conflicts with the Knights began in 1886, when the brewery workers' union and the Knights began to compete for members in the ale and porter breweries of New York. Traditionally, the workers in these firms were English and Irish, and with the German brewery workers showing no interest in them, they organized into a Knights of Labor Assembly in 1886. By the end of that year, however, the German brewery workers' union did make belated attempts to organize the increasing number of German workers in those breweries under their auspices. After much disagreement and an open break with the Knights, the German brewery workers' union organized a separate local for German workers in ale and porter breweries, which had a stormy coexistence with the English Ale and Porter Union for years to come. The union of lager beer brewers thus continued to identify itself primarily as an ethnic craft organization, which limited its ability to forge an effective industrywide coalition or widen its political influence in the labor movement.[30]

The repercussions of the conflict between the brewery workers union and the Knights had little effect during 1887–1888, since these years were a time of prosperity for the city's brewing industry. Because of the generous wages fixed in the contract of 1886, and renewed in 1887, the brewery workers took part in this prosperity, in a modest way. The contract made them the best-paid brewery workers in North America. The favorable conditions of the contract were unusual enough to attract hundreds of German immigrants to the city's breweries after 1886. "Since the contract has been signed, New York has been swamped with brewery workers," New York's lager beer union reported, a bit worried. "Every steamer arriving from Germany has lately brought a great many colleagues from overseas who, drawn by high wages, have left the fatherland to make their fortunes."

Despite generally good business prospects in New York, this influx of immigrant brewers soon created unemployment problems in lager beer breweries. In order to protect its interests and the status of its members, Local 1 therefore decided to implement a drastic measure: beginning in March 1887, prospective candidates for union membership had to be nominated by union members and, upon acceptance, had to pay the high initiation fee of $20. A month later, the fee was raised to $50, a measure of no immediate consequence, since no new members were being accepted for the time being. Newly arrived workers were told to find work in the hinterland. In officially barring new members, the union had once again affirmed its role as a guardian over the status of the craftsmen who were its constituents.[31]

But despite their concern for craft preservation, the union leaders were, unlike their pre-industrial predecessors, well aware that the ultimate solution to the competition for jobs lay in a national union movement. Only if a unified organization of brewery workers succeeded in forcing up wages for brewery workers everywhere in the country could the New York workers hope to retain their relatively comfortable position. Encouraged by local labor groups, socialist activists and, in some cities, the Knights of Labor, activists helped lager beer workers in the brewing centers of Milwaukee, Chicago, St.Louis, Detroit, Cincinnati, and Newark, and a number of other cities to form unions by the spring of 1887. Most of these groups espoused a mix of craft consciousness and socialist politics similar to the New York union, although in some cities the socialist leanings were predominant, while in others the union remained more decisively conservative. Five of the local groups met in August 1886 to form the National Union of United Brewery Workmen of the United States (NUUBW). The head of the New York brewery workers union, Louis Herbrandt, was elected as Secretary, and New York City became the headquarters of the new National Union. During its first 18 months the NUUBW grew to encompass 21 locals. New York City's Local 1 led in membership size and political influence, although the National Union remained a heterogenous group without the strict hierarchical leadership of other unions.[32]

In 1887, during its second year, the National Union began to expand its reach beyond the traditional community of skilled lager beer brewers and started to organize skilled workers in brewery-related trades such as brewery firemen (who tended the kettles), beer wagon drivers, and maltsers. The union was also making efforts to organize brewery machinists and coopers. Without compromising its craft union beliefs, this expansion served to expand the membership base of the union, especially significant because of the increasing importance of workers in supply and distribution for many breweries. Although no changes were made in the union's emphasis on craft preservation, the organization of brewery-related trades under the auspices of the NUUBW in fact meant that the union was adjusting to the need for industrial union organization.[33]

The response of the brewery owners all over the country to the unionization of their work force varied. In a few smaller cities such as Albany and Buffalo they shared the cooperative approach of the New York brewers and signed a contract amicably. But on the whole the tactics of the New York brewery owners were not widely emulated. In Detroit, Baltimore, and San Francisco the union gained recognition and a contract only after a strike. In the Midwestern breweries of St. Louis and Milwaukee, the union met almost continuous resistance from employers. Although agreements were reached for about a year at least in Milwaukee and St. Louis, the unions there did not win the right to a closed shop. Big shippers, such as Milwaukee's Pabst and Anhauser-Busch in St. Louis, shared little of the cooperative spirit of the New York brewers. They remained adamantly opposed to the unionization of their work force under the auspices of the NUUBW. For them there was nothing to gain from the stability that a union contract would bring, since expansion of the market and a higher profit margin was their main goal. Rather than carefully delineating one's market share through sales agreements with the competition and wage contracts with the workers, the big shippers preferred to meet the competition head-on and to win new markets with lower prices. The big firms tried to win over a majority of the members of the United States Brewers Association (USBA) to their hard-line stand against the union as early as 1886, but at first they were not successful in doing so.[34]

It was not until a national consolidation of the beer market was complete that the hard-liners' position prevailed. By the late 1880s, conditions had stabilized again and the market was expanding practically everywhere. With the price wars over and labor-saving technology (artificial refrigeration, steam engines, and bottling machinery) in place in all larger breweries, the union was perceived as the major national stumbling block to higher profits. Wages had risen nationwide for skilled brewers, and by 1887 the union was also beginning to raise the wage levels of workers in the auxiliary trades. Despite the simplification of many tasks through the use of machines, employers could not replace their journeymen brewers with semi-skilled workers, for in many cities the union saw to it that only skilled union members found employment. "Conditions have become intolerable," complained the United States Brewers Association in 1888; "the unwonted power conceded to these unions has in innumerable instances been abused for the perpetration of tyrannical exactions and petty, humiliating annoyances." The obstacles placed by the union in the way of expansion of the brewing business was perceived by the brewery owners as a national problem by 1887, and the USBA looked for a national solution for it.[35]

The opportunity to strike out against the brewery workers organization presented itself in the fall of 1887 when a strike of malthouse workers in Milwaukee for higher wages led to a union-sponsored nationwide boycott of Milwaukee beer. The Milwaukee malthouse strike not only led to a unilateral cancellation of the local union contract by the Milwaukee brewers, but also proved to be the catalyst for a series of secret meetings of the United States Brewers Association in New York City in late 1887 and early 1888 in which an aggressive anti-union stand was adopted by most members of the Association. By the spring of 1888 the New York brewery owners had, after two years of accomodationist policies, decided to adopt the hard-line stance of their Midwestern colleagues, and the USBA had decided to make New York the proving ground for its new tactics. On March 26, 1888, less than two weeks before the beginning of a new labor contract, the United States Brewers Association published a lengthy list of accusations against the brewery workers union, alleging that "On a comparatively small number of men, the leaders in the national and local brewery workmen's unions rests the responsibility for the misdirection and wilful abuse of power mistakenly granted to labor organizations in the settlement of labor questions." More specifically the owners alleged that the union leaders had gone so far as to "prostitute their sway over the minds and actions of brewery workmen, by drawing them into affiliation with anarchism. . . ."

The members of the USBA concluded that "after the expiration of the contract now existing, no new agreements between the brewery proprietors and the brewery workmen shall be entered into."[36] The breweries of greater New York, with their exemplary labor relations, were thus declared the first and primary battle zone in the USBA's attempts to break the union.

Since the leaders of Local 1 had been careful to keep the Milwaukee struggle from disturbing the cooperative mood of the industry in New York, the renunciation of the partnership by the bosses came as a complete surprise for the unionists. Even after the publication of the manifesto, the New York unionists could not quite believe that the employers had abandoned their cooperative stance. The local's leaders were unwilling to call for a strike or boycott; instead of espousing the aggressive, confrontational tactics that were part of their socialist ideology, the union's leaders told their fellow workers to "wait patiently" and tried to start negotiations with individual breweries about a new contract. But the union's negotiating attempts yielded only meager results, with fewer than five small breweries signing contracts in the New York area; it became clear that, while the New York brewery workers' commitment to cooperative labor relations was as strong as ever, the employers had now abandoned their partnership with organized labor.[37]

Still, for the time being, the union was unwilling to adopt a more aggressive stand against the employers. Instead, the leaders of Local 1 called on the New York State Board of Mediation and Arbitration to settle the conflict. But before this panel could intervene, the Central Labor Unions of New York, Brooklyn, and Newark resorted to more militant tactics and declared a boycott against all beer made by the United Lager Beer Brewers on April 13. The brewery workers union itself did not endorse the boycott officially. The brewery owners for their part seem to have waited for a pretext for attack; disregarding the fact that the workers were still waiting to negotiate, they immediately published a declaration stating that "if the boycott was not lifted from a certain date, they would reorganize their workers." Since the central labor bodies showed no signs of dropping their boycott, the employers locked out five thousand workers in the Greater New York area on April 13. Brewery workers willing to sign a no-union pledge were accepted for re-employment a day later. But the majority of brewers stuck with the union and remained on the street, locked out from their own standpoint, on strike from the standpoint of the employers.[38]

Despite the fact that thousands of brewery workers were out of work, the operation of most firms was not in serious jeopardy. As it turned out, the brewery owners had long prepared for this conflict. Large quantities of beer had been brewed and delivered in the weeks before the lockout. Many breweries immediately hired unskilled workers, "Slovaks and Italians" as a union journal remarked disparagingly. But to fill all the gaps left by the locked-out journeymen, employers also recruited recent German immigrants from within the trade. Most of these "Greens" had been out of work since their arrival in the New World, in part because Local 1 had closed its membership a year earlier. The newly hired workers were also attracted by the fact that, at least for the time being, the brewery owners continued to pay the same wages as under the old contract and kept similar working hours. Soon, a rather large number of skilled brewers had taken the place of the locked-out unionists. The employers adopted a more flexible stand towards technical maintenance workers (engineers, firemen, etc.), who were harder to replace. These workers, many of whom were not unionized in any case, did not have to be part of the owners' no-union policy, since they had refused to join their colleagues and had stayed on the job. The brewmasters also remained in the breweries, although the foremen were locked out with the other workers.[39]

While the members of the United States Brewers Association were ready for the lockout, the union was not only ideologically but also organizationally unprepared for a showdown. The brewery workers' union could try to help its members in two ways: it could rely on its own financial and organizational resources, or it could ask for help from New York's labor community. At the beginning of the lockout, the union attempted to practice self-reliance. Offers of money from unions and individuals outside the brewers' trade were politely refused. But as time wore on, it became clear that the union could not survive on its own. Since neither the national nor the local union had regular strike support funds or unemployment benefits to offer to its members, the union had to draw on its regular funds and appeal to the generosity of brewery workers' unions in other cities. But the unions were not wealthy, and locals in other cities proved hesitant in their contributions. Local community support therefore became indispensable for the striking workers. Only by receiving energetic financial and political support from a wide variety of unions and working-class people in the city could the brewery workers' local hope to win its battle.[40]

A number of New York unions gave money and some workers' musical societies organized benefits, but only one thousand dollars were donated during the first month of the lockout, certainly not enough to support five thousand locked-out workers. And donations did not pick up much thereafter. Parts of the New York labor movement did try to lend organizational support by initiating a beer boycott. Since the union was locked out of virtually all lager beer breweries in New York and vicinity, very little union beer was available to the city's beer drinkers. A boycott of the hostile firms would therefore have come close to beer prohibition. Nevertheless, the member organizations of the Central Labor Union in New York and Brooklyn, especially the German-speaking trade unions, stood behind the idea of a boycott—at least officially. Some one hundred saloon keepers, whose support was crucial, were also won for the cause.

Despite energetic promotion of the boycott by the Central Labor Unions and the labor press, however, community support was far from universal. Almost all the organizations involved in the boycott were made up of German-Americans and were mostly socialist. District Assembly 49 of the Knights of Labor, which passed a token resolution of solidarity shortly after the lockout began, showed no further interest. Workers in the ale and porter breweries did nothing to promote the boycott, and very few English organizations showed any involvement at all in the brewers' conflict. The beer boycott turned out to be an issue only for the German-American community.[41]

As the failure of the boycott became evident after the first weeks of the lockout, hundreds of brewery workers decided to renounce their membership in the union and return to work. By late May, only five hundred workers – one tenth of the original number – were still locked out of the lager breweries in the greater New York area. After much political infighting, the Central Labor Unions of Newark and Brooklyn suspended the beer boycott in the middle of June. Only the New York Central Labor Union maintained the boycott, though without actually doing much to enforce it. By the early summer the employers had effectively destroyed the union's position as a powerful representative of New York's lager beer workers.[42]

But the brewery workers' union of New York City was not completely eliminated in 1888 as it had been in 1881. The locals of the lager beer brewers and the beer drivers survived, although with only about two hundred members between them. A dozen smaller breweries continued to recognize the union, which doubled within the next ten years thanks to the continuing work of the union to win back territory. But despite such efforts and growing attempts from unions affiliated with the American Federation of Labor, New York's brewery workers had to wait until 1903 to gain a new citywide contract. By the time a new contract had been negotiated, New York's brewers were among the lowest paid and longest working brewing workers in the country. Not that brewery workers' unions elsewhere had easily gained higher wages for less work. Following the example of their New York colleagues, employers locked out union members in most major brewing centers along the East Coast and in the Midwest in the spring and summer of 1888. But despite many initial defeats, the locals of the National Union of United Brewery Workmen survived this onslaught of the employers elsewhere better than in New York City. Especially in Midwestern cities with dominant German-American populations, the brewery workers' unions were less isolated than in New York. With the help of a relatively cohesive labor movement in many localities, many brewery workers' locals were therefore able to reorganize and win a contract back after a few years.[43]

The story of New York's German lager beer workers is an extreme case of the preservation and reformulation of European craft politics in the context of an industrializing trade. The solid persistence of quasi-feudal ways of work and life among the lager beer workers of the city was unusual and made it peculiarly difficult for unions to take hold. After years of struggle, the union was temporarily successful but only because it tried to fit into the traditions of the industry in two ways: First it assumed the position of a traditional craftmen's guild for the brewery workers of New York, and, second, it accepted the employers as partners in the task of preserving certain craft traditions in the industry.

But the union's tactic was based on flawed premises. By organizing on the basis of German craft traditions, the union isolated itself politically and culturally from large parts of the multi-ethnic New York labor movement. Instead of drawing support from a large group of other unions, the German brewery workers were forced into an uneasy alliance with either the none-too-powerful German-American socialists or with the employers with whom they presumably shared a special understanding of labor relations.

Ultimately brewery owners were ideologically much less committed to cooperative craft relations than the unionists. The union only slowly began to define itself in terms of an industrial labor organization and was unprepared for a large-scale confrontation in 1888. The brewery owners, on the other hand, entered the industrial age with less hesitation and dispensed with traditional notions of craft politics rather quickly in the late 1880s once this met their business needs.

Considering the size and the financial might of the brewing industry, the German-American brewery workers would perhaps have been unable to take on such a formidable enemy even if they had been better prepared ideologically and organizationally. In the mix of conflicting traditions and of increasing industrialization, the brewery workers' adherence to a strong ethnic craft unionism made union survival tenuous. Culturally defined unionism inhibited the development of a strong, politically defined industrial labor organization in one of New York's premier industries.

CHAPTER 11

Catholic Corporatism, French-Canadian Workers, and Industrial Unionism in Rhode Island, 1938–1956

GARY GERSTLE

What first attracted the practitioners of the new labor history to the turbulent 1930s was the hope of recovering a radical working-class tradition. Indeed, historians like Jeremy Brecher, Staughton Lynd, and James Green thought they had found a radical democratic spirit within the ranks of the country's mass production workers. This radical spirit, they claimed, is what gave workers the strength to escape the torpor of the American Federation of Labor, challenge the autocratic might of their employers and establish new (and potentially revolutionary) industrial unions. Pressed to explain the failure of this radical spirit to revolutionize American society, these historians have pointed an accusing finger at bureaucratic labor leaders and their willingness to crush the radical spirit of their followers to gain the support of employers and government officials for union activity.[1]

This interpretation, however, did not survive long. The more historians dug into the materials of the 1930s, the more elusive this radical spirit proved to be. Detailed reconstructions of the milieux of mass production workers—both at work and in their communities—revealed that radicalism was generally confined to small groups of skilled workers with long histories of trade union and political activity. These radical skilled workers played a central role in establishing the new industrial unions, but they did not radicalize the masses of semiskilled and unskilled workers who formed the majority of the rank and file. Historians have poured considerable energy into

209

describing the nonradical majority, and they have given us a much firmer grasp of the composition and character of the American working class of the 1930s. We have a much greater appreciation for the significance of ethnicity, generation, age, and skill in shaping the outlook and behavior of rank-and-file workers. We now know how central the ethnic experience is to an understanding of the American working class; mass production industries – auto, steel, coal mining, electrical manufacturing, Northern textiles – depended especially heavily on the labor of first-, second- and third-generation immigrants, mostly from southern and eastern Europe, but from Ireland and French Canada as well.[2] What remains somewhat obscure, however, is the relationship of that ethnic experience to the particular course of development followed by organized labor.

John Bodnar is one of the few historians to confront this problem directly. He claims to have found among his Slavic steel and coal workers of western Pennsylvania an overriding preoccupation with economic security and family sustenance that bred a distrust of abstract ideas like equality, social justice, or democracy, so important to radical movements. Bodnar locates the source of this "working-class realism" partly in the ethnic culture of these Slavic workers, and partly in the structure of employment opportunity that they experienced in twentieth-century America. Although he does not carry his analysis into the post–World-War-II era, the implications of his work for the character of organized labor in the 1950s seem clear: The realistic, pragmatic values of these workers explain the increasing preoccupation of unions with minimalist, bread-and-butter demands for higher wages, more employment security, better pensions, and adequate medical insurance.[3]

Bodnar's effort to explain the postwar labor movement in terms of the aspirations of the rank and file represents an important innovation in the study of American labor. But his determination to show his Slavic workers as without interest in abstract ideas or ideology seems curiously reductionist. A lack of interest in radical ideas does not imply a lack of interest in ideas, per se. How do we fit a fictional character like Dobie – a third-generation Slavic steel worker in Thomas Bell's novel, *Out of This Furnace*, who sees unionism as the fulfillment of America's revolutionary heritage – into Bodnar's portrait of pragmatic, non-ideological workers? Likewise, how do we incorporate all those churches – next to the steel furnaces, the most ubiquitous and striking physical presence in steel towns – into Bodnar's portrait?[4] Is not religion a source of ideas and idealism? Should we not consider its influence on the world of the 1930s worker?

The answer should be a resounding yes. Yet what is striking is how little we know about religion and the working class in the 1930s and 1940s. David O'Brien and Mel Piehl have written fine books on the ferment within the Catholic Church hierarchy and among small groups of radical Catholic activists in the 1930s that led to much greater involvement of priests and lay Catholics in movements of social reform.[5] Ronald Schatz, in his book on electrical workers and unionism in the 1930s, has made one of the first efforts to move beyond the institutional walls of the church and examine the actual relations between particular priests and particular groups of workers. And Schatz has been one of the few labor historians to look into the Catholic contribution to the doctrine of corporatism as it developed in the first half of this century. His work, rich in description of actual campaigns undertaken by priests to rid local unions of communists, and of schools set up by Catholic dioceses to disseminate their views of the proper relation between capital and labor, has given us a much firmer grasp of the efforts of the Church to shape the character of the American labor movement.[6]

What were the effects of such efforts? Schatz, and O'Brien as well, have shied away from general conclusions about the influence of religion and of the Church on the American labor movement. Their reluctance stems in part from the flawed generalizations put forward by Marc Karson, a political scientist who claimed, in the 1950s, that Catholic influence on the American Federation of Labor in the years 1900 to 1918 explained the AFL's conservative, non-socialist character; by extension, he implied, the control exercised by an anti-radical Church over American Catholics—who formed a majority of the American working class—explained why socialism failed to take root in the United States. Karson, of course, had difficulty explaining how the heavily Catholic working classes of France, Germany, and Italy made possible the rise of powerful socialist and communist parties in those countries. Even more damaging to his argument was the fact that American socialism thrived for much of the period that Karson studied, from 1900 to 1918. Its sorry state in 1919 owed much more to its opposition to American participation in World War I than to priest-ridden American workers.[7]

What misled Karson were two erroneous convictions: first, that the Church inevitably stood on the side of privilege, and, second, that the Church's centralized hierarchical structure made Catholic parishioners passive recipients of whatever values their pope, cardinals, or bishops told them to hold dear. The first conviction led Karson to ignore the radical interpretations that could be extracted—and that groups of bishops, priests, and lay Catholics occasionally did extract — from papal encyclicals. The second conviction induced Karson to think that any anti-radical, anti-labor edict issued by a well-placed churchman quickly became the law for Catholic America.

Schatz and O'Brien, unlike Karson, have stressed the progressive side of Catholic doctrine. And both have realized that the influence of religious doctrine on lay Catholics workers must be traced, not simply assumed. Their efforts to track such influence have reinforced their appreciation for the complexity of the task. Papal encyclicals calling for social activism, they discovered, were susceptible to varying interpretations. Interpretations of these encyclicals varied from diocese to diocese and from one community to another. Moreover, even if one could demonstrate that the attitudes of a community of Catholics closely resembled those set forth in a papal encyclical, could one prove that rank-and-file Catholics learned those attitudes through their Church? O'Brien has suggested that the popularity of anti-communism in Catholic communities may have stemmed not simply from religious doctrine but also from the desire of Catholics to prove the compatibility of Catholicism with Americanism. "As nothing was more Catholic than anticommunism," he has written, "so there was nothing more fully American."[8] Similarly, Schatz has noted that "the very popularity of the anti-Communist, quasicorporatist brand of industrial unionism espoused by the church [in the 1930s] . . . makes clerical influence . . . difficult to isolate."[9]

Complicating matters even further was the manner in which the Church chose to exercise influence. Clerical activists did not attempt to set up Catholic unions along the European model; rather they set up cadre organizations, like the Association of Catholic Trade Unionists, to work as pressure groups within the existing unions. Members of such organizations sought power not by enrolling as many unionists as possible but by persuading them, through agitation and argument, to support ACTU positions. Thus their success cannot be measured by the number of members of Catholic labor organizations.[10]

Such empirical difficulties underscore the hazards of generalization. They point to the need for detailed studies of the relations between the Church and labor in particular locales and a case-by-case evaluation of the influence of the Church on union affairs. Only then will we be able to draw some general conclusions about the degree to which Catholicism served as a source of "working-class idealism" that not only helped Catholic workers endure the realities of their lives but also encouraged them to imagine ways in which those lives might be transformed.

This case study focuses on the influence of religion and the church on the predominantly French-Canadian work force of Woonsocket, a major woolen and worsted textile manufacturing center of fifty thousand inhabitants in northern Rhode Island. In Woonsocket, a small group of skilled workers set out in 1931 to organize the city's textile workers into an industrial union. In the next eight years, the union, the Independent Textile Union (ITU), conducted 41 strikes involving more than twenty thousand workers. It won recognition and collective bargaining agreements from three-fourths of the 50 textile manufacturing plants in the city. It became a powerful and progressive force in city politics, and emerged as the leading voice for labor in the state of Rhode Island. It made Woonsocket into a city of militant trade unionists who through their union achieved significant measures of control over their jobs and elements of social democracy in their city life.[11]

A group of European socialists from northern France and Belgium founded the union and provided its early leadership. From the beginning, however, the union's success depended on the ability of a secondary leadership group of French-Canadian skilled workers to forge links between the Europeans and the predominantly French-Canadian rank and file. The two leadership groups – (European and French Canadian) – had a great deal in common – a sense of economic injustice, a desire to secure the rights and privileges of citizenship for American workers and make American society more responsive to working-class aspirations. But the two groups had great difficulty in reconciling their contrasting aspirations and in hammering out a common political program.

The radicals – close to but not members of the Socialist Party – hoped to use the Wagner Act and the language of industrial democracy to democratize capitalist enterprise and gradually inaugurate a socialist society. French-Canadian skilled workers enthusiastically participated in the class insurgency embodied in the rise of Woonsocket's industrial union but did not imbibe the radicals' commitment to a fundamental transformation of the social order. Their enthusiasm for the ITU was tied much more to a desire to defend themselves and their families from further economic calamity, and to find a way of adapting their rich but burdensome ethnic identity to the realities of American industrial society.[12] These desires did not really cohere into a political vision of how American society should be transformed until the French Canadians discovered in the late 1930s, through their local Catholic clergy, the notion of corporatism.

Corporatist doctrine offered them a potent way to merge their class and ethnic identities. It provided religious sanction to the strug-

gles of these French-Canadian workers to establish strong industrial
unions to represent class interests. It allowed them to justify their
decade-long fight against unregulated capitalism at the same time that
it opened up an avenue of rapprochement with their traditional
religious authorities. In other words, it allowed these workers to
legitimate their claims as American workers while reconciling
themselves to the most important traditions within their ethnic
heritage. The desire of these workers for rapprochement pulled them
toward the Church and away from the radicals. Long smoldering
feuds erupted into open battles in 1939 and continued until the
French-Canadian skilled workers ousted the radicals in 1945.

Two aspects of the Woonsocket story are of particular interest
here: first, the role of local Catholic clergy in promoting the triumph
of the French-Canadian skilled workers, and second, the consequences of that triumph for both the Church and the union.

Woonsocket Catholic clergy's embrace in the 1930s of corporatist
industrial relations doctrine required a fundamental reorientation in
the character and practice of their Catholicism. Most Woonsocket
clergy, trained in Québecois seminaries, had long defined their role
not only in terms of the propagation of the faith but also in terms of
the preservation of a French-Canadian ethnic identity. Since the
establishment of Woonsocket's first French-Canadian national parish
in 1875, clergy from Québec had extolled from their pulpits the virtue
and godliness of pre-industrial French-Canadian society, when their
people had formed a nation of subsistence farmers devoted to the
land, their families, and their church; and the clergy impressed on
their parishioners the importance both of preserving the language,
faith, and manners of their ancestors and of looking forward to the
day when they might escape industrial labor and return to the land.
Their preachings and parish activities contributed to the formation of
vigorous ethnic communities in places like Woonsocket, where, in the
1920s, the children and grandchildren of French-Canadian immigrants frequently spoke French before they learned English.[13]

Such tightly-knit ethnic communities, steeped in the pre-industrial
and corporatist values of its clergy, would have been among the first,
it seems, to embrace the critique of laissez-faire capitalism and the
advocacy of corporatism imbedded in Pope Leo's pathbreaking 1891
encyclical, *Rerum Novarum*. Nowhere were the ill effects of industrial
capitalism clearer than in textile cities like Woonsocket: The
chronically low wages and long hours and the heavy reliance on the
labor of women and children offered sobering confirmation of the
evils of unregulated capitalism noted by the Pope[14]

But Woonsocket Catholic clergy did not support or even condone
the establishment of unions, not even Catholic ones. Only in the

encouragement they gave to parishioners to escape industrial labor and return to the land in rural Québec can one detect an opposition to capitalism. Thus in communities like Woonsocket where the influence of the Catholic clergy was considerable, trade unionism was weak. In stark contrast to textile cities like Fall River and Lawrence with large populations of English, Irish, and Italian workers, movements of working-class protest in Woonsocket remained small and ineffectual.[15]

The involvement of thousands of Woonsocket French Canadians in the ITU in the 1930s was not the first time that these parishioners had gone against the wishes of their church. In fact, union involvement among French Canadians in Woonsocket had been on the rise since 1910, especially among French-Canadian workers who had moved into the skilled ranks where they encountered the traditions of craft unionism. In the 1920s, the combined force of a depression in cotton textiles, an Americanizing Irish diocese in Providence, and nativist legislation passed by the Rhode Island legislature generated considerable conflict within Woonsocket's ethnic community, weakened the authority of the clergy, and stimulated interest in unions.[16] But no union effort prior to the ITU's had gained the power or numbers necessary to challenge the primacy of *la survivance* – the survival of French-Canadian religion, values, and customs in Woonsocket life.

The radical leaders of the ITU intended to do just that. Ultimately the success of their union, they felt, depended on their ability to wean French-Canadian workers from their ethnic vision and their ethnic authorities, and induce them to accept secular and radical visions of social transformation.

Woonsocket clergy first reacted with bewilderment to the emergence of a powerful union among their parishioners. They were stunned by the militance displayed by French-Canadian workers in a citywide strike in 1934 that left two dead and more than a score wounded. A few realized that something was seriously wrong in their local society, and that the Church ought to involve itself more in the social problems of its parishioners.[17] But not until the Depression had continued for another four years and the union had grown to the point where it was bidding to become the city's most powerful institution did the local clergy find the will to reform their religious practice and a way to re-establish the power of their church in Woonsocket French-Canadian society.

In a striking turnaround in 1938, local clergy and their supporters quite suddenly began advocating the rights of labor and the positive role that trade unions would play in a reconstructed social order. The clergy learned its industrial relations from Pope Pius XI's encyclical,

Quadragesimo Anno, issued in 1931, on the fortieth anniversary of *Rerum Novarum,* to reaffirm the Church's commitment to social action. The twin evils of greedy capitalists and godless communists, wrote Pius XI, had seriously weakened the social order; the clergy had a vital role to play in social reconstruction. Pius XI advocated a middle way between the laissez-faire of the right and the collectivism of the left. Such a way had to address the grievances of wage earners, increase their stake in society and encourage them to look beyond their own interests to the general social welfare. The social doctrine of corporatism, Pius XI suggested, should guide clergy in their efforts. Corporatism meant a humane and regulated capitalism made possible by the organization of society's main occupational groups – capitalists, workers, farmers, professionals, small businessmen – into guild-like bodies that would simultaneously promote the interests of their members and enlarge each group's consciousness of its dependence, for its own well-being, on the welfare of other groups. In this doctrine a substantial role was accorded the state; it would both promote the self-organization of various occupational groups and negotiate and resolve group conflicts.[18]

The willingness of some European religious leaders to use corporatism as justification for support of Mussolini's regime led European liberals and radicals to label the doctrine "fascist" in the 1930s. But there was nothing intrinsically fascist about corporatism. Papal corporatist theory did not glorify the state or justify the subordination of society's corporate groups to the will of the state. The state was merely an instrument for resolving group conflicts; it was an artificial, human creation that could never achieve the status accorded those occupational groups that sprang naturally (and thus divinely) out of society's social division of labor. Thus clergy could easily find in *Quadragesimo Anno* a justification for a more limited kind of state intervention than the sort Mussolini and other fascists advanced.

Indeed, a significant group of American clergy, inspired by the writings of Monsignor John Ryan, believed that Roosevelt's New Deal conformed to corporatist theory far better than Mussolini's fascist state. They became unabashed supporters both of the new industrial unions and of the state's efforts, through the Wagner Act, to establish order and stability in capital-labor relations.[19] Other clergy believed that even the New Deal represented too great an exercise of state power, as it threatened unacceptable interference with such essential underpinnings of the social order as the family and private property. Such disagreement within the Church makes it impossible to link papal corporatism to a single political vision; what made the theory so important was the impetus it gave clergy to participate in secular political debates and social movements seeking to define a new social order. Even those Catholics, like Peter Maurin of *The Catholic Worker,* who rejected the corporatist paradigm altogether, found in the papal encyclicals a powerful spur to Catholic social activism.[20]

Woonsocket priests and their lay allies advocated a form of corporatism similar to the one put forward by Monsignor Ryan and his followers. Setting aside a fifty-year tradition of anti-unionism, they began to speak in support of the rights of labor and to argue for the positive role that trade unions would play in a reconstructed corporatist social order. *L'Indépendant,* the city's French weekly with close ties to local clergy, introduced readers in 1940 to the concept of corporatism and emphasized its endorsement by the Pope. The newspaper reported approvingly the statement by a group of American bishops that laissez-faire capitalism "exploited workers and violated their human rights." It hailed the Wagner Act as legislation that would reduce exploitation, protect human rights and thus procure the social stability so central to a corporatist vision. Never before in the ethnic community's history had its leaders shown such a willingness to align themselves with capitalism's critics. For the first time as well, they advocated collective bargaining and worker organization into unions. Such developments, the editors of *L'Indépendant* pointed out, would restore rights to workers, guarantee their liberty and permit the reconstruction of the social order.[21]

Changing conceptions of spirituality reflected the local Catholic clergy's new concern for labor as well. To mark Labor Day in 1940, *L'Indépendant* published a piece entitled "La Noblesse du Travail." The author, a Montréal Jesuit, emphasized that the fate of labor under capitalism was "to become an instrument of degradation," resembling "the ancient slavery from which Christ delivered us." He rejected the view of Christian pessimists that work was inevitably drudge-like and alienating, as yet another price paid by humans for their sins. Earthly labor, he contended, could be ennobling. Labor that expressed the "original personality" of the worker produced a worthy, spiritual object, and fulfilled both divine and social purposes; it could serve as a providential bond linking the worker to society, the universe, and God. Through the noble labor of the individual, society could become like a single, harmonious city.[22]

The expression of such views in Woonsocket's French newspaper revealed how much the orientation of the local Catholic churches vis-à-vis labor had changed. The rise of organized labor in the city had compelled the local religious leaders to take the material concerns of its parishioners to heart and develop a view of the social order that accorded unions a prominent place. Some clergy went so far as to talk about the spirituality of labor and how work that was fulfilling brought men closer to God and brought the divine project on earth closer to completion. "La Noblesse du Travail" began to compete with *la survivance* for a central place in the Church's self-definition.

Clerical activism was motivated not only by a noble vision of heaven on earth but also by a fear of the social degeneration that would result from communism's triumph. In 1931 Pius XI spoke of laissez-faire and communism as comparable evils, but by 1937 communism frightened him more. His 1937 encyclical, *Divini Redemptoris*, sounded the tocsin against international communism and called on clergy to join an anti-communist crusade. This militant anti-communism, stimulated by such European events as the establishment of successful Popular Fronts in Spain and France, quickly crossed the Atlantic and powerfully influenced American Catholics.[23] American clergy moved easily from condemning communist participation in the anti-fascist loyalist forces in Spain to lashing out at the CIO for accommodating communists in its ranks. Some became so obsessed with identifying and condemning individuals with any connection, apparent or real, to the Communist Party, that they lost sight of the larger goal of social reconstruction. Many proved quite willing to dismiss the dangers of fascism in Europe and embrace uncritically the views of anti-communist conservatives at home.[24]

The clergy naturally had to oppose an ideology that denied the existence of God. And the Church's conception of the individual as simultaneously sacred and flawed had long made it a sharp critic of the omnipotence that communists wanted to confer on the state and the faith they expressed in human perfectability. But in places like Woonsocket, the church's anti-communism reflected more than a fear of communism itself. Rather, communism became in clerical hands an evocative representation of the secularist evil that had befallen the modern world. Priests in Woonsocket worried about their parishioners' waning commitment to ethnic survival and the consequent erosion of the clergy's own power and authority. They feared the success of a union in their midst, led by radicals who cared little for religion and who advocated an unabashedly secularist message. For some local priests, anti-communism became a way of justifying attacks on radicals, communist or not, who had done the most to promote the secularization of society. The sudden interest of clergy in union affairs in the late 1930s, then, was in part a calculated effort to oust the radical leaders of the ITU from their authoritative positions in the community and to re-establish the power of the church and the authority of its religious doctrines.[25]

Local clergy tried first to undermine the European-born radical leaders of the ITU by denouncing them in sermons. This strategy backfired: in 1938, union members attending mass at St. Anne's, the city's largest parish, walked out *en masse* in the midst of one Father Morin's anti-radical sermon.[26] Church leaders turned quickly to a more covert strategy. They organized a Catholic Workers' League, the Ligue Ouvrière Catholique, comprised of individuals selected for their leadership potential and their status in the working-class community, with the goal of reinjecting Christian values into the labor movement and re-establishing the importance of the parish as the institution best equipped to offer Catholic workers guidance in the problems of daily life. So successful was the church's covert strategy that union radicals knew nothing of this organization.[27]

The inspiration and direction of this Ligue came from Québec.[28] Québecois Jesuits helped to select for membership in the Ligue individuals who occupied strategic positions in the community and who had demonstrated leadership potential. Those selected were taken on retreats to Québec and instructed in subjects ranging from theology and papal encyclicals to leadership skills to family economics. Though many of the tasks they were called upon to undertake in Woonsocket, such as teaching mothers how to design family budgets, were simply meant to ease the day-to-day burdens of working-class life, one had a specific political aim; they were instructed to infiltrate Woonsocket's labor movement, propagate religious values, and oust the radicals.[29]

The Ligue took elaborate measures to disguise its counter-insurgency. It was designed not as a mass membership organization but as a vanguard group that would succeed (like the Communist Party) through the intelligence, dedication, and charisma of its cadre. Only a few individuals who demonstrated unshakable religious convictions were invited to join the organization. There were perhaps fifty members altogether, spread out among the city's six French-Canadian parishes. Each parish group, called a "cell," accepted directives from the "federation," the Ligue's governing council. The leaders of the federation, the Secretary and Chief Propagandist, worked closely with a local priest to develop plans to Christianize the labor movement in their midst. The two men who held these positions for much of the Ligue's ten-year existence, Arthur Fortin and Phileas Valois, were drawn from the ranks of the city's petty bourgeoisie. They occupied strategic positions at the crossroads of social intercourse in Woonsocket, one at a service station and the other at a grocery store. They orchestrated plans by Ligue members to make themselves available to Catholic workers in need, to inject their religious values into the currents of daily discourse and to stimulate opposition in the ranks of the union to its radical leadership.

The Ligue first took on the radical leadership of one of the union's largest locals. The Ligue's Chief Propagandist, Valois, recalls how a "whole bunch . . . maybe 15 or 20" European workers "were controlling . . . everybody there," making the local the one "we really wanted to go into." The Ligue wisely chose a sensitive religious issue to galvanize the French-Canadian rank and file into action. The radicals, charged Valois, had scheduled a meeting on Easter Sunday, "and all of our people were at Mass on Easter Sunday." This issue involved much more than religious freedom; it involved democracy as well. "I wanted to have the [French-Canadian] people working together, to have some part in the administration of the union – not just a little bit of it," Valois recalls.[30] The Ligue, in other words, intended to use the ITU's most potent ideological tool – democracy – against the radical leadership. By pushing their religious demands, French-Canadian workers would actually strengthen union democracy and thus fulfill the ideal most central to their union experience.

The Ligue's method of operation, however, was hardly a model of democratic procedure. Ligue cadre did not acknowledge their own role in the campaign to oppose the Easter Sunday union meeting. They chose the brother of a Ligue member who was also a representative of management – an overseer – to "pass the word" to ITU members in his department and to overseers in other departments. This overseer quickly mobilized sufficient support to force the meeting's cancellation.[31]

The episode was minor but significant, revealing a great deal about an alternative conception of unionism taking shape in Woonsocket. Most obviously, this conception put religion at the very center of union affairs; the religious habits of ITU members, the Ligue insisted, were to be respected, not merely tolerated or, at worst, subjected to the radicals' contempt. But the Ligue did not intend to substitute religion for democracy as the union's guiding principle. It argued, rather, that Catholicism and democracy were intimately linked, and that French Canadians, who made up the majority of union members, should shape union development and practice. The introduction of religiosity into union affairs, it asserted, represented the will of the majority and thus the fulfillment, not the denial, of the democratic ideal.[32]

This new conception of unionism also called for a vastly different set of relations between employer and employee. The fact that the Ligue was willing to work through an agent of management, as in the case of the Easter Sunday affair, is indicative of its members' desire to replace the radicals' commitment to class struggle with one of class harmony. Ligue members believed that the ties of religion could overcome the divisions resulting from class. Employers and employee would best serve their own interests by working together for the general welfare of their enterprise. The Ligue's perspective on industrial relations fit well with a mutualist ethic emerging from the shop-floor experience of many French-Canadian workers.

The emergence of this alternative conception of unionism posed a serious problem for union radicals. The strength of their union had long depended on their alliance with a group of French-Canadian skilled workers. The radicals had never seen eye-to-eye with these skilled workers with their ethnic ties. The latter had long resented the radical Europeans' higher socio-economic status – the French and Belgians held a disproportionate number of skilled and foremen positions in the mills – and bridled at the Europeans' tendency to assume the superiority of their secular Continental culture to the provincial Québecois heritage.[33] French Canadians were committed to the union and believed in the practice of democracy at the workplace and in the union. But they also wanted to reconcile their class and American identity with their ethnic heritage. Once clergy began to respond positively to the union in their midst and established the Ligue, reconciliation with the traditional ethnic leaders became possible. Ligue leaders worked closely with the French-Canadian skilled workers to develop an opposition to the radicals.[34]

In 1939, the French-Canadian skilled workers tried to oust the union's leading radical, Joseph Schmetz, from the union presidency. The manner in which this opposition group phrased its chief grievance – they depicted Schmetz "as a Hitler who rules with an iron hand" and labelled his leadership "autocratic and destructive" – resembles the tack used by the Ligue in the Easter Sunday affair.[35] In both instances, the radical leadership found itself stigmatized as an authoritarian European clique. In the short-term the opposition movement failed. The radicals rallied their supporters and won a stirring endorsement for their leadership. But the opposition had won its spurs in this fight and continued to gain in strength.

Local clergy, emboldened by the appearance of a strong conservative caucus in the union, went public with their denunciations of the radical leadership. Early in 1940, Reverend Stephen Grenier, pastor of Woonsocket's most prestigious French-Canadian parish, charged "that a communistic organization masquerading as an agency for the promotion of the industrial worker's welfare has established itself in Woonsocket and is working to sow the seeds of discord among employers and employees." He assured his parishioners that he believed in "the banding together of workers under a union standard," but declared his implacable opposition to "workers' organizations that looked to communists for leadership." He warned against supporting movements dedicated to "undermining . . . those principles on which this nation was founded."[36]

Though Grenier did not mention its name, the ITU was his target. It mattered little that none of the important ITU radicals could be identified as Communist Party members; a number of Catholic activists who supported Grenier's anti-communist campaign would later admit that many of the accusations they hurled against particular ITU leaders had little basis in fact.[37] At the time, however, what mattered was to strengthen the hand of the ethnic opposition in union affairs. Internal dissent spread in the union, increased the pressures on the radicals, and, in 1942, produced a serious split in their ranks. By 1945, the French-Canadian skilled workers had ousted the radicals and installed themselves in their place.[38]

The Ligue leaders who were interviewed claim an important role for their organization in removing the radicals from office. The character of the new ITU leadership certainly suggests the influence of the Ligue. References to God and Christianity became central to ITU discourse, marking a fundamental rejection of the secularism of the radical founders. ITU leaders opened the pages of their newspaper to the opinions of a Father Crépeau, a clerical expert on industrial relations. They endorsed the establishment of a diocesan labor school in Woonsocket and encouraged their members to attend. And their anti-communism increasingly became a mechanism for denouncing not just communists but all those who dissented from their constricted vision of a religious and patriotic America.[39]

The role of the Ligue in promoting this conservative triumph certainly seems to point to the re-establishment of clerical authority. This was true up to a point. But there were important limits to the clergy's authority. Just as the Church had not created the conservative caucus in the union, it did not control it. If Woonsocket Catholic clergy had enjoyed control over the conservative caucus, they would certainly have used it to re-establish the primacy of la survivance – a devotion to French-Canadian faith, language, and mores – among their unionist parishioners. Indeed, the decision of local clergy to model their Catholic workers' organization on the Québecois Ligue rather than on the native Association of Catholic Trade Unionists reflects their determination to preserve the connection with Québec and to continue their resistance to incorporation within the American Catholic Church.

But the cause of ethnic survival benefitted little from the triumph of the conservative unionists. On the contrary, the triumph of these ethnic corporatists pulled Woonsocket Catholics even further into the world of American Catholicism. Local clergy had long tried to maintain as great a distance as possible between their national parishes and the Americanizing influences of the Irish-controlled Providence diocese chancery twenty miles away. But as a result of their union experience—and especially their decade-long cooperation with class-conscious radicals—the new French-Canadian leaders of the ITU identified more as members of the American working class than of an exiled French-Canadian nation. They saw no reason to bar Irish priests from Woonsocket or obstruct diocesan policies; they welcomed pro-labor Irish priests into their communities and avidly participated in the activities of the diocesan Social Action Institute. They thus strengthened the ties of Woonsocket Catholics to the Providence diocese and accelerated the incorporation of French-Canadian Catholics into the American Church.

A poignant symbol of this incorporation was the dissolution of the Ligue in 1949 and the transfer of its membership to the Chicago-based Christian Family Movement. An earlier generation of French-Canadians in Woonsocket would have repudiated such a step as an unacceptable breach of *la survivance*, ethnic survival. This generation, however, saw the merger as an affirmation of their Catholic American identity. "The preamble of our American Constitution," noted ITU President Edwin Van Den Berghe in 1947, was as important an inspiration for ITU labor leaders as "the gospels of Jesus Christ."[40]

What were the consequences of the triumph of these ethnic workers for the union? It would be wrong to label the triumph reactionary or even conservative, for it preserved much of what the radicals in the 1930s had fought for. Drawing on the corporatist doctrines that local clergy had begun to disseminate in their ranks, the new leadership continued to speak out against the social evils of unbridled capitalism and to insist on the importance of union organization for social peace and industrial prosperity. They found in religious doctrine justification for their demands for a living wage, secure employment, and social security, and wholeheartedly committed themselves to the institutionalization of the welfare state. For a brief moment after their ascendancy to union power in 1945, they even endorsed a program of democratic national planning put forward by labor movement progressives Walter Reuther and Philip Murray and their left-liberal allies in the Democratic party. Nevertheless, these ethnic unionists still harbored a series of conservative political tendencies that, in the increasingly anti-labor climate spawned by the Cold War, would soon overwhelm their more radical inclinations. They increasingly exhibited, in 1946 and 1947, a discomfort with long and bitter strikes; a desire to dull the edge of class division through alliances with local clergy and local politicians; an excessive faith in the possibility of establishing a peaceful industrial order on the basis of mutual goodwill between employers and employees; and an excessive suspicion of dissenters and radicals, whether or not they had any connection to the Communist devil that these Catholics so deeply feared.

These tendencies might simply have secured Woonsocket labor a powerful niche in the emerging postwar political-economic order – which featured some of the corporatist arrangements that earlier papal encylicals had proposed – and brought a generation of northern Rhode Island workers secure jobs and high wages. But Rhode Island's textile industry entered a steep decline in the early 1950s as the area's industrialists began shutting down their Woonsocket operations. Capital flight caught the ITU organizationally and ideologically unprepared. The textile union, which had been one of New England's largest in the 1930s and 1940s, met a quick and bitter end. Most French-Canadian workers, suffering the loss of their jobs and the collapse of their union, despaired of politics altogether.[41]

In the few surviving mills where the union lived on, however, so did the corporatist values that this community of workers had recently embraced. In the Falls Yarn mill, a small woolen mill specializing in high quality yarn, for example, industrial relations approximated the corporatist dream from the 1940s through the 1970s. In this mill, a union veteran, Leonel Galipeau, reflected in 1980, "union and management worked for the same . . . goals. The owner makes a bunch, we make a bunch. And we had pride in workmanship. I don't want that . . . case of yarn going out if I can't put my name on it. He [the owner] doesn't want it to go out unless he can sell it at top price." Out of this sense of shared goals came an appreciation for the rights and duties of labor and of management. The union had a right to demand that management redress legitimate grievances that arose on the shop floor, but never would the union represent "a slacker," a worker too lazy to do his job. Management had a right to appoint its own foremen, but they "had to be promoted from within the family," which encompassed those already working at the mill and committed to the union. The union steadily enlarged the scope of its managerial responsibility through collective bargaining agreements and by gaining the appointment of more and more unionists to foremen positions. The owners accepted such encroachments because of their belief that the union was committed to the company's welfare. Management and workers, Galipeau explained, were part of the same "family."[42]

Galipeau frequently used the word "family" to describe both his union experience and labor-management relations at the Falls Yarn. His emphasis on family brings us back to Bodnar's point about the preoccupation of twentieth-century ethnic workers with the economic well-being of their families. Galipeau certainly shared that preoccupation, but his notion of family encompassed not just his kin but his entire workplace. For him, "family" was a vernacular expression of corporatism. It was the word he chose to express a vision of industrial relations that he had fashioned from his cultural background and work experience.[43] Some might emphasize the naivete of such a vision – though Galipeau himself was keenly aware of the unusual circumstances that made it work at the Falls Yarn – but no one should doubt the fervor with which he embraced it. That fervor underscores the enduring influence of corporatism on Catholic workers and their American unions. And it suggests the need to reconsider, if not dispense with, the notion of the twentieth century as an age of working-class realism.

CHAPTER 12

British and Irish Militants in the Detroit UAW in the 1930s

STEVE BABSON

"And if you...went to the Ecorse
plant [of Murray Body], you would
be hired. But not if you had a British
accent or Scotch. The English and
the Scotch...could not get by the
personnel manager."
Elizabeth McCracken

For any labor historian concerned with the tumultuous events of the 1930s, McCracken's comment suggests a new perspective for evaluating the rise of the United Auto Workers. In a period when union militants of every nationality had to go to great lengths to conceal their identity—changing their dress, assuming aliases, falsifying their personal histories—it appears that one entire group of foreign-born workers was indelibly stamped as "subversive." Being British was, at least in the eyes of Murray Body's personnel manager, proof enough that you were a bad risk.

Such stereotyping was common enough in the nineteenth century, when British skilled tradesmen and Irish laborers together provided the American labor movement with many of its most prominent leaders. Yet by the 1930s, the descendents of these nineteenth-century immigrants were more often associated with the conservative "labor aristocracy" of the American Federation of Labor; indeed, many had become employers. Immigrant workers certainly played a critical role in the rise of the UAW, but for good reason, historians have usually focused on the Poles, Slavs, Ukrainians, Italians, and other immigrant groups represented in the unskilled labor force of the 1930s.

227

Often overlooked is the stream of British and Irish immigrants arriving in Detroit throughout the first three decades of the twentieth century. Many of these new arrivals were skilled workers; many were also veterans of the political, trade union, and economic upheaval that characterized British and Irish society between 1900 and 1926. And many, in turn, participated in the organization of the UAW.

Skilled workers were the key leaders in the formation of the UAW, and the British millwrights, tool makers, electricians, and other craftsmen who made up such a large population of these trades were often the most prominent champions of industrial unionism. Irish workers, skilled and semi-skilled, were nearly as prominent. Four of the first six presidents of the union at Ford's massive River Rouge plant came from the British Isles: Bill McKie, a Scottish sheet-metal worker and President of the Ford "Federal" local at its founding in 1934; W.G. Grant, a tool and die maker from England, elected President of Local 600 in 1944; Joe McCusker, a toolmaker and former coal miner from Lanarkshire, Scotland, elected local President in 1945 for the first of two terms; and Tommy Thompson, an Englishman and former coal miner, elected President in 1947. Even Thompson's opponent came from the United Kingdom: the Irishman Michael Magee, a veteran of the 1926 General Strike.

If they hadn't been so dependent on foreign-born skilled workers, Detroit's auto companies might well have profited by adopting the screening device used at Murray Body. Management might then have snared Pat Quin, the Irish millwright and former IRA soldier, who in 1939 became the first elected President of Dodge Local 3 – then the biggest single-plant local in the UAW. Or Dave Miller, the former tram driver and paint chemist from Scotland, a founding officer of the Ford Federal local, and later the founding President of Local 22 at Detroit Cadillac. Or John Anderson, the Scottish toolmaker at GM's Ternsledt plant who helped organize the Mechanics Educational Society of America (MESA) with Matt Smith (another English toolmaker), and who later became the founding President of the UAW's East Side Tool and Die Local 155. Or Bill Stevenson, like Anderson a native of Glasgow, who became President of MESA's Local 91 at Fisher Tool and Die in Detroit, and later became founding President of the UAW's West Side Tool and Die Local 157.

When twenty-five thousand white workers went on a wildcat strike against the upgrading of Black workers at Packard in 1943, it was an Englishman, Norman Mathews – an electrician by trade and the newly elected President of Local 190 – who denounced their actions and moved aggressively to break the strike. Four years later, when Walter Reuther finally won control of the UAW's Executive

Board, the Presidency of his home local 174 was won by yet another Englishman, Harry Southwell, a machine grinder and former President of a company union.

Britons were found at every level of the union's hierarchy. There wasn't a plant in Detroit without at least one "Scotty" in the toolroom maintenance unit, or at least one member of the bargaining committee who spoke with a brogue or a Yorkshire accent. At the other end of the scale, by 1948, at least eight of the UAW's Executive Board members were Scottish, Irish, or English. Leonard Woodcock, the union's fourth President and the son of an English toolmaker, was born in Rhode Island but raised until 1926 in England; Doug Fraser, the union's fifth President, was born in Glasgow.

This essay will make a tentative effort to evaluate the role played by British and Irish workers in the formation of the United Auto Workers. The first section will examine the nature and causes of English, Scottish, and Irish immigration to Detroit. A second section will review the problems inherent in any effort to isolate the specific impact of these immigrant workers on the UAW. The final section will outline those aspects of their collective experience which set them apart from – and ahead of – their Detroit co-workers.

1

For the generation of British and Irish workers who played such a key role in the rise of the UAW in Detroit, the decision to emigrate was shaped by the ongoing crisis of post-war British society. The salient economic features of that crisis were prolonged depression and continued restructuring of British industry; the salient political features were bitter class conflict and an eventual defeat for organized labor.

As Britain emerged victorious from World War 1, its economy spiraled downward in a collapse "so sudden, catastrophic, and irreversible," says Eric Hobsbawm, "that it stunned incredulous contemporaries."[1] Where unemployment had never exceeded 3.3% during the pre-war boom,[2] by June of 1921, 23 percent of all trade unionists found themselves on indefinite layoff.[3] As the crisis deepened, its long-term causes became increasingly evident: the failure of British capitalists to invest over the previous half-century in the new electrical and chemical industries; their failure to modernize plant and equipment, to develop mass production and mass marketing techniques, and to consolidate production into efficient units able to compete in world markets. Collapse had been postponed only by the same parasitic economy that undermined entrepreneurial dynamism; the availability of still protected markets within the empire, and of "acceptable" profits from fully amortized (and obsolete) fixed capital.[4]

The dismal scenes that became commonplace around the world after 1929 got a ten-year head start in Great Britain. "The grimy, roaring, bleak industrial areas of the nineteenth century—in Northern England, Scotland and Wales—had never been very beautiful or comfortable, but they had been active and prosperous. Now all that remained was the grime, the bleakness, and the terrible silence of the factories and mines which did not work, the shipyards which were closed."[5]

Two of the hardest-hit industries were shipbuilding and coal mining—not coincidentally, the same two industries that drove the largest (or at least the most visible) proportion of British immigrants to Detroit. The decline in shipbuilding along the Clydeside was especially precipitous. Following a brief post-war boom, the sudden decline in orders in late 1920 had, by 1921, cut capacity utilization along the Clydeside in half. Output continued to fall over the next two years, with many yards going completely without orders between 1921 and 1923; by 1925, there wasn't a single liner on the Clydeside stocks. The combined impact of subsidized foreign shipping, lowered freight rates, and the fierce competition of U.S. and continental shipbuilders kept the industry in a near-permanent state of depression until World War II.[6]

For skilled metal workers along the Clyde, future prospects looked bleak. Bill Stevenson, as bad luck would have it, finished his five-year apprenticeship as a fitter and turner in 1921, the very year the bottom fell out of the job market. "The depression was in its full depth," he later recalled. "As a matter of fact, I never worked in the trade in Scotland." After two years of unbroken joblessness, Stevenson— 22 years old and apparently single—made the momentous decision "to escape boredom": he left for the United States in September 1923, arriving in Detroit "after several stops."[7]

He was joined by a mounting stream of emigrants from Britain's coal mines. British coal owners had traditionally resisted amalgamation of their scattered, small-scale operations into more efficient units; mechanization and improved methods (favored by the trade unions) were likewise shunned by the owners, who sought wage cuts as a cheaper way of maintaining profits in the face of revived foreign competition and falling prices. Only government subsidies prevented a complete collapse in wages. When the occupation of the Ruhr in 1924 brought German coal into Britain, prices fell still further, resulting in bankruptcies and accelerated erosion of work standards. Over the decade, some fifty thousand coal miners were driven from the pits by these worsening conditions.[8]

Among them was Henry McCusker, member of the Lanarkshire County (Scotland) Miners Union and an activist in the British Labor Party. A nine-year veteran of the pits by age 23, Henry surveyed the post-war conditions and decided he'd had enough. "I thought there was some better horizons," as he put it, "than to be continually working like a mole in the coal mines of Great Britain." In 1923, he left the 27-inch-high seam of coal that he had worked with his father and three brothers, and emigrated to Pennsylvania, where he eventually re-entered the mines as a member of the United Mine Workers. His entire family, his fiancé, and her entire family, all joined him over the next four years. In the meantime, Henry had moved to Detroit, bluffing his way into the Ford Highland Park plant as a grinder-hand in 1925. Coal miners "by the hundreds" had by then left his hometown near Edinburgh for the United States, all of them seeking the same "better horizons."[9]

Economic collapse was not the only pressure that pushed Britons across the Atlantic. The post-war era was also marked by a series of sharp defeats for the British labor movement. For skilled metal workers, the challenge to their workplace organization and power actually began during the war, when government-enforced de-skilling or "dilution" of the engineering trades provoked a series of bitter strikes in the sprawling munitions plants, particularly along the Clyde. The Clyde Workers Committee, made up of stewards from the plants as well as delegates from the mines and railroads, delayed the pace of dilution, leading significant (and unauthorized) strikes in 1915 and 1916. But government repression—the closing of shop and left-wing newspapers, the imprisonment and deportation of CWC leaders—had by April 1916 destroyed the organization. The shop stewards move-ment subsequently spread, with varying degrees of organization and revolutionary commitment, to industrial centers like Sheffield and Tyneside; a massive strike in May 1917 by some two hundred thou-sand metal workers temporarily blocked dilution of civilian produc-tion. But in the opening months of 1918, the revolutionary stewards movement collapsed when the Clydeside engineers failed to win the support of their militant brethren in Sheffield and Manchester for a "strike to end the war."[10]

Following the armistice, employers systematically rooted the mili-tant stewards from their plants, inflicting a particularly sharp defeat on the Clydeside engineers (with the help of troops and tanks to pre-vent mass picketing) in 1919.

The final post-war defeat for the metal workers was administered in the four-months lockout of the Amalgamated Engineering Union in 1922, with the employers successfully re-establishing control over overtime and all other matters of "managerial function."[11]

The depression and a general assault on unions drove membership in the affiliated unions of the TUC down by over two million between 1921 and 1923. The short-lived Labor Government of 1924 served only to demoralize the movement further, as Ramsay McDonald repudiated virtually every plank of his election platform, invoking the Emergency Powers Act against the London tram drivers, denouncing the railroad strikers, expanding naval and air force expenditures, maintaining colonial policy, supporting the Versailles Treaty and the Dawes Plan.[12] The Labor Party's leadership won the plaudits of *The Times* for "rising above the deep-rooted prejudices of many among their adherents," but many of these same adherents were profoundly demoralized by these collaborative policies.[13]

The defeat of the 1926 General Strike was the culminating blow to the hopes of those who had seen in the militancy of 1910–1925 the basis for a revolutionary challenge to British capitalism. The strike itself – precipitated by government and industry demands that the coal miners accept wage cuts and longer hours – was an inspiring demonstration of working-class solidarity. For nine days, millions of workers in 82 separate unions brought British industry to a grinding halt, defying mass arrests and intervention by the army. But even as the strike expanded (or perhaps because it expanded) the TUC leadership suddenly capitulated to the government, leaving the coal miners in the lurch. With the strike defeated, employers set about a thorough purging of union militants.[14]

Over the next few months, some of the victimized men decided to leave England. Many simply could not find work, both because of the depression, but now also because of blacklisting. Matt Smith, the Manchester-born machinist who'd refused conscription and spent much of World War I in jail, emigrated in 1927, according to Elizabeth McCracken, "after a period of insecurity . . . in which he had seven jobs in three weeks."[15] It didn't take long, apparently, for employers to identify Smith as a participant in the shop steward movement and a past leader of striking apprentices in the engineering trades.[16] Joe McCusker, Henry's younger brother, left Scotland in July 1927 to join his family in Detroit.[17] Bill McKie, a 30-year veteran of the National Sheet-Metal and Braziers Union, came to Detroit in the same year with his wife Bess, joining his "now American" daughter in a small house on Cabot Street in Springwells.[18] Others had already left England during the earlier bouts of government and employer repression. Dave Miller, for example, who had spent nearly four years in prison for his refusal to fight in World War I, left his native Dundee when the town "spurned" him after the war.[19]

Overlaying the post-war industrial and political confrontations in Britain was the continuing violent upheaval in Ireland, sparked by the Easter Rising of 1916. The insurrection, announced Easter Monday by Padraic Pearse from the steps of Dublin's General Post Office, failed to mobilize public support and ended in defeat after nearly a week of bloody fighting. But the British government's hasty execution of 14 rebel leaders provoked widespread indignation, and over the next three years, the independence movement not only survived but grew in prestige and power, building upon the popular program of land seizures and opposition to conscription. By the General Election of 1918, Sinn Fein could win 73 of 105 Irish Parliamentary seats, but 47 of the winning candidates were already in prison, and most of the remainder were arrested in early 1919 after the formation of Ireland's first Dail. Significantly, the British War Cabinet initially refused to release these patriots for fear (as paraphrased by Dangerfield) "it would be taken as a sign of weakness by the industrial agitators in England and Scotland."[20]

By September 1919, Sinn Fein, the Irish Volunteers (Irish Republican Army), the Gaelic League, and the Dail had all been declared illegal, forcing their members underground or overseas. The exodus of political refugees continued over the following years as a bloody and prolonged insurrection wracked the 26 Nationalist counties, with IRA ambushes, assaults on police stations, and assassinations of British officers answered by retaliatory raids on Irish civilians – the slaughter of Dublin football spectators in November 1920; the destruction of downtown Cork the following month. The Treaty of December 1921 granting the 26 counties de facto independence was followed by inter-Irish feuding and civil war, postponing peace until April of 1923.[21]

Among the IRA refugees from these wars was Pat Rice, who escaped the British army by fleeing to the Canary Islands. By the 1930s he had made his way to Detroit, becoming an operating engineer in the Ford River Rouge power house, and later winning election as President of Local 600's Maintenance and Construction Unit.[22] Hugh Thompson, another IRA veteran, came to Detroit in 1925, hiring on at Murray Body (apparently without detection), where he helped organize a "Federal" AFL local in 1934.[23] Pat Quinn, the future President of Local 3, joined the IRA in Ireland at age 17 and fought through the "civil commotion" of 1922. He thereafter received a small pension from the Republic, and as President of Detroit's Gaelic League, was honored by an IRA testimonial dinner as late as 1956.[24]

Not all Irishmen refused to fight with the British during World War I. Jack Thompson, for example, joined the British Army and fought in France before coming to Detroit in the early 1920s to work at Ford; fired in 1922, he moved to Toledo and later took a leading role in the 1934 Auto Lite strike.[25] Michael Magee also served in the British Army during World War I, spending much of the war in France as a member of the Irish Brigade. An organizer for the Transport Workers Union, he very probably had taken part in the 1913–1914 Dublin lockout and strike. Following the war he rejoined the TWU, became an activist in the Labor Party, and "took a leading part in the General strike of 1926," before emigrating to Detroit in 1930.[26]

Whether Irish or British, coal miner or metal worker, all these men had one thing in common: for them, Britain and Ireland could no longer sustain their hopes for the future. Some, like Harry Southwell, considered going to Australia, but apparently thought better of it after considering the limited job opportunities for industrial workers.[27] The United States, in contrast, was booming during the 1920s, paced by the new mass-production industries: steel, rubber, electronics, auto. For some, the realities of American industrial life, frequently covered in the left press, had perhaps penetrated the veil of popular conceptions about the "land of opportunity." Even so, anything seemed better than the British Islands of the 1920s. To the haggard British and Irish worker, "the word had also penetrated that an American manufacturer, Henry Ford . . . would pay common laborers $6 a day to work for him."[28] The lure, for some, was irresistible.

2

Determining the impact of these British and Irish immigrants on the UAW is a complicated matter. Even identifying them is difficult, for unlike the cohesive immigrant communities of Polish or Italian workers – separated by name, language, and religion from the surrounding society – British workers (if not the Irish) tended to quickly assimilate with their brethren who had arrived earlier. The nineteenth-century Irish concentrated in Detroit's Corktown, immediately south of Tiger stadium, but there was no comparable concentration of British immigrants. Newly arrived Scotsmen very often crowded into the boarding houses along Pine and Buchanan just north of Michigan Avenue, but these were temporary homes, a refuge for single men still saving money to start a family or bring their wives and children over from the old country.[29] Polish, Italian, and Slovakian organizations all provided space for union meetings and strike kitchens; the sole British-owned hall, St. Andrew's on East Congress, remained a bastion of upwardly mobile Scotsmen, indifferent if not antagonistic to the CIO. The only working-class benefit organization in Detroit headed by a Scotsman was the International Workers Order, with John Anderson as Secretary.

British immigrants, in short, had little organizational presence as Britishers in Detroit; consequently, the task of tracing their collective presence is made that much more difficult. Even their individual backgrounds frequently become muddled in the 1930s, when many assumed one or more aliases to conceal their identities from management. What can we say about Tom Parry—also known as Tom Parrot, Tom Parrie, Tom Parrish? He was English. In 1934 he was fired from Hudson Motors for pasting Communist literature inside car bodies as they passed his work station. He turns up in 1935 as Secretary of the strike committee at Motor Products. In 1936 he was arrested during the Kelsey Hayes strike while setting up a picket line outside the company's Canadian plant. He either was or he wasn't an organizer for Local 155, or maybe 157. The confusion here stems from the unfamiliarity and hostility of Parry's only biographer, Leo Kirchner, who wrote brief profiles on Detroit Communists for the Chamber of Commerce weekly, *Detroit Saturday Night*.[30] After 1937, Parry (Parrot, Parrie, Parrish) doesn't show up in published accounts of the UAW.

Fred William's background is even harder to untangle. Among those who remember him opinion is divided over whether he was Welsh, English, or American. Or even if he was Fred Williams: *Detroit Saturday Night* describes him as Jack Wilson, also known as Jack Wilkes, and "best known as" Fred Williams. "Fred Williams" was later the Business Agent for Local 208 at Bohn Aluminum, and a well-known supporter of the UAW's Communist Party/left-wing bloc. In the 1950s, the federal government tried to deport him as an "undesirable alien," but by then Fred's (or Jack's) background was so muddled the government apparently couldn't determine whether he was actually Welsh or not. To the end, he insisted he was from Pennsylvania.[31]

This kind of ambiguity was apparently not uncommon. In 1935, when the Detroit police arrested Joseph McClellan, a carpenter at Plymouth, Michigan, for selling subscriptions to the *Daily Worker*, they had first to determine which of his three names—McClellan, Joe Leland, or W.J. Howard—was "real." Was he a citizen or not? On the assumption that McClellan's political leanings warranted closer scrutiny, he was turned over to federal immigration authorities.[32]

For those we can conclusively identify as British or Irish, it is tempting to interpret their prominence in Detroit's labor movement as a contributing cause of the United Auto Workers' class-conscious and militant style in the 1930s. After all, most of these men had gone through the searing heat of class struggle in Great Britain or insurrection in Ireland. And all of them, in contrast to many of their American counterparts, came from trade union backgrounds. More significantly, a considerable portion of these British and Irish had played active roles in organizing industrial unions like the Transport Workers, or shop-floor stewards committees that cut across occupational lines and challenged the centralized craft-oriented structure of the Amalgamated Society of Engineers. Their subsequent leadership of Detroit's biggest and most militant UAW locals suggest the principles of industrial unionism, in Michigan at least, were often articulated with an English, Scottish, Welsh, or Irish accent.

No such generalization can be made, however, without three important qualifications. First, by the 1930s, capitalism had long since become a global system, one in which capital, labor, raw materials, and finished goods moved with increasing velocity and mass. Regional distinctions and experience certainly varied, but all within the parameters of an increasingly dense world market. The same process that by the twentieth century had made wars into "world wars," also tended to transmit economic trends and crises worldwide, with Europe and North America the dynamic centers of this global system.

The crisis of post-war British and Irish society must be seen, therefore, not as a peculiarly British phenomenon, but as a bellwether of the same worldwide crisis that would engulf the United States after 1929. The British Islands certainly had unique features: the ferocity of the Irish conflict, the extreme polarization of the classes, the peculiar (for Americans) nature of its parliamentary system. But the basic elements of crisis took on a roughly equivalent form in Detroit. "Dilution," after all, received its highest articulation in the assembly line techniques inaugurated by Henry Ford. Polarization likewise proceeded rapidly in Detroit, measured by the transformation of the Ford Sociology Department into the infamous Ford Service Department, and marked with stunning finality by the Hunger March Massacre of March 1932.

These conditions generated among native-born and immigrant workers of all nationalities a new orientation, one which rapidly narrowed the gap between the class-conscious British and Irish and their increasingly militant co-workers. The worldwide process of crisis and change had, since at least 1914, indelibly stamped people like Walter Reuther, Bud Simmons, Genore Dollinger, and Stanley Nowak, leaving a distinctly heightened sense of class consciousness and militancy; we can imagine any one of them easily and unobtrusively inserted into the General Strike of 1926 or the Dublin lockout of 1913.

Second, this same world system that so readily standardized working conditions and generalized crisis, and which made feasible the mass emigration of European workers to the United States, also involved a reverse movement of ideas and, less frequently, people. In this regard, it is important to remember that from the time of the American Revolution, British and Irish radicals and trade unionists had found many of their most compelling models for social change in America.

Radical reformers in particular automatically invoked American institutions—public education, universal manhood suffrage, Workingman's Democracy—in their efforts to widen the franchise in Great Britain. During the campaign for the Second Reform Act during the 1860s, the columns of radical weeklies like *Reynolds's Newspaper* were filled with a partisan enthusiasm for the union "that can only be paralleled in modern times with the enthusiasm of the Communist *Daily Worker* for the Soviet way of life," the only difference being that *Reynolds's* had a circulation of 350,000 at a time when the daily circulation of even *The Times* of London was 70,000. At the mammoth reform demonstrations in London in 1867, the crowds, appropriately enough, sang "John Brown's Body" and "Yankee Doodle."[33]

Liberal enthusiasm for American ways was dimmed in the closing decades of the nineteenth century by the appearance of huge trusts and their steadily mounting war on American unions. But for British and Irish trade unions, the American experience continued to provide a critical preview of the ideological and organizational forms needed to counter industrial capitalism. A key influence was Henry George, "the prophet of San Francisco," whose book *Progress and Poverty* was widely circulated in England and Scotland. More than a few British socialists traced their rejection of laissez-faire liberalism to George's work. Bernard Shaw, for example, later recalled how one of George's London lectures "struck me dumb and shunted me from barren agnostic controversy to economics.[34] James Keir Hardie, first chairman of the Independent Labor Party (ILP) and later first chairman of the Parliamentary Labor Party, described his eventual conversion to socialism as beginning with *Progress and Poverty*:

> It unlocked many of the industrial and economic difficulties which beset the mind of the worker . . . and led me, much to George's horror in later life when we met personally, into communism.[35]

Both *Reynold's Newspaper* and Friedrich Engels agreed that George's New York mayoralty campaign and the United Labor Party were the best models for a British workingman's party.[36]

American precedent was equally compelling as a model for industrial unionism, so much so that among the earliest industrial organizations in Britain, many consciously modeled themselves after the Knights of Labor. "The Sons of Labor," for example, organized themselves in the western coalfields of Scotland, and several branches of Knights were organized among dockworkers in Glasgow and Ayrshire. In 1887, the Irish labor leader Michael Davitt, after attending the Knight's Minneapolis convention, was engaged by the organization "to aid in developing the order in Europe."[37]

When industrial unionism took root in Britain in the pre-war years, its advocates made repeated references to their chief model and inspiration, the Industrial Workers of the World. The germ of Wobbly theory was spread by men like James Connolly, the Irish socialist and trade union leader later executed for his leadership of the Easter Rising. Connolly lived in the United States between 1903 and 1910, actively involving himself first in the Socialist Labor Party and, after 1905, in the IWW. His subsequent proselytizing provided numerous British and Irish with their first exposure to syndicalist theory, like James Larkin, Connolly's colleague and founder of the Irish General Workers and Transport Union, and Tom Mann, former secretary of the ILP, later editor of the *Industrial Syndicalist*, who co-founded the National Minority Movement. Syndicalists like Noah Abblet, a leader of the South Wales Miners, welcomed Big Bill Haywood to their strike councils during the 1910–1911 Cambrian Coal strike, as did Larkin when Haywood visited Dublin during the 1913 lockout.[38]

When Scottish militants and advocates of industrial unionism broke with the Social Democratic Federation in 1903, they readily took the name of their American mentor, Daniel DeLeon's Socialist Labor Party. Copies of the *Weekly People*, the American party's newspaper, were regularly distributed in London and Glasgow; *The Socialist*, published by the Glasgow SLP, frequently reprinted DeLeon's articles while advertising "American pamphlets" for sale.[39] The significance of their commitment to American models is underlined by their subsequent involvement in the wartime strikes along the Clyde, when virtually the entire leadership of the CWC was drawn from the ranks of the SLP.[40]

In short, any effort to identify the "British" contribution to the rise of industrial unionism in Detroit has to acknowledge that British industrial unionism was, in turn, an amalgam of British, Irish, French, and American ideas, continually recast in the heat of particular struggles. McKie, McCusker, Smith, and Quin all spoke with distinctly British and Irish accents, but the discriminating ear can also pick out a bit of Haywood's Western drawl.

Finally, it is important to recognize that the British and Irish workers who helped to build the UAW were not all of the same mind about how the union should be organized and directed. Norman Mathews, in his public support for upgrading Black workers at Packard, is probably representative of the progressive attitude towards race relations that characterized most British and Irish trade unionists. But at least one English worker in Detroit, Jimmy Walters, apparently played a role very different from Mathews. When Hodges Mason, a Black worker at Bohn Aluminum's Plant 2, ran for President of Local 208 in 1944, Walters (a skilled worker at Plant 1) countered with a "No Nigger President" campaign. When Mason won, becoming the first Black local union President in the UAW, Walters successfully broke his plant away from Local 208 and became President of the newly chartered Local 29.[41]

Intra-union conflicts divided the British and Irish along several distinct lines. The chief organizers of MESA in Detroit were disproportionally British; they agreed on certain elementary aspects of how and why a union should be organized. They did not, however, agree on whether or not that same union should merge with the fledgling UAW, and on May 5, 1936, the two Britishers who led the organization, John Anderson and Matt Smith, reportedly engaged in a fist fight over the issue in front of a room full of startled shop stewards.[42]

Ten years later, the UAW was wracked by a different sort of feuding, as "left" and "right" fought for control of the union's Executive Board. The British and Irish leaders of the union in Detroit seemed to line up on both sides. McKie, Grant, Stevenson, Quin, Anderson, Miller, Fraser, and Tommy Thompson supported Addes and Thomas on the left, and Mathews, Southwell, the McCuskers, Magee, Hamilton, and Doherty supported Reuther on the right. The two organizations recruited with equal success among the British and Irish, with the Communist Party winning the allegiance of men like Anderson and McKie, and the Association for Catholic Trade Unionists garnering the support of McCusker, Pat Hamilton (an Irishman from the Rouge Gear and Axle building), and Tom Doherty (a Chrysler worker, also from Ireland).[43] On these and other issues, British and Irish workers divided along distinctly American lines, exhibiting little inclination to define themselves as distinct ethnic blocs.

3

In evaluating the role of British and Irish workers in the early UAW, clearly we cannot assume that everything they articulate is a uniquely

"British" or "Irish" attitude. It could bear, as we have noted, the echo of an American innovation or the mark of an international crisis. What, then, can we finally say about their impact upon the union?

Chiefly this: As possessors of critical skills acquired either as metal-workers in Britain or, as with many former coal miners, after arrival in Detroit, they had a singular bargaining leverage with management. As experienced trade unionists, they had a "sense of the possible" and a practical knowledge of organization missing in many American workers. And as former citizens of the United Kingdom, they possessed a degree of class consciousness considered peculiar before 1929 in most American settings, but peculiarly suited, in any case, to the articulation of mass insurgency in the 1930s.

Men in skilled trades played a key role in the early years of the UAW for the simple reason that their skills were indispensable to production and difficult to replace. Management in any metal-working industry needed to attract millwrights, tool makers, lathe hands, fitters, and turners, but the need was probably greater than usual in Detroit's auto industry after the mid-1920s. In the latter half of that decade, Henry Ford completely retooled his plants to build the Model A; by the 1930s, General Motors had formally adopted the policy of annual model changes, requiring extensive retooling of its plants every 12 months. Both events generated a demand for skilled metal workers to build and maintain the machinery.[44]

These workers, possessing skills irreplaceable in the short run, were in a position to exert greater pressure on management than the more expendable semi-skilled and unskilled workers in the assembly departments and foundries. Management simply could not find enough skilled workers to easily replace striking toolmakers, which emboldened the tradesmen and made them the most aggressive sector of the auto industry's labor force. Significantly, the first massive walkout of auto workers in the United States, in the winter of 1933, was sparked by a successful strike of five hundred toolmakers at the Vernor plant of Briggs Manufacturing, one of Detroit's biggest suppliers of car bodies to Chrysler and Ford. Between then and World War II, the ligaments of autoworker organizing were provided by the organized toolmakers and other crafts from the MESA strikes of 1933 and 1934 to the "tool and die" strike of 1939, when the toolmakers carried the entire burden of the UAW's successful strike against GM.

By Stevenson's estimate, as many as 70 percent of the tool and die men in his skilled-trade local were Europeans: "Germans, Swedes, Poles, Italians, and British."[45] In Detroit, a disproportionate number of leaders were drawn from among the British, perhaps because the language and culture they shared with Americans made them more effective organizers; certainly their trade union experience in Britain was the equal of their counterparts from the continent.

For these men, the absence of unions in American industry was not simply lamentable, but unnatural. Harry Southwell's incredulity was characteristic:

> I immediately made inquires as to the existence of a union, which an expert grinder ought to have been able to find without any difficulty, based upon my experience in England. I was rather amazed to find that while there was such an organization nationally, it had very few members and was very inactive. . . . This caused me quite a bit of concern because I had been led to believe through my upbringing that every group of workers aspired to some form of security through a union.[46]

Stevenson, who initially worked at the Chrysler Jefferson plant, found the absence of a union "odd," since in Britain you could not even get a job unless you were a union member.[47]

So while many Americans accustomed to AFL inertia believed industries like auto and steel were "unorganizable," British and Irish workers not only knew it could be done, but found it uncanny that it had not already happened. The potential for a mass-based mobilization of workers was, for them, a practical experience, not a theoretical possibility.

That practical experience in Britain included the day-to-day need to counter both the opposition of British management and the craft-oriented exclusiveness of the Amalgamated Society of Engineers. The skills learned in these twin struggles served the Britishers well. In 1934, when the AFL organized "Federal" locals in the auto industry to represent all the workers in a particular plant, the threat always hung over these organizations that skilled workers would eventually be separated from the main body and parcelled out to one of the 18 craft unions claiming jurisdiction in the industry. Such a policy would weaken the bargaining position not only of production workers who had no essential skills to withdraw, but of the skilled trades as well, since their leverage declined once retooling ended and the production season got well under way. The two groups needed each other; McKie insured their continued merger by the simple expedient of signing everyone up in the Ford Federal local as production workers, then sending phony names to the AFL's chief auto organizer, Francis Dillon. It is not known what Dillon thought of a local headed by skilled tradesmen but made up entirely of "production workers."[48]

The structure of MESA, one of the key nuclei around which the UAW in Detroit was later formed, was similarly shaped by a British skilled trades worker, Matt Smith. As McCracken later recalled,

> It was his influence, his British influence, that resulted in the Secretary's job being the most important job inside the MESA. He did not have the tradition behind him that the President was tops. In England, the General Secretary of the union is the top man. When the election came up inside the MESA, he naturally chose to run for Secretary.[49]

Smith was criticized by his chief rival, John Anderson, for failing to open up MESA to production workers. Anderson, backed by MESA's Detroit locals, prevailed on Smith to let him broaden the 1933 strike – an effort that failed, but nevertheless established a precedent that rapidly changed the organization. In its first three years, MESA went well beyond the 1914–1922 transformation of the Amalgamated Society of Engineers in Britain. In 1934, the first MESA convention resolved to organize production workers, but in a separate section; in 1935, this segregated structure was dropped; in 1936, the union's largest locals in Detroit, both led by Scotsmen, bolted from MESA and merged with the UAW, becoming Locals 155 and 157 of the new organization.[50]

It was from this base – specifically, Local 155 – that the first sit-down strike in Detroit was launched at the Midland Steel auto-frame shop in November 1936. The key organizers were Nat Ganley and John Anderson, both officers of Local 155.

The militancy of these skilled trades workers stemmed from several sources, many of them generalized features of capitalist developments. De-skilling naturally had a major impact on the skilled trades. Automatic turret and capstan lathes made it possible to replace skilled turners with semi-skilled operators; higher-precision tools and gauges made it possible to replace skilled fitters with semi-skilled assemblers; specialized mechanical grinders, millers, and borers made it possible to replace skilled lathe operators with semi-skilled machine hands; repetition processes using specialized jigs and fixtures made it possible to dispense with certain skilled workers altogether.[51]

These technical changes didn't necessarily eliminate skilled workers. Fitters and turners were still needed as set-up men to supervise the semi-skilled workers; toolmakers were needed to make the growing number of jigs and fixtures; and millwrights and electricians were needed to install and maintain the increasingly complex machinery. The militancy of skilled workers, then, stemmed not from the outright elimination of their skills (although that happened), but from their continual transformation, a process that, paradoxically, preserved their bargaining leverage but perpetually clouded their future. "It was this combination," Hinton aptly summarizes, "of a very powerful bargaining position with a very strong sense of insecurity that made the engineers . . . such an explosive force.[52]

This explosiveness was probably heightened for the foreign-born skilled workers who emigrated to Detroit, since "dilution," mechanization, and Taylorism had proceeded further in the United States than in Europe. McKie's background in the workshops and engineering firms of Scotland, "where handcrafting was still something of an art and still a matter of pride," left him ill-prepared for the pace of production at the Ford Rouge plant. In the old country, lunch "was the time you relaxed, talked with your buddies, maybe even snatched 40 winks before going back to the job. In England, you sent the boy out for hot tea." Not at the Rouge, where harried workers ate standing up next to the lunch wagon, "swallowing rapidly, their eyes fixed in a stare, among the dirt and dust and open barrels of cyanide." McKie's work "was a far cry from his apprenticeship days, when he lovingly shaped the copper. Now, it was hard straight lines of grey tin."[53]

Among the many consequences of skill-leveling in metal-working centers like Detroit and Coventry was the corresponding erosion of the craft distinctions that divided workers. Cronin describes this process in the British context:

> Semi-skilled workers in the large plants characteristic of these industries formed an intermediate layer between the old "aristocrats" and the mass of casual unskilled laborers. . . . By 1918, a much less divided and internally stratified working class had come into existence, at least at the level of the workplace.[54]

This flattening of occupational distinctions served, in Britain and Ireland, to broaden the sense of commonality rooted in the family history of working-class individuals. Class consciousness was instilled in most long before they became wage earners. "As far as I personally was concerned," Stevenson later recalled, "I literally sucked this in with my mother's milk because my father before me was interested in the labor movement."[55] Harry Southwell, raised by his grandfather, would accompany him "to various union meetings, and he would always instill in me the necessity for becoming an active union member in any trade that I might become involved in."[56] Doug Fraser senior, the Scottish electrician and socialist who emigrated to Detroit in 1923, also took his son to union and political meetings; in such families, it was an automatic part of the child's education.[57] Dave Miller took the lessons to heart; his refusal to serve in World War I was the logical extension of his father's example, refusing to fight in the Boer war.[58]

These childhood lessons in solidarity were repeatedly underlined in Britain and Ireland by adult experience. Working-class society was a world apart, separated from bourgeois society by the independence wars in Ireland and the repeated industrial/political confrontations in Britain. Young British workers learned a brand of socialism made all the more vital by continual mass-based struggles. "Apprenticeship," as Stevenson describes it, took on a new meaning:

> The boys serving an apprenticeship in most of the shops on the Clydeside probably came under the supervision of a shop steward who at lunch time had classes on the industrial history of England, and on Political Science. This is where we gradually began to pick up the drift of the whole system of capitalism and its economic impact on society. So this was our training.[59]

The same atmosphere pervaded the British coal mines:

> For all day down in the headings 1000 feet below it has been little but a succession of Bolshevist meetings. . . . At the face near us [miners] were either arguing lustily or singing most of the day about the beauty of the "red flag of revolution" to the tune of "Maryland, my Maryland."

"Studying and reading we are," said one Welsh miner of this ferment, "so now we're fit and ready to govern . . . We'ave classes in Marx and all the others right 'ere and now we're ready to take over the job of runnin' the country."[60]

They failed of course, to take over the country, and in that failure many decided to leave their disappointment behind and emigrate to America. But the legacy of those heady moments of struggle and occasional victory was at least as enduring as the eventual defeat. Memory is not simply washed away by each succeeding wave of experience; it grows like a coral reef, with succeeding events modifying and building over the past, never eliminating it altogether. Even in defeat, the British and Irish militant carried with him to Detroit an unbroken pride in his class and its accomplishments.

"Pride is one of the essential ingredients of class consciousness."[61] This statement, made by Marc Bloch in reference to feudal nobility, seems equally relevant for these skilled tradesworkers and industrial unionists from the British Isles. It was a pride that in extraordinary cases resulted in a complete breach with bourgeois notions of patriotism and national identity. When prison officials during World War I ordered Matt Smith to put on an army uniform, he readily complied by putting it on—inside out. After emigrating to Detroit, Smith never bothered to become an American citizen. "I'm an internationalist," he explained, "a citizen of the human race."[62]

Smith and his compatriots cannot be described as the catalysts of the CIO in Detroit but they were the most *articulate* advocates of the shop-floor militancy, industrial unionism, and worker solidarity that characterized the CIO. As such, they were quickly elevated to positions of leadership by their Polish, Ukrainian, and native-American co-workers. From these positions of power, the British and Irish, in turn, sharpened and accelerated the UAW's breach with AFL orthodoxy.

Southern and Eastern Europe

Women's Work, Family Economy, and Labor Militancy: The Case of Chicago's Immigrant Packinghouse Workers, 1900–1922

JAMES R. BARRETT

Maggie Condon and Hannah O'Day worked side by side, painting tin cans in one of Chicago's largest meat-packing plants at the beginning of this century. Both were young, single, and working to help support their families, as did so many of the women working in the industry at the time. Maggie was the quick one—an efficient piece rate worker, a glib speaker, and a natural leader among the young Irish-American women. Hannah was slow with her hands and her head and always in trouble with the forelady. Maggie hoped one day to move out of her parents' cramped flat and have a place of her own, but her dreams were continually frustrated by a succession of piece-rate cuts.

In the spring of 1900 Maggie gathered together a small group of young women to discuss their grievances and map out a plan of action. Steeped in the lore of the Chicago labor movement and the heroic deeds of their parents' generation, the women first wrote to the Knights of Labor. At one time a great power among the Irish butchers in the stockyards, the Knights had organized thousands of Chicago's women workers during the 1880s. By the turn of the century, however, the Order was a mere shadow of its former self. The women received no reply, so Hannah took matters into her own hands. Tying a red scarf to her umbrella she paraded through the yards, calling the women out from their work.[1]

This spontaneous strike was crushed and its leaders blacklisted. In the following two decades, however, women continued to organize

249

in the stockyards, and the traditions and lessons of labor activism were passed on from one generation of immigrant women to another.

Labor activists like Maggie and Hannah, and the Polish and Lithuanian women who followed them into the stockyards unions have begun to attract the attention of historians.[2] But the question of why the great mass of American working women did not turn to trade unionism continues to trouble labor historians, particularly those concerned with the relationship among gender, ethnicity, and class.

Part of the answer lies in the changing occupational structure of the U.S. female labor force during the early twentieth century. In addition to those—particularly Black and recent immigrant women—who remained in traditionally unorganized domestic service, a disproportionately large number of women entered retail sales, clerical, and telephone work. These new industries were staffed by workers with little or no trade union experience. Even in manufacturing, where unions had gained a foothold in a few industries by the turn of the century, women were concentrated in sweatshops and large mass-production factories which presented formidable obstacles to any organizer, regardless of sex.[3] There, widespread ethnic and racial divisions, low skill levels, high labor turnover, and other factors made organizing extremely difficult.

Historians have also noted the hostility of many unions, particularly the conservative American Federation of Labor craft unions, to women's work and women's organization. At best, the organized labor movement tended to disregard working women's problems; at worst, unions actively opposed women's unionism. Where the women were recent immigrants, as was the case in many industries during this era, the effects of gender prejudice were compounded by those of nativism.[4]

Finally, even some recent feminist studies have stressed the importance of women's dependent position in shaping what the authors see as a docility that provided a poor foundation for industrial militancy. "Since many women failed to see in the job a source of essential income," Leslie Woodcock-Tentler argues, "they were cushioned from the reality of low wages by male breadwinners." According to this analysis, most women working for supplementary wages saw their work situation as transitory—a stopping off place between school and marriage. So bosses tended to pay them less and they themselves seemed content to work for less.[5] If this argument is correct, it is easy to see how such a frame of mind offered little encouragement to organizers. But this analysis tells us little about those women who in fact were aggressive and fought back.

Women did organize in fairly large numbers during the great labor upsurges of the early twentieth century and the First World War. The proportion of organized women workers doubled during the first two decades of the twentieth century, a rate of growth twice that for men.[6] Union strength among all workers fluctuated throughout these decades, of course, and was influenced by a variety of factors that have not always been clearly delineated by scholars studying trade union organization, or the lack of it, among women.

In the case of Chicago's meat-packing industry during the period 1900–1920, the limited success and ultimate failure of women's trade unionism can be explained in terms of a confluence of several factors. The relative importance of each of these factors and the ways in which they interacted probably varied from one industry and city to another, but most are relevant to women workers and indeed to most immigrant industrial workers during this era. After analyzing the social composition of the female labor force and the character of "women's work" in the industry, this essay describes women's responses to labor organizing and protest, and then considers the forces affecting women's organizations: the role of women in the family economy, the attitude of male-dominated unions, and especially the broader social and economic context within which organizational efforts took place. This context comprised such factors as business cycles and level of unemployment, the strength of the local labor movement, the response of ethnic and racial communities, and the role of the state.

Who were these women packinghouse workers? Throughout the late nineteenth and early twentieth centuries, the great majority of them came from families living in the immediate vicinity of the Union Stock Yards. Even the blacklisted 1900 strikers looked for work only in neighboring slaughterhouses and rendering plants.[7] But if the sources for the female labor force remained local, its various demographic characteristics changed during these decades. In fact, the industry's entire labor force went through a process of social recomposition, as extreme division of labor transformed skilled butchering into an assembly line operation. Slavic immigrants took up jobs as common laborers and machine tenders, displacing an older generation of Irish and German "knife men." By the turn of the century at least two-thirds of Chicago's packinghouse workers were unskilled, and the vast majority of these were recent immigrants from Poland, Lithuania, and other parts of Eastern Europe. During the First World War these new immigrants were joined by a flood of Black migrants from the Deep South and soon after by a steady stream of Mexicans.[8]

The result was an ethnic and racial heterogeneity equal to that of any American industry in this era.

Until World War I, the vast majority of meat-packing workers in Chicago (from 80% to 95%) were single and most were young, the average age remaining about twenty. Up to the turn of the century less than half were foreign-born, while the rest were primarily the American-born daughters of Irish, German, and Bohemian butchers. By the 1890s there was a slight shift from Irish and German to Bohemian and Polish, paralleling the more general shift in the ethnic composition of the Chicago labor force as a whole. Over ninety percent of a small sample of women in meat-packing investigated in 1892 were single. More than half came from homes that investigators considered "poor" or "bad," and more than a third had fathers who were unemployed, injured, departed, or dead. Most had entered the industry quite young and had been working in it for several years.[9]

The ethnic make-up of the packinghouse labor force continued to change at the turn of the century, so that the constituency for women's unionism in 1901–1904 was quite heterogeneous, a mixture of more experienced second-generation Irish, German and Bohemian women and a mass of younger, more recent Polish, Russian, and Lithuanian immigrants. A 1906 Illinois Bureau of Labor Statistics study of 451 women in packing plants found that nearly two-thirds of them were native-born, and well over half of the foreign-born were from Eastern Europe, most of them Polish. While many of the native-born were daughters of immigrants, the fathers were now more apt to be Polish laborers than skilled Irish butchers. Still, most of the women were single and lived at home. More women in meat packing walked to work than in any other Chicago industry considered in the 1906 study.[10]

During the next decade the ethnic shift in Chicago meat packing continued. By 1911 Edith Abbott and Sophinisba Breckinridge found very few Irish women except as foreladies. A 1918 study conducted by the meat-packing companies discovered that nearly two-thirds of the six hundred women questioned were first- or second-generation Polish or Lithuanian. During the First World War and the early 1920s, Black women entered the meat-packing industry in large numbers, so that by 1928 they accounted for over a quarter of the female labor force.[11]

During World War I, married women entered meat-packing plants in large numbers for the first time. As late as 1914, almost ninety percent of the women in Armour's Chicago plant were single. However, after World War I started, the combination of conscription, increased

TABLE 13.1
Growth of Women's Employment in Chicago Meat Packing, 1890 to 1920

Year	Women		Men		Total[a]	
	%	(N)	%	(N)	%	(N)
1890	1.6	(243)	95.5	(14,875)	97.1	(15,523)
1900	5.7	(1,421)	92.3	(23,205)	98.0	(25,141)
1905	11.1	(2,477)	88.7	(19,857)	99.8	(22,391)
1910	12.0	(2,647)	87.9	(19,384)	99.9	(22,064)
1920	12.6	(5,649)	87.4	(39,341)	100.0	(45,011)

Sources: *Eleventh U.S. Census, 1890, Manufactures* (Washington, D.C., 1895), 144–145;
Twelfth U.S. Census, 1900, Manufactures (Washington, D.C., 1902), 184–185;
U.S. Census of Manufactures, 1905, Part 2 (Washington, D.C., 1906), 236;
Thirteenth U.S. Census, 1910, Manufactures (Washington, D.C., 1912), 298;
Fourteenth U.S. Census, 1920, Manufactures (Washington, D.C., 1923), 364.

[a]Total (N) includes gender unknown.

production, and a dramatic decline in immigration produced a severe labor shortage in packing as in many other industries. Thousands of married women, including many with small children, joined the industry's labor force.[12]

These women labored in one of the most advanced mass-production industries of their time. By the turn of the century, the Big Five packers had developed a national mass-marketing network, a sophisticated corporate bureaucracy, and assembly-line slaughtering and packing operations. Henry Ford formulated the basic ideas behind his famous Highland Park Model T assembly line while watching the slaughter of steers at Swift's plant in Chicago. The new production system's speed demanded an enormous capacity. The Union Stock Yards and adjacent packing and rendering plants resembled a city unto themselves. With a labor force of over twenty-five thousand and a daily capacity of more than four hundred fifty thousand animals in 1900, the complex covered a full square mile and dominated Chicago's South Side working-class neighborhoods with its size, noise, pollution, and smell.[13]

Within the slaughterhouses and packing plants, extreme division of labor, mechanization of tasks in some departments, and reorganization of the flow of animal products into disassembly lines, all diluted the skill and strength required for most jobs, and so facilitated the introduction of women into one department after another. As technology and management innovation transformed the production process, they also changed the notion of "women's work."[14] Although originally confined to canning and some by-product departments in the late nineteenth century, by the 1920s women could be found in virtually every department of a modern packing plant – making, labelling, and filling cans; trimming meat; making sausage casings; packing lard, butter, butterine, chipped beef, cheese, and other items; and even working on the hog and cattle kill floors of a number of packing houses. Their representation in the industry's Chicago labor force grew consistently, from 1.6 percent in 1890 to 12.6 percent in 1920, although the most rapid increases came around the turn of the century.[15]

Yet even as women came to play a more important role in the industry, their work tended to be different in a number of ways from that done by most men in meat packing. From the time they entered the Chicago plants in the 1880s and throughout the early twentieth century, women were excluded from all skilled jobs. They received lower wages, even in those rare instances when they did the same tasks as men, and they suffered from chronic unemployment even more than male common laborers. In those departments where they replaced men, women worked in the poorly-paid positions, while men retained the few coveted higher-paying jobs. In sausage making, for example, women twisted, linked, and tied, while men tended the steam-driven stuffing machines – and received a higher rate of pay.[16]

Regular lines of promotion were established for men in many departments during the late nineteenth century, but advancement was virtually nonexistent for women as late as the 1920s. Occasionally a woman production worker might make the giant leap to a clerical job or even become a forelady, but most spent their careers doing low-skill work.[17]

Wages for women packinghouse workers compared unfavorably not only with those of their male counterparts, but also with working women in other Chicago industries. In 1906, over 84 percent of the packinghouse women studied by the Illinois Bureau of Labor Statistics earned less than the common laborer rate, that is, the lowest rate for men, and this pattern persisted over the next two decades. Women also contended with different pay systems than men. While men seldom worked for piece rates, departments with large numbers of women generally used piece rates. Packers sometimes tried to increase productivity by organizing the women into small piece-rate teams with payment based on team rather than individual output.[18]

In an industry infamous for its casual hiring practices and extremely erratic employment patterns, women were also far less secure in their jobs even than male employees. Women in packing and by-product departments were laid off for shorter periods of time than men on the killing floors, but the problem of seasonal layoffs affected a larger proportion of them than of the men. Even after some packers made attempts to stabilize their work force during the early twentieth century, women still suffered disproportionately from seasonal unemployment. In her careful study of payroll records for the 1920s, Alma Herbst found that much of the industry's high labor turnover was concentrated within a fairly small segment of the labor force consisting almost entirely of foreign-born women and Blacks.[19]

Women faced their problem of low pay and employment insecurity in a number of ways. One was through union organization. The earliest impulse for women's labor organization in meat packing did not come from the leadership of the AFL Amalgamated Meat Cutters and Butcher Workmen (AMC & BW) but rather from the women themselves, and particularly from the second-generation Irish women in the canning departments of the various plants. In the wake of an unsuccessful, spontaneous piece-rate strike in 1900 came the Maud Gonne Club. The club was a social group of young Irish-American women. With a mixture of ethnic and class solidarity characteristic of Chicago's South Side neighborhoods in those years, the young women named their club for a contemporary young Irish woman active in the movement for independence. But Maude Gonne was also recognized as the leader of *Inghinidhe na h'Eireann*, a feminist-nationalist group. In addition to those handed down to them from their parents, then, the Maude Gonne Club members had some ideas of their own.[20]

The club, with the support of Mary McDowell of the University of Chicago Settlement House, provided the nucleus for Local 183 of the Amalgamated Meat Cutters and Butcher Workmen of North America, which led to a highly successful organizing drive in the Union Stock Yards between 1901 and 1904. At its high point, the local claimed a membership of almost two thousand (about ninety percent) of the women in the yards and played a crucial role in the great stockyards strike of 1904.[21] But this strike was defeated, and labor organization in the industry was snuffed out.

During the First World War, the strongest response to the organizing drive of the Stockyards Labor Council came in the Polish community. One union organizer noted that "the union became almost a household word among these workers." Ten thousand Polish and Lithuanian workers were recruited within one month at the end of 1917. By the end of the War in late 1918, over twenty thousand East European workers had joined; about one-fourth of these were women.[22]

This strong response to unionism from recent immigrant women is important for a number of reasons. It contradicts the conventional wisdom in labor history that has held that such workers were unorganizable. The response is also important because it calls attention to the question of why women organized when and where they did.

But an exclusive focus on trade unionism certainly obscures the depth and the breadth of women's responses to class issues. Women participated in protests, particularly in moments of crisis, whether as wage earners or as housewives and mothers. The role of women in strikes underscores the importance of considering them in both roles.

Rioting during strikes in "Packingtown"–the neighborhood adjacent to the stockyards–was a product of both the labor market in the industry and the ecology of the community. In an industry with such a large proportion of unskilled laborers, aggressive picketing was essential, particularly in periods of high unemployment. It was fairly easy to recruit strikebreakers from outside the community during such times, and only force could keep them out of the yards. Because the stockyards represented the physical as well as the economic focal point of the community, it was extremely difficult for scabs to pass into or out of the yards undetected. Once recognized, they were invariably attacked. Although women composed a large proportion of the crowds in both the 1904 and 1921–1922 strikes (judging from arrests and reported injuries), they were particularly active in the later conflict. When two thousand mounted policemen invaded Packingtown on December 9, 1921, to enforce a sweeping injunction, they were pelted with rocks, bricks, and bottles and fired on by snipers from rooftops and windows. Polish women threw red pepper in the eyes of the horses, screaming "Cossaks, Cossaks!", and they poured tubs of scalding water down on the policemen from their tenement kitchens.

While such responses were more or less spontaneous, neighborhood women also organized themselves. During the 1921 strike, a Polish Women's Auxiliary drew five thousand women to its meetings, and staged a strike parade of nearly fifteen thousand. The matriarch of this organization was Mary Janek, "the Polish Mother Jones." Photographs show a middle-aged women wearing a heavy black overcoat, a babushka, and a look of grim determination.

Neither the strong response of immigrant women to trade union organizers nor the desperation with which they fought mounted policemen and scabs can be understood without carefully analyzing the role of women in the working-class economy. As in so many other communities of this era, Packingtown's families depended on a complicated local economy aimed at supplementing the insufficient earnings of family heads. The development of women's employment in packing was a product of this development. Data for the turn of the century and the First World War demonstrate that most families relied directly – many entirely – upon women's earnings for their survival.

Wages for most male packinghouse workers were extremely low. The wage for common labor in meat packing fluctuated between 15 and 20 cents per hour from the turn of the century until 1917. By around 1900, two-thirds of the industry's work force was considered unskilled and paid at, near, or even below this rate.[23] The packinghouse workers won important gains in real wages during the First World War, but these largely disappeared during the post-war depression of 1921.

Real earnings were far lower than these rates suggest because of the volatility of employment in the industry. Thousands of laborers in cattle- and hog-slaughtering gangs were laid off for two or three months during the slow summer season. As the number of cattle fell off, the packers reduced gang size and skilled men often took over common laborer jobs at reduced wages. Even on a daily basis the butcher workmen could not depend on anything like regular hours and pay. Thousands of workers, always more than were needed, milled around the Union Stock Yards gates and the employment offices of the various packers. They were called to work only when the killing was about to begin, and they were discharged once it was finished. On a Monday or Tuesday, when the flow of cattle was heavy, the gangs worked fourteen to sixteen hours; on Thursday and Friday, only two or three. Although some firms made efforts to regularize hours to undercut union agitation over the issue, seasonal unemployment and erratic scheduling remained problems for many workers throughout the 1920s.[24] As a result of these low wages and irregular employment, the earnings of male family heads in Packingtown fell far short of meeting their families' minimum budget requirements. A meticulous 1911 study by University of Chicago investigators estimated the average weekly wage for laborer husbands at $9.67, and the minimum weekly expenditures needed to support a family of five (based on family budgets) at $15.40. (In fact, average family size in the community was 5.33.) When *all* sources of income were considered, 30 percent of the 184 families in the study showed budget deficits. Estimates did not include such "extraordinary" expenses as weddings and funerals. The latter were probably not unusual in a Catholic community with a very high infant mortality rate.[25]

Packingtown's families survived because male family heads' earnings comprised only a fraction of family income (54.4% in this 1911 study).[26] The rest was made up through children's earnings, taking in boarders, and even scavenging for fuel and food. Families with teenage children sent them to work in the stockyards or in the surrounding factories and plants. Many young women working in the packing plants were primary breadwinners. The 1906 Illinois Bureau of Labor Statistics Report showed that 55 percent of such women came from families where fathers' earnings were either impaired or non-existent due to death, disease, divorce, desertion, injury or some other cause of chronic unemployment, many more than in 1892.

Packingtown's wives and mothers took in boarders to further supplement family income. The relative importance of the boarder system was related to the life cycle of the family but not, apparently, in the sense that Tamara Hareven, John Modell, and others have suggested. Rather than a "life choice" employed by older families to make up income lost through the departure of a mature child, taking in boarders in Packingtown was primarily a means by which younger families made ends meet. Thus, boarders was especially prevalent in young Lithuanian and Polish families whose children were too small to work. Boarders were quite rare in the older, more established Bohemian families. This was in part a reflection of the higher status of Bohemians in the packinghouse occupational structure, but in addition the older age of the children in these families meant extra income on which they could depend.[27]

More striking than the ethnic and family cycle variations however, is the extremely high proportion of families with boarders. Averages for communities studied in this era range from 20 to 50 percent, while the U.S. Commissioner of Labor's 1901 national survey found an average of 24 percent. But in Packingtown in 1905, 70 percent of the families studied had at least one boarder, and many had far more: University of Chicago investigators found the average in 1911 to be between two and three. These figures suggest that, like that of young working women, the contribution of wives and mothers to the family income was extremely important, as it was in many other working-class communities.[28]

Packingtown's intricate family economy, based almost as much on boarders and children's earnings as on father's contribution, faced a crisis during World War I. Just as rapid wartime inflation was placing greater pressure on family budgets, the boarder system went into eclipse: Hostilities in Europe and the draft at home cut off the flow of young unattached immigrants who had provided the bulk of the boarder population. At the same time, severe labor shortages offered greater employment opportunities for women. Without the income from boarders, thousands of Packingtown's wives and mothers entered the slaughterhouses for the first time.[29] Their contributions, now in the form of wages, remained a crucial component of the family economy. Analysis of data on the 600 working mothers who were studied in 1918 by the meat-packing companies' own research organization revealed that approximately thirty percent of the women were working because their husbands' earnings were impaired or cut off entirely due to illness, death, desertion, or divorce. Another fifty percent, including presumably many who had formerly taken in boarders, gave "insufficient income" or debts due to illness or death as explanations for their seeking employment. Less than eighteen percent said they were working to buy property, pay for their children's educations, or increase their savings.[30]

Thus, while employers may have considered women's earnings strictly supplementary, many of Packingtown's women workers could not afford to do so. Their wages were essential to the maintenance of their families. With women playing such a vital role in the community's local economy, it is hardly surprising that low wages, irregular hours, and other grievances were seen as attacks on the welfare of the immigrant family and the community as a whole. Such grievances provided a basis for solidarity and organization among the women and perhaps also a greater inclination on the part of the butcher workmen to support women's initiatives.

So long as women remained confined to traditional "women's work"—wrapping, sewing ham bags, painting and labeling cans—there was little opposition from the Amalgamated Meat Cutters and Butcher Workmen to women's employment and union membership. Apart from specific low-wage tasks that had always been assigned to women, the main distinction between men and women's work was the use of the knife, work traditionally considered degrading to women.

During a 1903 strike, Slavic women were introduced as strikebreakers in sausage departments, and many of them remained when the strike was lost. In some plants women were even picking up the knife to do the work of male trimmers. In response, sausage markers' locals offered a resolution at the union's 1904 convention. The resolution charged that the introduction of women downgraded men's work, and it called for the expulsion of women from all sausage departments and their exclusion from any job involving the use of the knife. Molly Daly of Local 183, who had been organizing the women sausage markers, took the floor. She argued forcefully against the resolution and for the principle of equal pay for equal work. Daly was supported by several male delegates, one of whom noted the importance of unionization to women who were often primary breadwinners. "It would be unfair now," he argued, "to discourage their organization, as many of them have families to support." The sausagemakers' resolution was defeated by a large margin. Instead, the convention adopted a compromise resolution that called for confinement of women to jobs that were not "brutalizing" but also demanded that women and men receive equal pay for equal work.[31]

In some cases, the Amalgamated union's support took concrete form. During the 1902–1904 organizing campaign, the union remitted the per capita tax for women. This meant, in effect, that the local union was not required to turn over any dues to the national organization. The Amalgamated did this at first because women's wages were so low and later so that the local could hire its own women organizers. Michael Donnelly, the Amalgamated's president, was particularly supportive of women's unionism. He worked with Mary McDowell of the University of Chicago Settlement House to build not only Local 183 of the Amalgamated but also the Women's Trade Union League (WTUL). In the leadership of the Stockyards Labor Council, which spearheaded the First World War organizing drive, William Z. Foster and Jack Johnstone were key figures. Both came out of the pre-war syndicalist movement and later became prominent Communists. The Council appointed several women organizers and worked closely with the WTUL on an educational program for immigrant workers. Partly as a result of these educational efforts, the strongest response in this period came from the Polish community "Back of the Yards," which provided the backbone of women's and men's organization.[32]

It would be easy to overemphasize the Amalgamated's commitment to the organization of immigrant packinghouse women. Certainly there is little evidence that the butcher workmen were willing to move beyond their support of the idea of equal pay for equal work to embrace a broader vision of women's social equality. Most were probably closer to the position of the union's conservative Secretary-Treasurer who argued that women worked because of economic necessity and that they should be organized and supported, if only to protect men's wages. Even this position, however, contrasts sharply with the more typical trade union demand of this era for the total exclusion of women from union and shop.[33] Clearly, the Amalgamated offered more support for women's organization than most unions at this time. Why?

The key seems to lie in the industry's production process and labor market. No turn-of-the-century industry could match meat packing in its extreme subdivision of labor and assembly line organization of work. By subdividing tasks and grossly reducing the degree of skill and experience required for most jobs, the packers opened to women all but the heaviest slaughtering and hauling work. The consistent expansion of the proportion of women to total labor force reflects these changes in production methods and technology. (See Table 13.1.) As it became increasingly difficult to keep "cheap female labor" out of most departments in the modern packinghouse, it became necessary to fight to raise women's wages in order to protect the men's rates. It was one thing for men in highly skilled trades or unskilled labor engaged in heavy work to exclude women; it was more difficult for mass-production workers to do so in an industry where women made up an increasingly important part of the labor force.[34]

The structure of the unions themselves also affected the prospects for successful women's organizations. All women workers joined one local union in the 1902–1904 period. This facilitated the acculturation of recent arrivals into the broader movement and maximized class solidarity across racial and ethnic lines. The union locals provided a context for "Americanization from the bottom up."

Mary McDowell saw this process at work when she visited a Local 183 meeting. A young Black women rose to accuse a Polish member of insulting her. The Irish-American president asked both to come forward.

Now what did yez call each other?

She called me a nigger.

She called me a Pollock first.

Both of yez oughta be ashamed of yourselves.

You're both to blame. But don't you know that this question in our ritual don't mean that kind of griev-e-ances, but griev-e-ances of the whole bunch of us?[35]

The episode suggests not only the potential for ethnic and racial conflict in this highly diverse force but also a conscious effort by local union leaders to discourage such thinking and promote a concentration on common interests and problems.

During World War I the structure of women's unions became more complicated and fragmented than it had been at the turn of the century. In addition to dividing men and women into separate locals, the Stockyards Labor Council also made the sincere, but tragic decision to organize along ethnic and racial lines. Thus there were Polish and Lithuanian, English-speaking, and "colored" women's locals. Some union locals were strong throughout the 1917–1922 period, particularly among the Poles, where all segments of the ethnic community provided moral and material support for unionization. Efforts were much less successful in the Black community, which contributed a growing proportion of women workers from the beginning of the war on. The Chicago Urban League and many Black ministers resisted the unions' overtures and generally sided with the packers. But even the strength of the Polish women's organization was based less on the sort of painstaking department-by-department effort in the meat-packing plants that had produced the 1902–1904 movement, and more on the results of wartime economic conditions and a massive organizing campaign run from the top down.

The reasons for shifting from ethnically and racially mixed locals to segregated community-based locals is not entirely clear. The first plan had been to create a number of mass locals composed of workers from all ethnic and racial backgrounds. When some leaders in the Black community opposed this plan, fearing that the Black minority would have little voice in such large organizations, the Stockyards Labor Council opted instead for a series of locals based on neighborhoods. The wartime movement also included trades locals composed largely of skilled, native-born and old-immigrant workers—Irish, Germans, and Bohemians. Given the high degree of residential segregation in Chicago by World War I, such a scheme was bound to result in de facto segregation. It is possible that "clan leaders" within the various ethnic communities also supported the idea of neighborhood locals, hoping to maximize their own influence by building the movement on the basis of nationality and residence rather than occupation.

The reasons for separate ethnic and racial organizations may be somewhat obscure, but the long-term results of such a structure were clearly disastrous. In the repressive political and cultural environment of post-war America, the organizational divisions within the movement tended to accentuate the social fragmentation among workers. This rendered the movement fatally vulnerable in an era of reaction.[36]

All of these factors—the character of work in meat packing; the importance of women's contributions to the family economy; the strategy and structure of the unions involved—shaped the experience and behavior of immigrant women. It is impossible, however, to fully explain the strengths and weaknesses of women's organizations without considering, however briefly, the general political and economic context within which they lived and worked. In Chicago during the early twentieth century, this problem of context may have played a more important role than it did in other situations.

As always with wage labor, economic conditions had a significant impact. Union strength was greatest during the economic boom just after 1900 and during the severe wartime labor shortage. The union was weakest during the 1904 recession and the post-war depression. These, of course, were the periods in which the meat-packing companies launched their attacks. Meat-packing unions were particularly susceptible to such downturns because most of the male labor force and virtually all women workers were unskilled. As a center for railroads and contract labor agencies, Chicago was filled with an army of casual laborers during depressions. These anonymous crowds provided the meat-packing companies with strikebreakers.[37]

More important, union strength peaked as part of an unusually strong local labor movement with a tradition of women's organization. Chicago boasted one of the most highly-organized and militant labor movements in the world during the early twentieth century. "The city could possibly challenge London for the title trade union capital of the world," writes David Montgomery. By the end of 1903, the Chicago Federation of Labor had a membership of more than two hundred forty-five thousand. It organized women workers, with more than thirty-seven thousand drawn from 26 different occupations, ranging from scrub women, waitresses, and laundry workers to teachers, box makers, and garment workers. Again during the First World War the city's labor movement was "more closely organized, more self-conscious, more advanced in its views" than any other in the country. Immediately following the War, the Federation launched its own independent labor party to fight for control of the city government and provided much of the impetus behind the move for a national labor party.[38]

This strength and militancy facilitated the organization of packinghouse workers in a number of ways. During the 1904 strike the teamsters and other trades went out in sympathy, and contributions flowed in from unions throughout the city. During the wartime organizing, the progressive wing of the city's labor federation created, staffed, and partially funded the Stockyards Labor Council, which directed the campaign. In both periods the crowds picketing the stockyards gates or listening to union rallies included workers from many other industries who viewed meat-packing companies as the vanguard of corporate capitalism in the city.[39]

But labor strength, especially for women, consisted of more than organizers and money. A working woman in early-twentieth-century Chicago was surrounded by what might be termed a labor ethos. Her father, brothers, sisters, cousins, and neighbors within the city's ethnic communities were apt to be union men and women. Labor values — class solidarity, industrial militancy, and a pride in the movement — were alive around her in sympathy strikes, demonstrations, independent labor politics, and other successful union organizing campaigns.

During World War I, the leaders of the multi-racial, multi-national stockyards labor unions struggled to build a united labor movement.

Black workers were actively recruited. Black union shop stewards, long-term residents of Chicago who had absorbed the ethos of trade unionism, played a crucial role in the organizing drive in the stockyards, as did Polish socialists. A union shop and an unprecedented stipulation banning employer discrimination based on "creed, color or nationality" was forced upon the meat-packing corporations in 1918 when the threat of a strike by the mobilized workers led to federal intervention. Following the First World War, the Chicago labor movement was hit particularly hard as economic depression, political factionalism within the Stockyards Labor Council and allied unions, and the emergence of nativism and racism – demonstrated most dramatically in the 1919 Chicago race riot – all weakened the nurturing environment within which stockyards organization had thrived.[40]

State power played a crucial role in the fate of packinghouse organization generally and thus the relative success and ultimate failure of women's unions. In the early-twentieth-century round of unionization and the 1904 strike, the federal government played no role, and the Democratic city government, sensitive to union power, was slow to repress the workers' movement in the yards. Police showed restraint in handling large crowds, and at times even fraternized with the strikers. When arrested, strikers were often released, with charges dropped, or they were given suspended sentences.[41] Only after the 1904 strike had dragged on for more than eight weeks did police provide enough protection for scabs to keep plants operating effectively. Because Chicago was the home of a large casual labor market, and unemployment in the city was high, the meat-packing firms had a large pool of potential strikebreakers on which to draw. Once it became clear that the police, and not the union or the crowd, controlled the streets around the stock yards, the battle was lost.

State power at both the federal and local levels was more resolutely interventionist during and immediately after the First World War. Wartime arbitration allowed the unions temporary, limited recognition and brought short-term improvements in wages and hours, but it did not represent a commitment by the government to a new form of industrial relations in the industry. The arbitration agreement provided the meat-packing corporations with a degree of flexibility in the midst of wartime market conditions highly unfavorable to them. The agreement not only outlawed unofficial strikes but also saddled union officials with the responsibility for disciplining their members when they engaged in such actions. During the period of government arbitration, the meat-packing companies erected an elaborate welfare system and an employee representation plan.

Federal support was withdrawn precisely at the moment when union organization was weakest—during the depression of 1921.[42]

When the meat-packing corporations attacked the unions in the winter of 1921–1922, local government power was thrown decisively on the side of the companies. The critical factors in crushing the strike were a sweeping injunction, which virtually outlawed any picketing, and the invasion of the stockyard neighborhoods by hundreds of heavily armed mounted policemen. Polish women played a particularly important part in the street fighting surrounding this strike, but the overwhelming numbers and force of the mounted police carried the day. Union organization was wiped out and did not reappear until the CIO campaign of the late 1930s.[43]

What can the story of Maggie Condon, Hannah O'Day, and the other women packinghouse workers tell us about women's organization in the early twentieth century? At the very least it suggests that the relative lack of organization among women workers in the United States was not in any sense inevitable, and it encourages us to analyze more precisely the factors affecting women's organization.

The behavior of women packinghouse workers underscores the fact that when offered the opportunity to improve their conditions, they grasped it eagerly. Leslie Woodcock-Tentler has emphasized the conservative impact of traditional immigrant values on women's mentality and behavior, but the experience in Chicago's Packingtown suggests that these same values could contribute to women's militancy. John Bodnar has noted recently that the worldview of early-twentieth-century immigrants was far less concerned with workplace than with family issues. "After all other arguments have been heard," Bodnar writes, "one is left with a recurring suspicion that for the rank and file in the twentieth century, labor issues were essentially family issues."[44] The importance of women's contributions to the family economy in Packingtown exemplifies the significance of Bodnar's argument, but the behavior of the women themselves in joining unions and participating in strikes suggests a firm link rather than a dichotomy between family and workshop issues. If the family was indeed the focus of working class women's lives, and its maintenance and protection their paramount goal, then union organization was a means by which they might fulfill these responsibilities.

Traditional values regarding women's roles did not always inhibit militancy, then. In some cases they may indeed have produced fear and submission to authority; in others, resistance. If such values are not sufficient in themselves to explain the history of women's labor organization, then it might be necessary to look beyond the position of women in the family, or stereotypical personality traits shaped by this role, to broader social factors in order to fully explain the success and failure of women's organizing efforts. Here, the Chicago case study is quite instructive. In both periods of Chicago meat-packing unionization success came as part of a general upsurge nurtured by a militant, well-organized labor movement and by mobilized ethnic working-class communities. Failure came within the context of economic depression, heavy unemployment, intense nativism, virulent racism, and a general decline of the local and national labor movements. All of this reminds us that it is difficult to understand the experience of any particular group of workers outside of the context of class relations in the society in which they lived.

CHAPTER 14

Anthony Capraro
and the Lawrence Strike of 1919

RUDOLPH J. VECOLI

Lawrence, Massachusetts, about thirty miles north of Boston in the
Merrimack River Valley, was in the early decades of this century the
scene of several of the most bitterly fought labor struggles in the textile industry. These strikes captured national attention and had far-
reaching significance for the American labor movement. Of these, the
strike of 1912 has been the subject of extensive historical study;
perhaps because of the role of the Industrial Workers of the World
(IWW) and the celebrated case of Ettor and Giovannitti, it appears to
hold a particular fascination for labor historians. But the strike of
1919, which in some ways was of greater consequence, has been
almost totally ignored. Involving more workers, half of whom were
women, and lasting longer than the 1912 conflict, it embodied the
post-war spirit of labor militancy, inspired in part by the Russian
Revolution, and was sustained by an established, powerful union, the
Amalgamated Clothing Workers of America (ACWA). In certain
respects, the Lawrence strike of 1919 prefigured the mass organizing
drives of the CIO in the 1930s.[1]

The American Woolen Company, the most powerful textile corporation in the United States, which had four of its largest mills in
Lawrence, dominated the life of the city. Of Lawrence's population of
more than ninety-six thousand in 1919, nearly half were immigrants,
the majority employed in the woolen mills. Incorporating some fifteen
nationalities, this labor force was predominantly "new immigrant" in
character, two-thirds from eastern and southern Europe and the Middle East. The Italians, numbering about twelve thousand and compris-
ing more than a third of all mill workers, were by far the largest ethnic

267

group. But Germans, Ukrainians, Syrians, Poles, and Lithuanians were also present in force, while smaller contingents of Russian Jews, Armenians, Portuguese, Greeks, and Belgians further spiced the ethnic mix. Only about ten percent of the mill operatives were designated as "English-speaking," a category which included persons of British and Irish background.[2]

The distinction between English-speakers and non–English-speakers demarcated a basic cleavage in the social structure of Lawrence. The latter were tagged as "foreigners," a term loaded with pejorative connotations. The older immigrant stocks, themselves once victims of prejudice, having achieved respectability, shunned the newcomers as pariahs. An astute observer commented:

> The English-speaking, whether British or American, whether employers or employed, have always shown a surprising degree of intolerance toward those of other tongues and other manners. The American laborer, the Irishman, and – strange to say – the French-Canadian, regard the Italian or Greek or Jew as a being who occupies in the scheme of creation a place a little higher than that of the Fiji islander, but far beneath that held by the most depraved English-speaking tramp that was ever kicked off a freight car. The foreigner, in short, is a wop, a sheeny, or a Polack.[3]

Living in ethnic enclaves, housed in shabby, crowded tenements, providing for their needs through their own institutions, these "foreign elements" had little social intercourse with the English-speaking residents of Lawrence. This pattern of ethnic segregation was also reflected in the mills, where preference for the highest-paying and more pleasant jobs, such as weavers and menders, was given to the English-speaking workers, while the "dirty work" was assigned to the recent immigrants. Not only did this reflect the bias of the bosses, but also the prejudices of the older ethnic groups, who refused to work with the "greenhorns."[4]

The ethnic hierarchy in work assignments translated into differentials in earnings and standards of living. Because of rapid technological developments in the textile industry, the demand for machine tenders had increased while the need for skilled workers diminished. Thus raw immigrant labor was welcomed and became the preponderant element in the work force. In 1919 the minority of skilled operatives had average weekly earnings of more than twenty five dollars, while the unskilled brought home about thirteen dollars a week. True, the wages in both categories had more than doubled since the 1912 strike; however, the cost of living had also doubled during the war years, especially with respect to essentials such as food and clothing. Moreover, immediately following the armistice, a cutback in the production of textiles resulted in widespread unemployment and underemployment. The upshot was that the vast majority of the Lawrence mill workers in 1919 had annual incomes of at least five hundred dollars less than the "minimum existence wage" for a family of four, which was estimated to be fifteen hundred dollars.[5]

Given these economic conditions, it is not surprising that the strike was precipitated by the threat of a wage reduction. In November 1918, the United Textile Workers of America (UTWA), an American Federation of Labor (AFL) affiliate, initiated a campaign for an 8-hour day in the industry. Only some two hundred of the more than thirty-two thousand mill operatives in Lawrence belonged to the UTWA (another five or six hundred belonged to an independent union). In order to press the demand for a reduction of the work week from 54 to 48 hours, the support of the unorganized workers was enlisted. Since demand was in any case down, the American Woolen Company and other Lawrence firms readily agreed to the shorter work week, but with a commensurate reduction in earnings. When the non–English-speaking workers learned that the result would be a 12½ percent reduction in their already meager pay, they balked at the agreement. Despite the entreaties and threats of the UTWA officers, a general committee composed of representatives of all the nationality groups demanded a 48-hour work week, but with 54 hours' pay. At a mass meeting, the textile workers voted unanimously to strike if this demand was not met by January 31. Accordingly, on February 3, practically all of the thirty-two thousand hands walked out, shouting the strike slogan "48-54."[6]

The solidarity of the woolen workers, however, was short-lived, for the ethnic and skill distinctions soon expressed themselves in a breaking of ranks. Gradually the generally better-paid English-speaking workers, including the Irish and French-Canadians, began to drift back into the mills; they were followed by some of the smaller groups – Greeks, Portuguese, Turks. But the main body of immigrant workers remained impressively intact through the gruelling ordeal. Harvell L. Rotzell observed in retrospect: "The Italians, Poles, Lithuanians, Russians, Ukrainians, Syrians, Franco-Belgians, Germans, and Jewish [sic], numbering between fifteen and twenty thousand were the backbone of the strike and there was never a serious break among them in the 16 long weeks of the strike."[7] The conflict thus assumed the character of an ethnic as well as economic struggle, pitting the newcomers against the older groups. At issue appears to have been not only the specific matter of wages, but also the resentments engendered by the maltreatment that the "new immigrants" had received at the hands of "American" workers and bosses alike. Out of this common experience of degradation, they fashioned a pan-ethnic unity:

> Clad thus in the same mantle of opprobrium, the denizens of Lawrence's Little Babel have come to see one another more or less as comrades, in opposition both to their employers and to their English-speaking, unionized fellow-workers.[8]

The strike divided Lawrence into two hostile camps along lines of class and ethnicity. The city was described as in the grip of a civil war. On one side were some twenty to thirty thousand mill workers, foreign-born, polyglot, and unorganized. On the other was arrayed the city's power structure, City Hall, the Chamber of Commerce, the churches (especially the Roman Catholic Church), the press, and the conservative labor organizations, all allied with the Woolen Trust. The strike opponents quickly advanced the view that "the trouble in Lawrence" was not a conflict over wages but part of "the worldwide revolution of the proletariat." No less than Secretary of Labor William B. Wilson characterized the strike as "a deliberate organized attempt at a social and political movement to establish soviet governments in the United States."[9] The mill owners quickly seized upon this interpretation of the dispute. Winthrop L. Marvin, speaking for the National Association of Wool Manufacturers, wrote to Secretary Wilson: "Manufacturers of the Lawrence district are in harmony with you and with leaders of organized labor in this vicinity that Bolshevist propaganda in Lawrence is the real cause of the continuing troubles there." In rejecting conciliation of the strike the mill owners declared: "There can be no arbitration between Americanism and Bolshevism." The AFL-affiliated Lawrence Central Labor Union and the UTWA condemned the strike as due to the influence of "alien Bolshevik I.W.W. agitators" who had seduced the non-English speaking non-organized textile workers" with "un-American promises."[10]

But the person identified as "the most persistent and bitter opponent of the strikers" was Father James T. O'Reilly, pastor of St. Mary's Church. The General Strike Committee declared that he "has done more than any other single individual in Lawrence to try to discredit our cause and inflame the public mind against us by circulating false reports to the effect that we are a body of Bolshevists, anarchists, etc." O'Reilly, who had been a leading foe of the IWW-led strike of 1912, perceived himself as engaged again in a fight against "foreign, anti-American, revolutionary forces." A master of invective, he declared the issue in Lawrence to be "whether such a combination of local and imported revolutionists, real dyed-in-the-wool foreigners, radical socialists, avowed bolshevists, shall hold this city by the throat in the name of honest labor."[11] Although O'Reilly was the most vocal clerical opponent, the evidence suggests that other Catholic priests generally shared his views.

Early in the strike, The Citizens Committee of Lawrence, composed of prominent business and professional men drawn from the various ethnic groups, was formed to seek a solution to the recurring labor troubles that were giving their city "an international bad name." Moderate and reformist in temper, the committee called for improvements which would make Lawrence "a cleaner, finer, and better city in which to live and work." Specifically, it advocated programs of Americanization, neighborliness, and civic betterment for the immigrant population. The committee advised its "foreign-born friends" that America provided abundant opportunities for them and their children, but that these could only be enjoyed through obedience to, not defiance of, American laws. Its efforts to mediate the strike were unsuccessful and despite its stance of impartiality, the committee was in the final analysis on the side of law and order and property rights.[12]

The high-sounding rhetoric of the Citizens Committee about "true Americanism" was at odds with the heavy-handed repression pursued by the public authorities throughout the strike. With the memory of the 1912 dispute still fresh in mind, Commissioner of Public Safety Peter Carr and City Marshall Timothy J. O'Brien determined from the beginning upon a policy of *force majeure*. Since this was not a bona fide labor conflict but part of the worldwide Bolshevik revolution, they gave the police a free hand in using arbitrary force against the strikers. Reinforced by officers from surrounding towns, mounted and foot patrols instituted a "reign of terror," assaulting, arresting, and incarcerating strike leaders, pickets, and innocent bystanders alike. Police on horseback rode their mounts down sidewalks, chasing, trampling and clubbing pedestrians. Rights of free speech and assembly were denied the workers by city officials, who prohibited them from holding parades or open air meetings, even on private property. Protests against police brutality to President Wilson and Governor Coolidge were to no avail, but the plight of the strikers did arouse sympathy in liberal quarters.[13]

Despite the opposition of church, state, business, and labor, the despised foreigners maintained an unbroken resistance through sixteen long weeks. In the early days of the strike, H. J. Skeffington and James A. Sullivan had been assigned as Commissioners of Conciliation by the U.S. Department of Labor to mediate the dispute. Their initial report embodied the view of the strike as Bolshevik-inspired and also the expectation that it would be short-lived. Summarizing their discussion with the strike leaders, Skeffington reported:

> We told them that we [sic] our judgement the strike was lost, that they had attempted to kick up a violent agitation such as obtained in Lawrence in 1912, that the State officials had organized so effectively and produced such a show that [sic] force that it was impossible for them to make any headway, that they would need at least $10,000 a week to carry on the strike and that they couldn't possibly do that. . . . Surely the strike for 54 hours' pay for 48 hours work will not succeed in Lawrence. The employers are as firm as a rock on that point and the City officials, and as far as we could find out the general public, are all in favor of the mills opening up on a 48-hour week for 48 hours' pay.[14]

Such appears to have been the general expectation.

How then did these workers who ordinarily lived on the verge of destitution sustain the struggle for almost four months? How from their kaleidoscopic ethnic diversity did they create such an impressive unity of purpose and action? What was the source of leadership in the strike movement? Was there any substance to the charge that the leaders were "imported agitators" and Bolsheviks? And finally, did the strike succeed or fail in its objectives? This study will attempt to provide at lest partial answers to these questions.

Contrary to the allegations that they were outside troublemakers, many of the strike leaders came from the rank-and-file mill workers and local labor. The most prominent of these were Samuel Bramhall and Imre Kaplan, who respectively served as chairman and secretary of the General Strike Committee. Bramhall was an Englishman, a long-time socialist and anti-clerical, and president of the Lawrence carpenters' union. Kaplan, a twenty-seven-year-old Russian Jew, was a delegate of the Mulespinners' Union and a professed revolutionary. With customary restraint, Skeffington described them as "red-eyed socialists of the most violent type," adding that "Kaplan is the agent of the Russian bolsheviki crowd if there is any agent in Lawrence."[15] Other leaders emerged from the various nationality groups to mobilize and organize their countrymen; they served on the General Strike Committee and its subcommittees. Strategy and tactics had to be communicated, picket lines organized, rumors and fears dispelled, and relief administered to some fifteen ethnic groups diverse in language, custom, and temperament. The success of this inter-ethnic collaboration moved A. J. Muste to comment: "If the League of Nations has been realized nowhere else, it has been realized in Lawrence. Fifteen nationalities are represented on the strike committee and are working together harmoniously."[16]

Feeding the strikers and their families was the most urgent task. Each nationality elected a relief committee, and the chairmen of these committees formed a General Relief Committee. Soup kitchens and food stations were established; tickets were issued to strikers for meals and provisions. A "Strikers' Cross" provided medical care for the ill and injured. The maintenance of morale was a second pressing concern. Meetings were held daily at which speakers in various languages exhorted the strikers to remain firm and songs of resistance were sung. One labor organizer, Anthony Capraro, noted that "the struggles of the Lawrence strikers have been put into song by one of their own members," but their favorite song was the "Internationale," which they sang at the opening and closing of their meetings.[17] *Victory Bulletins* were published periodically to provide news and to bolster the spirits of the strikers. *Bulletin* Number 8, for example, reported: "Sunday was another *May Day*. We visited our comrades of other nationalities, talked with them, sang with them. National lines are disappearing. We are making our Union one solid international organization."[18] One wonders to what extent this was wishful thinking and to what extent a fusion of ethnic elements did occur in the heat of the strike.

The leadership of the 1919 strike was distinguished by restraint, effective organization, and prudent management. These qualities owed much to the contribution of certain "outsiders" who did rally to the cause of the strikers. Among the most important of these were three former clergymen, A. J. Muste, Cedric Long, and Harvell L. Rotzell; all three had progressed during the war from radical Christianity and pacifism to social radicalism. Having formed the Comradeship of the New World in Boston in January 1919 to combat all forms of injustice, they hastened to Lawrence the following month to put their convictions into practice. Each played an important role in the strike, but Muste soon became a key figure as chairman of the executive committee and as the major spokesman and negotiator.[19] In addition to their organizing work in Lawrence, the ex-ministers brought the strike to the attention of a larger public through their speeches and writing. *Forward*, a Boston monthly, for example, devoted several supplements to documenting "The Truth About Lawrence."[20] The "intellectual gang," as they were called, enlisted the moral and financial support of well-to-do liberals and radicals. The appearance on the picket lines of such socialites as Elizabeth Glendower Evans inspired conservative diatribes against "Parlor Socialists" and "Boudoir Bolsheviki."[21]

Muste and his colleagues also broadened the ideological scope of the Lawrence strike. Beyond the issue of "48–54" was the struggle for industrial democracy to prepare the day when "the workers of the world shall own and control their own industries." While the end was socialism, the revolution was to be bloodless. Eschewing violence, the former clergymen urged the workers to respond to police assaults with folded arms. The relative lack of violence on the part of the strikers was attributed to the teaching and example of these disciples of the Quaker principle of passive resistance.[22] The moderating influence of the former ministers was resented by the more radical element among the strike leadership who wished the struggle to take on a more direct revolutionary character. Capraro was himself troubled by the Christian rhetoric and attitudes which the ex-preachers sometimes introduced in discussions of the General Strike Committee. On one occasion he challenged Muste to refute the radical charge that he, Long, and Rotzell were really not radicals but clergymen who were seeking "to promote peace between capital and labor, capitalistic peace, of course."[23]

On February 24, the *New York Call* carried a lengthy article on the Lawrence strike which concluded:

> Despite all the powers arrayed against them, the strikers are courageously keeping up the struggle, but there is a limit to their endurance, and that limit is the hungry cry of their little children. The suffering of the little ones is the weakest point in the armor of the workers as it is the strongest weapon that the bosses can wield.[24]

Indeed, the limited resources of the workers were quickly depleted. Citing these desperate straits, Muste appealed to Sidney Hillman, president of the Amalgamated Clothing Workers of America, for organizers and money. After consulting with August Bellanca, a vice-president of the ACWA, Hillman sent two organizers to Lawrence, Anthony Capraro and H. J. Rubenstein.[25]

A major source of opposition to the strike within the Italian community was the Catholic clergy. Father Mariano Milanese, pastor of the Italian Church of the Holy Rosary since 1905, was accused of betraying the interests of his parishioners, who were mainly workers. As in 1912, it was rumored that he had been paid by the woolen companies to oppose the strike, that he urged the police to beat the strikers, and that he had denounced the Italians as dangerous criminals. Given the traditional anti-clericalism rampant among the Italians, such allegations found fertile soil. Milanese felt compelled to issue a published statement in which he denied the ugly rumors and declared that the Italians had allowed themselves to be deceived by "those who are sworn enemies of the Priesthood, of Catholicism, of our faith and of your religion." Milanese complained that even "our most intimate friends look at us with rancour and disgust." Yet he admitted that he had counseled workers to return to the mills because he knew for a certainty that the manufacturers would never accept their demands. By this admission, the pastor convicted himself of the worst charge of his enemies. Not surprisingly, feelings against Father Milanese ran high. Windows in his church were broken; religious functions were boycotted; and even physical assaults took place.[40] Capraro, after witnessing an altercation involving Milanese and Salerno, commented.

> This, indeed, is a very small incident. Yet in Lawrence it may assume considerable proportions. Milanese is such a rascal that I shouldn't be a bit surprised if he was either to hire thugs to attack me or to incite the Irish Catholic element against us. Do you realize what this would mean here? The Italians are terribly anti-priest. And if the Irish took upon themselves the task to avenge the priest a race riot of the most serious character would ensue.[41]

Capraro also had to contend with a small, but extreme element among the Italians who agitated for more radical measures. *Maestra Cacici*, a leader of this faction, it was said, could arouse an audience to murder with her violent rhetoric. This group demanded that Arturo Giovannitti and Carlo Tresca, the heroes of the 1912 strike, be brought to Lawrence. In response to an invitation delivered by Signora Cacici herself, Giovannitti and Tresca demurred on the grounds that their presence in Lawrence would impede negotiations which promised to bring a speedy settlement to the strike. However, should the strike continue, Giovannitti and Tresca assured their comrades that they would be with them "in body as we are now in spirit."[42] In this they were following the advice of cooler heads, including Capraro, who believed that such a provocation would incite the authorities to harsh retaliation. But the revolutionary element would not be appeased. Also, after twelve weeks, Capraro noted that the strikers' morale was flagging and that some dramatic event was needed to revive their spirits. He then engineered a theatrical coup which did generate renewed enthusiasm among the workers but which also placed his life in jeopardy.[43]

While Giovannitti was reluctant to return to Lawrence, Tresca was willing, although City Marshall O'Brien (whom Tresca had slapped in an encounter in 1912) vowed that he would be killed if he set foot in the city. Securing acquiescence from a reluctant General Strike Committee, Capraro demanded complete control over the timing and staging of Tresca's visit. Meeting with Tresca in Boston on May 1, Capraro was stymied by the problem of how to evade the tight police security. By chance they were dining in the North End when Dr. Calitri entered the restaurant. It turned out that he was a friend and *paesano* of Tresca; despite his personal views, Calitri agreed to take Tresca in his car to Lawrence and to harbor him in his home. Capraro then spread the news by word of mouth that an important meeting would be held at Lexington Hall the evening of May 2. With Tresca hidden beneath the speakers' platform and guards preventing anyone from leaving, Capraro opened the meeting before a capacity crowd of Italians. Sensing the mounting tension, he gave strict instructions that no one was to leave the hall, there was to be no fighting, and no applause until he said the word. Then he turned and said:

> "Carlo." Carlo Tresca came up and stood along beside me. Well, have you ever heard the stunning detonation of silence? Not a word was uttered, not a sound made, and yet there was a situation which was about to explode. The intensity of the emotion that was generated by the presence of Carlo Tresca . . . was such that it was an absolute pity to continue to keep these people without giving vent to their emotions. . . . I said, "Comrades, *compagni*, you may applaud if you want to." The explosion was absolutely incredible and immediately after that, I saw that they let a little steam out, so I said, "Silence." There was perfect orchestration of sound and silence, and then Carlo started to speak."[44]

Tresca gave a fiery speech urging the strikers to remain steadfast in their cause and then was spirited out of town.

The next day, the *Lawrence Telegram* carried the headline: "Tresca Smuggled in and out of City – I.W.W. Leader Delivers a Vicious Speech against the Police." The article, which quoted Capraro at length, described the meeting in detail and even mentioned that "a prominent Italian doctor and lawyer [Calitri and Rocco?] had been active in shielding Tresca during his stay here."[45] The Lawrence police had been made to look like fools; they responded by setting up machine guns manned by ex-soldiers. Even before the Tresca incident, the mood in Lawrence was becoming uglier. The *Leader*, on April 27, citing the example of western cities where citizens had herded IWW leaders into freight cars and shipped them away, asked in bold type: "WHERE ARE THE VIGILANTES?" On April 30, City Marshall O'Brien announced that police protection had been withdrawn from the strike leaders. On May 3, the *Lawrence Telegram* commented that if the authorities did not take steps against the radicals, "the common people of America will, even if they have to form mobs to do so." On May 5, a Liberty Loan speaker urged the use of the lamp post for foreign-speaking strikers.[46]

At two o'clock in the morning of May 6, a gang of masked men broke into Capraro's room in the Hotel Needham, kidnapped him and Nathan Kleinman, as well as an ACWA organizer, took them out of the city, and beat them. Capraro was brutally assaulted and threatened with lynching, but managed to escape his assailants. Capraro had the presence of mind to have a photograph taken of his bloodied body prior to receiving medical attention, a photograph which was widely published. Soon after the attack, he wrote a vivid account of the incident, "How the Lawrence Ku-Klux Gang Taught Me American Democracy."[47] During his night of terror, Capraro recalled that he had decided to return to Lawrence as soon as he could: "[to] wash myself of the stain that I had procured for myself when I promised my assailants that I would not if they spared my life." While still recovering from his injuries, Capraro did return to Lawrence on May 18 to a hero's welcome. In his speeches to enthusiastic crowds, he disclaimed any claim to heroism: "I am back to tell you, Comrades, that I am not a hero, but a mere victim of the capitalistic system we are all fighting."[48]

The murderous attack upon Capraro, however, appears to have backfired. After visiting Lawrence, Bellanca wrote that the "villanous act," rather than intimidating the workers, had "electrified them all, men and women, Italians, Syrians, Germans, Lithuanians, French, Irish, Armenians, and disposed them to the greatest, the most noble sacrifices." A. J. Muste commented: "These brutal tactics instead of breaking the strike have only welded more firmly together the various race elements and imbued them with revolutionary ardor." The outrage also stimulated an outpouring of financial contributions. Evelyn Bramhall comforted Capraro with the thought that "the spreading of the news of such brutality will bring us thousands and thousands of dollars to continue this war—for such it is."[49]

Capraro's near martyrdom elicited the following tribute from the General Strike Committee:

> We have found you tireless and efficient even in ill health in the work you have undertaken with your Italian comrades, on the Finance Committee and as editor of our paper. But most of all we have found you a lovable [sic] comrade and friend, and . . . we shall treasure your friendship as one of the priceless byproducts of our struggle which gives us hope that a cooperative commonwealth will come in which men shall no more be brutalized by the competitive struggle for bread.[50]

The Italians were particularly affected by the attack upon Capraro. A thousand of them visited him, pooling their pennies and nickels for a gift as an expression of their appreciation and affection.[51]

As the strike entered its fourth month, the endurance of the workers appeared to be reaching the breaking point. For several weeks in May, the strike fund was depleted, ending regular relief. Yet an effort to reopen the Everett Mill on May 19 failed, with only a handful of the former fifteen hundred employees reporting for work. The very next day the mill owners announced that a 15 percent increase in wages would go into effect June 2, and that there would be no discrimination against strikers. Writing to Capraro, Rotzell exclaimed: "Hurrah we have a real victory and every one is jubilant." At a huge mass meeting outside Lexington Hall, the workers voted unanimously to accept the recommendation of the General Strike Committee that the strike be declared at an end. In Muste's words:

> Thus, amid the gay shouting and singing of thousands of men, women, and little children, the weary struggle came to a glorious end. AND NO SENTIMENT WON SUCH LONG AND WILD APPLAUSE FROM THAT IMMENSE MULTITUDE AS THE APPEAL TO STICK TO THE AMALGAMATED TEXTILE WORKERS OF AMERICA, THEIR OWN ONE BIG UNION, BORN OUT OF THE AGONY OF THEIR STRUGGLE![52]

At a victory picnic held on May 25, Capraro was singled out for a tumultuous ovation. Speaking to the assembled Italians, he was presented with a bouquet of carnations, which he returned, saying: "I am honored only in so far as I am able to honor you."[53]

For Capraro, as for Muste, Bellanca, and others, the victory in Lawrence was not the end of the struggle but the first step toward the creation of One Big Union in the textile industry – and beyond that, the workers' commonwealth. The recently formed Amalgamated Textile Workers of America was to be the vehicle for realizing those objectives. When Capraro was sent to Lawrence, one of his assignments was to establish a textile workers' union affiliated with the ACWA. Within a matter of weeks, he was able to report that "the central executive and general strike committees and the masses of the workers voted unanimously and enthusiastically for affiliation with the Amalgamated."[54] The Lawrence strike committee also endorsed the draft of a constitution for the Amalgamated Textile Workers of America which defined its purpose as follows:

> Our ultimate aim is, by whatever methods of proletarian action may be most effective, to help achieve the abolition of capitalism and the

system of wage-slavery; and to establish the ownership and control of industry by the workers; for the workers.[55]

The movement for the formation of such a union culminated in an organizing convention held in New York City on April 12 and 13. Under the patronage of the ACWA, and with the particular encouragement of Bellanca, seventy-five delegates from various textile centers assembled in the Labor Temple at 14th Street and Second Avenue. Just as the ACWA had been born of a revolt against the United Garment Workers Union, so the ATWA was the product of disaffection with the United Textile Workers of America. The Lawrence strike had demonstrated the capacity of the unskilled immigrant workers, who had been hitherto ignored by the UTWA, to organize and wage a drawn-out struggle. With Muste in the chair, the convention adopted the preamble of the ACWA constitution as its own. Based on the Marxist doctrine of the class struggle, it called for the organization of labor according to the principles of industrial unionism and for the education of the workers in preparation for the time when they would assume control of the system of production. The radical spirit of the convention was also expressed in its resolutions, which called for the observance of May First, extended greetings to Soviet Russia, communist Hungary, and Bavaria (the salutation concluded "Long live the Soviets!"), demanded the immediate withdrawal of American troops from Russia, and protested the political and industrial prisoners in the United States. In its "Call to Organize," the convention invited "our fellow workers in [the textile] industry to join with us in organizing a class conscious, industrial union which shall be organized and controlled by the rank and file of the workers themselves."[56]

The ATWA set up its headquarters in New York City with Muste as general secretary, and Capraro, after he recovered from the beating, as editor of its organs, the *New Textile Worker* and *Il Tessitore Libero*, Capraro had nurtured the idea of a textile workers' union in Lawrence affiliated with the ACWA, but his hope was that one day the two would merge to form "One Big Industrial Union of the Textile and Clothing Workers," a vertical organization of labor from the weaving of the cloth to the sewing of the garment.[57] Although the Amalgamated Clothing Workers in its 1920 convention voted for unity with the Amalgamated Textile Workers, the merger was never consummated. One reason was that Sidney Hillman was opposed to the idea. However, there was also growing opposition to the proposed amalgamation among Capraro's old comrades in Lawrence. Some now viewed the ACWA as not sufficiently revolutionary.[58] A conflict over this issue in the Lawrence local of the ATWA led to Capraro's resigning his position in the union. In a letter to Muste of March 1, 1920, he explained his reasons:

> I was accused by Kaplan in the midst of a Central Council meeting of being an agent of the Amalgamated Clothing Workers of America. The members of this body took cognizance of the incident by various expressions but failed, as a body, to repudiate Kaplan's explicit accusations and its mean implications. . . . Now, you will understand that a lack of pronouncement on the part of the Central Council to the effect that the executive body of the Lawrence Local did not entertain the same belief with regard to my role in our organization justifies me to believe that the opinion of that body coincides with that of Kaplan. That being the case I could not with any amount of dignity remain in the organization. . . .[59]

As a Sicilian, Capraro had a high sense of personal honor and this attack upon his integrity was more than he could brook. But he also felt out of place in the textile workers' union and wished to return to his work as an organizer for the ACWA.[60]

What appears to have happened in Lawrence is that a man, known to us only by his last name, Legere, had gained ascendency, particularly among the younger militants in the union. It was said of Legere that "a great number of workers . . . are ready to go with him wherever he decides, so great is the confidence which they have in him as a leader of tremendous imagination, energy, and experience in the labor movement." A syndicalist, Legere favored One Big Union along the lines of the Winnipeg model. He was so opposed to fusion of the ATWA with the ACWA that he favored secession of the Lawrence local if that should happen.[61] Capraro viewed this development from afar with growing displeasure: "In Lawrence the supreme need is a strong class-conscious textile organization. Whatever fosters such an organization is good; whatever does not foster such an organization is the work either of spies or of fools." He concluded that Legere must be either one or the other.[62]

But ideological disputes were not the major obstacle confronting the infant ATWA. The Amalgamated Textile Workers initially spread rapidly through the mill towns of New England, New Jersey, New York, and Pennsylvania. Using foreign-language organizers and literature, it was especially successful in attracting immigrant workers. ATWA membership reached a peak of fifty thousand in 1920. However, the severe depression which struck the textile industry beginning in April 1920 caused widespread unemployment and mill closings.[63] Under such conditions the strength of the union was rapidly eroded. In the textile strike of 1922, the longest and largest such dispute in New England, the Amalgamated Textile Workers controlled the strike only in the Pawtuxet Valley of Rhode Island. The United Textile Workers directed the struggle in other areas, except for Lawrence, where the majority of the strikers followed the leadership of One Big Union (evidently Legere had carried the day!).[64] A leading labor scholar of the day, William M. Leiserson, observed: "While the Amalgamated Textile Workers made rapid progress in the first year or two of its existence, it has more recently shown it is not any more successful in organizing and holding the unskilled foreign-born workers in the industry than the United Textile Workers."[65] The 1922 strike was the ATWA's "last hurrah." Its final convention was held in New York City in the spring of 1923; its leaders discouraged, the organization collapsed, leaving surviving locals to fend for themselves.[66]

In the 1930s, the Textile Workers Organizing Committee of the CIO, funded by Hillman's Amalgamated Clothing Workers and David Dubinsky's International Ladies' Garment Workers, succeeded where the ATWA had failed. The textile workers finally were organized into an industrial union, encompassing skilled and unskilled workers, foreign-born and native, white and black. Neither Muste nor Capraro was to play a part in the delayed realization of their dream of one big textile union. However, one might ask the extent to which the experience of the 1919 strike (and similar strikes elsewhere) contributed to the shaping of an American working class ready to make the most of the New Deal of the thirties. The connections between the earlier, if largely failed efforts of immigrant workers to redress their grievances and the mass organizing drives of the 1930s in which they and their children played prominent roles remain to be studied systematically.

Regardless of its consequences, the Lawrence strike of 1919 is in itself instructive as an episode in ethnic labor history. First, it is clear that, apart from the hysteria of the Red Scare, there were real immigrant radicals afoot in the land. "Comrade Fellow Worker Anarchist Communist Radical Revolutionary Anthony Capraro," as he was addressed by one correspondent, was one of these.[67] There were others who viewed the strike in Lawrence as a battle in the class war. Not all were avowed Communists, but some were. The fear of Bolshevik influence then was not simply a bogeyman born of the conservatives' fevered imagination. Nor was such radicalism limited to "outside agitators"; rather it appears to have been widespread among the laboring people of Lawrence, and especially the "new immigrants."[68] The 1919 strike gives the lie to both Donald Cole's assertion that the immigrants "would follow alien leaders for better conditions but would never adopt un-American [i.e., radical] views" and Gerald Rosenblum's dictum that the conservatism of the American labor movement can be attributed to the "new immigrants,"[69]

What the Lawrence strike did not do was to create class conscious working-class solidarity among all wage earners. Rather, it brought to the surface those cleavages of ethnicity and status that divided the workers into antagonistic, competing groups. The basic dichotomy, as indicated earlier, appears to have been between the English-speaking and the non–English-speaking. The strike then was not only a conflict between labor and capital, but also a struggle between the older established ethnic elements and the more recent arrivals. This was a struggle involving both socio-economic interests and cultural values. Capraro observed that the Irish Americans had proven to be the "greatest enemies of the strikers."[70] As a still-marginal ethnic group, the strike gave the Irish the opportunity to reinforce their position by demonstrating to the Yankee establishment their utility as guardians of law and order. Father O'Reilly and City Marshall O'Brien, the leading antagonists of the immigrant strikers, personified this role. Thus, while the common struggle generated a trans-ethnic unity among the non–English-speaking groups, the conflict widened the abyss that separated them from the English-speaking portion of the working class. Certainly the heritage of the 1919 strike must have continued to influence intergroup relations, politics, social life, and economic arrangements in Lawrence for years to come.

The Transformation of Working-Class Ethnicity: Corporate Control, Americanization, and the Polish Immigrant Middle Class in Bayonne, New Jersey, 1915–1925

JOHN J. BUKOWCZYK

Despite America's darkening anti-labor climate after 1900, the decade prior to U.S. entry into World War I showed that industrial protest and labor radicalism had not disappeared. These years witnessed great strikes at McKees Rocks (1909), Lawrence (1912), Paterson (1913), and Akron (1913), and also saw an upsurge of labor militance in countless less celebrated incidents.[1] The significant part of this record, however, is the strikers' identity. They were not the same native-born men in skilled trades who had acquired a reputation for protest in the late nineteenth century, but unskilled immigrants. These men and women who so dramatically reshaped the American working class during the mass-production years had often remained outside the American labor movement. But as their attitudes hardened and their numbers grew, immigrant workers now posed the first serious challenge to America's industrial capitalist order since the great labor upheaval of the 1890s.

In this immigrant working-class revolt American labor therefore found a unique opportunity, but by 1919 that opportunity had simply evaporated. The opportunism of AFL leaders during the War isolated radical, militant, and often spontaneous protest. Repression – by corporate security forces, extra-legal middle-class "citizens" groups, and the enforcement arm of the State – crushed protest. Finally, "welfare

283

capitalism" diffused or coopted working-class dissent, while Americanization programs suffused American society with ruling-class values that suffocated working-class resistance. As a result, union organizing and working-class protest fell into disarray, and the 1920s became "lean years" for American labor.

The major theme in the history of class relations in the late 1910s and early 1920s was thus the re-establishment of corporate control over a heavily immigrant, "re-made" American working class. Accordingly, much of the historical literature on the period focuses on the external process of cooptation and repression.[2] Subsidiary developments within immigrant working-class communities, however, also affected working-class history during the period. If we look inside those communities, we discover a complicated social world populated not only by workers but also by assorted small proprietors, petty entrepreneurs, and ethnic professionals who, taken together, constituted the immigrant middle class in process of formation.[3] Sometimes allied with their working-class co-nationals but often coupled with corporate managers and civic officials, middle-class immigrants, in order to advance their own political and economic interest, manipulated malleable ethnic symbols. In the 1910s and 1920s, these middle-class immigrants created an ethnic variant of the "American Creed," which also helped contain their new fellow-nationals' labor militance.

The place to investigate this development is the burgeoning industrial towns and cities of America's Second Industrial Revolution, whose mass-production industries attracted unskilled immigrants from Southern and Eastern Europe who streamed into the country in search of work in the years before the Great War. Bayonne was such a place – a bastion of heavy industry in New York harbor, the site of major labor turmoil in 1915 and 1916, its population heavily Polish and foreign-born.

From the outset, Polish immigration to Bayonne mirrored developments in Bayonne's industrial economy, particularly in the oil-refining industry. Poles first arrived in significant numbers between 1880 and 1885, as refining operations in the city expanded. In 1883, managers mechanized a large refinery barrel factory and hired Poles, Slovaks, and Ruthenians to break a strike by American and Irish coopers. In the next fifteen years, this pattern recurred. In 1885 and again in 1901, more Poles won jobs after factory enlargement and mechanization, and because they were "available and made satisfactory laborers"; in 1903 and 1904, still more entered the refineries as strikebreakers. From an estimated two hundred families in 1900, the Polish population in Bayonne climbed to about nine hundred families ten years later. Along with the Slovaks, Poles dominated the refinery barrel factories and held many of the unskilled jobs in the refineries, in the stills, and in other Bayonne industries. Occupationally, they had made inroads into semi-skilled fields too—as helpers, machine operators, coopers, headers, and occasionally as foremen.[4]

Factory work represented a great change for the vast majority of Polish refining industry workers who had been farm laborers or small peasant proprietors in the old country.[5] Though working conditions in the refining industry compared favorably to those in other industries during the period, immigrants accustomed to the intermittent rural workplace still found the conditions extraordinarily taxing. Most refinery workers labored nine hours a day, six days a week, but men in the refining department followed staggered-hour, day-and-night shifts for a weekly average of 84 hours. Moreover, despite so-called "excellent" general sanitary conditions, the industry still took its toll in broken health and shortened lives. Lead burners in the scaling departments chronically suffered from "lead colic."[6] Still cleaning, another occupation heavily populated by Poles, posed hazards so graphic that it attracted the attention of radical journalist John Reed, who described it in chilling detail in a *Metropolitan Magazine* article:

> A gang of two to five men . . . are set to clean each still. Wearing iron shoes, and wrapped in layers and layers of sacking, they enter the still in turns to break out the red-hot "cokes" left by the oil. In a temperature of over two hundred degrees they work furiously—a man can only stand it for three or four minutes at a time—from three to four hours a day. Almost every day someone collapses in the still and has to be rescued, sometimes with his clothing on fire. When they come out, after their spell, they strip and throw themselves down in the snow, if it be winter, or dash buckets of water over each other. One man said they looked like "boiled meat."

In order to refresh themselves, still-cleaners usually downed buckets of beer after they emerged from this noxious inferno. About the men who endured this harsh regimen, one doctor commented:

> the average working-life of a still-cleaner is *ten years*. Take a twenty-year-old Polish or Lithuanian peasant who has worked out of doors all his life; a big, strong, healthy animal—the finest human material in the world. At thirty he will be a bent old man, with white hair. At thirty-two he will be dead.[7]

Peasant fatalism, reinforced by the dolorous world view of Polish Roman Catholicism, helped inure Polish immigrant workers to these harsh conditions. But it was the purpose that many Poles had in mind when they emigrated which actually encouraged them to endure industrial hardship. Many young Galician and Russian Poles left behind families in Poland who struggled to hold on to undersized parcels of land.[8] Less immigrant than migrant, these Poles considered their sojourn in American factories a temporary expedient. They fully intended to return to Poland and use their American wages to buy land or to bail out debt-ridden rural households.

Yet however transient, Polish immigrant workers in cities like Bayonne could not afford to overlook some features of factory labor and urban life. The very precariousness of conditions in industrial America continually threatened to wreck all of their plans, since injury, sickness, layoff, discharge, wage cuts, and industrial depression could unexpectedly disrupt immigrant financial calculations at any time. Other chronic problems also worried even the temporary sojourner. Without financial resources or skills, unable to speak English, sometimes unable even to read or write, immigrant workers found themselves vulnerable even when employed.

Against this insecurity, Bayonne's Polish immigrant working people took shelter within their own growing community. For many, immigrant families helped cushion the shock of uncertainty in a new and alien world. Here the unmarried immigrant also sought refuge as boarder or lodger.[9] Other immigrant institutions also helped working-class immigrants keep body and soul together. In 1898, Bayonne Poles founded the Roman Catholic parish of Our Lady of Mount Carmel, which henceforth would shape the identity of Bayonne's Polish community. As in other Polish settlements, Bayonne's Polish Roman Catholic Church became the religious, cultural, and social center of gravity for Bayonne's Polish neighborhoods.[10]

Yet Polish immigrant workers in Bayonne did not sit back content and passively accept pastoral assistance, religious comfort, and parochial aid. Drawing on the principle of mutual aid which already had taken root in the Polish countryside in peasant land banks and village cooperative societies, Bayonne Poles joined together in fraternal benevolent associations "for mutual moral and material assistance."[11] Finally, working-class immigrants discovered still another institution which could shield them from industrial hazards and a host of alien laws, practices, and customs. Bayonne's Polish newcomers depended heavily upon assistance from the settlement's "go-betweens," i.e., from immigrant shopkeepers and small-business proprietors.

Despite dire predictions by European social critics that the development of industrial capitalism would push the lower strata of the middle class – including artisans and shopkeepers – into the growing industrial proletariat, by the early 1900s this had not happened.[12] The number of skilled crafts dropped precipitously during these years, while the autonomy of surviving artisans and shopkeepers often declined. But on the whole, the spread of capitalism often multiplied rather than shrank opportunities for petty enterprise and small business. One of the ways in which this occurred involved international mass migration. The great influx of European migrants to an alien United States between the 1880s and the 1920s created myriad opportunities for immigrant entrepreneurs – shopkeepers, fraternal insurance operators, agents, liquor dealers, small-time bankers, and occasionally confidence men – who together constituted a separate stratum within immigrant working-class communities like Bayonne.

The corporate strategy of divide-and-conquer notwithstanding, aspects of Polish working-class culture already had helped make the immigrants into tractable, docile, obedient workers.[24] Transplanted peasant fatalism; Roman Catholic attitudes about suffering, martyrdom, and salvation; deep attachments to family and household which produced a preoccupation with "steady" work; and political interests directed away from conditions in America and toward affairs in partitioned Poland all tended to blunt class resentments among immigrant workers and to foster acceptance of the industrial status quo.[25] Rapid turnover, return migration, and considering industrial labor in America a momentary opportunity or a temporary cross to bear had a similar effect. Yet not all such "traditional" and migrant attitudes meshed so easily with the industrial capitalist order. The Poles' belief in a customary social right to work challenged patterns of cyclical unemployment and arbitrary discharge which played such a pivotal role in the American industrial economy of the period. Community cohesiveness likewise threatened managerial authority. Finally, a host of transplanted rural values and practices – the observance of religious holidays, "pre-industrial" work rhythms, alcohol consumption – continually interfered with the factory regimen. As a result, beneath the apparent calm that prevailed in Bayonne's oil refineries, subterranean tensions remained a more or less constant feature of immigrant working-class employment throughout the early decades of Polish migration to the city.[26]

By the early 1910s, the changing character and composition of Bayonne's working-class Polish immigrant community caused these chronic tensions to erupt. First, by the 1910s, the temporary character of Polish settlement in Bayonne had begun to fade, as more and more immigrants sent for families or married, joined the parish, formed organizations, and otherwise set down roots in the oil-refining city.

When the outbreak of the World War in 1914 cut off the possibility of re-emigration, even more Polish sojourners postponed or abandoned plans to return to Poland. In the process, temporary migrants who had readily endured transitory hardships now suddenly became permanent settlers with a newfound concern about the character of the work and the conditions of employment, and a deeper stake in community life.[27]

Second, while migrants from rural Poland had little acquaintance with radical ideologies or progressive politics in the 1880s, the opposite held true for post-1890 migrants. Leaving a rural society now gripped by popular agitation for peasant land reform, strikes by agricultural wage laborers, and a full-fledged rural socialist movement, they carried an assortment of democratic and egalitarian notions that hardly fitted contemporary—and laterday—stereotypes. Moreover, after the repression of the Revolution of 1905 by Tsarist authorities in Russian Poland, Polish settlements in America also received an infusion of political radicals, trade unionists, and insurrectionaries who had literally fled for their lives. That many settled in New York City and environs is evident from the sudden rise of the Polish left there during the subsequent period. The Alliance of Polish Socialists (*Zwiazek Socjalistów Polskich*), founded in 1896, experienced a burst of support after 1905. Polish socialists also played a leading role in the Polish nationalist Committee for National Defense (*Komitet Obrony Narodowej*), which operated between 1912 and 1914, with much of its strength in the New York area. Blending Polish nationalism with a radical social and economic program, these Polish leftists appealed strongly to other working-class Poles and helped galvanize workplace tensions and class resentments into an upsurge of labor militance in the 1910s.[28]

In Bayonne, the spark which exploded the city's vaunted "industrial peace" soon came at the Standard Oil Company works. Because company foremen functioned virtually as independent labor contractors, with broad power over hiring, discipline, work pace, working conditions, and firing, supervision in the plant operated on a direct, personal, and often arbitrary basis.[29] Polish migrants from an often still quasi-feudal Polish countryside might have accepted such supervisory relations as commonplace. But denied customary reciprocal rights in the workplace, which typically had helped contain class tensions between laborer and landlord in rural Poland, immigrant workers now found the "pull-and-tug" of class relations in the Bayonne refinery brutal, capricious, and very lopsided: Foremen took far more than they gave in return.[30] Polish immigrant workers chronically brooded about "being fleeced out of a portion of their earnings by unscrupulous 'bosses' and 'supervisors.'"[31] Ethnic differences between immigrant workers and native-born – often Irish – foremen only aggravated the problem, as did the intense wartime speedup then underway in the plant.[32] Thus primed, Bayonne's industrial powderkeg merely awaited a match. On July 15, 1915, the heavily Polish gang of still-cleaners at the Standard Oil works complained that they were continually "cursed out" by the foremen, subjected to physical intimidation and ethnic abuse, and that, "to settle grudges, foremen were detaining cleaners in the hot stills, with temperatures up to 250° F." When refinery officials refused to hear their grievances, the still-cleaners – about one hundred men – walked out, to be joined a few days later by about nine hundred workers in the cooperage and barrel departments.[33]

For a while, affairs in Bayonne hung in the balance. Intransigent refinery managers imported a crew of strikebreakers – mostly Italians – while the strikers, grown more resolute, began to organize. Soon picketing and similar grievances at other Bayonne plants spread the strike to the Tide Water Oil, Vacuum Oil, and Bergen Point Chemical companies. With fifteen hundred of its five thousand employees out, Standard Oil shut down its Bayonne operations on July 20. Later in the day, striking workers – joined by their wives – stoned local police guarding the plant and started a full scale riot. That evening a second smaller riot ensued after striking workers attacked a Polish non-striker. Shortly, an American Federation of Labor representative and Frank Tannenbaum, an IWW organizer, arrived in Bayonne to assist the strikers. The Bayonne refinery strike had entered a new phase.[34]

With its major factories closed and its streets swollen with striking Poles and other immigrant workers, Bayonne now faced open revolt by its working class; and its corporate and civic authorities responded decisively. The fact that Pierre Garven, counsel for the New York office of Standard Oil, also served as Bayonne's mayor, already guaranteed that the Bayonne Police Department would vigorously aid any corporation attempt to break the strike.[35] When the police proved inadequate to the task and their use seemed politically unwise, however, Mayor Garven himself urged refinery officials to hire private armed guards to protect company property and help pacify the city. Upon Garven's advice, Standard engaged the nefarious Pearl L. Bergoff, a recent resident of Bayonne and proprietor of a notorious New York City "industrial service" firm. Bergoff already had six labor spies planted at Standard Oil. Now Bergoff furnished Standard with a barge full of guards, guns, and ammunition, and dispatched a second contingent to Tide Water.

For the next four days, Bergoff's private army of so-called "nobles" terrorized the strikers by sniping at pickets and launching armed sortees into the assembled crowds. No fewer than five strikers died and several more sustained gunshot wounds before the corporate reign of terror at the hands of Bergoff's "armed thugs" finally subsided. In the end, force—and persuasion—applied from another quarter finally restored order to the city of Bayonne. Hudson County Sheriff Eugene K. Kinkead broke up the strikers' organization, beat up their young socialist leader Jeremiah Baly, dispersed Bergoff's forces, arrested IWW organizer Tannenbaum, and banned the sale of the radical newspaper the *New York Call*.[36] Yet Kinkead also tried to mollify the strikers by manipulating ethnic sentiments. "I told them they were Poles and had suffered much at the hands of Russia," the Sheriff said, "and that I was an Irishman and my people had suffered at the hands of England." Also citing their common religion, Kinkead tried to make the strikers "feel that he was one of them."[37] Despite Standard Oil's refusal to deal with federal mediators, Kinkead's iron fist, silver tongue, and relative impartiality brought the immigrant strikers back to work. They soon received part of the wage increase they had sought—at a time when the earnings of the Bayonne plant were rising from $332,000 in 1914 to $6,552,000 the following year.[38]

The way corporate and civic officials handled the 1915 refinery strike reflected the underside of their attitudes about immigrants. Moved by class consciousness, race hatred, and simple fear, and convinced that outside agitators were manipulating ignorant foreigners, Bayonne's ruling elite resolved to teach the immigrant a lesson. The instructions that Standard Oil General Manager George B. Gifford gave Pearl Bergoff amply revealed the refiners' intentions. "Get me two hundred and fifty husky men who can swing clubs," Gifford told Bergoff. "If they're not enough, get a thousand or two thousand. I want them to march up Bayonne's East Twenty-second Street through the guts of Polacks."[39] Bayonne's police harbored their own resentments against the striking Poles. One graphic strike vignette described how officers wrecked a Polish saloon frequented by strikers. According to the account, one policeman "amused himself by shooting holes in framed paintings of the Kings of Poland and put a bullet through *the picture of Kosciuszko*—the Pole who fought so gallantly in the American Revolution."[40] This climate of repression affected Bayonne's foreign- and native-born residents alike. The United States Commission on Industrial Relations called the collapse of the strike "a complete victory for the Standard Oil Company as to its vital policies,"[41] Even more important to bolstering Standard Oil's power in the city, the strike deepened anti-immigrant attitudes. Native-born residents interviewed in 1916 divided Bayonne's population into two classes: "'white' men and foreigners."[42]

But repression failed to teach the Poles a lesson which would stick. The following year, in October 1916, the now far better organized immigrant workers again struck Standard and Vacuum protesting wages, hours, the high cost of living, and abuses by some of the foremen.[43] In milder form, workers, officials, and police repeated the 1915 scenario. Once again, force eventually defeated the strike. Yet the 1916 strike showed that force alone could not prevent still another such outbreak. The chronic volatility of the immigrants, Bayonne authorities believed, irrepressibly stemmed from their very foreignness.

Despite its racist overtones, a kernel of truth lay at the heart of this observation about immigrant working-class ethnicity: it did underpin both refinery strikes. As evident from the list of strike casualties and from the fact that Poles began both strikes, common language and culture fostered common action and widespread community support. In turn, the refineries' tactic of engaging non-Poles—mostly Italians—as strikebreakers reinforced the social boundaries of the ethnic working-class community. Class and ethnicity overlapped to provide a powerful bond for Bayonne's strikers, which realized the worst fears of the refinery managers. "Clannishness"—cohesiveness arising from shared ethnic culture—was dangerous. Finally, those Polish strikers who wore buttons which read "Liberty for Poland" showed that rising Polish nationalism—that is, ethnicity as ideology—also was dangerous.[44] Instead of diverting immigrant attentions abroad, Polish nationalism—when fused with radical ideologies like socialism and populism—buttressed immigrant working-class militance here.

This working-class understanding of ethnicity wrenched social relations within Bayonne's Polish settlement. Striking Poles demanded that their middle-class countrymen and their priests live up to ideals of "community" cohesion and mutual obligation on which their patron/client networks rested. During the 1915 strike, workers actually fired at the Rev. Sigismund Swider, pastor of Our Lady of Mount Carmel parish; by urging strikers to return to work, he had breached community solidarity.[45] They also demanded that refinery officials dismiss "a foreman, a fellow Pole named Anthony Jozwicki, whom they regarded as one of the most brutal bosses *and* who refused to go out with them" [emphasis added].[46] Jozwicki's real crime was not brutality, for that the men would have forgiven. Jozwicki's unforgivable offense was disregarding the claims of ethnic cohesiveness which should have obliged him to join them. By demanding his dismissal, striking Poles insisted that mutual duties and obligations should accompany common nativity and should constrain foremen who expected obedience from their men.

Yet not all of Bayonne's immigrant middle class violated this assumed trust. Rushing to catch up with their radicalized working-class countrymen, Bayonne's Polish shopkeepers and professionals avoided Swider's and Jozwicki's mistake and supported the strikers. Local merchants extended credit which sustained the strikers' families throughout the conflict. Paul Supinski, a Polish attorney from neighboring Jersey City, translated speeches into Polish, presided over a strike meeting, and represented his striking countrymen to refinery officials. Polish saloonkeepers also lent critical support. In both years, strikers met at saloonkeeper John Mydosh's hall, while several saloonkeepers like Anthony Dworzanski actually helped lead the strikes. Dworzanski sat on the 1916 strike committee as a Standard Oil worker, while also running a grocery store and tavern business in the city. After the strike, the ambitious and upwardly mobile Dworzanski inspired the founding of St. Anthony Society for Mutual Aid and Benefit, a fraternal insurance operation which members appropriately named after his own patron saint. During the 1916 strike, police recognized the role of men like Dworzanski and arrested John Mydosh's son and five other saloonkeepers on charges of inciting to riot.[47]

Perhaps feelings of ethnic solidarity motivated these Polish proprietors and professionals, but they also stood to gain by supporting the strike. First, by backing the strikers, middle-class Poles showed up Bayonne's Polish pastor and thereby won another small victory in their long-standing competition for political and social authority within the immigrant settlement. Second, by siding with the workers, middle-class Poles also countered the small but vocal Polish socialist minority that had challenged their leadership in the last few years. Finally, supporting the strike reaffirmed ethnic ties which redounded to their economic benefit. At the time of the strikes, Polish saloonkeepers and small proprietors faced stiff competition from Irish-owned saloons and from Jewish immigrants "extensively engaged in small business enterprises."[48] As a result of the strikes, however, the precarious market position of Bayonne's Polish businessmen improved measurably.

The middle-class Poles' market position improved in two ways. First, strikers attacked the Poles' competitors. We may never know for certain why rioters sacked one Bayonne business street during the 1915 refinery strike. Perhaps rumors that one saloonkeeper harbored company guards and tipped off police touched off the violence. But the identity of the storeowners whose businesses were wrecked suggests that class antagonism alone did not motivate the rioters. Four men owned saloons that fell victim to the riot: Samuel Schwartzberg, Richard Flood, David Weinberg, and Samuel Greenberg – three Jews and an Irishman, apparently. Jacob Cohen, owner of a drygoods store which rioters sacked, obviously also was Jewish.[49] Interestingly, crowds attacked not a single Polish business during the two strikes. The prevalence of Jewish-owned businesses in Bayonne may account for this pattern of violence, but not entirely. Historic tensions between Poles and Jews in Poland conditioned immigrant working-class behavior. The fact that Pearl Bergoff and probably at least one of his lieutenants, John ("Jew Stoney") Speiser, both were part-Jewish exacerbated intergroup resentments.[50]

Second, supporting the strikes aided Polish businessmen in a positive way: it strengthened their own claim to immigrant working-class patronage as against their Jewish competition. The rumor that Jewish lawyers conspired with Bayonne saloonkeepers to fleece arrested immigrant strikers of their savings in a bail-bond racket may explain why mobs sacked Samuel Greenberg's saloon: he was one of Bayonne's notorious "bail sharks."[51] But it also may explain why strikers selected Paul Supinski of Jersey City instead of a local lawyer to serve as their counsel. Middle-class Poles were harnessing both ethnic and religious ties to cordon off immigrant business patronage during these turbulent years.[52]

Out of the two refinery strikes, ethnicity thus emerged as a far more complicated thing than Bayonne's refinery managers may have anticipated when they hired the first Pole for their plants in the 1880s. While ethnic differences still divided the work force, foreignness proved increasingly difficult to manipulate. In both strikes, unskilled immigrants like the Poles behaved far more militantly than English-speaking workers.[53] Since it heightened labor unrest, Bayonne authorities therefore concluded, foreignness was a dangerous thing which they had to render harmless.

In the wake of the 1916 strike, Standard Oil managers instituted a wide range of welfare capitalist measures designed to wean immigrant workers from virulent foreignism. Wage increases, coupled with accident, sickness, and death provisions, sought to convince the immigrants that "capital and industry are partners" and led one local newspaper to conclude that Bayonne stood "on the threshold of becoming a workmen's paradise."[54] Standard also reformed its supervisory apparatus, organizing a "Foremen's Club" in order to impart loyalty and professionalism to critical frontline personnel and introducing its celebrated "Industrial Representation Plan." Designed at the behest of John D. Rockefeller, Jr., after the infamous Ludlow Massacre of 1914, the Industrial Representation Plan established a company union, work rules, a progressive system of fringe benefits, and a formal grievance procedure.[55]

To augment these efforts, Standard also sharpened ideological weapons. In September 1920, Standard established *The Messenger*, a company magazine "published every Saturday in the interest of the Employees of the Bayonne Refinery." Trying to build a rapport between labor and management, *The Messenger* attempted to inculcate a work ethos into working-class readers. Front-page editorials railed against "The Chronic Kicker," "The Anonymous Letter," and the "Industrial Drifter," while the magazine constantly extolled a version of the Protestant ethic: "Don't let any bewhiskered Bolshevik tell you that there is a royal road to success or that we can achieve success without work." In a notice for a corporation-sponsored recreational event, *The Messenger* revealed how Standard Oil viewed its relationship with its employees. "Old Mamma Standard Oil," the magazine advised:

> is going to have big family gathering at Pershing Field, Jersey City, tomorrow, where she expects to meet and greet all the thousands and thousands of children. You being one of these you are, of course, invited to attend and expected to accept the invitation.[56]

While the corporation flourished its mailed, motherly fist, other benevolent constraints fell into place. In 1918, for example, corporate money financed a block of model apartment houses in Bayonne.[57] This measure, like all the rest, encouraged working-class loyalty and gratitude to serve corporate purposes.

However effective, the carrot-and-stick blend of welfare capitalism and repression could remain only a stopgap so long as one basic condition remained: Foreignness itself was dangerous. That conclusion seemed increasingly true during the xenophobic World War I years. Accordingly, as war with Germany neared, Bayonne authorities acted to protect the city's large industries against sabotage. Standard Oil officials took a "census" in their plant "with a view toward ascertaining the nativity and sympathies of their employees."[58] If nativity and sympathies were thus linked, saboteurs would be foreigners. And if foreignness was dangerous, there followed only one logical next step: to stamp it out wherever possible by Americanizing the immigrants.

Already in 1915, at the end of the refinery strike, Bayonne industrial leaders had witnessed how Americanism could quell social ferment among the foreign-born when Sheriff Eugene Kinkead opened a meeting of strikers. Kinkead began by having two of his deputies unfurl a large American flag, which started the workers cheering. Then, he told them to go back to work in the name of the United States, the flag, and himself. "If there is any foreigner," he said, "who is dissatisfied with conditions in the United States, for God's sake let him go where he has come from."

Kinkead's performance impressed the Poles, who returned to work and henceforth called the sheriff "godfather" (*"Kresni Ocec"* [sic]) for his role in ending Bergoff's reign of terror in Bayonne.[59] Bayonne industrial managers, smarting from the strikes, themselves later instituted private efforts to Americanize the foreign-born. As early as October 1917, a committee of Bayonne manufacturers considered how to convert immigrants into Americans and thereby "help the immigrant work out his salvation." During this time, Standard Oil and the International Nickel Company also sponsored "industrial classes" inside their plants, with respectively 180 and 160 "students," who posted an impressive 89% attendance rate.[60] These Americanization lessons not only sought to impart patriotism, but also to instill work discipline. Along with English and civics lessons, the Bayonne Chamber of Commerce lectured that, "it is necessary that [immigrants] be taught to realize the baneful influences of the saloon and the dance hall — not by means of enforced abstinence, but that they be taught to realize the virtues of moderation. . . ."[61]

Despite these efforts, civic officials complained that local industrial managers showed little interest in Americanization work. It therefore remained for civic rather than industry officials to spearhead Bayonne's public Americanization drive.[62] Because the city depended upon Standard Oil for half of its revenues by 1881 and because Standard and Tide Water contributed to the police and firemen's pension funds "in appreciation of services rendered" during the strikes, we might surmise that city officials merely did the bidding of the refiners.[63] But this was not the case. By trying to diffuse immigrant working-class militance, public officials promoted notions of law and order and private property rights which they too shared, strengthening their own influence over Bayonne civic affairs, and enhancing the importance and autonomy of Bayonne's municipal bureaucracy.[64]

Bayonne officials relied upon persuasion and threat in order to Americanize the immigrants, and settled upon citizenship as the most tangible measure of their own success. As the 1920 Federal census enumeration approached, Bayonne citizenship statistics gave cause for hope. While 30 percent of Bayonne's population was still "alien," during the past twelve months alone 5,179 aliens in Hudson County had filed declarations of an intention to become a citizen and over twenty-nine hundred petitioned for naturalization. Immigrants responded to the Americanizers' citizenship campaign for obvious reasons. Without citizenship, immigrants faced severe disabilities in post-war America. After a January 1920 Red Raid in New Jersey netted 68 Bayonne residents—"the largest number of any municipality in the country," at least a third of them Poles—citizenship applications flooded into the Hudson County Bureau of Naturalization at the rate of 80 to 100 a day.[65] Citizenship offered protection, and also conferred other positive benefits. These included preferment in employment, access to political patronage, and that most singular gift, according to American mythology, prized since the days of the Yankee yeoman farmer: the right to vote.

But that Bayonne's city fathers and refinery managers should have encouraged immigrant citizenship and thus enfranchisement raises a perplexing question. After immigrant strikers twice threatened corporate power in Bayonne, were industrial and political leaders not afraid that immigrant citizens now would use votes to accomplish the same end? Apparently they were not. Bayonne's Americanizers believed that foreign vices could be shed and American virtues learned through civic education. Still, education alone would hardly have ensured responsible immigrant voting had it not been for the immigrant middle class, which would soon play a powerful role in the Americanization drama.

Even as Bayonne's middle-class Poles aided their striking countrymen, they themselves were changing. And as they changed, they redefined their social position within the immigrant working-class world. In terms of the group's socio-economic composition, immigrant shopkeepers slowly gave way to ethnic entrepreneurs and professionals who shouldered the mantle of leadership as Polish Bayonne entered the 1920s. Business tied these men to the larger economy and society, via property law, government and financial bureaucracies, and electoral politics. In the process, it drew them beyond the working-class world that immigrant shopkeepers had inhabited. In terms of ideology, middle-class immigrants also changed. Disappointed with events in post-war Poland and increasingly absorbed in their own business affairs, middle-class Polish immigrants adopted two slogans in the early 1920s which no longer invoked the progressive principles that had characterized Polish nationalism a few decades earlier. The two slogans were "Wychodztwo dla Wychodztwa" and "Swój do Swego."[66] The first meant "The Emigrants for Themselves" and signified a shift away from Poland's politics and toward Polish affairs in America—language maintenance, cultural preservation, political and ecclesiastical representation, resistance to nativism, and upward social and economic mobility. The second, loosely translated, meant "Patronize Our Own," i.e., Buy Polish. In middle-class hands, Polish nationalism (ethnicity as ideology) thus became a benign and malleable creed that buttressed political patronage and economic clientage networks and increased their influence over working-class immigrants.

Withal, Bayonne's middle-class Poles had found themselves in an awkward position during the recent refinery strikes. From one side, Polish socialists challenged their leadership. Yet as they jockeyed for their countrymen's loyalty by siding with the strikers, civic and corporate officials now menaced their fragile economic and political position in the city. Not only did Bayonne police wreck John Mydosh's saloon for his role in the 1915 strike – an obvious form of pressure – but authorities also coerced Polish middle-class strike sympathizers in more subtle ways. Bayonne officials equated support for the strikes with disloyalty and subversion, for example, the company's charge that one Polish lawyer – probably Paul Supinski – was "an agent of the German emperor" for the part he played in the 1915 strike.[67] Later the Americanization program attacked the economic underpinnings of the immigrant middle-class. By equipping immigrants to do things for themselves, it would eliminate many middle-class service occupations.[68] This accumulated pressure may clarify why local merchants finally withdrew credit from the strikers in 1915.[69] They did so amidst a wave of repression as the strike turned steadily left.

Bayonne's middle-class Poles thus welcomed the overture that Bayonne's civic and industrial leaders now extended. Perhaps following the guidelines laid out by Peter Roberts, architect of YMCA Americanization work, Bayonne Americanizers invited middle-class Poles to join the Americanization campaign.[70] Their enlistment caused few pangs of conscience. Americanization could aid business and professional advancement. Moreover, as Polish nationalism itself had come to mean "The Emigrants for Themselves," promoting Polish interest in America, the Americanization ideology converged with the credo middle-class Poles soon would adopt: "Polish-Americanism."

Polish involvement in Americanization work in Bayonne had begun in fact before the War. In September 1912, Joseph Derowski, the son of a Standard Oil timekeeper and the first Pole appointed to Bayonne's Police Department, formed the Young Men's Democratic Political Club, the first such Polish organization in the city.[71] Though Derowski's club arose at a time when some national Polish-American fraternal organizations urged Poles to become American citizens in

order to lobby more effectively for Poland, Bayonne's Polish Democrats apparently promoted self-advancement.[72] After the refinery
strikes and American entrance into the First World War, Bayonne's
middle-class Poles grew steadily more involved in Americanization
work and related activities which boosted their social, economic, and
political standing in the city. The U.S. military intelligence department
dispatched one young Pole to Bayonne on secret orders to "see how the
Polish people are doing"; although he reportedly turned up no sub-
versives, possible espionage among his countrymen nonetheless
launched a future career in Bayonne Polish-American politics.[73]

From these beginnings, Bayonne's middle-class Poles soon plung-
ed into less clandestine Americanization work. In February 1919,
Bayonne Poles met at Mydosh's Hall to reorganize the Polish Democratic Club as the Polish Citizen's Club. Present and active were tavern
keeper Leon Pejkowski, undertaker Stanley Fryczynski, and attorney
Paul Supinski, the strikers' erstwhile counsel. Two months later, the
club joined the Bayonne Board of Education in sponsoring a Polish
Americanization rally. Held at Mydosh's Hall, the saloon sacked by
police during the 1915 strike, the meeting feature several speakers,
including Superintendent of Schools Preston H. Smith, Mayor Pierre
Garven, undertaker Fryczynski, and lawyer Supinski. A later gathering in September 1919, however, best illustrates how much Bayonne
immigrant affairs had changed. This "mass meeting in the interest of
the evening schools and especially the Americanization classes"
brought together Alexander Debski of the socialist newspaper, the
Polish Daily Telegram (Telegram Codzienny); the Rev. W. Slominski of
Our Lady of Mount Carmel Church; attorney Supinski; and representatives from the Texas Oil Company in Bayonne and from the Standard
Oil Company plant. Police officer Joseph Derowski provided musical
entertainment.[74]

The careers of two Bayonne Poles reveal much about how middle-
class Poles mixed professional ambition and Americanization work.
Saloonkeeper and Standard Oil worker Anthony Dworzanski had
served on the refinery strike committee in 1916 and founded St.
Anthony Society for Mutual Aid and Benefit in the aftermath of the
strike. In 1923, Dworzanski joined Bayonne's police force, rising to the
rank of lieutenant sixteen years later. Eventually Dworzanski became
Bayonne's Commissioner of Public Works. Stanley Fryczynski's career
parallels Dworzanski's. Working himself up through a series of
manual labor jobs, Fryczynski opened a provisions business in 1911.
After a stint in night school, in 1916 Fryczynski became an undertaker. Two years later, the ambitious Pole joined the Bayonne Elks,
whereupon he won appointment to the community Americanization

Committee. In 1926, Fryczynski opened a private bank and in 1930 formally entered Bayonne politics. Through his Americanization and political work, Fryczynski helped twenty-seven hundred immigrants become citizens.[75] One Polish lawyer in Bayonne suggested why Fryczynski performed so Herculean a task:"Well, you know, to pick up the business and at the same time to help out the Polish people."[76]

The Polish middle class targeted Bayonne's Americanization campaign for success. As trusted leaders, middle-class Poles had access to the heart of Polonia. As recruits to the Americanization cause, they opened that heart to Bayonne's native-born Americanizers. Part-seduced, part-coerced, middle-class Poles thus bolstered the power structure in Bayonne during very difficult years. They did so by transforming Polish-American ethnicity from the vital core of the ethnic working-class community into an effective control mechanism. Yet we must not jump to the conclusion that the immigrant middle class in Bayonne – and probably in countless other American industrial cities during the period – was mere puppet or hireling in the piece. Middle-class immigrants also advanced their own interests during Bayonne's oil refinery strikes and thereafter. The ideology of "Polish-Americanism" countered the dual threat of Americanization and assimilation.

What needs explanation, however, is why working-class Poles followed the middle class. Several factors seem to have influenced Polish working-class thinking. With the outbreak of the Polish-Soviet War in 1920, patriotic working-class Poles recoiled from Bolshevism because it endorsed traditional Russian territorial aims and therefore menaced their resurrected and expanded homeland, post-Versailles Poland. Drawn by middle-class anti-Bolshevism, they also identified with the middle-class Poles; upwardly mobile working-class immigrants themselves aspired to become small-business proprietors. Working-class Poles also found practical reasons to follow middle-class leaders. Because the defeat of the second refinery strike extinguished many other options, immigrant working-class interest now often did lie within the supportive patron/client networks of the ethnic community. Finally, working-class Poles could have perceived a hidden benefit from middle-class politics. As strikers learned in 1915 and 1916, he who controlled politics ran the police, the fire department, and the courts. Through politics they might decide the outcome of future strikes.

The fragile control that Bayonne's corporate and civic leaders achieved with the cooperation of the immigrant middle class would prove recurrently susceptible to pressure from below. Even while Sheriff Kinkead repressed the 1915 strike, he had to underscore a hitherto unstated point. "It has got to be understood," the Sheriff said, "that these wealthy people with their palatial homes can't hire men to shoot down poor people just to protect their property. They can't be allowed to kill human beings to save mere plants and machinery."[77] If nothing else, Bayonne Poles had won an important concession in principle, however routinely reneged on in the years ahead. Thereafter, Poles intermittently asserted their rights in organizing efforts during 1920 and 1924.[78] With their votes, meanwhile, Polish working people purchased a measure of social responsiveness from their middle-class leaders and pressed for those legislative reforms which altered American capitalism during the 1930s. The great welfare state erected by the New Deal undoubtedly became a powerful new means of controlling social ferment, but it also brought significant improvement to working-class lives, improvement that only working-class protest could have made possible.

Notes

Chapter 1: Introduction

1. *USA Today*, July 3, 1986.

2. On ethnic mixtures in the French labor force, see the excellent study by Gary S. Cross, *Immigrant Workers in Industrial France: The Making of a New Laboring Class* (Philadelphia: Temple University Press, 1983).

3. Terrance V. Powderly to William B. Wilson, March 8, 1890, Reel 55, Terrance V. Powderly Papers, Catholic University of America, Washington D.C.

4. Samuel Gompers, "Mr. Hunter's Dilemma Proven," *American Federationist*, 17 (1910), 486.

5. Rose Pesotta to David Dubinsky, Dec. 13, 1933, Box 1, Rose Pesotta Papers, New York Public Library.

6. Pesotta to Max Danish, Dec. 15, 1933, Pesotta Papers.

7. Robert Asher, "Union Nativism and the Immigrant Response," *Labor History*, 23 (Summer 1982), 325–348.

8. See especially Herbert Gutman, "The Braidwood Lockout of 1874," *Journal of the Illinois State Historical Society*, 53 (Spring 1960), 5–28, and "Reconstruction in Ohio: Negroes in the Hocking Valley Coal Mines in 1873 and 1874," *Labor History*, 3 (Fall 1962), 243–264. Gutman synthesized these articles in "The Workers' Search for Power," in H. Wayne Morgan, *The Gilded Age* (Syracuse: Syracuse University Press, 1970), 31–54.

9. H. Feldberg to Joseph Schlossberg, Sept. 29, 1915, Amalgamated Clothing Workers of America Archives. (The author used these materials when they were still in New York City and were in file drawers; hence there is no box number. The Amalgamated Papers are now available at the Labor-

Management Documentation Center of theNew York State School for Industrial and Labor Relations, Cornell University.)

10. David Goldberg, "Immigrants, Intellectuals and Industrial Unions: The 1919 Textile Strikes and the Experience of the Amalgamated Textile Workers of America in Passaic and Paterson, New Jersey, and Lawrence, Massachusetts." Ph.D. diss., Columbia University, 1984.

11. Isaac Hourwich's 1912 study of the economic impact of immigration on labor markets in the short and long run is still the best discussion available. Hourwich points out that in the long term, immigration increased the size of the national market, thereby contributing to the prosperity of native-born as well as foreign-born workers. See *Immigration and Labor: The Economic Aspects of European Immigration to the United States* (New York: Putnam, 1912).

12. Wisconsin, Bureau of Labor and Industrial Statistics, *Third Biennial Report, 1887–1888* (1888), 1.

13. William Preston, Jr., *Aliens and Dissenters: Federal Suppression of Radicals, 1903–1933* (Cambridge: Harvard University Press, 1963).

14. See P. T. Sherman to August Belmont, October 27, 1911, Box 127, National Civic Federation Papers, New York Public Library; State of Pennsylvania, Industrial Accident Commission, *Sixth Tentative Draft of a Workmen's Compensation Act*, 1912; *St. Paul Pioneer Press*, December 3, 1912; Henry F. Hilfers, Secretary New Jersey State Federation of Labor to John B. Andrews, Feb. 7, 1919, Box 18, Andrews Papers, Labor-Management Documentation Center, Cornell University.

15. Manuel Castels, "Immigrant Workers and Class Struggles in Advanced Capitalism: The Western European Experience," *Politics and Society*, 5 (1985), 33–66.

16. Edna Bonacich, "Split Labor Market Theory," in Cora Bagley Marrett and Cheryl Leggon, eds., *Research in Race and Ethnic Relations*, 1 (1979), 20–62. See the cogent critique of Bonachich's analysis in Alexander Saxton, "Historical Explanations of Racial Inequality," *Marxist Perspectives*, 2 (Summer 1979), 148–149.

17. Mike Davis, *Prisoners of the American Dream: Politics and Economy in the History of the U.S. Working Class* (London: Verso, 1986), 24.

18. Moses Rischin, "The Jewish Labor Movement in America: A Social Interpretation," *Labor History*, 4 (1963), 227–247.

19. Victor Greene, *The Slavic Community on Strike* (South Bend, Ind.: University of Notre Dame Press, 1968).

20. See discussions in Asher, and in Michael Nash, *Conflict and Accommo-*

dation: Coal Miners, Steel Workers and Socialism, 1895–1920 (Westport: Greenwood Press, 1982).

21. See analysis in Goldberg.

22. Alexander Saxton, *The Indispensable Enemy* (Berkeley and Los Angeles: University of California Press, 1968).

23. Melton A. McLaurin, *Paternalism and Protest: Southern Cotton Mill Workers and Organized Labor, 1875–1905* (Westport, Conn.: Greenwood Press, 1971).

24. Daniel Rosenberg, *New Orleans Dockworkers: Race, Labor and Unionism, 1892–1923* (Albany: State University of New York Press, 1988).

25. David Brody, *Steelworkers in America: The Nonunion Era* (Cambridge: Harvard University Press, 1960).

26. Philip S. Foner, *History of the Labor Movement in the United States,* 1 (New York: International Publishers, 1947), 155.

27. William M. Leiserson, *Adjusting Immigrant and Industry* (New York: Harper, 1924) Chapter 8, n.25.

28. Illinois State Federation of Labor, *Proceedings,* 1913, 12.

29. *Miami Valley Socialist* (Ohio), September 28, 1923.

30. United Electrical Workers, *Proceedings,* 1937, 8.

31. Edward Jennings, "Ethnicity and Class: Detroit's Polish Workers and the Organization of the United Automobile Workers," Ph.D. diss., Northern Illinois University, 1984; John Paul Sade, "Ethnic Assimilation and the Congress of Industrial Organizations" (honors thesis, History Department, University of Connecticut, 1975).

32. Robert Asher, *Connecticut Workers and Technological Change* (Storrs, Conn.: Center for Oral History, 1983); Barry Bluestone and Bennett Harrison, *The Deindustrialization of America: Plant Closings, Community Abandonment, and the Dismantling of Basic Industry* (New York: Basic Books, 1982); Tom Forester, ed., *The Microelectronics Revolution* (Cambridge: Massachusetts Institute of Technology Press, 1981); Colin Norman, *Microelectronics at Work: Productivity and Jobs in the World Economy,* Worldwatch Paper 39 (Washington, D.C.: The Worldwatch Institute, 1980); Colin Norman, *The God That Limps: Science and Technology in the Eighties* (New York: Norton, 1981).

33. Leslie Woodcock Tentler, *Wage-earning Women: Industrial Work and Family Life in the United States, 1900–1930* (New York: Oxford University Press, 1979); Sallie Westwood, *All Day, Every Day: Factory and Family in the Making of Women's Lives* (Urbana: University of Illinois Press, 1984).

Chapter 2: Ethnicity and Class in Hawaii

The Epigraph appeared in the Hawaii Herald, Feb. 2, 1973.

1. Hawaii Laborers' Association, *Facts about the Strike on Sugar Plantations in Hawaii* (Honolulu, 1920), 1.

2. William Hooper Diary, Sept. 12, 1836, in William Hooper Papers, Hawaiian Collection, University of Hawaii Library.

3. Hooper to Ladd and Company, Nov. 16, 1836, and Hooper to Ladd and Company, Dec. 1, 1838, Hooper Papers.

4. Theo. Davies and Company to C. McLennan, Aug. 22, 1889, July 2, 1890, May 7, 1896, January 3, 1898, Laupahoehoe Plantation Records, microfilm, University of Hawaii Library; William G. Irwin and Company to George C. Hewitt, Oct. 12, 1894, Hutchinson Plantation Records, U.H. Library; Vice-President of H. Hackfield and Company to G.N. Wilcox, May 5, 1908. G.P. Wilcox, Director of H. Hackfield and Company to Grove Farm Plantation, July 3, 1918; Grove Farm Plantation Records, Grove Farm Plantation Archives, Grove Farm, Kauai.

5. Robert Hall, George F. Renton, and George H. Fairfield, in Republic of Hawaii, *Report of the Labor Commission on Strikes and Arbitration* (Honolulu, 1895), 28, 23–24, 36.

6. *Planters' Monthly*, 2 (Nov. 1883), 177, 245–247. A.S. Cleghorn, in Republic of Hawaii, *Report of the Bureau of Immigration* (Honolulu, 1886), 256–257.

7. Theo. Davies and Company to C. McLennan, Sept. 24, 1894 Laupahoehoe Plantation Records; U.S. Commissioner of Labor Carrol Wright, quoted in *Honolulu Record*, Jan. 12, 1950; G.C. Hewitt to W.G. Irwin and Company March 16, 1896, Hutchinson Plantation Records; H. Hackfield and Company to George Wilcox, Sept. 26, 1896, Grove Farm Plantation Records.

8. H. Hackfield and Company to Grove Farm Plantation, Dec. 22, 1900, Grove Farm Plantation Records; *Honolulu Advertiser*, "Sixty Years Ago," Sept. 19, 1960; *Maui News*, Jan. 21, 1961, reprint of article published originally Jan. 19, 1901.

9. *Report of the Commissioner of Labor*, reprinted in *Planters' Monthly* (1903), p. 296; H.F. Glade to F.M. Hatch, September 10, 1895, quoted in Bernhard Hormann, "The Germans in Hawaii," unpublished M.A. Thesis, University of Hawaii, 1931, p. 29; Theo. Davies and Company to C. McLennan, Nov. 19, 1896, Laupahoehoe Plantation Records; Walter Giffard to Manager of the Hutchinson Sugar Plantation, October 3, 1898, quoted in Wayne K. Patterson, "The Korean Frontier in America: Immigration to Hawaii, 1896–1910." unpublished Ph.D. Thesis, Univ. of Pa., 1977, p.100; Giffard to William Irwin, Dec.

18, 1901, quoted in *ibid.*, p.129; Giffard to Irwin, Feb. 25, 1902, quoted in *ibid.*, p. 134: Giffard to Irwin, April 30, 1902, quoted in *Ibid.*, p. 146; J.P. Cooke to Rithet, October 14, 1902, quoted in *ibid.*, pp. 169–171.

10. Giffard to Irwin, Feb. 3, 1903, quoted in Patterson, "Korean Frontier," p. 255; Director of Theo. Davies and Company to C. McLennan, n.d., Laupahoehoe Plantation Records; Manager of the Hutchinson Sugar Plantation to W.G. Irwin and Company, April 11, 1905, Hutchinson Sugar Plantation Records.

11. *Pacific Commercial Advertiser,* January 22, 1906; December 21, 1906; *Honolulu Evening Bulletin,* February 21, 1907.

12. *Board of Immigration Report* (1909), quoted in Mary Dorita, "Filipino Immigration to Hawaii," unpublished M.A. Thesis, University of Hawaii, 1954, p. 11; Manager, Hawaiian Agricultural Company to C. Brewer and Company, July 1, 1920; Aug. 7 and 27, 1913, Hawaiian Agricultural Plantation Records, microfilm, U.H. Library.

13. Hawaiian Sugar Planters Association, resolution, November 18, 1904, Grove Farm Plantation Records; Hawaiian Sugar Planters Association, resolution, in director of H. Hackfield and company to G.N. Wilcox, June 14, 1911, Grove Farm Plantation Reocrds.

14. *Royal Hawaiian Agricultural Society Transactions,* 1, no.5 (June 1852), pp. 6,7,70.

15. Experiment Station, Hawaiian Sugar Planters Association Circular, "The Labor Question," May 7, 1917, in Grove Farm Plantation Records; Virgilio Felipe, "Hawaii: A Pilipino Dream" unpublished M.A. Thesis, University of Hawaii, 1972; pp. 170, 177.

16. *Pacific Commercial Advertiser,* March 17, 1899

17. Morris Pang, "A Korean Immigrant," *Social Process in Hawaii,* 13 (1949), p. 114; Milton Murayama, *All I Asking For Is My Body* (San Francisco, 1975), pp. 28, 96.

18. *The Higher Wage Question,* excerpts reprinted in U.S. Bureau of Labor Statistics, *Report of the Commissioner of Labor on Hawaii* (Washington, D.C., 1910), 76.

19. *Hawaii Herald,* Feb. 2, 1973.

20. Yasutaro Soga, *Honolulu Record,* July 7, 1949; Take and Allen Beekman, "Hawaii's Great Japanese Strike," reprinted in Dennis Ogawa, *Kodomo no tame ni* (Honolulu, 1978), 158.

21. Takashi Tsutsumi, *History of Hawaii Laborers' Movement,* trans. (Honolulu, 1922), 194–198.

22. Tsutsumi, 161, 175.

23. Tsutsumi, 238–243.

24. President of C. Brewer and Company to James Campsie, Manager of the Hawaiian Agricultural Company, Feb. 3, 1920, Hawaiian Agricultural Company Records; *Pacific Commercial Advertiser*, Jan. 30, 1920; *Honolulu Star-Bulletin*, Feb. 13, 1920; R.D. Mead, Director of the Labor Bureau, to Manager of Grove Farm Plantation, Feb. 13, 1920, Grove Farm Plantation Records.

25. "The Five O'Clock Whistle," *Kohala Midget*, April 27, 1910.

26. Tsutsumi, 19.

27. Tsutsumi, 12, 44.

28. Tsutsumi, 17, 13, 22.

29. Milton Murayama, *All I Asking For Is My Body*, 28, 96.

30. Walt Whitman, in Horace Traubel, *With Walt Whitman in Canada*, 2 vols. (New York, 1915), 34–35.

Chapter 3: Chinese-American Agricultural Workers in Los Angeles

1. A preliminary version of this essay was presented at the 1981 Annual Conference of the American Historical Association. Data presented here are taken from a larger work, Raymond Lou, "The Chinese-American Community of Los Angeles, 1870–1900: A Case of Resistance, Organization, and Participation," Ph.D. diss., University of California, Irvine, 1982.

2. Unless otherwise stated all demographic statistics and occupational categories are based on my analysis of the U.S. Census manuscripts of 1870, 1880, and 1900. Examples of other agriculture-related occupations listed in the Census data: "digs roots," "fruit picker," "fruit and vegetable dealer," "seed grower." The category "gardener" can be misleading. The term does not refer to a grounds keeper. Chinese-American farmers were listed frequently as "gardeners" rather than "farmers." To avoid confusion, the term "farmer" will be used in this essay.

3. These figures do not include room and board. Los Angeles *Times*, Sept. 23, 1886, Sept. 26, 1890; Ng Poon Chew, "The Chinaman in America," *Independent*, 54 (1902), 801–803.

4. Los Angeles *Times*, Sept. 23, 1886.

5. By the 1880s, in order to remain competitive with Euro-American-owned steam laundries, Chinese laundries lowered their rates and promised faster service. The latter was accomplished by working long hours, often beyond midnight. The evening operation of laundries gave an additional reason

for the anti-Chinese movement to demand the exclusion of Chinese. See Lou for a discussion of the anti-Chinese movement in Southern California.

6. During the last major anti-Chinese boycott of the century in the spring of 1886, all businesses that employed Chinese as well as Chinese-owned and -operated establishments were targeted for a policy of "non-intercourse." Because of the skills of Chinese-Americans who filled positions as chef and chief cook, their employers were reluctant to discharge them.

7. Good ironers were in high demand. However, it is estimated that it required two to three years of apprenticeship before one became a skilled ironer. Los Angeles *Star*, March 22, 1872.

8. Initial expenses included rent, purchase of equipment, payment for utilities such as firewood and water, and operating licenses.

9. In 1872, a reporter for the Los Angeles *Star* conducted a survey in which he found 11 Chinese laundries in the town. By 1890 this number had grown to 52 (Los Angeles *Times*, Sept. 26, 1890). It appears that the Chinese laundry industry entered a period of decline shortly afterwards.

10. Los Angeles *Times*, Sept. 12, 14, 1899.

11. These choices were not voluntary. Life chances for Chinese-American wrokers were not only restricted by their class position, they were further reduced by their race.

12. In 1880, those listing "farmer" or "gardener" as their occupation numbered 203 or 19% of the Chinese-American population. By 1900, the absolute number increased to 412.

13. Los Angeles *Times*, Jan. 1, 1896.

14. At the turn of the century, it was still possible for the average household to purchase a daily supply of fresh vegetables for five to ten cents. Owners of canneries began to complain about their inability to purchase vegetables from Chinese farmers in the early 1880s. For example see Los Angeles *Times*, June 6, 1883.

15. This view was held by many and can be found in numerous sources. See Harris Newmark, *Sixty Years in Southern California, 1853–1913* (New York: Knickerbocker Press, 1926); Ludwig Salvatore, *Los Angeles in the Sunny Seventies* (Los Angeles: Bruce McCallister-Jake Zeitlin, 1929); Marshall Stimson, *Fun, Fights and Fiestas in Old Los Angeles: An Autobiography*; Leo Carrillo, *The California I Love* (Englewood Cliffs, N.J.: Prentice Hall, 1961): Helen Raitt and Mary Wayne, eds., *We Three Came West* (San Diego: Tofua Press, 1974). References to a Chinese-American "monopoly" in the agricultural sector are also found in the early stages of Chinese immigrant settlement in the region, e.g. see *Los Angeles Evening Express*, Jan. 25, 1872.

16. Los Angeles *Times*, Jan. 1, 1896.

17. Ibid., and June 2, July 7, 1883, May 23, 28, 1886, Aug. 26, 1893.

18. Los Angeles *Times*, Jan. 1, 1896.

19. Evidence indicates the opposite may have occurred; i.e., Euro-American workers underbidding and/or forcing Chinese-American workers out of work. See Ping Chiu, *Chinese Labor in California: An Economic Study* (Madison: University of Wisconsin Press, 1963). There are data that point to the fact that Chinese growers began to hire white workers in the 1890s, rather than Chinese laborers, as a money-saving tactic. See Los Angeles *Times*, August 26, 1893, August 27, 1894. In 1886, at a mass meeting of Euro-American women in Los Angeles, Chinese workers were credited with raising the wage standards of "women's" work. Los Angeles *Times*, March 28, 1886.

20. Los Angeles *Times*, Jan. 1, 1896.

21. The figures are based on calculations found in a feature article entitled "Chinatown" in the Los Angeles *Times*. Jan. 1, 1896.

22. See Stimson, Ng, Newmark, Salvatore, Carrillo.

23. Los Angeles *Express*, June 9, 1876.

24. Los Angeles *Express*, June 2, 1876.

25. This tactic was not new. Euro-American settlers had used high taxes and license fees against Chinese immigrants since the initiation of the Foreign Miners's Tax of 1853.

26. Los Angeles *Herald*, Jan. 28, 1879.

27. Los Angeles *Herald*, Feb. 4, 1879.

28. Los Angeles *Herald*, Feb. 7, 1879.

29. Los Angeles *Herald*, Feb. 14, 1879. Although the Council was dominated by anti-Chinese members, this increase passed by a vote of 8–6.

30. Los Angeles *Herald*, Feb. 19, 1879.

31. Los Angeles *Herald*, Feb. 19, 1879.

32. Los Angeles *Herald*, April 11, 15, 1879; Los Angeles *Express*, July 27, 1880.

33. Grace H. Stimson, *Rise of the Labor Movement in Los Angeles* (Berkeley and Los Angeles: University of California Press, 1955), 11, 25, 129–131.

34. Los Angeles *Herald*, April 14, 1879.

35. Los Angeles *Express*, Sept. 26, 1879.

36. Los Angeles *Express*. July 27, 1880.

37. Los Angeles *Herald*, Aug. 19, 1880. The euphemism "alien ineligible to citizenship" was not used with great frequency to enact discriminatory laws against Chinese settlers. Many laws designed for this purpose were written with non-discriminatory language but were selectively enforced. The Chinese harassment laws enacted by the City of San Francisco in the early 1870s are examples of these; see Elmer C. Sandmeyer, *The Anti-Chinese Movement in California* (Urbana: University of Illinois Press, 1939). During the first two decades of the twentieth century, the term became a popular way to avoid questions of constitutionality in discriminating against Japanese settlers.

38. Los Angeles *Express*, July 28, 1880.

39. Los Angeles *Express*, July 30, 1880.

40. Los Angeles *Herald*, Aug. 19, 1880.

41. San Francisco *Bulletin*, quoted in the Los Angeles *Herald*, Sept. 26, 1880.

42. Los Angeles *Times*, June 6, 1883. By this time, the majority of vendors used wagons.

43. For a description of this period, as well as a survey of the anti-Chinese movement, see Sandmeyer, and Alexander Saxton, *The Indispensable Enemy* (Berkeley and Los Angeles: University of California Press, 1971).

44. Paul Crane and Alfred Larson, "The Chinese Massacre," *Annals of Wyoming*, 12 (Jan. 1940) 47-55, (April 1940) 153-160.

45. Los Angeles *Times*, Feb. 23, 1886.

46. Los Angeles *Express*, Oct. 5, 1877.

47. Los Angeles *Times*, March 9, 1882.

48. Los Angeles *Times*, May 10, 1886.

49. It appears that the boycott organizers were subjected to some ridicule after its outcome became obvious. This was a significant change in public sentiment. While a small group of people, mostly missionaries, defended the Chinese in some manner throughout the nineteenth century, the anti-Chinese movement was seldom denigrated. Objections to the movement were usually made on moral agruments in defense of the Chinese rather than addressing the character of its Euro-American proponents. In a satirical letter to the editor of the *Times*, a local resident made it clear that the members of the anti-Chinese movement were no longer immune from criticism. Los Angeles *Times*, May 16, 1886.

50. Los Angeles *Times*, Feb. 27, March 23, April 1, May 10, 16, 1886.

51. Los Angeles *Times*, April 28, 1886.

52. Los Angeles *Times*, Feb. 27, March 28, 1886.

53. Los Angeles *Times*, March 28, 1886.

55. Los Angeles *Times*, Sept. 8, 11, 13, 14, 15, 16, and 23, 1893.

56. Not only were Chinese-American workers effectively excluded from primary occupations by the anti-Chinese movement, but Congress also passed the Chinese Exclusion Act in 1882, which prevented further immigration of Chinese to the United States.

57. For some historians there is no debate. The anti-Chinese movement has been seen as a class war that Euro-American workers had to wage successfully in order better their class position. An example of this interpretation can be found in Selig Perlman, *A History of Trade Unionism in the United States* (New York: Macmillan, 1950).

58. For a discussion of these and other accusations see Lou.

59. The implied assumption is that all Chinese laundrymen were carriers of syphilis.

60. Advertisements of this type appeared regularly in the local press. Often these claims were bogus. During periods of intense anti-Chinese agitation such as the 1886 boycott, many Euro-American business establishments displayed signs stating that "No Chinese Employed Here" when their Chinese employees were still working. For example, see advertisements for the Los Angeles Steam Laundry in the Los Angeles *Express*, April 25, 1884, and Los Angeles *Times*, March 12, 1886. The *Express* advertisement solicited Euro-American patrons with the claim of "No Chinese Labor". During the boycott of 1886, the firm put a notice in the *Times* that all Chinese workers had been discharged. Also see *Times*, March 13, April 10, 17, 29, 1886, for further evidence of this ploy by other businesses during the boycott.

61. Los Angeles *Express*, Oct. 5, 1875.

62. Newmark, Salvatore, Stimson, Raitt and Wayne.

Chapter 4: Ethnic Life and Labor in Chicago's Filipino Community

1. See, for example, Carlos Bulosan's poignant memoir, *America Is in the Heart: A personal History* (Seattle: University of Washington Press, 1973 [1943]), 99–112; interview with Phillip A. Lontoc, Chicago, Aug. 10, 1979.

2. The best general study of Filipinos in the United States is in H. Brett Melendy, *Asians in America: Filipinos, Koreans, and East Asians* (Boston: Twayne Publishers, 1977); see 50–57.

3. Melendy, 99; Bulosan, 307.

4. Interview with Florentino Bella, Oakbrook, Ill., April 30, 1979; Lontoc interview; Miriam Sharma, "The Philippines: A Case of Migration to Hawaii, 1906–1946," in Lucie Cheng and Edna Bonacich, eds., *Labor Immigration under Capitalism: Asian Workers in the United States Before World War II* (Berkeley and Los Angeles: University of California Press, 1984), 337–358.

5. On the Filipino West Coast experience, see: Roberto B. Ballangca, *Pinoy: The First Wave (1898–1941)* (San Francisco: Strawberry Hill Press, 1977); Fred Cordova, *Filipinos: Forgotten Asian Americans—A Pictorial Essay/ 1763-Circa-1963* (Cubuque, Iowa: Kendall/Hunt Publishing Company, 1983); Edwin B. Almirol, "Ethnic Identity and Social Negotiation: A Study of a Filipino Community in California," Ph.D. diss., University of Illinois at Urbana-Champaign, 1977, and "Filipino Voluntary Associations: Balancing Social Pressures and Ethnic Images," *Ethnic Groups, 2 (1978)*, 65–92; Jack K. Masson and Donald L., Gulmary, "Philipinos and Unionization of the Alaskan Canned Salmon Industry," *Amerasia*, 8 (Fall 1981), 1–30; Cletus E. Daniel, *Bitter Harvest: A History of the California Farmworkers, 1870–1941* (Berkeley and Los Angeles: University of California Press, 1981).

On the Hawaiian experience, see: Miriam Sharma, "Labor Migration and Class Formation among the Filipinos in Hawaii, 1906–1946," in Cheng and Bonacich, eds., *Labor Immigration under Capitalism*, 579–615, and "Pinoy in Paradise: Environment and Adaptation of Pilipinos in Hawaii, 1906–1946," *Amerasia*, 7 (Fall/Winter 1980), 91–117; Ruben R. Alcantara, *Sakada: Filipino Adaptation in Hawaii* (Washington, D.C.: University Press of America, 1981); Ronald Takaki, *Pau Hana: Plantation Life and Labor in Hawaii, 1835–1920* (Honolulu: University of Hawaii Press, 1983); Robert N. Anderson, *Filipinos in Rural Hawaii* (Honolulu: University of Hawaii Press, 1984).

An early account covering both areas is Bruno Lasker, *Filipino Immigration to the Continental United States and Hawaii* (Chicago: Institute of Pacific Relations, University of Chicago Press, 1931).

6. See: Barbara M. Posadas, "The Hierarchy of Color and Psychological Adjustment in an Industrial Environment: Filipinos, the Pullman Company, and the Brotherhood of Sleeping Car Porters," *Labor History*, 23 (Summer 1982), 349–373, and "Crossed Boundaries in Interracial Chicago: Philipino American Families since 1925," *Amerasia*, 8 (Fall/Winter 1981), 31–52; Posadas and Roland L. Guyotte, "From Student Community to Immigrant Community: Chicago's Filipinos before World War II," Philippine Studies Group Conference, Ohio University, Aug. 1983; Posadas, "Concluding a Cohort's Experience: Filipino American History and the Old-Timers' Generation." *Amerasia*, forthcoming.

7. On the *pensionados*, see William A. Sutherland, *Not by Might: The Epic of the Philippines* (Las Cruces, N.M.: Southwest Publishing Company, 1953).

8. Sutherland.

9. Robert W. Rydell, *All the World's a Fair: Visions of Empire at American International Expositions, 1876–1916* (Chicago: University of Chicago Press, 1984), 137–144, 167–178; "Igorrotes in the Shows," *The Filipino Students'*

Magazine, July 1906, 2, American Historical Collection, American Embassy Library, Manila; "Seeks Exhibit," *The Filipino Students' Magazine,*, Dec. 1906, 10-11.

10. On education in the Philippines, see: Encarnacion Alzona, *A History of Education in the Philippines, 1565-1930* (Manila: University of the Philipines Press, 1932); Glenn A. May, *Scoial Engineering in the Philippines: The Aims, Execution, and Impact of American Colonial Policy, 1900-1913* (Westport, Conn.: Greenwood Press, 1980), Part Three, "Schooling," 75-126; The Board of Educational Survey, *A Survey of the Educational Syustem of the Philippine Islands* (Manila: Bureau of Printing, 1925), 313-400, 609-672.

11. Interview with Jose Marasigan, Manila, Dec. 14, 1982.

12. Benny F. Feria, *Filipino Son* (Boston: Meador Publishing Company, 1954), 32.

13. Lontoc interview.

14. Interview with Juan B. Barreras, Chicago, Aug. 13, 1979.

15. Interviews with Eulogio C. Tolentino, Manila, Oct. 3, 1982, and Carlos Quirino, Manila, Oct. 6, 1982. Tolentino, who attended Ohio State University, and Quirino, who graduated from the University of Wisconsin, returned to the Philippines after completing college. For details on the Chicago student community, see *The Filipino Student Bulletin*, in the archives of the University of Washington, Seattle, especially IV (Jan. 1926), 6, on the Crane Filipino Club; and *Bagumbayan* [1928] in the Philippine National Library, Manila.

16. Leopoldo T. Ruiz, "Filipino Students in the United States," M.A. thesis, Yale University, 1925, 37; Manuel A. Adeva, "Filipino Students in the United States," *Mid Pacific Magazine* (Aug. 1932), 119-123; Melendy, 251; interview with the Rev. Fernando A. Laxamana, DeKalb, Ill., Sept. 27, 1985.

17. "Free Literary Program and Dance . . . ," *Associated Filipino Press*, 6 (Dec. 30, 1934), Bessie Louise Pierce Notes, Chicago Historical Society; *Filipino Students' Magazine*, Dec. 1906, 21; *Filipino Student Bulletin*, 4 (Jan. 1926), 6; *Filipino Student Bulletin*, 1 (Feb. 1923), 2; *Filipino Student Bulletin*, 1 (May 1924), 2-3; The Filipino Association of Chicago to Manuel Quezon, Aug. 4, 1924, Quezon Papers, the Philippine National Library, Manila.

18. Paul G. Cressey, *The Taxi-Dance Hall: A Sociological Study in Commercialized Recreation and City Life* (Montclair, N.J.: Patterson Smith, 1969 [1932]), 145-174; Albert W. Palmer, *Orientals in American Life* (New York: Friendship Press, 1934, 94-102.

19. Marasigan interview.

20. Marasigan interview.

21. Pedro T. Orata, "My Life and Work, Mostly Work!" (unpublished manuscript).

22. Bella interview; interview with Fred A. Bernal, Worth, Ill., Aug. 9, 1979.

23. Feria, 80.

24. Interview with Pedro L. Cabillener, Lombard, Ill., May 2, 1979; Laxamana interview.

25. Donn V. Hart, *Compadrinazgo: Ritual Kinship in the Philippines* (DeKalb: Northern Illinois University Press, 1977), 203–210; J. J. Carroll, *Changing Patterns of Social Structure in the Philippines, 1896 and 1963* (Quezon City: Ateneo de Manila University Press, 1968), 34–36, 63.

26. Lontoc interview.

27. Interview with Ruth Gutierrez Konetshny. Wooster Lake, Ill.

28. Allan H. Spear, *Black Chicago: The Making of a Negro Ghetto, 1890–1930* (Chicago: University of Chicago Press, 1968), vii–x, 11–27, 147–166.

29. Interview with Laxamana, DeKalb, Ill., March 17, 1986.

30. Interview with Frances Lontoc, Chicago, April 23, 1981.

31. Luis S. Quianio, "A Mother to Them All," *Graphic*, June 22, 1933, 10–11, 53, 60.

32. "Chicago Hoodlums Attack Filipinos," *Filipino Nation*, 9 (Dec. 1931), 24, 26.

33. Palmer, 97.

34. Palmer, 99–102; Laxamana interviews.

35. Laxamana interviews.

36. Interview with Baldomero Olivera, Manila, Dec. 22, 1982; Posadas, "Hierarchy of Color," 356.

37. Olivera intrerview.

38. Laxamana interviews.

39. Posadas, "Crossed Boundaries," 48.

40. Feria, 78.

41. Feria, 78.

42. Feria, 78.

43. Feria, 80.

44. Feria, 82. In 1940 median years of schooling for Chicago Filipinos stood at 12.2 years; for native-born white males, 9.4 years; for foreign-born white males, 7.5 years, U.S. Department of Commerce, Bureau of the Census,

Sixteenth Census of the United States: 1940, "Population: Characeristics of the Nonwhite Population by Race" (Washington, D.C.: Government Printing Office, 1943), Ill, and Vol. 2, "Characteristics of the Population," 642.

45. Feria, 80.

46. Feria, 81.

47. *Pullman News* (Nov. 1925), 221; William H. Harris, *Keeping the Faith: A. Philip Randolph, Milton P. Webster, and the Brotherhood of Sleeping Car Porters, 1925-1937* (Urbana: University of Illinois Press, 1977), 33–35.

48. Harris, 1–3. Pullman's decision to hire Filipinos came at a time of heavy Filipino immigration to the United States, almost a decade prior to immigration restriction. It can thus be argued that Pullman saw the Filipino population in Chicago as an expanding labor pool of potentially significant size.

49. *Pullman News*, March 1929, 371; *Railway Age*, April 16, 1932, 667.

50. Harris, 63.

51. *The Black Worker*, Feb. 1, 1930, 4. In 1933 and 1934, however, Randolph supported Washington Senator Clarence A. Dill's proposed legislation excluding non-citizens from work in railroad service positions.

52. Posadas, "Hierarchy of Color," 365–367. A 1952 St. Louis attendants' seniority list indicates that only Filipinos held seniority dates between June 1926 and December 1937. Rufino Adamas held the oldest seniority date, November 9, 1925, on the St. Louis list. In 1952, Adamas was preceeded on the list by eight "colored" attendants with seniority dates between December 22, 1919 and June 24, 1925. "Colored" attendants were indicated by a "(C)" while "Native Philippines" was shown by an "(F)". In the absence of a similar list for the Chicago Commissary Department, it is impossible to tell whether, and if so, how many Black attendants were returned to the Commissary Department's seniority list in Chicago after the 1937 agreement. "Record of Seniority Roster, St. Louis, Jan. 9, 1952," Brotherhood of Sleeping Car Porters, New York Division, Chicago Historical Society.

53. Posadas, "Hierarchy of Color," 368–369.

54. National Railroad Adjustment Board (NARB), Third Division, Award No. 3218, Docket No. PM-3247, Transportation Library, Northwestern University, Evanston, Ill., Award No. 3260, Docket No. PM-3251, and Award No. 3341, Docket No. PM-3272; Milton P. Webster to NARB. The Brotherhood of Sleeping Car Porters (For and in behalf of E. J. Domantay, Petitioner, *vs.* The Pullman Company, Respondent), Exhibit B, "Transcript of the Hearing of Attendant E. J. Domantay," Sept. 29, 1944, Brotherhood of Sleeping Car Porters Papers, Chicago Division, Chicago Historical Society.

55. Webster to NARB, 5.

56. NARB, Third Division, Award No. 3218, Docket No. PM-3247.

57. Domingo C. Manzon to Barbara M. Posadas, December 1979.

58. Lontoc interview; interview with Honesto P. Llanes, Chicago, Aug. 15, 1979; interview with Claudio R. Alcala, Chicago, Aug. 13, 1979.

59. Posadas, "Hierarchy of Color," 358, 365, 369–370.

60. Milton P. Webster to NARB. The Brotherhood of Sleeping Car Porters (For and in behalf of S. F. Balais, Petitioner, *vs.* The Pullman Company, Respondent), Exhibit B, "Transcript of the Hearing of Attendant S. F. Balais," Oct. 23, 1944, 2, Brotherhood of Sleeping Car Porters Papers, Chicago Division, Chicago Historical Society.

61. Manzon to Posadas, Dec. 1979.

62. Bella interview.

63. Manzon to Posadas, Dec. 1979.

64. Bella intereview.

65. Bernal interview.

66. Posadas, "Hierarchy of Color," 370–371; Manzon to Posadas, Dec. 1979.

67. Pedro Villegas Padilla, "Still in Clover," *Graphic,* April 27, 1932, 8–9.

68. Laxamana interviews.

69. Lontoc and Bella interviews.

70. Nueva Viscaya Association, "Just Yesterday: History Exhibit of Chicago's Filipino Americans" (Chicago: Alamar, Inc., 1985), 25.

71. Interview with Dionisio P. Fortich, Chicago, Aug. 11, 1979.

Chapter 5: Mexican-Americans and the International Union of Mine, Mill and Smelter Workers

1. On Afro-American workers and the CIO see, for example, Roger Biles, "Ed Crump Versus the Union: The Labor Movement in Memphis During the 1930s," *Labor History* (Fall 1984), 533–552; Stephen Brier, "Labor, Politics, and Race: A Black Worker's Life, *Labor History* (Summer 1982), 416–421; Horace Cayton and George S. Mitchel, *Black Workers and the New Unions* (Chapel Hill, N.C., 1939); Donald T. Critchlow, "Communist Unions and Racism: A Comparative Study of the Responses of the United Electrical Radio and Machine Workers and the National Maritime Union to the Black Question during World

War II," *Labor History* (Spring 1976), 230–244; Philip S. Foner, *Organized Labor and the Black Worker 1619–1973*, especially Ch. 16, "The CIO and the Black Worker, 1935–1939" (N.Y. and Wash., D.C., 1974), 215–237; Foner and Ronald L. Lewis, eds., *The Black Worker from the Founding of the CIO to the AFL–CIO Merger, 1936–1955*," Vol. 7 in The Black Worker Series (Philadelphia, 1983); Hosea Hudson, *Black Worker in the Deep South* (New York, 1972); Horace Huntley, "Iron Ore Mines and Mine Mill in Alabama, 1933–1952," Ph.D. diss., University of Pittsburgh, 1976); Charles Martin, "Southern Labor Relations in Transition: Gadsden, Alabama, 1930–1943," *Journal of Southern History*, 47 (1981), 545–568; August Meier and Elliot Rudwick, *Black Detroit and the Rise of the UAW* (New York, 1979); Meier and Rudwick, "Communist Unions and the Black Community: The Case of the Transport Workers Union, 1934–1944," *Labor History* (Spring 1982), 165–197; Gilbert W. Moore, "Poverty, Class Consciousness and Race Conflict in the UAW-CIO, 1937–1955," (Ph.D. diss., Princeton University, 1978); James S. Olson, "Organized Black Leadership and Industrial Unionism: The Racial Response, 1926–1945," *Labor History* (Summer 1969), 475–486; Roderick Ryan, "An Ambiguous Legacy: Baltimore Blacks and the CIO, 1936–1941," *Journal of Negro History*, 65 (1980), 18–33; Philip Taft, *Organizing Dixie: Alabama Workers in the Industrial Era* (Westport, Conn., 1981).

On Mexican-Americans and the CIO, see Luis Arroyo, "Industrial Unionism and the Los Angeles Furniture Industry, 1918–1954," (Ph.D. diss., University of California at Los Angeles, 1979); Cletus Daniel, *Bitter Havert: A History of California Farmworkers, 1870–1941* (Berkeley and Los Angeles, 1982); Douglas Monroy, "Mexicans in Los Angeles, 1930–1941: On Ethnic Group Relations to Class Forces," (Ph.D. diss., University of California at Los Angeles, 1978); Victor B. Nelson-Cisneros, "La Clase Trabajadora en Tejas, 1920–1940," *Aztlan*, 6 (Summer 1975), 239–266; Vicki Ruiz, "UCAPAWA and Mexican Women Workers," (Ph.D. diss., Stanford University, 1982).

2. On El Paso, see Mario T. García, *Desert Immigrants: The Mexicans of El Paso, 1880–1920* (New Haven, 1981). On labor segmentation and "colonized labor," see Mario Barrera, *Race and Class in the Southwest: A Theory of Racial Inequality* (Notre Dame, 1979); Tomas Almaguer, "Class, Race, and Chicano Oppression," *Socialist Revolution* (July–Sept. 1975), 71–99; Edna Bonavich, "A Theory of Ethnic Antagonism: The Split Labor Market," *American Sociological Review* (Oct. 1972), 542–559. Richard Edwards, et al., eds., *Labor Market Segmentation* (Lexington, 1975); Mario T. García, "Racial Dualism in the El Paso Labor Market, 1880–1920," *AZTLAN* (Summer 1975), 192–218; Robert Staples, "Race and Colonialism: The Domestic Case in Theory and Practice," *Black Scholar* (June 1976), 37–48.

3. See Abraham Hoffman, *Unwanted Mexican Americans in the Great Depression: Repatriation Pressures, 1929–1939* (Tucson, 1974); Francisco Balderrama, *In Defense of La Raza: The Los Angeles Mexican Consulate and the Mexican Community, 1929 to 1936* (Tucson, 1982).

4. El Paso *Times*, Jan. 28, 1930, in "El Paso" Vertical File, "Smelting Industry" in Southwest collection, El Paso Public Library (hereafter cited as SW Col.).

5. Unpublished article by D.H. Dinwoodie, "The Rise of the Mine-Mill Union in Southwestern Copper," 2, in Humberto Silex private collection, El Paso.

6. Interview with Humberto Silex, El Paso, Dec. 11, 1982, by Mario T. García.

7. See Interview No. 505 with Silex by Oscar J. Martinez and Art Sadin, El Paso, April 28, 1978, in Institute of Oral History, University of Texas at El Paso (hereafter cited as IOH).

8. Silex interview, Dec. 11, 1982.

9. As quoted in Frank Arnold, "Humberto Silex: CIO Organizer from Nicaragua," in *Southwest Economy & Society* (Fall 1978), 5.

10. See García, 127-154; Mark Robinson to Harold [no last name given], El Paso, Jan. 14, 1941, in Archives of the International Union of Mine, Mill and Smelter Workers, Western History Collection, University of Colorado, Box 553, Folder "Local 501" (hereafter cited as UMMSW).

11. Silex interview, April 28, 1978, IOH, 15-16.

12. Silex interview, Dec. 11, 1982.

13. As quoted in unidentified clipping from SW Col., El Paso Public Library, "El Paso" Vertical File, "Industries—American Smelting and Refining Co."

14. Interview with J. B. Chavez, El Paso, Jan. 18, 1983, by Mario T García.

15. El Paso *Herald-Post*, July 7, 1939, 2; July 10, 1939, 1; July 12, 1939, 2; July 6, 1939, 8; July 11, 1939, 12.

16. El Paso *Herald-Post*, July 13, 1939, 10; July 15, 1939, 10; Aug. 1, 1939, 5.

17. El Paso *Herald-Post*, Aug. 10, 1939, 1, 10. Other than its formation, nothing else is known about the Union of Protective Latin Americans.

18. Silex interview, Dec. 11, 1982.

19. Chávez interview, Jan. 18, 1983.

20. See Mario T. García, "Americans All: The Mexican American Generation and the Politics of Wartime Los Angeles, 1941-1945," *Social Science Quarterly* (June 1984), 278-289; García, "Mexican Americans and the Politics of Citizenship: The Case of El Paso, 1936," *New Mexico Historical Review*, 59:2 (1984), 187-204; and "Mexican American Labor and the Left: The Asociacion Nacional Mexico-Americana, 1948-1954" in John A. Garcia, et al., eds., *The Chicano Struggle: Analyses of Past and Present Efforts* (Binghamton, N.Y., 1984), 65-86.

21. Chávez interview, Jan. 18, 1983.

22. Silex interview, Dec. 11, 1982.

23. Silex interviews, Dec. 11, 1982, and April 28, 1978, IOH, 17.

24. Silex interview, April 28, 1978, IOH, 18; Dinwoodie, 4.

25. Chávez interview, Jan. 18, 1983.

26. Silex interview, Dec. 11, 1982.

27. Chávez interview, Jan. 18, 1983.

28. Silex interview, Dec. 11, 1982 and April 28, 1978, IOH, 4.

29. As quoted in Arnold, 7.

30. Arnold, 8.

31. El Paso *Herald-Post*, March 11, 1940, 1–2; March 22, 1940, 16; March 7, 1940, 1, 11; March 8, 1940, 1, 16.

32. El Paso *Herald-Post*, March 8, 1940, 1, 16. For the "Brown Scare," see Ricardo Romo, *East Los Angeles: History of a Barrio* (Austin, 1983), 89–111.

33. El Paso, *Herald-Post*, March 9, 1940, 1, 6.

34. El Paso, *Herald-Post*, March 12, 1940, 4.

35. El Paso, *Herald-Post*, March 11, 1940, 4. Sheriff Fox later testified before the Dies Committee and reiterated his charge of Communist ties between Juárez and El Paso labor leaders; *Herald-Post*, March 26, 1940, 1; March 27, 1940, 1; July 24, 1940, 1; El Paso *Times*, July 21, 1940, 8. A few months later, Fox endorsed a U.S. State Department nullification of border-crossing cards and the stricter control of "alien" visits. He reasserted his belief in the linkage between "Communist subversion" and Mexican "aliens": "What is the use of fighting vigorously against persons who wade the river when other persons, possibly far more dangerous, have been allowed to simply walk into the United States over a dry bridge?" See *Herald-Post*, June 12, 1940, 2; El Paso *Times*, July 20, 1940, 1, 2.

36. El Paso *Herald-Post*, March 12, 1940, 1, 4.

37. El Paso *Herald-Post*, March 19, 1940, 1. Of the remaining three men in jail, Pedroza was turned over to U.S. immigration officials and repatriated to Mexico; Oaxaca was released from county jail and allowed a "voluntary departure" by U.S. immigration officials; finally, Frank Sener was tried and convicted on a charge of "vagrancy," fined $200, and sentenced to 74 days in jail. See *Herald-Post*, March 11, 1940, 1, 12; March 12, 1940, 1, 11; March 13, 1940, 9; March 15, 1940, 1; March 18, 1940, 1, 8; March 19, 1940, 1, 7; March 21, 1940, 1–2; March 22, 1940, 1, 16; March 23, 1940, 1.

38. El Paso *Herald-Post*, April 12, 1940, 2; Nov. 4, 1940, 1, 12; El Paso *Times*, Nov. 8, 1940, 9; *Herald-Post*, Nov. 13, 1940, 1, 8; Nov. 6, 1940, 1–2; Nov. 9, 1940, 1, 6; Nov. 12, 1940, 1, 12; Nov. 15, 1940, 1; Nov. 4, 1940, 1, 12; May 7, 1940, 7; Feb. 6, 1941, 1.

39. El Paso *Herald-Post*, Feb. 1, 1941, 1, 6; Feb. 3, 1941, 1, 10; Feb. 4, 1941, 1, 12; Feb. 7, 1941, 1; Robinson to "Harold," El Paso, Jan. 25, 1941, in UMMSW, Box 553, Folder "Local 501"; *Herald-Post*, Sept. 4, 1941, 10.

40. As quoted in *Mine-Mill Union*, May 4, 1942, 10.

41. As quoted in *Mine-Mill Union*, May 25, 1942.

42. *Mine-Mill Union*, July 6, 1942, 3, see agreement, May 6, 1942, in UMMSW, Box 131, Folder "509."

43. Silex to Reid Robinson, El Paso, July 14, 1942, in UMMSW, Box 41, Folder 15.

44. Silex to Allen D. McNeil, El Paso, Oct. 19 and Nov. 14, 1942, in UMMSW, Box 41, Folder 15.

45. Leo Ortiz to McNeil, El Paso, Aug. 3 and 6, 1942, in UMMSW, Box 41, Folder 3; Jess Nichols to Reid Robinson, El Paso, March 24, 1943, in UMMSW, Box 41, Folder 1.

46. Nichols to Robinson, El Paso, March 24 and 10, 1943, in UMMSW, Box 41, Folder 1.

47. *Mine-Mill Union*, Aug. 28, 1942.

48. See Leo Ortiz to Reid Robinson, Miami, Arizona, Feb. 16, 1943, Robinson to Ortiz, Denver, March 18, 1943, Ortiz to McNeil, El Paso, Aug. 3 and 6, 1942, Ortiz to Robinson, El Paso, Sept. 11, 1942, all in UMMSW, Box 41, Folder 3. Also see Nichols to Robinson, El Paso, June 23, July 10, 1943, in UMMSW Box 41, Folder 1; Robinson to Silex, Denver, June 8, July 19, 1945, and Silex to Robinson, El Paso, July 3, 1943, all in UMMSW, Box 134, Folder "509."

49. See Leo Ortiz to Edwin A. Elliot, El Paso, Aug. 6, 1942, in UMMSW, Box 41, Folder 3; Ortiz to W.L. Allison Chalmer, El Paso, Aug. 17, 1942, in UMMSW, Box 173, Folder "501"; Ortiz to Ben Riskin, El Paso, Aug. 19, 1942, in UMMSW, Box 41, Folder 3; Silex to Allen D. McNeil, El Paso, Nov. 14, 1942, in UMMSW, Box 41, Folder 15; Antonio M. Salcido and J.A. Reyes to Herbert Heasley, El Paso, Oct. 20, 1942, in UMMSW, Box 173, Folder "501"; Jess Nichols to Allen D. McNeil, El Paso, n.d. [sometime in Dec. 1942], Nichols report, Dec. 3, 1942, Nichols to Reid Robinson, El Paso, March 24, 1943, Robinson to Nichols, Denver, April 29, 1943, Nichols to Robinson, El Paso, March 24, 1943, Nichols to McNeil, El Paso, Dec. 4, 1943, all in UMMSW, Box 41, Folder 1; Ortiz to McNeil, El Paso, Aug. 6, 1942, in UMMSW, Box 41, Folder 3. Blacks as well as women were hired at P-D only during the war years.

50. Ortiz to McNeil, El Paso, Aug. 6, 1942, in UMMSW, Box 41, Folder 3.

51. Ortiz to McNeil, Aug. 6, 1942.

52. Quoted in *The Union*, Oct. 11, 1943, 15.

53. *Union News*, Sept. 26, 1944, in UMMSW, Box 136, Folder 616.

54. Arthur Martinez and Nichols to J.B. Beaty, El Paso, July 26, 1944, in UMMSW, Box 134, Folder "501"; Robinson to Nichols, Denver, May 6, 1943, in UMMSW, Box 41, Folder 1; Robinson to Silex, Denver, May 18, 1943, and Silex to Robinson, El Paso, May 10, 1943, in UMMSW, Box 41, Folder 15; R.F. Gafford to Robinson, El Paso, June 4, 1945, in UMMSW, Box 134, Folder "509"; NLRB document, June 25, 1945, in UMMSW, Box 134, Folder "501."

55. See contract, Jan. 24, 1944, in Archives of U.S. Steelworkers, El Paso Public Library.

56. See "Abuses, Discriminacion en el Suroeste," in *The Union*, Aug. 28, 1944, 12; also R.F. Gafford to Reid Robinson, El Paso, June 4, 1945, in UMMSW, Box 134, Folder "509."

57. El Paso *Herald-Post*, March 2, 1946, 1, 2; Feb. 16, 1946, 1; Feb. 25, 1946, 1, 8; Feb. 26, 1946, 1; Feb. 27, 1946, 14; Feb. 28, 1946, 3; March 2, 1946, 1, 2; March 11, 1946, 1.

58. El Paso *Herald-Post*, Feb. 28, 1946, 3; Feb. 16, 1946; Feb. 25, 1946, 1–8; Feb. 16, 1946, 1, 4, 7.

59. El Paso *Herald-Post*, March 4, 1946, 1–2; Feb. 18, 1946, 3; March 2, 1946, 1–2; March 9, 1946, 1; March 18, 1946, 1.

60. *The Union*, April 3, 1946, 2; El Paso *Herald-Post*, March 13, 1946, 1 and 11; March 28, 1946, 1.

61. *The Union*, May 13, 1946, 19; May 27, 1946, 4.

62. *The Union*, El Paso *Herald-Post*, Feb. 26, 1946, 1, 7; March 8, 1946, 1, 15; April 3, 1946, 2.

63. El Paso *Herald-Post*, Feb. 26, 1946, 1 and 7; March 12, 1946, 3.

64. El Paso *Herald-Post*, March 22, 1946, 4.

65. El Paso *Herald-Post*, April 3, 1946, 4.

66. El Paso *Herald-Post*, June 21, 1946, 1–2.

67. El Paso *Herald-Post*, June 21, 1946, 1–2.

68. El Paso *Herald-Post*, June 28, 1946, 1 and 18; June 29, 1946, 1; *The Union*, June 24, 1946, 2.

69. *The Union*, June 24, 1946, 2; Sept. 16, 1946, 3.

70. See García, "Americans All;" "Politics of Citizenship;" and "Labor and the Left."

71. See Juan Gomez-Quiñones, "The First Steps: Chicano Labor Conflict and Organizing, 1900–1920," *Aztlan* (Spring 1972), 13–49; Gomez-Quiñones and David Maciel, *Al Norte del Rio Bravo (Pasado Lejano), 1600–1930* (Mexico City, 1981; Maciel, *Al Norte del Rio Bravo (Pasado Immediato), 1930–1981* (Mexico City, 1981).

72. In 1967, Minc Mill, due to declining membership and other causes, finally merged with the U.S. Steelworkers. Many of the Mine-Mill veterans are still active today with the U.S. Steelworkers. See Robert S. Keitel, "The Merger of the International Union of Mine, Mill and Smelter Workers into the United Steel Workers of America," *Labor History* (Winter 1974), 36–43.

Chapter 6: Puerto Ricans in the Garment Industry of New York City

1. Raymond Vernon, *Metropolis, 1985: An Interpretation of the Findings of the New York Metropolitan Region Study* (Cambridge, Mass.: Harvard University Press, 1960), 34.

2. Blacks also began to enter the industry after 1900. For a brief account of the history of Blacks in the needle trades, see Robert Laurentz, "Racial/Ethnic Conflict in the New York City Garment Industry, 1933–1980" (Ph.D. diss. State University of New York at Binghamton, 1980), 81–94.

3. Laurentz; Virginia Sanchez Korrol, "Settlement Patterns and Community Development among Puerto Ricans in New York City, 1917–1948," (Ph D diss. State University of New York at Stony Brook, 1981), ch. 4. This work has been published under the title, *From Colonia to Community: The History of Puerto Ricans in New York City, 1917–1948* (Westport, Conn.; Greenwood Press, 1983). In 1986, the Centro de Estudios Puertorriquenos at Hunter College of the City of New York conducted a series of oral interviews with Puerto Rican female garment workers, held a conference on the subject, and prepared a slide show and radio program, entitled, "Nosotras Trabajamos en la Costura" (We Work in Needlework). The Oral History Task Force that has been in charge of these projects intends to follow up this research with a publication on the experiences of Puerto Rican women in the garment industry.

4. Marcia Rivera Quintero, "Educational Policy and Female Labor, 1898–1930," in Iris M. Zavala and Rafael Rodriguez, eds., *The Intellectual Roots of Independence: An Anthology of Puerto Rican Political Essays* (New York: Monthly Review Press, 1980), 350–351; For implications of this policy see Celia Fernandez Cintron and Marcia Rivera Quintero, "Bases de la Sociedad Sexista en Puerto Rico," *Revista Interamericana*, 4, (Summer 1974) 239–45.

5. Virginia Sanchez Korrol, "On the Other Side of the Ocean: The Work

Experiences of Early Puerto Rican Migrant Women," *Caribbean Review* (Jan. 1979), 22–23. See also Blanca G. Silverstrini Pacheco, "The Needlework Industry in Puerto Rico, 1915–1940: Women's Transition from Home to Factory," paper presented at the Twelfth Conference of Caribbean Historians, Trinidad, (April 1980), 1–30.

6. Charles Wright Mills, Clarence Senior, and Rose Kohn Goldsen, *Puerto Rican Journey: New York's Newest Migrants* (New York: Russell and Russell, 1967 [1950]), 34–37).

7. Sanchez Korrol, "Settlement Patterns," 164–168.

8. Sanchez Korrol, "Settlement Patterns," 167–168.

9. Sanchez Korrol, "Settlement Patterns," 168; Lawrence R. Chenault, *The Puerto Rican Migrant in New York City* (New York: Russell and Russell, 1970 [1938]), 72, 76.

10. Sanchez Korrol, "Settlement Patterns," 164–165; See also Caroline Manning, *The Employment of Women in Puerto Rico*, U.S. Department of Labor, Women's Bureau, Report No. 8, (Washington, D.C.: Government Printing Office, 1934).

11. Chenault's work was one of the first secondary publications to refer to Puerto Ricans who settled in the United States as "migrants." Subsequent studies also referred to Puerto Ricans as "migrants" rather than "immigrants" because Puerto Rico is considered an integral part of the United States. Recently, however, Puerto Rican scholars have begun to use the term "immigrant," for they see the Puerto Rican situation as politically and culturally different from those of the North American states. In connection with this, see Manuel Maldonado-Denis, *Puerto Rico y Estados Unidos: emigracion y colonialismo: un analisis socio-historico de la emigracion puertorriquena* (Mexico: Siglo Veintiuno Editores, 1976).

12. Chenault, 76.

13. Sanchez Korrol, "Settlement Patterns," 169–170.

14. Interview with Julia Rodriguez, daughter of Georgina Feliciano, Brentwood, New York, Nov. 17, 1984.

15. Dan Wakefield, *Island in the City: The World of Spanish Harlem* (New York: Arno Press, 1975 [1959]), 198.

16. Wakefield, 198–199.

17. Sanchez Korrol, "Settlement Patterns," 161, 194.

18. Chenault, 72–73.

19. Sanchez Korrol, "Settlement Patterns," 194–196.

20. Barbara Wertheimer and Anne H. Nelson, *Trade Union Women: A Study of Their Participation in New York City Locals* (New York: Praeger, 1975), 60–61.

21. Laurentz, 43–44.

22. Philip S. Foner, *History of the Labor Movement in the United States*, vol. 4 (New York: International Publishers, 1965), 66–67.

23. Hyman Berman, "Era of Protocol, A Chapter in the History of the I.L.G.W.U., 1910–1916," Ph.D. diss., Columbia University, 1956; Alice Kessler-Harris, *Out to Work: A History of Wage-Earning Women in the United States* (New York: Oxford University Press, 1982), 150–161; Michael Meyerson, "ILGWU: Fighting for Lower Wages," *Ramparts* 8 (Oct. 1969), 51.

24. Steve Fraser, "Dress Rehearsal for the New Deal: Shop-Floor Insurgents, Political Elites, and Industrial Democracy in the Amalgamated Clothing Workers," 212–255 in Michael H. Frisch and Daniel J. Walkowitz, eds., *Working-Class America: Essays on Labor, Community, and American Society* (Urbana: University of Illinois Press, 1983).

25. Jesse T. Carpenter, *Competition and Collective Bargaining in the Noodle Trades, 1910–1967* (Ithaca, N.Y.: New York State School of Industrial and Labor Relations, 1972); Kathy Claspell, "Sexual Harassment in the Garment Trade, 1900–1925," seminar paper, History Department, The University of Connecticut, 1986; Daniel Nelson, *Unemployment Insurance: The American Experience, 1915–1935* (Madison: University of Wisconsin Press, 1969), 92–101.

26. Robert Asher, "Jewish Unions and the American Federation of Labor Power Structure, 1903–1935," *American Jewish Historical Quarterly* 65 (March 1976), 223–226; William Green to Abraham Baroff, September 8, 20, 1927, Correspondence with Affiliates, A.F.L.-C.I.O. Archives, Silver Spring, MD.; David Gurowsky, "Factional Disputes within the International Ladies' Garment Workers' Union, 1919–1928," Ph.D. diss., State University of New York at Binghamton, 1978; Irving Howe and Lewis Coser, *The American Communist Party* (New York: Frederick A. Praeger, 1962), 245–251.

27. Roger Waldinger, "Another Look at the International Ladies' Garment Workers' Union: Women, Industry Structure and Collective Action," 86–109, in Ruth Milkman, ed., *Women, Work and Protest: A Century of U.S. Women's Labor History* (Boston: Routledge & Kegan Paul, 1985); Gary Edward Endelman, "Solidarity Forever: Rose Schneiderman and the Women's Trade Union League," Ph.D. diss., University of Delaware, 1978; Mercedes Stedman, "Skill and Gender in the Canadian Clothing Industry, 1890–1940," 161–167 in Craig Heron and Robert Storey, eds., *On the Job: Confronting the Labour Process in Canada* (Kingston: McGill-Queens University Press, 1986); Charlene Gannage, *Double Day, Double Bind: Women Garment Workers* (Toronto: The Women's Press, 1986); Rose Pesotta to David Dubinsky, Sept. 30, 1933, Box 1, Rose Pesotta Papers, New York Public Library.

28. Alice Kessler-Harris, "Problems of Coalition-Building: Women and Trade Unions in the 1920s," 110–138 in Milkman; Alice Kessler-Harris, "Organizing the Unorganizable: Three Jewish Women and Their Union," *Labor History* 17 (Winter 1976), 14–28; William H. Harris, *The Harder We Run: Black Workers since the Civil War* (New York: Oxford University Press, 1982), 138–141; Sumner M. Rosen, "The CIO Era, 1935–1955," 188–208 in Julius Jacobson, ed., *The Negro and the American Labor Movement* (New York: Doubleday, 1968); Bert Cochran, *Labor and Communism: The Conflict That Shaped American Unions* (Princeton, N.J.: Princeton University Press, 1977).

29. Chenault, 79; Laurentz, 125, 127, 147.

30. Laurentz, 151–52.

31. Laurentz, 147.

32. Relocation, also, was a reaction to a declining immigrant labor population in the East. Vernon, 120.

33. Laurentz, 137, 175, n.16. The use of trucks made relocation more feasible than ever. Vernon, 43–44, 70–71, 109.

34. Meyerson, 51.

35. Transcript from article in *La Prensa*, December 23, 1933 in the International Ladies' Garment Workers' Union Archives, Charles S. Zimmerman Collection Records, Box 33, File 11.

36. Strike leaflet of 1934, ILGWU Archives, *Zimmerman Collection*, Box 33, File 11.

37. Will Herberg, "The Old-Timers and the Newcomers, Ethnic Group Relations in a Needle Trades' Union," *Journal of Social Issues* (Summer 1953), 161.

38. Laurentz, 123–124, 167, 105, 163.

39. Abraham J. Jaffee, "Demographic and Labor Force Characteristics of New York City Puerto Rican Population," in Abraham J. Jaffee, ed., *Puerto Rican Population of New York City* (New York: Arno Press, 1975 [1954]), 22.

40. Carl Raushenbush, "A Conmparison of the Occupations of First- and Second- Generation Puerto Ricans in the Mainland Labor Market, and How the Work of the New York State Department of Labor Affects Puerto Ricans," in Jaffee, 57.

41. Centro de Estudios Puertorriquenos, *Labor Migration under Capitalism* (New York: Hunter College, 1979), 150.

42. Clarence O. Senior, *The Puerto Ricans: Strangers—Then Neighbors* (Chicago: Quadrangle Books, 1965), 93.

43. The decline of the garment industry is discussed in: Leon H. Keyserling, *The New York Dress Industry: Problems and Prospects* (Washington, D.C., 1963); Roy B. Helfgott, "Women's and Children's Apparel," in Max Hall, ed., *Made in New York: Case Studies in Metrtopolitan Manufacturing* (Cambridge, Mass.: Harvard University Press, 1959), 21–134; Raymond Vernon and Edgar Malone Hoover, *Anatomy of a Metropolis: The Changing Distribution of People and Jobs within the New York Metropolitan Region* (Cambridge, Mass.: Harvard University Press, 1959); Vernon, *Metropolis, 1985.*

44. Laurentz, 238, 315; Vernon, 60–61; Vernon and Hoover, 27.

45. Imports hurt the Puerto Rican workers because large numbers of them were employed in these industries. Laurentz, 238–239, 263–270.

46. Adalberto Lopez, "The Puerto Rican Diaspora: A Survey," in Adalberto Lopez and James Petras, eds., *Puerto Rico and Puerto Ricans: Studies in History and Society* (New York: Wiley, 1974), 318; José L. Vazquez Calzada, "Demographic Aspects of Migration," in Centro, 225.

47. The ILGWU encouraged de-skilling of the needle trades in order to make use of inexpensive and unskilled wage workers to avoid relocation of firms to other low-labor cost areas. Laurentz, 239–242.

48. Vernon and Hoover, 65.

49. Meyerson, 51–52; Vernon, 70–71, 109.

50. Wakefield, 200–201.

51. Wakefield, 191–195; Roy B. Helfgott, "Puerto Rican Integration in the Skirt Industry in New York City," in *Discrimination and Low Incomes: Social and Economic Discrimination against Minority Groups in Relation to Low Incomes in New York State* (New York: Studies of New York State Commission against Discrimination, New School for Social Research, 1959), 255.

52. Herbert Hill, "Guardians of the Sweatshops: The Trade Unions, Racism, and the Garment Industry," in López and Petras, 392.

53. Helfgott, "Puerto Rican Integration in the Skirt Industry;" see also: Roy B. Helfgott, "Puerto Rican Integration in a Garment Union Local," *Proceedings of the Tenth Annual Meeting, Industrial Relations Research Association*, 10 (1958), 269–275.

54. Joseph P. Fitzpatrick, *Puerto Rican Americans: The Meaning of Migration to the Mainland* (Englewood Clifs, N.J.: Prentice-Hall, 1971), 61–62; Hall.

55. Will Herberg maintained in his 1953 study that although the new ethnic groups were not adequately represented in the Dressmakers' Local 22 leadership positions, the ILGWU was not responsible for this. He believed that the union's leaders were "sincerely desirous" of developing leaders among the newcomers. Herberg's explanation for the lack of minorities in the leadership

structure rested on what he termed the breaking up of an "organic process" that historically had created leaders in the union's militant past. In other words, the conditons that had given rise to Jewish and Italian leaders, who learned their leadership abilities on the picket line and in the conflicts within the union, did not exist any longer. Consequently, it was difficult for the new workers to develop leadership skills. Herberg, 12–19.

56. Hill, 386–87; Meyerson, 54.

57. Hill, 387; Laurentz, 186–87.

58. The 1975 study of Local 22 by Wertheimer and Nelson revealed that men were still in control of this union local, and that this may have accounted for the low participation of women in union activities in general. Wertheimer and Nelson, 62–63.

59. Hill, 403.

60. Wakefield, 211.

61. Meyerson, 54.

62. Hill, 402.

63. Meyerson, 55.

64. Herberg, 14–15.

65. Helfgott, "Women's and Children's Apparel," 95. In the skirt industry, Helfgott noted, there was movement to higher skills. See also "Puerto Rican Integration in the Skirt Industry," 256; "Puerto Rican Integration in a Garment Union Local," 3.

66. U.S. House of Representatives, 87th Cong., 2nd sess., "Investigation of Labor Irregularities and Discrimination in the Garment Industry," Hearings before the Ad Hoc Subcommittee on the Investigation of the Garment Industry, August 7, 1962, *Congressional Record*, pt. 12–14, vol. 108.

67. Hill, 396.

68. Hill, 399.

69. Laurentz, 307.

70. Skilled Puerto Rican cutters, in time, found employment in "cut-up" shops that specialized in cutting of garments only. These shops, however, were not unionized, and, of course, paid wages that were far below those of union shops. Laurentz, 244–245.

71. In their studies dealing with the participation of Puerto Rican women in the labor force during the 1960s Rosemary Santana Cooney and Alice Colon attribute the decline of the numbers of Puerto Rican women in the labor

market to several other factors: the Hispanic family structure that pressures women to marry and remain at home; the high fertility rates among Puerto Rican women; the relocation of low-skill industries outside the city. Rosemary Santana Cooney and Alice Colon, "Work and Family: The Recent Struggle of Puerto Rican Females," in Clara E. Rodriguez, Virginia Sanchez Korrol, and José Oscar Alers, eds., *The Puerto Rican Struggle: Essays on Survival in the United States* (New York: Puerto Rican Migration Research Consortium, 1980), 58–73.

72. Herberg, 13.

73. Helfgott, "Puerto Rican Integration in the Skirt Industry;" "Women's and Children's Apparel."

74. Helfgott, "Women's and Children's Apparel," 96.

75. Helfgott, "Women's and Children's Apparel," 97–98.

76. Vernon, 76.

77. Vernon, 75 76.

78. Clara E. Rodriguez, "Economic Factors Affecting Puerto Ricans in New York," in Centro, 214–215.

79. Rodriguez, 213.

80. Rodriguez, 197–198.

81. In accordance with its low wage policy, the ILGWU negotiated contracts with manufacturers that did not represent the interests of the vast majority of Puerto Rican workers. Hill concluded that: "For many locals in New York City in which the overwhelming membership is Negro and Puerto Rican, the wage schedules provided in the collective bargaining are a disgrace to the American labor movement. In these agreements the so-called 'minimum wages' are in fact most frequently the maximum wages." Hill, 404.

82. Federico Ribes Tovar, *The Puerto Rican Woman: Her Life and Evolution throughout History* (New York: Plus Ultra Educational Publishers, 1972), 194.

83. Lourdes Miranda King, "Puertorriquenas in the United States: The Impact of Double Discrimination," *Civil Rights Digest*, 6 (Spring 1974), 123.

84. Centro, 151.

Chapter 7: Black Workers in Alabama, 1945–1953

1. Thomas R. Brooks, *Toil and Trouble* (New York: Dell, 1974, 228). Constituent unions could be expelled by a three-fourths majority of the Executive Board.

2. Philip Foner, *Organized Labor and the Black Worker, 1619–1973* (New York: Praeger, 1974), 275.

3. Richard O. Boyer and Herbert M. Morais, *Labor's Untold Story* (New York: United Electrical Radio and Machine Workers of America, 1955), 341–342.

4. James C. Foster, *The Union Politic: The C.I.O. Political Action Committee* (Columbia: University ofMissouri Press, 1975), 53–55.

5. Art Preis, *Labor's Giant Step: Twenty Years of the CIO* (New York: Pioneer Publishers, 1964), 172.

6. Preis, 258.

7. "Report of the Committee to Investigate Charges against the International Union of Mine Mill and Smelter Workers" in the proceedings of the Senate, *Hearings on Communist Domination of Unions and National Security,* 82nd Cong., 2nd sess., 1952. These assaults were evidenced by the United Electrical Workers' President James Carey's accusations against former UE president James Fitzgerald of Communist involvement; the Farm Equipment Workers Union in jurisdictional disputes with the United Automobile Workers; Joseph Curran's decision to lead the National Maritime Union into the anticommunist camp; the allegation that support of Henry Wallace and the Progressive Party in 1947 resulted from Communist manipulation; the 1948–1949 CIO-Steelworkers raid of Mine Mill in Alabama; and finally censure and expulsion of the "Communist-dominated" unions.

8. U.S. Senate, Committee on Education and Labor, *Violations of Free Speech,* Hearings on S. 266, 75th Cong., 1st sess., pt. 3, 779.

9. U.S. Senate, *Violations of Free Speech,* 74th Cong., 2nd sess., pt. 2, 727.

10. *Birmingham News,* May 9, 1934, 1.

11. F. Ray Marshall, *Labor in the South* (Cambridge, Mass.: Harvard University Press, 1967), 157.

12. U.S. Senate, *Violations of Free Speech,* 75th Cong., 1st sess., pt. 3, 965.

13. U.S. Senate, *Violations of Free Speech,* 75th Cong., 1st sess., pt. 3, 966.

14. U.S. Senate, *Violations of Free Speech,* 75th Cong., 1st sess., pt. 3, 970, 971–972.

15. See Foner. Wilson Record, *The Negro and the Communist Party* (New York: Atheneum, 1971 [1951]). Theodore Rosengarten, *All God's Dangers* (New York: Knopf, 1974); Angelo Herndon, *Let Me Live* (New York: Random House, 1937); and Hosea Hudson, *Black Worker in the Deep South* (New York: International Publishers, 1973).

16. James M. McPherson, Laurence B. Holland, James M. Banner, Jr., Nancy J. Weiss, and Michael D. Bell, *Blacks in America: Biographical Essays* (Garden City, N.Y.: Doubleday, 1971), 231.

17. Record, 38, 41.

18. In addition to Record's account, also see Hudson.

19. The quest for social equality in Amnerica has often been associated with Communism, particularly by white reactionaries.

20. Horace Huntley, "The Nigger Union: Organization in Birmingham Iron Ore Mines, 1933–1938," paper presented at the 63rd Annual Convention of the Association for the Study of Afro-American Life and History, Los Angeles, Cal., Oct., 1978.

21. *U.S. Supreme Court Paper Books*, 321 US 590, Oct. term, 1943, vol. 4, 2481. Also, personal interview, Marion Reynolds, retired miner, May 1975.

22. U.S. House of Representatives, Committee on Education and Labor, *Federal Fair Employment Practices Act*, II.R. 4453, 81st Cong., 1st sess., 1949, 254. Also personal interviews conducted with retired miners.

23. Prior to 1949, several aborted attempts were made to take control of Mine Mill by disgruntled white workers.

24. See Vernon Jensen, *Nonferrous Metal Industry Unionism 1932–1954* (Ithaca, N.Y.: Cornel University Press, 1954). This was best exemplified in the "Brass Valley" of Connecticut.

25. Jensen, 208–234.

26. See Horace Huntley, "Mine Mill in Alabama," Ph.D. diss., University of Pittsburgh, 1977.

27. Agreement for Consent Election, in Mine Mill Papers

28. The term "popsicle" referred to those workers who had been members of the earlier company union.

29. *Iron Ore Miner*, April 14, 1949.

30. *Iron Ore Miner*, April 14, 1949.

31. Letter from Mine Mill Officials to Allan Haywood, dated March 22, 1949, in International Union of Mine, Mill and Smelter Workers Papers, Western Historical Collection, University of Colorado.

32. Report from Graham Dolan to John Clark, in Mine Mill Papers.

33. See Huntley, "Mine Mill in Alabama," 163–167; Jensen, *Nonferrous Metals Industry Unionism*, 267–268.

34. *New York Home News*, May 11, 1949.

35. Frank Allen, International Representative Semi-Monthly Reports, April 30, 1949, in Mine Mill Papers.

36. J. P. Mooney, International Representative Semi-Monthly Reports, April 30, 1949, in Mine Mill Papers.

37. Foner, 280.

38. CIO Resolution, in Mine Mill Papers.

39. See Huntley, "Mine Mill in Alabama," 186–193.

40. Gilbert Osofsky, *The Burden of Race* (New York: Harper and Row, 1967), 389.

41. Maurine Christopher, *America's Black Congressmen* (New York: Crowell, 1971), 198.

42. Adam Clayton Powell, Jr., *Marching Blacks* (New York: Dial Press, 1945), 69.

43. Jensen, 267–268.

44. Interviews with several retired miners, including Asbury Howard, who later became International Vice-President of Mine Mill.

45. Statement by Amzi Park, June 26, 1951, in Mine Mill Papers.

46. Interview, Asbury Howard, May 1975.

47. Howard, interview.

48. See Asbury Howard, International Representative Semi-Monthly Reports, Jan. 15, 1948, Feb. 28, June 15, July 31, 1949, Jan. 15, April 15, April 30, 1950, Feb. 28, 1951, in Mine Mill Papers.

49. Howard, interview.

50. Asbury Howard to John Clark, March 23, 1953, in Mine Mill Papers.

51. Howard Report, July 15, 1953, in Mine Mill Papers.

52. During the height of the Red Scare the NAACP was consistently critical of left-wing unions. According to Record in *Race and Radicalism*, just like the CIO, the NAACP felt threatened by communist infiltration and "was increasingly disposed to move in, revoke charters, and reorganize local branches when communists were even momentarily successful."

53. Howard Report, July 15, 1953, in Mine Mill Papers.

54. Howard, interview, May 1975.

55. Reynolds, interview.

56. Howard, interview.

Chapter 8: Immigration Ethnicity, and Working-Class Community

1. Oscar Handlin, *Boston's Immigrants* (Cambridge, Mass., 1941); Handlin's later work, *The Uprooted* (Boston, 1951) contains many of the same insights but expanded beyond the Boston Irish experience. For examples of revision of Handlin, see Rudolph Vecoli, "Contadini in Chicago; A Critique of the Uprooted," *Journal of American History*, Dec. 1964, 404–417; Virginia Yans-McLaughlin, *Family and Community: Italian Immigrants in Buffalo 1880-1930* (Ithaca, N.Y., 1977). Arthur M. Schlesinger, in his classic essay, "The Significance of Immigration on American History," *American Journal of Sociology*, 27:1 (July 1921), 27–85, was the first to argue for the importance of immigration in the study of American History.

To list all of the important works on various immigrant groups would absorb far too much space and be of limited use to the specialist and of limited interest to the non-specialist, but some of the important studies are: Marcus L. Hansen, *The Atlantic Migration* (Cambridge, Mass., 1940); and *The Immigrant in American History* (Cambridge, Mass., 1940); William I. Thomas and Florian Znaniecki, *Polish Peasant in Europe and America* (Chicago, 1918); Hubert Nelli, *The Italians in Chicago, 1880-1930* (New York, 1973); Josef Barton, *Peasants and Strangers* (Cambridge, Mass., 1975).

2. See John Bodnar, *Immigration and Industrialization. Ethnicity in an American Mill Town, 1870-1940* (Pittsburgh, 1977), and John Bodnar, Roger Simon, and Michael Weber, *Lives of Their Own* (Urbana, Ill., 1982). Herbert Gutman's work also stresses this conflict: see *Work, Culture and Society* (New York, 1977).

3. See Stephen Thernstrom, *Poverty and Progress* (Cambridge, Mass., 1964), particularly 164–165, and John Laslett and Seymour Lipset *Failure of a Dream* (Berkeley, 1974), for examples of this argument.

4. See Herbert Gutman, "Work, Culture, and Society in Industrializing America, 1815-1919," *The American Historical Review*, 78 (1973); Rowland Berthoff, *British Immigrants in Industrial America, 1790-1950* (Cambridge, Mass., 1953); Charlotte Erickson, *Invisible Immigrants, Part 2* (Coral Gables, Fla., 1972).

5. See Sam Bass Warner, *Streetcar Suburbs* (Cambridge, Mass., 1978 ed.), 10-11, for an example of this romantic nationalism.

6. During the fiscal year ending June 1909, 87,160 immigrants listed skilled occupations with immigration officials, while 171,310 were listed as

farm laborers. Commissioner General of Immigration, *Annual Report* (Washington, D.C., 1909), table 6.

7. See Clifton D. Yearly, Jr. *Britons in American Labor: A History of the Influence of the United Kingdom Immigrants on American Labor, 1820–1914* (Baltimore, 1957); David Montgomery, *Beyond Equality: Labor and the Radical Republicans, 1862–1872* (Boston, 1967).

8. Although it is true that 54% of the immigrants from Europe between 1907 and 1910 were from agrarian occupations, 15% had industrial occupations before emigrating. U.S. Senate "Report of the Immigration Commission," Cong., 2nd sess., Doc. 663, 19, 95. Later reports of the Commissioner-General of Immigration showed even a larger proportion of immigrants with non-agrarian backgrounds; although immigrants from certain regions, especially Poland, Russia (non-Jewish), southern Italy, and Slovakia, were predominantly farm workers, even these countries provided skilled workers as well. Reports of the Commissioner-General of Immigration, 1909–1911 (Washington, D.C.). See particularly Berthoff and Erickson.

Often the process of immigration was a long one, taking the peasant first to an industrial setting closer to home before the trip to America. Typical of this pattern was Thomas Dolerty, who was born in Ireland. Dolerty migrated to England with his wife, also born in Ireland, and lived there long enough to have two children, born in England. Later Dolerty migrated to Fall River where he took up the trade of spinner, presumably learned while in England. Thomas Sullivan was also born in Ireland, migrated to England, where he met and married his wife and then migrated to Fall River to find a job in a cotton mill. John Gorman was born in Ireland, as was his wife. They moved to England, where she gave birth to five children. After some time in England, Gorman moved to Fall River with his family. There his wife gave birth to three more children. Manuscript schedules of the 10th U.S. Census (1880) Mass., vol. 4, Bristol Co., Fall River.

9. Jonathan Lincoln, in a speech commemorating the opening of a new mill in Fall River, commented that in Boston and New York, Fall River was considered a culturally backward place because all its energy was put to the single task of industry and prosperity. J.Gilmer Speed, *Fall River Incident* (Fall River, Mass., 1895).

10. Despite the romantic claim that more northern New England towns like Lowell and Lawrence maintained on the nation's imagination with respect to textile manufacture, southern New England had a majority of the nation's spindles by the post–Civil War period. Southern New England practiced the Fall River system of labor more typical of England than the paternalistic Lowell system.

11. From a random sample of 523 Irish male heads of households working as textile workers in Fall River in 1880, 31% had either English-born wives (usually themselves born of Irish parents) or had children born in England.

This indicates that at the very least 31% of the Irish textile workers in Fall River spent considerable time in England before emigrating to Fall River. This percentage does not include those Irish who spent time in England but did not have children there or marry English-born wives. If it were possible to add those to our calculations, the percentage with English experience would be considerably higher, probably well above fifty percent. Sample from manuscript schedules of 10th U.S. Census (1880), N-523.

12. Henry Fenner, *History of Fall River* (New York, 1906), 146.

13. Address to International Textile Conference, England, 1894, quoted in *Fall River Herald*, Aug. 7, 1894.

14. Quoted in Berthoff, 32.

15. Thomas Young, *The American Cotton Industry* (New York, 1903), 1–2.

16. In Elizabeth Gaskell's *Mary Barton*, the story of the lives of textile operatives during the mid-nineteenth century, the heroine's father, a textile operative, belonged to a club so "that money was provided for the burial of his wife" (Middlesex, 1970), 58.

17. Sir Frederick M. Eden, *Observations on Friendly Societies* (London, 1801), 4. See also P.H.J.H. Gosden, *The Friendly Societies in England 1815–1875* (New York, 1967) and *Self-Help Voluntary Associations in Nineteenth-Century Britian* (New York, 1974).

18. Eden, 23, 24.

19. Eden, 7. Even more important, these clubs provided for an alternate ideology from that of the prevailing middle class. Central to the middle-class ideology was the concept of equality in opportunity for individual upward mobility. Although this ideology would find ultimate expression in the United States, it was the common core of western liberal middle-class democracy. The institutions of the working class provided them not only with institutions counter to those dominated by the middle class, but in ideological terms they reinforced the concept of mutual dependence. Workers learned to look not to individual hard work in the context of the impersonal forces of the economy, but to mutual and collective support of others caught in the same constraints of the industrializing system.

This in turn gave strength to working-class modification of the western ideology of individualism, that is, to collective equality and security. This sense of collective security provided the basis for the developing working-class concepts of collective equality manifested in the trade union movement. It also provided the means for translating the individual labor theory inherited from the craft stage of development to the sense of collective labor theory of value central to the working-class ideology of the industrial period. See John Cumbler, "Community in the Twentieth Century," paper presented at the Annual Meeting of the Organization of American Historians, Minneapolis, 1985.

20. John Foster, in *Class Struggle and the Industrial Revolution* (London, 1974), notes,

> It is also significant that they [the friendly societies] remained exclusively organizations of and for the working people. Despite periods of great financial difficulty, they never resorted to outside help. They remained free of the otherwise pervasive influence of the clerical establishment and the tradesmen, petty bourgeoisie.

Gosden's analysis, which stresses their relief functions, does not account for or look at the sharp differences between Lancashire's limited relief expenditures and other districts'. Gosden, *The Friendly Societies*. See Eden for the figures on relief expenditures.

21. See E.P. Thompson, *The Making of the English Working Class* (New York, 1963), 415, 418–427, for a discussion of these clubs; also Webb Collection, London School of Economics. See Friedrich Engels, *Conditions of the English Working Class* (Moscow, 1973), for a description of working-class areas in Lancashire.

22. Sydney Chapman, *The Lancashire Cotton Industry* (Manchester, 1904), 190–233.

23. Quoted in Chapman, 194.

24. Chapman, 194.

25. Thompson, 415, 418–427.

26. Webb Collection, vol. 36, folio 303, London School of Economics.

27. Chapman, 196, 233.

28. Henry Ashworth, "An Inquiry into the Origin, Progress and Results of the Strike of Cotton Spinners of Preston, October 1836–February 1837," paper presented at Manchester Statistical Society, 1838, 3–4, in Manchester Library Collection.

29. In Webb Collection, vol. 40. folio E./A., 76.

30. J.M. Baerneither, *English Associations of Workingmen* (London, 1889).

31. Baerneither. Foster estimated that by 1877 Oldham membership in the five main affiliated orders, the United and the Independent Oddfellows, Druids, Gardeners, and Foresters numbered 6,000. Unlike the Masons or Orangemen, these organizations lacked any link with the bourgeoisie or the clerical establishment. Foster, 217, 218.

32. John Taylor, *From Self-Help to Glamour: The Workingman's Club, 1860–1972* (Ruskin College, Oxford, 1972); Baerneither, 14.

33. See Gaskell's *Mary Barton* for a description of the deterioration of con-

ditions for the English working class from the 1830s through the 1840s. See also the *Industrial Renumeration Conference Report* (London, Jan. 1885), 50.

34. *Industrial Renumeration Conference Report*, 433.

35. See Raymond Williams, *Culture and Society* (London, 1958).

36. Gaskell, 59.

37. Quoted in Thompson, 432.

38. Most of Chartist Feargus O'Connor's northern base and readers for his *Northern Star* came from Lancashire. See also *Manchester Statistical Society Report* (Manchester, 1838), table 6; and Thompson, 428. See also Engels; J.T. Ward, *Chartism* (New York, 1973); and Dorothy Thompson, *The Early Chartists* (London, 1971).

39. See Eva Mueller, *Migration into and out of Depressed Areas* (Washington, D.C., 1964) for a discussion of chain-migration theory. See also Barton.

40. Erickson, 243.

41. *Cotton Factory Times*, June 10, 1892.

42. See notes 7, 9.

43. In the period 1882–1902, the records of the Bolton Operative Cotton Spinners Protective Association, which represented the most skilled textile operatives, listed members of their unions who migrated from Lancashire to the New World. Most of these operatives found their way to Fall River, which, in making fine cloth, had the greatest demand for skilled spinners, since less fine cloth manufacturing enterprises had switched to unskilled ring spinning. Of the spinners leaving Lancashire for Fall River 32% were of Irish origin (according to surnames). This corresponds roughly to the percentage of Irish in the skilled trades in Fall River. Moreover, the number of Irish coming over with less skills was much higher than that of the Irish spinners. This accounts for the large number of Irish textile workers in the Fall River mills who already had training and experience in industrial occupations and in the trade union and working-class institutions in England. Records of the Bolton Operative Spinners Protective Association, Bolton and District, 1882–1902, in Webb Collection.

44. *Cotton Factory Times*, Jan. 16, 1885.

45. *Cotton Factory Times*, Jan. 16, April 13, Dec. 18, 1885.

46. *Cotton Factory Times*, Feb. 20, 1885.

47. *Cotton Factory Times*, April 3, 10, 1885.

48. *Cotton Factory Times*, Feb. 27, 1885.

49. *Cotton Factory Times*, Sept. 30, 1892.

50. *Fall River City Directory*, 1887.

51. All but one of the officers of the Odd Fellows' Manchester Unity Lodge of Fall River were textile operatives or unemployed textile operatives. Most were weavers. The high numbers of unemployed operatives who were officers implies that the workers used the Lodge as an informal unemployment service. Unemployed workers also had more time to do the tasks of the lodge. The other Odd Fellow lodges were also primarily working class in makeup, with mostly working-class officers.

The Manchester Unity Lodge of Fall River was chartered directly from Manchester in 1881. It was not the only Odd Fellows lodge in Fall River with direct English ties, but the others had switched over to a U.S. charter by the late 1880s. The Unity Lodge was charter No. 6434 of a Manchester organization. Lancashire textile workers could then utilize their English membership to integrate themselves into Fall River through the Odd Fellows. *Fall River City Directory*, 1887.

52. The city's Ancient Order of Foresters Lodges, like the Odd Fellows, acted as a transitionary institution for Lancashire textile workers. The Foresters were widespread in England, and when Fall River began to fill up with English operatives they formed lodges of the Foresters there and applied for charters from their home districts. *Fall River City Directory*, 1887.

53. *Amalgamated Association of Operative Spinner's Quarterly Report*, Oct. 31, 1882, in Webb Collection. Both Robert Howard and John Golden, Fall River labor leaders, left Lancashire because of being blacklisted for their union activity.

54. *Annual Reports of Operative Cotton Spinners Provincial Association, Bolton, 1880–1900; Reports of the Amalgamated Association of Operative Cotton Spinners, 1880–1900*, in Webb Collection.

55. *Cotton Factory Times*, June 19, 1885.

56. Yearly, *Britons in American Labor*, 57.

57. Jonathan Baxter Harrison, *Certain Dangerous Tendencies in American Life* (Boston, 1880), 182–183.

58. Harrison, 182–183; Massachusetts Bureau of Labor Statistics, *Thirteenth Annual Report, 1882* (Boston, 1882), 254.

59. Quoted in Mass. Bureau of Labor, 254.

60. *Fall River Daily Herald*, Feb. 28, 1884. Any claim that this was unique to textile workers must be taken with a grain of salt. Each group of workers appeared to think that its work and nationality was special in its drinking habits. But the historian must be careful to distinguish between claims of uniqueness and genuine national or trade differences. The claim has its source

in nineteenth-century concepts of manliness, especially among unskilled and semi-skilled workers in cultural conflict with the middle class. The reality could be another thing entirely, and the historian must be careful not to confuse the two. Although David Bensman has written an otherwise excellent study of hatters in America, he makes the mistake of assuming their claims to be fact. Bensmen, *The Practice of Solidarity* (Urbana, Ill., 1985).

61. Jonathan Lincoln, *The City of the Dinner Pail* (Boston, 1909), 53.

62. Webb Collection, vol. 36, folio 303.

63. *Fall River Daily Herald*, April 28, May 2, 1884.

64. Berthoff, 150.

65. Quoted in Berthoff, 32.

66. *Cotton Factory Times*, April 10, May 18, 22, 1885; May 16, Sept. 2, 1892; April 16, 1904.

67. William Hale, "The Importance of Churches," *Forum*, 18, (Sept. 1894–Feb. 1895), 294.

68. John T. Cumbler, "Community in the Twentieth Century," paper presented at Annual Meeting, Organization of American Historians, Minneapolis, 1985.

69. Harrison, 163–164.

70. Gaskell, 45; See also her *North and South*, where the striking Nicholas Higgings explains to the middle class Margaret Hale the concept of class solidarity:

Du yo' think it's for mysel' I'm striking work at this time? It's just as much in the cause of others. . . . I take up John Bowher's cause as lives next door, but one, with'a sickly wife and eight children, none on'em factory age; and I don't take up his cause only though he's a good-for-nought, as can only manage two looms at a time, but I take up th'cause of "justice" (183).

He goes on to say that the masters "beat us down to swell their fortunes. . . ." (184)

71. For a study of other peasant and agrarian cultures interacting with existing English-Irish working-class communities, see John Cumbler, *Working Class Community in Industrial America* (Westport, Conn., 1979), chs. 8, 9, 10. See also Robert Berkhofer, "Space, Culture, and the New Frontier," *Agricultural History*, 38 (1964) for a discussion of the process of cultural adaptation and environmental factors.

72. Hugo A. Dubuque, *Guide aux Canadien-Francais de Fall River* (Fall River, Mass., 1889); *Fall River City Directory 1887, 1895*. See also Philip Silvia,

"The Spindle City: Labor, Politics, and Religion in Fall River, Massachusetts,"
(Ph.D. diss., Fordham University, 1973), 381–425.

73. See Philip Silvia for a discussion of religious conflict between French-
Canadian and Irish workers. This religious conflict led to pitched battles
between Irish and French-Canadian Catholics. In one case, the appointment of
an Irish priest over a French-Canadian church led to the burning of the church.

74. Dubuque.

75. "Testimony of George McNeill," in "Report of U.S. Industrial Commis-
sion," vol. 17, 56th Cong., 2nd sess., 1900, H. Doc. 495, 567; *Fall River Daily
Herald*, Feb. 13, 18, 20, 1884; U.S. Immigration Commission, *Immigration in
Industry* (Wash., D.C., 1909–1910), 123–125. For a description of how the French
Canadians arrived as strikebreakers but soon became strong unionists, see
"Testimony of Rufus Wade," "Report of U.S. Industrial Commission," 70.

Chapter 9: Scottish Americans and the Modern Class Struggle

1. For the role of British immigrant miners in pioneering the establish-
ment of mining towns in the immediate post–Civil War period, see Rowland
T. Berthoff, *British Immigrants in Industrial America, 1790-1950* (Cambridge,
Mass.: Harvard University Press, 1953), ch. 4; Andrew Roy, *A History of the
Coal Miners of the United States* (Westport, Conn.: Greenwood Press, 1970).

2. Anthony Slaven, *The Development of the West of Scotland, 1750-1960*
(London: Routledge and Kegan Paul, 1975), 92–98, 116–117; Alan B. Campbell,
The Lanarkshire Miners, A Social History of Their Trade Unions, 1775-1874 (Edin-
burgh: John Donald, 1979), 94–99.

3. Campbell, 33–35.

4. Thomas Stewart, *Among the Miners, Being Sketches in Prose and Verse,
With Rhymes and Songs on Various Subjects* (Larkhall: W. Burns, 1893), 60.

5. Quoted in Royden Harrison, ed., *Independent Collier, The Coal Miner
as Archetypal Proletarian Reconsidered* (New York: St. Martin's Press, 1978), 65.

6. Cited in Campbell, 266.

7. Campbell, 248.

8. Campbell, 104–109; Harrison, 68–70.

9. See, e.g., Jack McLellan, *Larkhall, Its Historical Development* (Larkhall:
H. Mathers, 1979), 27–28.

10. Gordon A. Wilson, *Alexander MacDonald, Leader of the Miners* (Aberdeen: Aberdeen University Press, 1982), 95.

11. Henry Pelling, *America and the British Left, From Bright to Bevan* (London: Adam & Charles Black, 1956), 24; James D. Young, "Changing Images of American Democracy and the Scottish Labour Movement," *International Review of Social History* (Amsterdam), vol. 18 (1973), Part 1, 67–77.

12. On the radical ideology of the newly established Republican Party, see Eric Foner, *Free Soil, Free Men, Free Labor, The Ideology of the Republican Party before the Civil War* (New York: Oxford University Press, 1970).

13. Campbell, 248; Edward A. Wieck, *The American Miners Association, A Record of the Origin of Coal Miners Unions in the United States* (New York: Russell Sage Foundation, 1940), 112–114.

14. For Scottish miners who went to the Maryland coal field, see Katherine Harvey, *The Best-Dressed Miners, Life and Labor in the Maryland Coal Region: 1865–1910* (Ithaca, N.Y.: Cornell University Press, 1970), 18–20.

15. Roy, ch. 12.

16. Michael McCormick, "A Comparative Study of Coal Mining Communities in Northern Illinois and Southeastern Ohio in the Late Nineteenth Century" (Ph.D. diss. Ohio State University, 1979), 28.

17. Berthoff, 54.

18. Richard P. Joyce, "Miners of the Prairie: Life and Labor in the Wilmington, Illinois, Coalfield, 1866–1897" (Ph.D. diss. Illinois State University, 1980), 15.

19. *Workingman's Advocate*, May 10, 1873, 2.

20. *Workingman's Advocate*, December 30, 1876, 2; March 31, 1877, 2; Amy Z. Gottlieb, "The Influence of British Trade Unionists on the Regulation of the Mining Industry in Illinois, 1872", *Labor History*, 19:3 (Summer 1978), 397–415.

21. Gordon A. Wilson, "The Miners of the West of Scotland and Their Trade Unions, 1842–1874" (Ph.D. diss., University of Glasgow, 1977), 98–100.

22. Illinois Bureau of Labor Statistics, *Third Biennial Report*, (Springfield. 1884), 432–434.

23. Amy Z. Gottlieb, "British Coal Miners, A Demographic Study of Braidwood and Streator, Illinois," *Journal of the Illinois State Historical Society*, 72:3 (Aug. 1979), 192.

24. Amy Z. Gottlieb, "The Regulation of the Coal Mining Industry in Illinois with Special Reference to the Influence of British Miners and British Precedents, 1870–1911" (Ph.D. diss., University of London, 1975), 303–338.

25. Wilson, "The Miners of the West of Scotland," 103.

26. Gottlieb, "The Regulation of the Coal Mining Industry," 97.

27. Joyce, 12; George Woodruff, *The History of Will County, Illinois, Containing a History of the County, Etc.* (Chicago, William Le Baron, 1878); Campbell, 64.

28. *Glasgow Sentinel*, Sept. 16, 1865, 6.

29. Tom Tippett, *Horse Shoe Bottoms* (New York: Harper, 1935), 4, 8.

30. Cited in Joyce, 37.

31. *Workingmen's Advocate*, Aug. 1, 1868, 3.

32. *Workingmen's Advocate*, Aug. 1, 1868, 3.

33. *Wilmington Advocate*, July 22, 1868, 2.

34. Joyce, chs. 1–2.

35. Joyce, 20; Harry M. Dixon, "The Illinois Coal Mining Industry" (Ph.D. diss., University of Illinois, 1951), 78.

36. Joyce, 20.

37. Illinoius Bureau of Labor Statistics, *Second Biennial Report* (Springfield. 1882), 24.

38. Keith Dix, *Work Relations in the Coal Industry: The Hand-Loading Era, 1880–1930* (Morgantown: West Virginia University, 1977).

39. *History of Will County*, 466–468; Jasper Johnson, "The Wilmington, Illinois Coalfield," in *Transactions of the American Institute of Mining Engineers*, 3 (Easton, Pa.: 1874–7a5), 188–202; Henry D. Lloyd, *A Strike of Millionaires against Miners, or the Story of Spring Valley* (Chicago, Bedford-Clarke, 1890), 11–15.

40. *Workingmen's Adovcate*, April 14, 1873, 2.

41. Joyce, 112–128.

42. *Glasgow Sentinel*, June 4, 1873, 5.

43. Joyce, 60–69; *Workingmen's Advocate*, May 3, 1873, 2; May 17, 1873, 2.

44. *Wilmington Advocate*, May 24, 1873, 2; July 7, 1873, 2.

45. *Workingmen's Advocate*, Aug. 16, 1873, 2.

46. Herbert Gutman, "The Braidwood Lockout of 1874," *Journal of the Illinois State Historical Society* (Spring, 1960), 5–28.

47. Joyce, ch. 6.

48. *National Labor Tribune*, May 28, 1877, 5.

49. *Glasgow Sentinel*, April 4, 1874, 3.

50. *Glasgow Sentinel,* Jan. 28, 1876, 3.

51. Clifton K. Yearley, *Britons in American Labor, A History of the Influence of the United Kingdom Immigrants on American Labor, 1820-1914* (Baltimore: John's Hopkins University Press, 1957), 136-137; *National Labor Tribune,* May 18, 1878, 5; July 6, 1878, 4; Aug. 24, 1878, 6.

52. *National Labor Tribune,* Dec. 15, 1877, 6.

53. Joyce, 178-197; *National Labor Tribune,* June 4, 1878, 3; June 12, 1878, 5.

54. *National Labor Tribune,* July 13, 1878, 5.

55. *Workingmen's Advocate,* July 12, 1880, 2.

56. Robert V. Bruce, *1877, Year of Violence* (Chicago, Quadrangle Paperbacks, 1970), 317-318; I. Unger, *The Greenback Era, A Social and Political History of American Finance, 1865-1879* (Princeton, N.J.: Princeton University Press, 1964), ch. 11.

57. Eugene Staley, *History of the Illinois State Federation of Labor* (Chicago, University of Chicago Press, 1930), 81-89.

58. For the impact of the Haymarket affair on the Knights of Labor and the labor movement generally, see Henry David, *The Haymarket Affiar, A Chapter in the History of American Violence* (New York: Russell, 1958), ch. 8

59. Karl W. Fivek, "From Company Town to Miners Town, Spring Valley: 1885-1905" (Certificate of Advanced Study Thesis, Northern Illinois University, 1976), 68 84.

60. For evidence on this point, see Staley, 208-211.

61. On relations between the Miners Federation of Great Britain and the Labor Party, see Roy Gregory, *The Miners and British Politics, 1908-1914* (London, Oxford University Press, 1968). For a discussion of the 1894 and 1897 strikes, and the rise of socialist influences in Illinois District 12 of the United Mine Workers of America, see John H.M. Laslett, *Labor and the Left, A Study of Socialist and Radical Influences in the American Labor Movement, 1881-1924* (New York: Basic Books, 1970), ch. 6.

Chapter 10: German Brewery Workers of New York

1. John Laslett, "Marxian Socialism and the German Brewery Workers of the Midwest," *Labor and the Left* (New York), 1970, 9-53; Herman Schlueter, *The Brewery Industry and the Brewery Workers' Movement of America* (Cincinnati, 1910).

2. Karl Friedrich Wernet, *Wettbewerbs und Absatzverhältnisse des Handwerks in historischer Sicht*, vol. 2, (Berlin, 1967), 231–238, 247–263.

3. Emil Struve, *Die Entwicklung des deutschen Braugewerbes im 19. Jahrhundert*, (Leipzig, 1893), 13–14, 19–24, 31–32, 50–57, 70; Erich Borkenhagen, *100 Jahre deutscher Brauerbund* (Bonn, 1971), 13–14.

4. *Statistisches Jahrbuch für das deutsches Reich* (Berlin, 1881), 15, 44–45, 49, 133; Borkenhagen, 16, 34.

5. Struve, 264–265, 268; Martin Weigert, *Arbeitsnachweis, Einigungsamt und Tarifgemeinschaft im Berliner Braugewerbe* (Leipzig, 1907), 10, 13–14; Borkenhagen, 19–20.

6. Weigert, 15–16; Borkenhagen, 19, Wernet, 266–267.

7. Eduard Backert, *Geschichte der Brauerbeiterbewegung* (Berlin: 1916, 73–76, 80–96, 151–154, 435–436, 490; Borkenhagen, 19–23, 31, 40; Weigert, 8–9, 21–23, 27–32.

8. Biographical data about brewery owners in New York City are from information on New York City brewing businesses provided in *One Hundred Years of Brewing, A Supplement to the "Western Brewer"* (Chicago, 1903); Schlueter, 67–68; George Ehret, *Twenty-Five Years of Brewing, with an Illustrated History of American Beer* (New York, 1891), 100; *New Yorker Volkszeitung*, Jan. 4, Sept. 8, 9, 1879, Jan. 18, 19, Dec. 23, 1880, Jan. 10, March 16–21, 1881.

9. *New Yorker Volkszeitung*, Feb. 8, 1881; Alfred Kolb, *Als Arbeiter in Amerika* (Berlin, 1904), 4, 52; most of the demographic data on New York City brewery workers are taken from a statistical sample of the 1880 Federal Census "Gewerkschaft undGemeinschaft," for New York City, discussed in greater detail in Dorothee Schneider, Ph.D. diss., University of Munich, 1983, 227–230.

10. Tenth Census of the United States, Population Schedules for New York County, 19th Ward, New York 1880; *New Yorker Volkszeitung*, Jan. 8, Feb. 18, 1881; Schlueter, 93.

11. Kolb, 40, 51; Schlueter, 92–93; *New Yorker Volkszeitung*, Jan. 8, Feb. 18, June 3, 1881, Feb. 25, 1888.

12. Ehret, 83–95; U.S. Internal Revenue Service, *Annual Report of the Commissioner*, vols. 13–34, table A: *One Hundred Years of Brewing*, 111–115; Stanley Baron, *Brewed in America* (Boston: 1964), 241–242; *Brauer-Zeitung*, Nov. 12, 1886, June 23, 1892.

13. A few earlier associations of brewers and brewery workers are known (the earliest groups had workers as well as employers among their members), see Schlueter, 96–99, 107; *One Hundred Years*, 549–557; International Union of United Brewery, Flour, Cereal, Soft Drink and Distillery Workers of America, *Seventy-Five Years of a Great Union* (Cincinnati, n.d.), 13.

14. *New Yorker Volkszeitung*, Jan. 7–10, Feb. 8–10, 1881; *New Yorker Staats-Zeitung*, Jan. 1, 28, 1881; *American Brewer*, Feb. 1881, 97.

15. *New Yorker Volkszeitung*, Jan. 10, Feb. 6, 8, 18, 24, 25, March 5, 7, 14, April 11, 14, 25, 1881.

16. *New Yorker Volkszeitung*, March 7, 16–23, April 7, 9, 11, 18, 25, 27, 31, May 19, 24, Aug. 16, 1881.

17. *New Yorker Volkszeitung*, June 3–6, 8, 10–18, 22–25, 28, July 2, 1881; *American Brewer*, April, June, July 1881; *Western Brewer*, June 12, 1881.

18. Schlueter, 106–107.

19. Schlueter, 114–116; *New Yorker Volkszeitung*, Jan. 26, Feb. 20, 23, March 6, 1881.

20. *New Yorker Volkszeitung*, March 9, 11, 16, 19, 20, 23, 24, 30, April 13, 20, May 4, 9, 30, June 18, July 6, 13, 20, Aug. 17, 24, Sept. 29, 1885; Schlueter, 116.

21. Donald Bull and Manfred Friedrich, *The Register of United States Breweries* (Trumbull, Conn., 1976), vol. 1; Baron, 270–271; Thomas Cochran, *The Pabst Brewing Company* (New York, 1948), 102–128.

22. Baron, 257–258, 265; *One Hundred Years*, 448–457; Bull and Friedrich.

23. New York State Board of Arbitration and Mediation, *Third Annual Report* (Albany, 1889), 37.

24. Board of Arbitration, 37 38, 122; *New Yorker Volkszeitung*, Feb. 11, March 8, 15, 22, April 20, 1885, May 4, 18, July 13, Oct. 2, 9, 10, 1885.

25. Board of arbitration, 107; *New Yorker Volkszeitung*, March 15, 1886.

26. Schlueter, 117; *Western Brewer*, May 1886, 98; *Brauer Zeitung*, Oct. 2, 1886.

27. *Brauer-Zeitung*, Oct. 2, 1886.

28. *Brauer-Zeitung*, Aug. 13, 1888.

29. Board of Arbitration, 107, *Brauer-Zeitung*, Oct. 9, 22, 29, Nov. 25, Dec. 9, 1887.

30. Schlueter, 122–123, 126–127, 198–199; *New Yorker Volkszeitung*, Feb. 14, June 13, 20, 1887; *Brauer-Zeitung*, Jan. 1, Feb. 19, March 5, May 7, 30, June 6, July 16, Dec. 3, 1887; Board of Arbitration, 67, 174.

31. *Brauer-Zeitung*, Feb. 12, April 23, June 25, 1887; *New Yorker Volkszeitung*, June 27, 1887.

32. Schlueter, 121–131; *Brauer-Zeitung*, Nov. 13, Dec. 18, 1886, April 23, 1887.

33. Schlueter, 135–137, 168, 172, 180–188.

34. Schlueter, 121–124, 144–145, 179; Cochran, 283–289; *Western Brewer*, May 1886, 994.

35. Board of Mediation, 45.

36. Schlueter, 144–152; Cochran, 385; Board of Mediation, 44–46.

37. Board of Mediation, 47, 162–163; *Brauer-Zeitung*, April 2, 7, 1888; *New Yorker Volkszeitung*, April 7, 1888.

38. *New Yorker Volkszeitung*, April 14, 21, 1888; *Brauer-Zeitung*, April 14, 21, 1888; Board of Arbitration, 165.

39. *Brauer-Zeitung*, Aprill 21, 1888; *New Yorker Volkszeitung*, April 28, 1888.

40. Schlueter, 167; *New Yorker Volkszeitung*, May 5, 1888; *Brauer-Zeitung*, June 9, 1888.

41. *New Yorker Volkszeitung*, April 14, 21, 28, May 5, 26, June 16, July 7, 1888 *Brauer-Zeitung*, May 12, 19, 25, June 2, 9, 16, 30, 1888.

42. *Brauer-Zeitung*, April 21, June 2, 9, 16, 1888; *Western Brewer*, May 5, 1888, 1064; *New Yorker Volkszeitung*, May 26, June 2 and 9, July 14, 21, 28, 1888.

43. Schlueter, 166–204; Schneider, 294–303.

Chapter 11: Catholic Corporatism, French-Canadian Workers and Industrial Unionism

I wish to thank Bob Asher, Steve Fraser, Liz Lunbeck, Mike Merrill, David O'Brien, Bruno Ramirez, Ron Schatz, and Robert Zieger for their comments on a 1985 Organization of American Historians paper that formed the basis of this essay. A far more extended analysis of the issues raised here will soon appear as part of my book, *Working-Class Americanism: The Politics of Labor in a Textile City, 1914–1960*, (Cambridge, Cambridge University Press, forthcoming).

1. Jeremy Brecher, *Strike!* (San Francisco, 1972); James Green, "Working-Class Militancy in the Depression," *Radical America*, 6 (Nov.–Dec. 1972), 1–36; Staughton Lynd, "The Possibility of Radicalism in the Early 1930s: The Case of Steel," *Radical America*, 6 (Nov.–Dec. 1972), 37–64. A version of this interpretation also appears in Frances Fox Piven and Richard Cloward, *Poor People's Movements: Why They Succeed, How They Fail* (New York, 1977), 96–180.

2. Peter Friedlander, *The Emergence of a UAW Local, 1936–1939: A Study in Class and Culture* (Pittsburgh. 1976); Ronald Schatz, *The Electrical Workers: A History of Labor at General Electric and Westinghouse* (Urbana, Ill., 1983);

Joshua Freeman, "Catholics, Communists, and Republicans: Irish Workers and the Organization of the Transport Workers Union," in Michael Frisch and Daniel Walkowitz, eds., *Working-Class America: Essays on Labor, Community and American Society* (Urbana, Ill., 1983); Steven Fraser, "Dress Rehearsal for the New Deal: Shop-Floor Insurgents, Political Elites, and Industrial Democracy in the Amalgamated Clothing Workers," Frisch and Walkowitz, 212-255; Gary Gerstle, "The Mobilization of the Working-Class Community: The Independent Textile Union of Woonsocket, Rhode Island, 1931-1946," *Radical History Review,* 17 (Spring 1978), 161-172; Robert H. Zieger, *American Workers, American Unions, 1920-1985* (Baltimore. 1986), 26-61; and Steve Babson, "Pointing the Way: The Role of British and Irish Skilled Tradesmen in the Rise of the UAW," *Detroit in Perspective,* 7 (1983), 75-96, reprinted in this volume.

3. John Bodnar, "Immigration and Modernization: The Case of The Slavic Peasants in Industrial America," *Journal of Social History,* 10 (Fall 1976), 45-60; Bodnar, "Immigration, Kinship, and the Rise of Working-Class Realism in Industrial America," *Journal of Social History,* 14 (Fall 1980), 45-65; and Bodnar, *Workers' World: Kinship, Community and Protest in an Industrial Society, 1900-1940* (Baltimore. 1982), 165-191. See also his *Immigration and Industrialization: Ethnicity in an American Mill Town, 1870-1940* (Pittsburgh. 1977).

4. Thomas Bell, *Out of This Furnace: A Novel of Immigrant Labor* (Pittsburgh. 1976). Bodnar has significantly modified his views of ethnic workers in his recent work, and has accorded more importance to the play of ideas in shaping their consciousness; see his *The Transplanted. A History of Immigrants in Urban America* (Bloomington, Ind., 1985) Nevertheless, the "working-class-realism" interpretation he did so much to pioneer remains prominent in much 1930s labor historiography.

5. David O'Brien, *American Catholics and Social Reform: The New Deal Years* (New York. 1968); Mel Piehl, *Breaking Bread: The Catholic Worker and the Origin of Catholic Radicalism in America* (Philadelphia. 1982).

6. Schatz, 188-221; Schatz, "American Labor and the Catholic Church, 1919-1950," *International Labor and Working Class History* (Fall 1981), 46-54; Schatz, "Connecticut's Working Class in the 1950s: A Catholic Perspective" *Labor History,* 25 (Winter 1984), 83-101; Schatz, "Domesticating the Unions, Liberalizing the Church: The Catholic Labor Schools of Connecticut, 1942-1964" (OAH paper, 1985). See also Neil Betten, *Catholic Activism and the Industrial Worker* (Gainesville, Fla., 1976); Thomas Becnel, *Labor, Church, and the Sugar Establishment: Louisana, 1887-1976* (Baton Rouge, La., 1980); Douglas P. Seaton, *Catholics and Radicals: The Association of Catholic Trade Unionists and the American Labor Movement, from Depression to Cold War* (Lewisburg, Pa., 1981); Joshua Freeman, "The Catholic Response to the Congress of Industrial Organizations: The Case of the Transport Workers Union" (unpublished paper, 1985).

7. Marc Karson, *American Labor Unions and Politics, 1900-1918* (Carbondale, Ill., 1958), 212-284; Karson, "The Catholic Church and the Political

Development of American Trade Unionism (1900–1918), *Industrial and Labor Relations Review*, 4 (1951), 527–542. For critiques of Karson, see Henry J. Browne, "Comment on Karson's *Catholic Anti-Socialism*," in John H. Laslett and Seymour Martin Lipset, eds., *Failure of a Dream: Essays in the History of American Socialism*, rev. ed. (Berkeley. 1984), 103–112; and Schatz, "American Labor and the Catholic Church." Irving Howe has recently argued that it was the excessive moralism and self-righteousness that Protestants brought to the socialist movement which explains the weakness of American socialism! See his *Socialism and America* (New York. 1985), 3–48, 105–144.

8. O'Brien, 95.

9. Schatz, "American Labor and the Catholic Church," 51.

10. On ACTU, see Betten, and Seaton.

11. The summary history of the ITU is taken from my book *Working-Class Americanism*

12. Gerstle, *Working-Class Americanism*, chs. 2, 3.

13. Gerstle, *Working-Class Americanism*, ch. 1; Richard Sorrell, "The Sentinelle Affair (1924–1929) and Militant 'Survivance': The Franco-American Experience in Woonsocket, Rhode Island" (Ph.D. diss., State University of New York at Buffalo, 1975); Pierre Anctil, "Aspects of Class Ideology in a New England Ethnic Minority: The Franco-Americans of Woonsocket, Rhode Island (1865–1929)" (Ph.D. diss., New School of Social Research, 1980); Bessie Bloom Wessel, *An Ethnic Survey of Woonsocket, Rhode Island* (Chicago, 1931).

14. Joseph M. Corrigan, ed., *Two Basic Encyclicals: On the Condition of Workers, Leo XII, and Forty Years After, on Reconstructing the Social Order, Pius XI* (Washington, D.C., 1943), 1–82; Herbert Lahne, *The Cotton Mill Worker* (New York. 1944), 102–174.

15. John T. Cumbler, *Working-Class Community in Industrial America: Work, Leisure and Struggle in Two Industrial Cities* (Westport, Conn., 1979) and "Transatlantic Working-Class Institutions," *Journal of Historical Geography*, 6 (1980), 275–290; Donald B. Cole, *Immigrant City: Lawrence, Massachusetts, 1845–1921* (Chapel Hill, N.C., 1964); Melvyn Dubofsky, *We Shall Be All: A History of the Industrial Workers of the World* (New York. 1969), 146–170; David J. Goldberg, "Immigrants, Intellectuals and Industrial Unions: The 1919 Textile Strikes and the Experience of the Amalgamated Textile Workers of America in Passaic and Paterson, New Jersey and Lawrence, Massachusetts" (Ph.D. diss., Columbia University, 1983).

16. Gerstle, *Working-Class Americanism*, ch. 1.

17. Gerstle, *Working-Class Americanism*, Ch. 4.

18. Corrigan, 83–195; O'Brien, 3–28. On the secular theory and practice of corporatism, see Charles S. Maier, *Recasting Bourgeois Europe: Stabilization*

in France, Germany and Italy in the Decade after World War 1 (Princeton, N.J., 1975); Philippe C. Schmitter, "Still the Century of Corporatism?" in *Trends toward a Corporatist Intermediation,* Philippe C. Schmitter and Gerhard Lehmbruch, eds. (Beverly Hills, Cal., 1982); Wyn Grant, *The Political Economy of Corporatism* (New York, 1983); Alan Cawson, ed., *Organized Interests and the State* (Beverly Hills, Cal., 1985); Suzanne Berger, ed., *Organizing Interests in Western Europe: Pluralism, Corporatism, and the Transformation of Politics* (Cambridge, U.K., 1981).

19. O'Brien, 47-69, 120-49; John A. Ryan, *A Better Economic Order* (New York. 1935), 148-90, and *Social Doctrine in Action: A Personal History* (New York, 1941); Francis L. Broderick, *Right Reverend New Dealer John A. Ryan* (New York, 1963), 211-243.

20. For the range of clerical positions in political debates and of clerical involvement with social movements, see O'Brien, 150-211; Alan Brinkley, *Voices of Protest: Huey Long, Father Coughlin and the Great Depression* (New York. 1982), 124-142; Piehl, 57-144; Robert P. Ingalls, *Herbert Lehman and New York State's Little New Deal* (New York. 1975), 118-119. For clerical involvement in labor questions and labor movements, see Schatz, *The Electrical Workers,* 188-221; Schatz "American Labor and the Catholic Church, 1919-1950"; Seaton; Betten; Becnel.

21. *L'Indépendant,* Feb. 9, 1940.

22. *L'Indépendant,* Sept. 3, 1940.

23. On European papal politics, see Richard A. Webster, *The Cross and the Fasces: Christian Democracy and Fascism in Italy* (Stanford, Cal., 1960); A. D. Binchy, *Church and State in Italy* (London, 1941); Guenter Lewy, *The Catholic Church and Nazi Germany* (New York. 1964), Martin Blinkhorn, *Carlism and Crisis in Spain, 1931-1939* (New York. 1975).

24. Piehl, 122; O'Brien, 70 119. See also George Q. Flynn, *Roosevelt and Romanism: Catholics and American Diplomacy, 1937-1945* (Westport, Conn., 1976); Leo V. Kanawada, *Franklin D. Roosevelt's Diplomacy and American Catholics, Italians and Jews* (Ann Arbor, Mich., 1982); Donald F. Crosby, "Boston's Catholics and the Spanish Civil War: 1936-1939," *New England Quarterly,* 44 (March 1971), 82-100; J. David Valaik, "Catholics, Neutrality, and the Spanish Embargo, 1937-1939," *Journal of American History,* 54 (June 1967), 73-85.

25. *L'Indépendant,* Jan. 27, 1938, May 1-3, 1939, Feb. 8, 10, 1940.

26. Interviews with Lawrence Spitz, Oct. 22, 1976, and Angelo Turbesi, Oct. 9, 1980; letter from Lawrence Spitz to author, Dec. 21, 1976.

27. Spitz interview, Sept. 14, 1984.

28. Québec clergy drew their inspiration from developments in France.

On French origins, see Joseph Debès, *Naissance de l'Action Catholique Ouvrière* (Paris, 1982), 23-62.

29. No written records on this organization have been found. This account is based on interviews with Arthur Fortin and Phileas and Yvonne Valois, July 7, 1983, leading members of the Ligue, and with Charlotte LeBlanc, July 14, 1981, a 1940s member of La Jeunesse Estudiante Catholique in Woonsocket.

30. Phileas Valois interview.

31. Phileas Valois interview.

32. The intimate link perceived between Catholicism and democracy emerged repeatedly in interviews, not only with Ligue members but with French-Canadian ITU activists. Interviews with Leona Galipeau, Oct. 22-23, 1980, and Arthur Rock and Lionel Harnois, Oct. 8, 1976.

33. Interviews with Spitz, Sept. 20, 1979, Ernest Gignac, June 25, 1981, and LeBlanc.

34. The precise relationship between Ligue members and French-Canadian ITU members is difficult to establish. Arthur Fortin recalled that a number of ITU elected officials wanted to join but the Ligue refused to accept them. The Ligue did not want prominent union leaders as members; it wanted unobtrusive infiltrators who seemed to spring naturally from the rank and file. The Ligue's prohibition of official links with union officials, however, did not prevent Fortin from developing close friendships with leaders of the French-Canadian skilled worker caucus. These friendships, rather than formal ties, made possible a working relationship between the two groups.

35. *Providence Journal*, Sept. 17, 1939.

36. *Woonsocket Call*, Feb. 5, 1940.

37. Interviews with Fortin and Monsignor Edmund R. Brock, July 7, 1983. In those interviews, both individuals retracted the charge – made frequently by them and others in the 1930s and 1940s – that Lawrence Spitz, the General Secretary of the ITU from 1937 to 1943, was a communist. This controversy over Spitz's alleged communism is discussed at length in my *Working-Class Americanism*, ch. 5.

38. Gerstle, *Working-Class Americanism*, ch. 8.

39. *ITU News*, 1945-1946. A letter from Father Henry Crépeau to Most Reverend Francis P. Keough, April 22, 1946, Social Action Institute, File 19-194, Folder 1, Providence Diocesan Archives, supports the claim of Ligue leaders regarding the role of their organization in ousting ITU radicals from office. Crépeau wrote Keough: "with the use of every medium of publicity at our command and with the cooperation of the L.O.C. members in the different

ngth to defeat Mr. Spitz [the
our campaign of opposition as
ch openly into an issue which
ıl affair of the Union. I feel that
rking-Class Americanism, chs. 8,

iew, 3.

ıWSU.

at Ford (New

RAWSU.

976), 309.

980.

ın, 1940.

ertical File,

ın, Veılıcal

campaign

nism, ch. 10.

Oct. 22–23, 1980.

if "family" to the consciousness of
owd Hall, James Leloudis, Robert
es, and Christopher B. Daly, *Like a
Mill World* (Chapel Hill, N.C., 1987).

ish Militants in the UAW

Oral History Interview, 30, in Reuther
eafter RAWSU).

l Empire (New York, 1968), 174.

iense of an Impending Crash': English
ıt World War," *American Historical Review*,

ı and Reaction in Britain, 1919–1926: A
aper, 1980, 18.

l Since 1707 (New York, 1965), 256–258.

story Interview, RAWSU, 1–2.

:h Henry McCusker, Nov. 11, 1980.

ıst Shop Stewards' Movement (London, 1973), ch.

Nov. 6,

5, 29.

ıd the
3, part

War History of the British Working Class (London,
ı, *The Legend of Red Clydeside* (Edinburgh, 1983),

12. Hutt, 76–88.

13. Hutt, 86.

14. Hutt, ch. 6.

15. Matt Smith, Vertical File, RAWSU; McCracken interv

16. "W.E.", Oct. 30, 1942 in Matt Smith, Vertical File.

17. *Solidarity*, July 1968 in Joe McCusker, Vertical File, R

18. Philip Bonosky, *Brother Bill McKie: Building the Union* York, 1953), 18–23.

19. Undated publication about Dave Miller, Vertical File, I

20. George Dangerfield, *The Damnable Question* (Boston, 1

21. Dangerfield, 312–325, 344.

22. Author's interview with Shelton Tappes, November 4, 1

23. Hugh Thompson, Vertical File, RAWSU; *CIO Reporter*, J

24. *Dodge Main News*, August 11, 1956 in Pat Quinn, V RAWSU; *Detroit News*, May 3, 1969, April 18, 1965.

25. UAW Convention flyer, probably 1942 in Jack Thomps File, RAWSU.

26. *Michigan CIO News*, Sept. 30, 1954, Detroit City Council brochure in Michael Magee, Vertical File, RAWSU.

27. Harry Southwell, Oral History Interview, RAWSU, 2.

28. Bonosky, 12.

29. McCusker interview.

30. *Detroit Saturday Night*, April 10, 1937.

31. Author's interviews with Tappes and with Hodges Mason, 1980; *Detroit Saturday Night*, March 6, 1937.

32. *Detroit Saturday Night*, Oct. 9, 1937.

33. Henry Pelling, *America and the British Left* (London, 1956), 2

34. Pelling, 56.

35. James Young, "Changing Images of American Democracy a Scottish Labour Movement," *International Review of Social History*, 18, 197 1, 81.

36. Pelling, 62.

37. Young, 84–84.

38. Pelling, 100–105.

39. Chushichi Tsuzuki, "The 'Impossible Revolt' in Britain," *International Review of Social History*, 1, 1956, 381–383.

40. Hinton, 122.

41. Hodges interview.

42. *Detroit Saturday Night*, March 20, 1937.

43. McCusker interview.

44. Alfred Sloan, *My Years With General Motors* (New York, 1965), 167.

45. Stevenson interview, 6.

46. Southwell interview, 3–4.

47. Typed biography dated Aug. 20, 1942 in Bill Stevenson, vertical file, RAWSU.

48. Bonosky, 121.

49. McCracken interview, 22–23.

50. Sidney Fine, *The Automobile Under the Blue Eagle* (Ann Arbor, 1963).

51. Hinton, ch. 2.

52. Hinton, 65.

53. Bonosky, 15–45.

54. Cronin, 15.

55. Stevenson interview, 4.

56. Southwell interview, 3–4.

57. *Current Biography*, Oct. 1977, 16.

58. Undated UAW publication in Dave Miller vertical file.

59. Stevenson interview, 4.

60. Cronin, 10–11.

61. Marc Bloch, *Feudal Society* (Chicago, 1974), 292.

62. McCracken interview, 30; Martin Glaberman, *Wartime Strikes* (Detroit, 1980), 84.

Chapter 13: Women's Work and Labor Militancy

The author wishes to acknowledge the comments of Susan Levine, Gail O'Brien, and Elizabeth Higginbotham, Hal Beneson, Diane Koenker and members of the Chicago Area Labor History Group.

1. Howard E. Wilson, *Mary McDowell, Neighbor,* (Chicago, 1928), 86–90, 95–97; Alice Henry, *The Trade Union Woman,* (New York, 1905), 52–58; Barbara Wertheimer, *We Were There, The Story of Working Women in America* (New York, 1977), 225–226. On the strength of the Knights of Labor in the stockyards during the 1880s, see: David Brody, *The Butcher Workmen, a Study of Unionization* (Cambridge, Mass., 1964), 13–18; Jonathan Garlock and N.C. Bilder, *Directory of the Local Assemblies of the Knights of Labor* (Westport, Conn., 1981); Edna Clark, "A History of Labor Controversies in the Slaughtering and Meat Packing Industry in Chicago," M.A. thesis, University of Chicago, 1922, ch. 1. On the Knight's commitment to organizing women, see Susan Levine, *Labor's True Woman: Carpet Weaver, Industrialization, and Labor Reform in the Gilded Age* (Philadelphia, 1984), especially ch. 5. For varying interpretations of the Order's decline in the stockyards, see: Norman Ware, *The Labor Movement in the United States, 1860–1895* (New York, 1929), 152–154; Joseph R. Buchanan, *The Story of a Labor Agitator* (New York, 1903), 316–321; *The Path I Trod, the Autobiography of Terrence V. Powderly* (New York, 1940), 140–162.

2. On women trade union organizers in various industries, see: Alice Kessler-Harris, "Organizing the Unorganizable: Three Jewish Women and Their Union," *Labor History,* 17 (1976), 5–23; Maurine W. Greenwald, *Women, War, and Work: The Impact of World War One on Women Workers in the United States* (Westport, Conn., 1980), 203–205.

3. Greenwald, ch. 1, esp. 5–32; W. Jett Lauk and Edgar Sidenstricker, *Conditions of Labor in American Industries, A Summarization of the Results of Recent Investigations* (New York, 1917), 20–24; Leslie Woodcock-Tentler, *Wage-Earning Women, Industrial Work and Family Life in the United States, 1900–1930,* (New York, 1979), ch. 2.

4. Alice Kessler-Harris, "Where Are the Organized Women Workers?" *Feminist Studies,* 3 (1975), 92–110; and, *Out to Work, A History of Wage-Earning Women in the United States* (New York, 1982), 153–159; Carl Degler, *At Odds, Women and The Family in America from the Revolution to the Present* (New York, 1981), 397–400; Philip Foner, *Women and the American Labor Movement, from Colonial Times to the Eve of World War One* (New York, 1979), 250–252. The International Ladies Garment Workers' Union and the Amalgamated Clothing Workers of America are notable exceptions, but both organized in industries characterized by large numbers of women workers, as well as extensive gender division of labor. Quite apart from the socialist politics of the activists involved, it was simply impossible to exclude women from such unions because they represented the bulk of the labor force.

5. Woodcock-Tentler, *Wage Earning Women*, 1-9, 15-17, 27-28, and elsewhere. The quote is on page 75. See also Degler, 398-399, and Kessler-Harris, *Out to Work* 153, 159.

6. Degler, 400; Kessler-Harris, "Where Are the Organized Women Workers?," 92-93; *Out to Work*, 152.

7. Edith Abbott and Sophinisba Breckinridge, "Women in Industry: the Chicago Stockyards," *Journal of Political Economy*, 19 (1911), 651.

8. For a full analysis of the changing composition of the labor force and relevant citations, see James R. Barrett, "Work and Community in 'The Jungle': Chicago's Packing House Workers, 1894-1922," Ph.D. diss., University of Pittsburgh, 1981, ch. 2.

9. U.S. Commissioner of Labor, *Fourth Annual Report, Working Women in Large Cities* (Washington, D.C., 1889), 92-93, 132-133, 178-179, 264-265; Illinois Bureau of Labor Statistics, *Seventh Biennial Report* (Springfield, 1893), 82, 312, 338, 345, 349, 340-342.

10. Illinois Bureau of Labor Statistics, *Fourteenth Biennial Report*. (Springfield, 1908), 180, 196, 198, 209, 211.

11. John R. Commons, "Labor Conditions in Slaughtering and Meat Packing," in John R. Commons, ed., *Labor and Trade Union Problems*, 1st Series (Boston, 1905), 238; Abbott and Breckinridge, 635; Stockyards Community Clearing House, "Community Study, 1918," Folder 20, in Mary McDowell Papers, Chicago Historical Society; Alma Herbst, *The Negro in the Slaughtering and Meat Packing Industry in Chicago* (Boston, 1932; reprinted, New York, 1969), xxi; Geo. Haynes, *The Negro at Work During the World War and During Reconstruction* (Washington, D.C., 1921), 52-53.

12. U.S. Commission on Industrial Relations, *Final Report and Testimony*, vol. 4 (Washington, D.C., 1916), 3527, Stockyards Community Clearing House.

13. Alfred Chandler, *The Visible Hand: The Managerial Revolution in American Business*. (Cambridge, Mass., 1977), 299-301; Charles J. Bushnell, "Some Social Aspects of the Chicago Stockyards," Part 1, *American Journal of Sociology*, 3 (1901), 149; Henry Ford, *My Life and Work* (Garden City, New York, 1923), 81. See also U.S. Bureau of Corporations, *Report of the Commissioner of Corporations on the Beef Industry* (Washington, D.C., 1905).

14. For a discussion of this transformation of work, see James R. Barrett, "Immigrant Workers in Early Mass Production Industry: Work Rationalization and Job Control Conflicts in Chicago Packing Houses, 1900-1904," in Hartmut Keil and John Jentz, eds., *German Workers in Industrial Chicago, 1850-1910: A Comparative Perspective* (Dekalb, Ill., 1983).

15. See Note 12. Abbott and Breckinridge, 637-644; Illinois Bureau of Labor Statistics, *Fourteenth Biennial Report*, 290-300: Mary E. Pidgeon, *The*

Employment of Women in Slaughtering and Meat Packing, Bulletin No. 88, U.S. Women's Bureau, Dept. of Labor (Washington, D.C., 1932), 17–32.

16. Abbott and Breckinridge, 638–639, 643–644.

17. Pidgeon, 32.

18. Abbott and Breckinridge, 639–641, 648–649; *Eleventh U.S. Census, 1890, Manufactures.* (Washington, D.C., 1895), Part 2, 144–145.

19. Abbott and Breckinridge, 645–647; Herbst, 71–77, 99, Table X, 102.

20. Henry, 52–58; Commons, 238–240. On Maude Gonne (Mrs. Maude McBride), see: C. Desmond Greaves, *The Life and Times of James Connolly* (New York, 1961), 81, 88–89, 116; Maude Gonne, *Servant of the Queen* (London, 1938).

21. Amalgamated Meat Cutters and Butcher Workmen of North America, *Official Journal*, 2 (Nov. 1903).

22. Theresa Wolfson, *The Woman Worker and the Trade Unions* (New York, 1926), 96, Table I, 213: Barrett, "Work and Community in 'The Jungle'" 303–305, 408–411.

23. Commons, 243–245.

24. U.S. Commission on Industrial Relations, *Final Report*, 3467, 3504–3505, 3513; Rudolf Celmen, *The American Livestock and Meat Industry* (New York, 1923), 608–609, 707, 710–711; Herbst, 111. For a discussion of the casual labor system in numerous other industries during this era, see Lauck and Sydenstricker, ch. 4.

25. Kennedy, *Wages and Family Budgets*, 75–76, 80. See also U.S. Commission on Industrial Relations, *Final Report*, 3464–3467.

26. Kennedy, 169.

27. Kennedy, 70; U.S. Immigration Commission, *Immigrants in Industry: Slaughtering and Meat Packing*, Part 2 (Washington, D.C., 1911), xiii, 221, 222–225; Barrett, "Work and Community in 'The Jungle,'" 169–175; Tamara K. Hareven and John Modell, "The Malleable Household: Boarding and Lodging in American Families," *Journal of Marriage and the Family*, 35 (1973), 474–475.

28. Martha Fraundorf, "The Labor Force Participation of Turn-of-the-Century Married Women," *Journal of Economic History*, 39 (1979), 402–403; Barrett, "Work and Community in 'The Jungle,'" 173.

29. Joseph Perry, "Rents and Housing Conditions among the Lithuanians in Chicago," M.A. thesis, University of Chicago, 1925, 8–16; Alice Miller, "Rents and Housing Conditions in the Stockyards District of Chicago, 1923," M.A. thesis, University of Chicago, 1923, 20–21; Stockyards Community Clearing House; Pidgeon, 123.

30. Stockyards Community Clearing House. See also Pidgeon, 122–131.

31. Amalgamated Meat Cutters and Butcher Workmen of North America, *Proceedings of the Annual Convention*, 1904, 51–52; Foner, 320.

32. Commons, 239–240; *AMC & BW Official Journal*, 4 (Nov. 1903); Emily Barrows, "Trade Union Organization among Women in Chicago," Ph.D. dissertation, University of Chicago, 1927, 117; Foner, 299, 313; Olive Anderson, "Chicago League Organizing Stockyards Women Workers," *Life and Labor*, 7 (April 1918); and her "The Women's Part in the Stockyards Organization Work," *Life and Labor*, 7 (May 1918), 102–104.

33. Amalgamated Meat Cutters and Butcher Workmen of North America, *Proceedings of the Annual Convention*, 1902, 23. For sources on union exclusion, see Note 3. The Amalgamated union was far more hospitable to unskilled new immigrants in general. As in the case of women's organizing, self-interest forced a more tolerant attitude toward the immigrants. See Robert Asher, "Union Nativism and Immigrant Response," *Labor History*, 23 (Summer 1982), 325–348.

34. Carl Degler argues that the decision of whether to include women in trade unions often turned on the question of whether or not they as unorganized workers represented a serious threat to men's wages. Maurine Greenwald's case studies of telephone operators, railroad workers, and streetcar conductors during World War I in *Women, War, and Work*, seem to support this generalization. See also Degler, 395–396.

35. Wilson, 100; Henry, 56. For a discussion of the local union as a vehicle for acculturating immigrant workers, in an "Americanization from the bottom up," see Barrett, "Work and Community in 'The Jungle,'" ch. 4.

36. On the First World War organizational structure, see Anderson, "Chicago League Organizing," 84; her "Women's Part in the Stockyards," 102–104; Barrett, "Work and Community in 'The Jungle,'" 318–339; Barrows, 119.

37. On the problem of casual labor in Chicago, see Grace Abbott, "The Chicago Employment Agency and the Immigrant Worker," *American Journal of Sociology*, (1908), 289–305; Carlton Parker, *The Casual Laborer* (New York, 1920), ch. 2.

38. David Montgomery, *Workers' Control in America* (New York, 1979), 57–58; Steven Sapolsky, "Class-Conscious Belligerents: The Teamsters and the Class Struggle in Chicago, 1901–1905," seminar paper, Univ. of Pittsburgh, 1974, esp. 1–2. Dorothy Richarson, *The Long Day* (New York, 1974), 19–21; Theodore Glocker, *The Government of American Trade Unions* (Baltimore, 1912), 24; John B. Andrews and W.D.P. Bliss, *History of Women in Trade Unions, Report on Condition of Woman and Child Wage Earners*, vol. 10 (Washington, D.C., 1911; reprinted, New York, 1974), 148. The second quote is from Ray Stannard Baker, *The New Industrial Unrest* (Garden City, N.J., 1920), 112, quoted in William Tut-

tle, *Race Riot: Chicago in the Red Summer of 1919* (New York, 1970), 141. On the long-standing tradition of women's unions in Chicago and the organizers who built them, see Meredith Tax, *The Rising of the Women* (New York, 1980), 38–89.

39. Barrett, "Work and Community in 'The Jungle,'" chs. 4, 5.

40. See materials in National Archives, Record Group 280, series 864, including the 1918 agreement on grievance procedures; Montgomery, *Workers' Control in America*, 96, 100; Tax, 91–92; Tuttle; Barrett, "Work and Community in 'The Jungle,'" 318–369. Compare with Greenwald, 172–180.

41. Howard B. Meyer, "The Policing of Labor Disputes in Chicago: A Study," Ph.D. diss. University of Chicago, 1929, ch. 9; *Chicago Tribune*, August 14, 1904.

42. Barrett, "Work and Community in 'The Jungle,'" 296–318, 377–400.

43. Dominic Pacyga, "Crisis and Community: Back of the Yards, 1921," *Chicago History*, 6 (1977), 167–177; *Dziennik Chicagoski*, Dec. 8, 9, 1921; *Chicago Herald Examiner*, Dec. 8, 9, 1921; Benjamin Stolberg, "The Stockyards Strike," *The Nation*, 114 (Jan. 25, 1922), 90–92. For personal testimony of women workers involved in the CIO organizing of the late 1930s, see: Stella Nowicki, "Back of the Yards" in Alice and Staughton Lynd, eds., *Rank and File, Personal Histories by Working-Class Organizers* (Boston, 1973), 69–88; "Anna Novak" in Ann Banks, ed., *First Person America* (N.Y., 1980), 62–65.

44. Woodcock-Tentler; John Bodnar, "Immigration, Kinship, and the Rise of Working-Class Realism in Industrial America," *Journal of Social History*, 14 (1980), 44–65, quote: 56.

Chapter 14: Anthony Capraro and the Lawrence Strike

Reprinted from *Pane E Lavoro*, George E. Pozzetta, ed., The Multicultural History Society of Ontario, 1980.

1. The 1912 strike is extensively treated in: Melvyn Dubofsky, *We Shall Be All. A History of the Industrial Workers of the World* (New York, 1969); Philip S. Foner, *History of the Labor Movement in the United States*, vol. 4 (New York, 1965); Donald B. Cole, *Immigrant City: Lawrence, Massachusetts, 1845–1921* (Chapel Hill, N.C., 1963). Although Cole's terminal date is 1921, he devotes less than two pages to the 1919 strike. His failure to analyze this conflict in depth and his overreliance on the English-language press lead Cole into factual errors and absurd conclusions.

The most detailed account of the 1919 strike is to be found in the contemporary study, J. M. Budish and George Soule, *The New Unionism in the Clothing Industry* (New York, 1920), 254–269. Brief mention is to be found in: Robert W. Dunn and Jack Hardy, *Labor and Textiles* (New York, 1931), 218–220; William M. Leiserson, *Adjusting Immigrant and Industry* (New York, 1924), 204–205. Otherwise the labor studies literature is silent on this strike.

2. A. J. Muste, "The Story," *The Truth about Lawrence, Forward Supplement,* (Boston), 3 (Feb. 1919), 2–3; Anthony Capraro, "Lawrence Textile Strikers," *New York Call,* March 14, 1919. An illuminating series of articles on the immigrant population of Lawrence by Norbert Weiner appeared in the *Boston Herald,* Feb. 23, 28, March 1, 1919. Clippings in Box 9, "Lawrence Strike," Anthony Capraro Papers, Immigration History Research Center, University of Minnesota (hereafter IHRC).

3. *Boston Herald,* Feb. 23, 1919.

4. "Interviews with Textile Workers," in Box 9, "Lawrence Strike," Capraro Papers. See for example, "Statement concerning Wood Mill of The American Woolen Company given by Rose and Grace Santora," and "Interview with Annie Trina."

5. "Interviews with Textile Workers"; *Boston Herald,* Feb. 23, 1919; Budish and Soule, 254–257; Harvell L. Rotzell, "The Issues," *The Truth about Lawrence, Forward Supplement;* James F. Hughes to Hugh L. Kerwin, Jan. 15, 1919, "Textile Workers. Lawrence, Mass.," Federal Mediation and Conciliation Service FMCS, Case 33/2694 – Record Group 280, National Archives (hereafter RG,NA). Hughes, Secretary of the Building Trades Council of Lawrence, wrote to Kerwin, Director of Conciliation, U.S. Department of Labor, that 70% of the textile workers were working 3 days a week while 30% were idle.

6. Budish and Soule, 257–59; Harvell L. Rotzell, "The Lawrence Textile Strike," *The American Labor Year Book 1919–1920* (New York, 1920), 172–173; Muste, 2; *New York Times,* Jan. 26, Feb. 1, 4, 1919; *New York Call,* Feb. 2, 1919; *Boston Herald,* Feb. 28, 1919.

7. Rotzell, "Lawrence Textile Strike"; clipping, April 29, 1919, in Box 9, "Lawrence Strike," Capraro Papers.

8. *Boston Herald,* Feb. 23, 1919; "Interviews with Textile Workers."

9. Demarest Lloyd to William B. Wilson, May 31, 1919, "Textile Workers, Lawrence Mass.," FMCS, Case 33/2694, in RG 280, NA. Writing as Secretary of the Harvard Liberal Club of Boston, Lloyd challenged Wilson to reconcile the economic settlement of the strike with his allegation that it was revolutionary in character. This file of the Federal Mediation and Conciliation Service fully documents the interpretation of the strike as Bolshevik in inspiration. This point of view is summarized by William H. Crawford, "Three Months of Labor Turmoil in Lawrence, Mass.," *New York Times,* May 25, 1919, Sec. 4.

10. Winthrop L. Marvin to William B. Wilson, April 12, 1919. James R. Menzie and others, Lawrence Central Labor Union, to Frank Morrison, Secretary, AFL., Feb. 10, 1919; John Golden to William B. Wilson, July 9, 1919; "Textile Workers. Lawrence, Mass.," FMCS, Case 33/2694, RG 280, NA. Budish and Soule, 259. The standard work on the anti-radical nativism of this period, Robert K. Murray, *Red Scare: A Study in National Hysteria, 1919-1920,* (Minneapolis, 1955), totally ignores the Lawrence strike.

11. General Strike Committee, Lawrence, Mass., to William B. Wilson, April 24, 1919; The Roman Catholic Strikers of Lawrence to Cardinal William O'Connell, May 2, 1919; Letter to the Editor, James T. O'Reilly, March 1, 1919 (clipping), all in Box 9, "Lawrence Strike," Capraro Papers.

12. The Citizens Committee of Lawrence, *Circular No. 1*, Oversize 2; Capraro Papers, clippings, Box 9, "Lawrence Strike" Capraro Papers; *New York Call*, March 27, May 16, 1919.

13. Crawford; *New York Call*, March 27, April 8, 15, May 7, 8, 1919; "Truth about the Lawrence Police," (Boston), 3 (April 1919). The latter includes affidavits and photographs documenting police brutality.

14. H. J. Skeffington to H. L. Kerwin, February 14, 1919, "Textile Workers. Lawrence, Mass.," FMCS, Case 33/2694, RG 280, NA.

15. Skeffington; *Boston Herald*, February 28, 1919; *New York Call*, March 14, 1919.

16. *New York Call*, May 14, 1919.

17. *New York Call*, March 14, 15, 1919; General Strike Committee, *Victory Bulletin*, nos. 5-8, Capraro Papers; Budish and Soule, 260-261.

18. General Strike Committee, *Victory Bulletin* No. 8, May 7, 1919.

19. "Autobiography in Miniature of Cedric Long," and "Biographical Sketch of A. J. Muste," in Box 9, "Lawrence Strike" Capraro Papers; *New York Call*, May 23, 1919; Interviews with Anthony Capraro, April 19, Aug. 11-12, 1975; *New York Times*, Feb. 17, 1919. See also: A. J. Muste's brief memoir in Rita J. Simon, ed., *As We Saw the Thirties* (Urbana, Ill., 1967), 123-150; *The Reminiscences of A. J. Muste* (The Oral History Office, Columbia University, 1965).

20. *Forward* (Boston), 3 (Feb., April 1919).

21. Crawford; *New York Call*, March 24, May 8, 27, 1919; *Truth about Lawrence; The Leader* (Lawrence), March 30, 1919; clipping, April 6, 1919, in Capraro Papers.

22. "Biographical Sketch of A. J. Muste"; Budish and Soule, 260; Crawford, *Truth about Lawrence*, 8; *Reminiscences*, 407.

23. Capraro to A. J. Muste, October 18, 1919, in Box 2, "Lawrence Strike," Capraro Papers; Vittorio Buttis, *Memorie di Vita di Tempeste Sociali* (Chicago, 1940), 105.

24. *New York Call*, Feb. 24, 1919.

25. Capraro interviews; Buttis, 108.

26. Capraro interviews. Because Giuseppe and Diego Capraro came to the attention of the Italian police for their anarchist activities, dossiers were

compiled on them: Ministero dell'Interno, Direzione Centrale di Pubblica Sicurezza, Casellario Politico Centrale, Archivio Centrale dello Stato (Rome). The Consul General of Italy in New York reported in 1911 that the Capraro brothers were very active propagandists, especially of the theories of Francisco Ferrer. Il. R. Console Generale al On. Ministero dell'Interno, Direzione Gen. P.S., New York, Nov. 18, 1911.

27. Capraro interviews; Board of Parole for State Prisons, State of New York, Anthony Capraro's Parole, Aug. 10, 1911, in Box 5, Prison Record and Pardon, Capraro Papers. The Capraro Papers also contain an extensive file of correspondence between Capraro and Cerafisi.

28. Capraro interviews. A copy of *State and Revolution* was given to Capraro by "Arthur Adams," the representative of the Soviet Government in New York City. One of Mr. Adams' cards is in the Capraro Papers.

29. Anthony Capraro, "Communism versus Victor Berger's Socialism" (typescript), in Box 9, "Capraro's Writings," Capraro Papers. This essay appears to have been written in 1921. Capraro was editor of *Alba Nuova* (New Dawn), the organ of the Federation of Italian Workers of America of the Workers (Communist) Party of America, Vol. I, nos. 2, 3 (Oct., Nov. 1921) and vol. II, nos. 1, 2 (Feb. 15, April 15, 1922) are in the IHRC.

30. Capraro to Joseph Schlossberg, March 19, 1919; Mrs. John Bateman and others to Capraro, May 8, 1919, in Capraro Papers. The activities of the Young People's International League can be followed in the letters from Bert Emsley to Capraro, Oct. 20, 1919–July 28, 1920, in Box 9, "Lawrence Strike," Capraro Papers; Capraro interviews.

31. Among the articles appearing under his byline were "Lawrence Strikers Shed Their Blood; Murdered and Maimed in Labor's Cause," March 27, 1919, and "Police Clubs Used in Vain to Break Textile Strikers' Solidarity in Lawrence," April 15, 1919.

32. Capraro to Schlossberg.

33. *New York Call*, March 20, 22, 1919.

34. *New York Call*, March 17, May 22, 1919; Rotzell, "Lawrence Textile Strike."

35. *Reminiscences*, 379–380. According to Muste, Capraro was a "very eloquent, persuasive talker in Italian." Buttis, 104–108; *New York Call*, March 14, May 19, 27, 1919; Capraro interviews; Capraro to "My Dear Maria" (Bambace), Aug. 4, 1919, in Box 3, "Nino's Letters to Maria," Capraro Papers.

36. Skeffington to Kerwin, Feb. 14, 1919, "Textile Workers. Lawrence, Mass." FMCS, Case 33/2694, RG 180, NA; *New York Call*, March 29, April 9, 1919; *Lawrence Telegram*, April 25, 1919, clipping, in Box 9, "Lawrence Strike," Capraro Papers; Budish and Soule, 261.

37. Letter of Tripoli Club di Mutuo Soccorso, n.d.; Società di Mutuo Soccorso della Basilicata to Comitato Generale dello Sciopero di Lawrence, Mass., March 2, 1919; Società Mutuo Soccorso (Duke of Abruzzi) to Comitato generale sciopero, March 3, 1919; Carlo Vespasiano to Comitato dirigente lo Sciopero, March 7, 1919. Vespasiano, the proprietor of a pharmacy, refutes the charge that he is an enemy of the working class and signs himself "L'amico del popolo."

38. Capraro interviews. According to the *Leader*, "in the foreign quarters, the milkmen, grocers and provision dealers, whose customers were almost wholly among the foreign peoples . . . trusted out many thousands of dollars. Some of this they may eventually get back, but what will happen to the grocers and milkmen who confidingly accepted orders from the strike committee for supplies to the amount . . . of 16,000 to 18,000 dollars?" April 6, 1919.

39. *New York Call*, March 27, April 9, May 16, 1919. Rocco and Calitri expressed their views in a letter to the editor, *Lawrence Sun American*, March 13, 1919. Calitri also published and distributed a handbill objecting to the gossip that he was an enemy of the workers; to the contrary, he declared, he was not opposed to the strike, but wished victory to the workers in the struggle. *A tutti gli Italiani di Lawrence*, in Oversize 2, Capraro Papers.

40. Cole, 187–188; M. Milanese, *Agli Italiani di Lawrence, Quaresima 1919; New York Call*, April 15, May 20, 1919.

41. Capraro to "My Dear Maria" (Bambace), Aug. 1–2, 1919, in Box 3, "Nino's Letters to Maria," Capraro Papers.

42. Arturo Giovannitti and Carlo Tresca to "Compagni Scioperanti di Lawrence, Mass.," n.d., (on Il *Martello* letterhead).

43. Capraro interviews; Buttis, 105–106.

44. Capraro's retrospective account conforms closely to contemporary reports.

45. Clipping, May 3, 1919, in Box 9, "Lawrence Strike," Capraro Papers.

46. *Lawrence Leader*, April 27, 1919; *New York Call*, May 7, 11, 1919; Crawford.

47. *New York Call*, May 23, 1919; Capraro interviews.

48. *Mew York Call*, May 19, 23, 1919.

49. *Il Lavoro* (New York), May 10, 1919; *New York Call*, May 14, 1919; Bramhall to Capraro, May 19, 1919, in Box 9, "Lawrence Strike," Capraro Papers; Budish and Soule, 261–262; *Reminiscences*, 399.

50. Mrs. John Bateman and others to Capraro, May 8, 1919, in Box 2, "Lawrence Strike – Rotzell," Capraro Papers.

51. *New York Call*, May 12, 1919.

52. Rotzell, "Lawrence Textile Strike"; *New York Call*, May 19, 22, 23, 1919; *Boston American*, May 19, 1919; *New Textile Worker* (New York), May 14, 1919; Rotzell to Capraro, May 20, 1919, in Box 2, "Lawrence Strike – Rotzell," Capraro Papers.

53. *New York Call*, May 27, 1919.

54. Capraro to Schlossberg; *New York Call*, March 14, 1919.

55. "Meeting of Executive Committee of General Strike Committee of Lawrence, March 10, 1919, " in Box 9, "Lawrence Strike," Capraro Papers. This draft appears to be in Capraro's hand; it bears the notation, "Telegraph of this resolution to Bellanca, March 10, 1919."

56. *New York Call*, April 9, 12, 14, 15, 1919; "Minutes of the First Convention of the Amalgamated Textile Workers of America," in Box 9, "Lawrence Strike," Capraro Papers.

57. Capraro to Muste, March 1, 1920, in Box 2, "Lawrence Strike," Capraro Papers; Capraro to Schlossberg, July 31, 1919, in Box 9, "Lawrence Strike," Capraro Papers.

58. Budish and Soule, 269; *New Textile Worker*, May 22, 1920; Bert Emsley to Capraro, June 8, 1920; Capraro to Emsley, June 22, 1920, in Box 9, "Lawrence Strike" Capraro Papers; Capraro interviews.

59. Capraro to Muste, March 1, 1920, in Box 2, "Lawrence Strike," Capraro Papers. One of the "insinuations" that offended Capraro was that he favored affiliation with the ACWA in order to secure an increase in organizers' wages. A sympathetic correspondent wrote to Capraro: "You have made great sacrifices for Lawrence, and almost lost your life here, and the Lawrence workers listen in apathy while you are calumniated." Bert Emsley to Capraro, February 27, 1920, in Box 9, "Lawrence Strike," Capraro Papers.

60. Capraro to Muste, March 1, 1920, in Box 2, "Lawrence Strike," Capraro Papers; Capraro interviews.

61. Bert Emsley to Capraro, June 8, 1920, in Box 9, "Lawrence Strike," Capraro Papers. This might have been Benjamin J. Legere, an IWW organizer, who was active in the Little Falls, N.Y., textile strike of 1912. Foner, 4: 351.

62. Capraro to Emsley, June 22, July 9, 1920, in Box 9, "Lawrence Strike," Capraro Papers.

63. Budish and Soule, 263; Dunn and Hardy, 204; Robert W. Dunn, "Unionism in the Textile Industry," *The American Labor Year Book 1921–1922*, 4 (New York, n.d.): 155–162; Leiserson, 204–205.

64. Dunn and Hardy, 220–221; *The American Labor Year Book 1923–1924*, 5 (New York, 1924): 104–106.

65. Leiserson, 206.

66. Dunn and Hardy, 203–204.

67. Bert Emsley to Capraro, October 20, 1919, in Box 9 "Lawrence Strike," Capraro Papers.

68. Expressions of radicalism are common in "Interviews with Textile Workers." Muste attributed "a good deal of working class solidarity" and "revolutionary fervor" to the strikers, *Reminiscences*, 398, 410.

69. Cole, 202; Gerald Rosenblum, *Immigrant Workers: Their Impact on American Labor Radicalism* (New York, 1973).

70. *New York Call*, May 23, 1919.

Chapter 15: Transformation of Working-Class Ethnicity

A version of this article was presented at the annual meeting of the Social Science History Association in Nashville, Tennessee, Oct. 23, 1981. The author would like to thank Alan Dawley, Herbert Gutman, Daniel Leab, John DeBrizzi, William Reddy, Chris Johnson, Bob Zieger, and Tom Klug for their helpful discussion and comments at various stages. He would also like to thank Di Miles of the Reuther Library, Wayne State University, Sigmund Woytowicz, formerly of the Bayonne Public Library, as well as Ron Grele and the New Jersey Historical Commission, which awarded a grant-in-aid that made the research for this article possible.

1. See David Brody, *Workers in Industrial America: Essays on the Twentieth Century Struggle* (New York, 1980), 37ff.; James R. Green, *The World of the Worker: Labor in Twentieth-Century America* (New York, 1980), 67ff.; David Montgomery, *Workers' Control in America: Studies in the History of Work, Technology, and Labor Struggles* (New York, 1979), 91ff.

2. See for example, Irving Bernstein, *The Lean Years: A History of the American Worker, 1920–1933* (Boston, 1960); William Preston, Jr., *Aliens and Dissenters: Federal Suppression of Radicals, 1903–1933* (Cambridge, Mass., 1963); Stephen Meyer III, *The Five Dollar Day: Labor Management and Social Control in the Ford Motor Company, 1908–1921* (Albany, 1981); Alan Dawley, "The State Made Visible: Policing Work and Loyalty in the United States, 1917–1922" (paper presented at the Third Annual North American Labor History Conference, Wayne State University, Detroit, Oct. 8, 1981).

3. More properly speaking, it was the petit bourgeoisie, a lower middle class. See Arno J. Mayer, "The Lower Middle Class as Historical Problem," *Journal of Modern History*, 47 (1975), 409–436; John J. Bukowczyk, "Polish Factionalism and the Formation of the Immigrant Middle Class in Brooklyn, 1880–1930," in *Immigrant Communities in America*, John Bodnar, ed. (Urbana, Ill., forthcoming).

4. Reportedly they came to exceed 20% of the work force in the oil-refining industry. This figure, however, is only approximate, as it includes only those employees for whom the Immigration Commission secured information. It is likely that, compared to the Irish, Poles were disproportionately under-counted and that they accordingly accounted for a far larger percentage of the total refinery labor force than Commission figures indicate. See U.S. Senate, *Immigrants in Industries: Reports of the Immigration Commission*, vol. 16, 61st Cong., 2nd sess., no. 633 (Washington, DC, 1911), 751, 760–762 (hereafter cited as *Immigration Commission*); *Our Lady of Mount Carmel Church, Bayonne, New Jersey, U.S.A., Seventy-five Years, 1898–1973* (n.p., n.d.), 30–32.

5. Of the Polish men in the oil-refining households reported on by the Immigration Commission in 1910, fully 80% had been farm laborers and another 8% had been independent farmers before coming to the United States. See *Immigration Commission*, 777–778.

6. *Immigration Commission*, 789, 800–802.

7. John Reed, "Industrial Frightfulness in Bayonne," *Metropolitan Magazine* (Jan., 1917), n.p., clipping in Clipping File, Bayonne Public Library (hereafter cited as CFBPL).

8. In 1909 Bayonne's Polish population numbered about fifty-five hundred; 40% of the Poles came from Russian Poland, 50% from Austrian Poland (Galicia), and only 10% form German Poland. See *Immigration Commission*, 758.

9. Of the Polish families selected for study in the Immigration Commission's general examination of employees in the oil refining industry, 42.3% took in boarders or lodgers. *Immigration Commission*, 795.

10. *Our Lady of Mount Carmel Church*, 30–38, 52. Shortly after its founding, a schism in the parish resulted in the short-lived St. Mary Carmelite Roman Catholic Polish Church. On the clergy and immigrant community leadership, also see John J. Bukowczyk. "Factionalism and the Composition of the Polish Immigrant Clergy," in S. Blejwas and M. Biskupski, eds., *Pastor of the Poles: Polish American Essays*, Polish Studies Program Monograph No. 1 (New Britain, Conn., 1982), 37–47.

11. See Victor Greene, *For God and Country: The Rise of Polish and Lithuanian Ethnic Consciousness in America, 1860–1910* (Madison, 1975), 39. Cf. Frank Renkiewicz, ed., *The Poles in America, 1608–1972* (Dobbs Ferry, N.Y., 1973), 62.

12. See Bukowczyk, "Polish Factionalism," ms. pp. 10ff.

13. *Bayonne Evening Times*, Nov. 20, 1959, Oct. 17, 1961, CFBPL; *Our Lady of Mount Carmel Church*, 29, 33, 34.

14. Victor Greene, "Poles," *Harvard Encyclopedia of American Ethnic Groups*, S. Thernstrom ed. (Cambridge, Mass., 1980), 793.

15. In middle-class areas, Richard Hoggart has observed, the shopkeeper "assumes, in manner at least, a lower status than his customers," but in working-class districts, "the shopkeeper is among his own class, though his income may sometimes be above the average of the neighborhood." See Richard Hoggart, *The Uses of Literacy: Aspects of Working-Class Life, with Special Reference to Publications and Entertainments* (London, 1957), 54.

16. Cf. John J. Bukowczyk, "Steeples and Smokestacks: Class, Religion, and Ideology in the Polish Immigrant Settlements in Greenpoint and Williamsburg, Brooklyn, 1880–1929" (PhD diss., Harvard University, 1980), 168–171.

17. See *The World* (New York), June 27, 1926, CFBPL.

18. Cf. Bukowczyk, "Steeples and Smokestacks," p. 169. On the general fragility of small businesses, see the essays in Stuart W. Bruckey, ed., *Small Business in American Life* (New York, 1980).

19. See Frank Renkiewicz, "An Economy of Self-Help: Fraternal Capitalism and the Evolution of Polish America," C. Ward, et al., eds., *Studies in Ethnicity: The East European Experience in America*, East European Monographs, no. 73 (Boulder, Colo., 1980), 71–91.

20. In that year, the New Jersey Superior Court awarded contested property to the Mount Carmel loyalist faction. See *Our Lady of Mount Carmel Church*, 31–32, 34. A similar conflict pitting saloonkeeper against pastor is discussed in John J. Bukowczyk, "The Immigrant 'Community' Reexamined: Political and Economic Tensions in a Brooklyn Polish Settlement, 1888–1894," *Polish American Studies*, 37 (1980), 5–16.

21. See Bukowczyk, "Steeples and Smokestacks," chs. 6 and 7.

22. *Immigration Commission*, 800, 802, 805–806.

23. *Immigration Commission*, 757, 800, 802, 804.

24. In recent years, the literature on working-class Polish immigrants in the 1880–1920 period has grown appreciably. See, for example, Victor R. Greene, *The Slavic Community on Strike: Immigrant Labor in Pennsylvania Anthracite* (Notre Dame, Ind., 1968); Greene, "The Polish American Worker to 1930: The 'Hunky' Image in Transition," *The Polish Review*, 21 (1976), 63–78; Edward Pinkowski, "The Great Influx of Polish Immigrants and the Industries They Entered," in Frank Mocha, ed., *Poles in America: Bicentennial Essays*, (Stevens Point, Wisc., 1978), 303–370; Dominic A. Pacyga, "Crisis and Community: The Back of the Yards, 1921," *Chicago History*, 6 (1977), 167–176; Pacyga, "Villages of Steel Mills and Packinghouses: The Polish Worker on Chicago's South Side, 1880–1921," paper presented at Conference on Poles in North America sponsored by the Multicultural History Society of Ontario and the University of Toronto, Canada (Oct. 23–25, 1980); Frank Renkiewicz, "Polish American Workers, 1880–1889," in S. Blejwas and M. Biskupski, eds.,

Pastor of the Poles: Polish American Essays, 116–136; John Bodnar, Michael Weber, and Roger Simon, "Migration, Kinship, and Urban Adjustment: Blacks and Poles in Pittsburgh, 1900–1930," *Journal of American History*, 66 (1979), 548–565; Bodnar, Weber, and Simon, *Lives of Their Own: Blacks, Italians, and Poles in Pittsburgh, 1900–1960* (Urbana, Ill., 1982); John J. Bukowczyk, "Polish Rural Culture and Immigrant Working Class Formation," *Polish American Studies*, 41 (Autumn 1984).

25. See Renkiewicz, "Polish American Workers"; John Bodnar, "Immigration and Modernization: The Case of Slavic Peasants in Industrial America," *Journal of Social History*, 10 (1976), 44–67; Bodnar, "Immigration, Kinship, and the Rise of Working-Class Realism in Industrial America," *Journal of Social History*, 14 (1980), 45–65; John J. Bukowczyk, "Polish Rural Culture."

26. See Renkiewicz, "Polish American Workers"; Bukowczyk, "Polish Rural Culture"; Lawrence D. Orton, *Polish Detroit and the Kolasinski Affair* (Detroit, 1981), 174–180; Herbert G. Gutman, "Work, Culture, and Society in Industrializing America, 1815–1919," *American Historical Review*, 78 (1973), 531–588.

27. Cf. Michael J. Piore, *Birds of Passage: Migrant Labor and Industrial Societies* (New York, 1979), 112–113, 154–157.

28. A less nationalistic Polish socialist body, the Polish Section of the Socialist Party of America, also was active during these years. See Stefan Kieniewicz, *The Emancipation of the Polish Peasantry* (Chicago, 1969), 214–220, 226–235; Bukowczyk, "Polish Rural Culture"; Renkiewicz, "Polish American Workers," 123; Victor Greene, "Poles," 795; Greene, "The Polish American Worker," 78.

29. George Sweet Gibb and Evelyn H. Knowlton, *The Resurgent Years, 1911–1927: History of Standard Oil Company (New Jersey)* (New York, 1956), vol. 2, 135, 139–141.

30. Renkiewicz, "Polish American Workers," 117.

31. *Our Lady of Mount Carmel Church*, 49.

32. *Immigration Commission*, 759.

33. Strikers reportedly demanded "a fifty-hour week, time and a half for overtime, a 15 per cent increase in wages, and no discrimination because of strike activity." See Stuart Chase, *A Generation of Industrial Peace: Thirty Years of Labor Relations at Standard Oil Company (N.J.)* (1947), 9–10; Gibb and Knowlton, 142. For recent accounts of the strike, also see George Dorsey, "The Bayonne Refinery Strikes of 1915–1916," *Polish American Studies*, 33 (1976), 21ff; Philip S. Foner, *On the Eve of America's Entrance into World War 1, 1915–1916: History of the Labor Movement in the United States* (New York, 1982), vol. 6, 41–64.

34. Dorsey, 22–24. Tannenbaum, a 22-year old busboy and member of the Waiters' International Union, had recently led an IWW drive to organize the unemployed during the winter of 1914. See Philip S. Foner, *The Industrial Workers of the World, 1905–1917; History of the Labor Movement in the United States* (New York, 1965), vol. 4, 444.

35. Contrast this with the 1939 Chrysler strike in Detroit, when the Hamtramck police responded to pressure from the city's heavily Polish-American working-class electorate and sided with the strikers. See *Union Town* (Detroit, n.d.), 21.

36. Dorsey, 23–27; Edward Levinson, *I Break Strikes!*, reprint edition (New York: Arno Press, 1969), 158, 161–164, 166–168; Chase, 9; Gibb and Knowlton, 141–142, 144–146. According to historian Philip Foner: "After his release from prison, Tannenbaum played little role in the IWW. The last mention of him as a participant in an IWW activity is in *The New York Times* of Sept. 2, 1915. He is listed along with Helen Gurley Flynn and Alexander Berkman as having been prevented from addressing a meeting of 1500 employees of the Standard Oil and Tidewater companies. Following this experience, Tannenbaum was helped to complete his education by several philanthropic-minded people. He abandoned the labor movement and later became a professor at Columbia University, specializing in labor relations, Latin America and anti-radicalism." See Foner, *Industrial Workers of the World*, 448.

37. *The Survey*, 34 (Aug. 7, 1915), 415. Along the same vein, Kinkead had his deputies remove their hats when they passed Bayonne's Greek Catholic Church, the place of worship of many strikers. See *Literary Digest*, 51 (Aug. 7, 1919), 257.

38. Gibb and Knowlton, 141–142, 144–146.

39. Levinson, 162.

40. Reed.

41. Levinson, 169.

42. John A. Fitch, "The Explosion at Bayonne," *Survey*, 36 (Oct. 21, 1916), 62; Dorsey, 28.

43. Gibb and Knowlton, *Resurgent Years*, Vol. II, 151–152; Dorsey, "Bayonne Refinery Strikes," 28–30; Levinson 169–170.

44. Reed.

45. Gibb and Knowlton, 146.

46. Dorsey, 22.

47. Dorsey, 22, 24, 25, 27, 30; *Bayonne Evening Times*, Oct. 17, 1916, and *Bayonne Evening Review*, Oct. 14, 1916, CFBPL; *Our Lady of Mount Carmel Church*, 50.

48. *Immigration Commission,* 759, 762.

49. *Bayonne Evening Review,* Oct. 10, 1916, CFBPL.

50. Levinson, 35, 165. Bergoff was born of a Dutch Protestant mother and a German Jewish father.

51. A proverb said to have circulated among Bayonne's "regular"– presumably non-Polish – attorneys held: "When a Polak comes around, get his money – or somebody else will." This professional tip found ready application in a bail-bond racket allegedly used by Jewish lawyers to defraud immigrant strikers. According to one strike account, immigrants often carried their bank books with them "as a sort of 'talisman.'" When arrested, immigrants summoned Jewish lawyers, the latter secured the immigrants' release, but only for the price of the bank book. The practice, reportedly termed "stripping the bank-roll," sometimes netted large sums, with one Pole losing $225 and another a $450 to the bail-bond gimmick. But the lawyers profitted less than would appear, for they allegedly shared their proceeds with co-conspirators – none other than Bayonne saloonkeepers – called in to provide the actual cash that secured the prisoners' release. See Reed.

52. For a full discussion of this issue, see Bukowczyk, "Steeples and Smokestacks," ch. 6.

53. Dorsey, 24; Gibb and Knowlton, 151–152.

54. *Bayonne Evening Times,* July 13, 1918, CFBPL.

55. *Evening Post* (Bayonne, N.J.), Nov. 8, 1919, CFBPL; *The Messenger,* 1 (Dec. 3, 1920), 2; Chase, 12 14, 17–21; Gibb and Knowlton, 136.

56. *The Messenger,* 1 (Sept. 11, 18, Oct. 2, Dec. 8, 1920; Jan. 28, June 24, 1921) The magazine was patterned after *The Lamp,* a corporation-wide organ which began publication in May 1918. See Dorsey, 30.

57. *Bayonne Evening Times,* July 13, 1918, CFBPL.

58. *Bayonne Evening Times,* Feb. 5, 1917.

59. Dorsey, 26–28.

60. *Jersey Journal* (Jersey City, N.J.), Oct. 25, 1917, CFBPL; *The Messenger,* 1 (Dec. 24, 1920; April 8, 1921); *Bayonne Evening Times,* Dec. 5, 1919, CFBPL.

61. *Jersey Journal,* Oct. 25, 1917, CFBPL. Cf. Stephen Meyer, "Adapting the Immigrant to the Line: Americanization in the Ford Factory, 1914–1921," *Journal of Social History,* 14 (1981), 67–82. I would like to thank the author for furnishing me with a copy.

62. *Jersey Journal,* May 22, 1919; *Bayonne Evening Times,* Mar. 13, 1919, CFBPL.

63. John A. DeBrizzi, "Class Formation and the State: Class, Status and the

Political Economy of an American Industrial Society," *Berkeley Journal of Sociology*, 26 (1981), 118; Alfred Davis, Fire Department Chief, Bayonne, to Henry Wilson, Director of Public Safety, Aug. 10, 1915, in *Minutes of the Board of Commissioners, Bayonne, N.J.*, Aug. 10, 1915, in *Minutes of the Board of Commissioners, Bayonne, N.J.*, Nov. 14, 1916.

64. DeBrizzi, 111–115, 118. DeBrizzi's article is especially helpful in relating these developments to the broader crisis over municipal finance.

65. *Bayonne Evening Times*, Mar. 1, 1920; *Bayonne Evening Review*, Jan. 7, 1920, CFBPL.

66. Bukowczyk, "Steeples and Smokestacks," 374–380.

67. DeBrizzi, 130.

68. Cf. *Americanizing a City* (Detroit, 1915), 8.

69. Dorsey, 27.

70. Cf. Peter Roberts, *The New Immigration: A Study of the Industrial and Social Life of Southeastern Europeans in America*, reprint ed. (New York: Arno Press, 1970), ch. 12. I should like to thank Thomas Klug for bringing the Roberts chapter and the National Americanization Committee pamphlet to my attention.

71. *Our Lady of Mount Carmel Church*, 39–46.

72. Joseph A. Wytrwal, *America's Polish Heritage: A Social History of Poles in America* (Detroit, 1961), 232–233. In 1934, Derowski, who "acted behind the scene, prodding and motivating the club," became Bayonne's first Polish police lieutenant. See *Our Lady of Mount Carmel Church*, 39, 48.

73. Anonymous interview no. 1 (Bayonne, N.J.). His assignment unknown to anyone except local police and, interestingly, Bayonne's Polish pastor, this Polish intelligence operative circulated in saloons, Polish clubs, and organization meetings, and filed written reports to his military superiors. He probably worked under Alexander Bruce Bielaski, grandson of a Polish political refugee, who directed the investigation of pro-German activities in the United States and reportedly "hired secret agents of Polish descent to ferret out radicals with Polish backgrounds." See Edward Pinkowski, 308.

74. *Bayonne Evening Times*, Feb. 2, April 1, 24, Sept. 29, 1919, CFBPL.

75. *Bayonne Evening Times*, Nov. 20, 1959; Oct. 16, 1961, CFBPL.

76. Interview with Casimar Tokarski (Bayonne, July 23, 1980).

77. *Survey*, 34 (Aug. 7, 1915), 415.

78. *Bayonne Evening Review*, Jan. 10, 13, 1920; April 11, 1924, CFBPL.

Contributors

ROBERT ASHER is Professor of History at The University of Connecticut. He is the author of *Connecticut Workers and Technological Change* and is co-editor of *Life and Labor: Dimensions of American Working-Class History.*

STEVE BABSON is a program coordinator for Wayne State University's Labor Studies Center, Detroit, Michigan. He is completing a dissertation on Anglo-Gaelic immigrant metalworkers in the UAW in the 1930s.

JAMES R. BARRETT is a member of the Department of History at the University of Illinois at Urbana-Champaign. He is the author of *Work and Community in the Jungle: Chicago's Packinghouse Workers, 1894–1922* and is co author of *Steve Nelson, American Radical*, and has edited a new edition of *The Jungle.*

JOHN J. BUKOWCZYK is Associate Professor of History at Wayne State University. He is the author of *And My Children Did Not Know Me: A History of the Polish-American.*

JOHN CUMBLER is Professor of History at the University of Louisville. He is the author of *Working Class Community in Industrial America* and *A Social History of Industrial Decline*. He has edited *The Moral Response to Industrialism.*

MARIO T. GARCIA is Professor of History and Chicano Studies and Chair of the Department of Chicano Studies at the University of California, Santa Barbara. He is the author of *Desert Immigrants: The*

Mexicans of El Paso, 1880–1920 and the forthcoming *Americans All: The Mexican-American Generation and the Struggle for Civil Rights and Identity, 1930–1960.*

GARY GERSTLE teaches American history at Princeton University. He has written *Working-Class Americanism: The Politics of Labor in a Textile City, 1914–1960* and has co-edited *The Rise and Fall of the New Deal Order, 1930–1980.*

HORACE HUNTLEY is Assistant Professor of History, University of Alabama at Birmingham.

JOHN H. M. LASLETT is Professor of History at The University of California, Los Angeles. He is the author of *Labor and the Left* and is co-editor of *Failure of a Dream? Essays in the History of American Socialism.*

RAYMOND LOU is an Associate Professor and Program Coordinator in the Asian American Studies Program, San Jose State University. His is a specialist on the history of the Chinese in Los Angeles.

ALTAGRACIA ORTIZ is Associate Professor of History at the John Jay College of the City University of New York.

BARBARA M. POSADAS is Associate Professor of History at Northern Illinois University. She has published articles in *Labor History, Amerasia Journal*, and *Chicago History.*

DOROTHEE SCHNEIDER is a member of the Department of American Studies at Occidental College. A former editor of the Samuel Gompers Papers, she is now preparing a book on the German Working Class in late nineteenth century New York City.

CHARLES STEPHENSON is Associate Professor of History at Central Connecticut State University. He is the author of *In the Shadow of LBJ: The Democrats of Texas and the Liberal Quest for Party Control* and co-editor of *Life and Labor, Proletarians and Protest*, and *Confrontation, Class Consciousness and the Labor Process.*

RONALD TAKAKI is Professor of Ethnic Studies at the University of California, Berkeley. He is the author of *Race and Culture in Nineteenth-Century America* and *Pau Hana: Plantation Life and Labor in Hawaii.*

RUDOLPH J. VECOLI is Professor of History and Director of the Immigration History Research Center of the University of Minnesota. He is general editor of Research Collections in American Immigration (University Publications of America). He recently edited *Italian Immigrants in Rural and Small Town America.*

Index